TRANSFORMATION AS CREATION

Transformation as Creation

ESSAYS IN THE HISTORY, THEORY AND AESTHETICS OF INDIAN MUSIC, DANCE AND THEATRE

(Volume I : Essays in English)

MUKUND LATH

ADITYA PRAKASHAN
New Delhi

First Published: 1998

ISBN 81-86471-16-2

Published by P.K. Goel for Aditya Prakashan,
F-14/65, Model Town II, Delhi – 110 009.
Printed at Replika Press Pvt. Ltd., A-229, DSIDC,
Narela Industrial Park, Delhi – 110 040.

For

Ram Swarupji

Sita Ramji Goel

Contents

	Preface	vii
1.	The 'Modern', the 'Traditional' and Criticism in the Indian Musical Tradition	1
2.	Transformation as Creation	16
3.	Ancient Indian Music and the Concept of Man	39
4.	Words and Music	51
5.	Why Study Ancient Musical Texts ?	54
6.	Taṇḍu: The First Theoretician of Dance	69
7.	Improvisation in Indian Music	87
8.	Bharata and the Fine Art of Mixing Structures	92
9.	Bharata Muni and Hindi Films	123
10.	Bharata and the Hindi Film revisited	150
11.	An Enquiry into the Rāga-Time Association in the Light of History	163
12.	Some Thoughts on the Early History of Rāgamālā Paintings	174
13.	Some Reflections on the Viṇā in Gupta Coinage	186
14.	The Music of Gītagovinda and its Antecedents: Some Historical Observations	205
15.	Music in the Ṭhāṇaṁga Sūtra	223
16.	The Body as an Instrument A Theoretical Choice Made by Sāṛṅgadeva	247

17. Reflections on the Logos of Music

i. The Search of the *Apauruṣeya*, or Absolute in Music 267

ii. The *Pauruṣeya* Logos, Immanent in Human Seeking 307

Appendix I 336

Appendix II 338

Index 342

Preface

The essays, or if one likes to use the term 'articles', collected here have been written over a period of about two decades, and have been published in various journals and collections over the years. I have been writing and deliberating about music both in English and in Hindi, and I strongly feel that essays in these two languages are part of the same enterprise; they complement each other and belong together. I have, therefore, also put them together as forming a single corpus, which has been divided into two volumes for the sake of convenience. Those who study music in India, not as 'ethnomusicologists' from the outside, but from within the culture, tend in our multilingual nation, to write their thoughts in more than one language, which, in our country today, is natural enough. Their oeuvre, I believe, should be taken as belonging together. Studying the music from within the culture, I would like to think of these essays as essays in self-understanding. Students who deliberate on cultural phenomena from an 'ethnic' point of view, do not really do so as an exercise in self-understanding. A two-pronged assumption which is debilitating for any true self-understanding, underpins their enterprise : they assume not only the phenomenon they study to be 'objects', but, in a significant sense, the people who have created them are also studied as 'objects'. The ethnomusicologist, thus, does not address what he has to say to the people whose culture he is studying, as he would if he had related to them as subjects, and not objects, but to a specialised 'peer group' claiming to be participants in a 'scientific' discourse, which is at the same time, like science itself, the only and truly 'universal' discourse, and is meant for those trained as experts in the discourse. Those who study the rich musical culture of the west from within, do not call themselves ethnomusicologists, and, tellingly, they address themselves to *rasikas* and others belonging to their own culture. I would like to think of my own study, as I said, as a species of self-understanding; it is, to my mind, the study of a realm of *puruṣārtha,* a realm of seeking, meaning and significance in which I feel myself to be a co-*puruṣārthī*, a part of the world I am studying. And, in any case, like most Indian students of music, I am not a specialised student of the discourse that is 'ethnomusicology', and cannot be a practitioner of it. This is, obviously, not to decry the spirit of a critical *draṣṭā-bhāva,* the absence of which will defeat my very purpose of being a *student*, and I hope I have been able to keep that spirit.

The essays reflect the different interests I have had in studying music, interests which I am sure I share with those who think and write about Indian music today. These interests concern both the *prayoga* and the *śāstra* of music, and the different ways in which the two can be seen to be related, venturing, as any deliberation naturally does today, into the contexts, the arenas of culture, of which music is a part, especially its history and aesthetics, as well as its ties with other areas of art and thought. They can also be described as essays in cultural history with an accent or focus on music. There are also essays concerning parallel areas, traditionally connected with music, namely, *nṛtya* and *nāṭya*, and their analogous *śāstra, prayoga,* and cultural history.

My interest in music began with an interest in its *prayoga,* as it does, I suppose, with most of us, and I began to learn the art as a practitioner. My interest in the *śāstra* of music was more accidental, and resulted through an assignment to work on the ancient text, *Dattilam* (the work was published as *A Study Of Dattilam*: *A Treatise On The Sacred Music Of Ancient India* by Impex India in 1978). The *Dattilam* may seem rather remote from *prayoga* — as well as *śāstra* — as we understand it today, but it bears a palpable relation with them, because of the remarkable continuity of our musical culture, parallel in this with many other fields of thought and creativity. The study of a text like *Dattilam* and others, to my mind, provides a greater depth and a broader perspective to the continuing *paramparā* of *śāstra* and *prayoga,* imparting to the *paramparā* a larger meaning and a rich grounding of historical strata, which is usually missing from its vision. More importantly, for me, the sagacity which the *Dattilam* demonstrates in the *śāstric* enterprise, conveyed an impulse of excitement for the enterprise itself. And these essays, which have been written after the *Dattilam,* can perhaps also be called ramifications of that *śāstra*-oriented impulse, though, of course, taking '*śāstra*' in a sense somewhat larger — or perhaps more 'scattered' and 'dissipated' — than that of *ācārya* Dattila.

There is in this collection an essay entitled, 'Why Study Ancient Musical Texts' ; in a sense, many of the following essays can be understood as answers to this question, although the particular essay I refer to, was not written with the idea of composing such a theme-paper in mind. But just as the *prayoga* of others inspires a practitioner to an independent *prayoga* of one's own, a study of *śāstra* leads to independent thought. Some of the essays collected here, I hope, bear the stamp of such thinking. These may not be, as I said, exactly classifiable as belonging to the category of what we know as *śāstra* in *saṅgīta,* but *śāstra* is grounded in a spirit of reflection, and that certainly is as open to new ventures as music itself. In *saṅgīta-śāstra,* as in 'musicology', the *śāstric* venture is traditionally tied down to *lakṣaṇa,* or, roughly speaking, a mapping of *prayoga.* The *śāstra* has a set of categories and devices of its own, which are thought of as embedded in the logic of knowledge itself, and which it brings to bear on an area of study such as the *prayoga* of *saṅgīta,* the *śāstra* of *saṅgīta*, or 'musicology', thus being logos, or thought, as it relates to music. But music can be said to have a logos, a *prajñā* of its own. It runs as deep as a universal human *puruṣārtha* as thought. Confucius, indeed, as opposed to Aristotle, defined man through music and not reason or thought. If this be so, the *śāstra* related to *saṅgīta,* the logos of music, need not only be *about* music, it can also be thought that thinks *through* music. Pythagoras, Confucius and the ancient singers of

Sāmaveda, were, I think, practioners of *saṅgīta-śāstra* in this sense. This, in a way, which might appear paradoxical, turns the table on the *śāstra-prayoga* relation, envisioning *prayoga* itself as a *śāstra,* a species of reflection or thought. But this should not appear strange, since music is a reflective activity of its own kind. It can be as profound an 'index of culture' as thought, as many thinkers have, indeed, taken it to be. The final essay of this volume of the collection of essays in English, contains a longish piece in two parts, entitled, 'Reflections On The Logos Of Music', which is an essay in looking at music itself as being imbued with logos. The essay was specially written for this collection.

There are numerous friends, colleagues and *gurus* to whom I must offer thanks. For me, they form the *sampradāya* within which I have written. The best way I can think of to acknowledge their debt is to offer this *vidyā-sampradāya* a *namaskāra* which, I hope, will also act as a *maṅgala* for the book itself.

I must, however, offer special thanks to Pradeep Goel of Aditya Prakashan who has published this book, for his extreme patience with me. He has waited for months for me to give final form to the book and write the final essay.

CHAPTER – ONE

The 'Modern', the 'Traditional' and Criticism in the Indian Musical Tradition

The word 'modern', and by implication the word 'traditional', are used in two very distinct senses today: an old sense, and one which is very much more recent. This dual use creates a basic confusion concerning modernity and tradition in the Indian context. I will attempt to show how it does so in the field of the arts, causing a strange mixing of categories. I shall then move on to discuss how the notion of *paramparā*, the Indian word for tradition, is articulated in India and the role assigned to criticism in it, before outlining a brief history of criticism in the *paramparā* of music.

The old, original sense of the word, 'modern', is a relative sense. The new meaning attached to it may, by contrast, be termed, 'absolute'. In both senses 'modern' is opposed to the 'traditional', that is, the old and established which it replaces. In the relative sense of modern, a living and dynamic continuity is maintained between the old and the new, the traditional and the modern. The modern, in this sense, is but a phase of an unbroken tradition which it transforms, and with the coming of a newer phase, a newer modern, it can itself become old and traditional. And so, today we have the phenomenon called post-modernism in the west where the tradition does flow into a newer modern. The Sanskrit analogue of such usage is the relative opposition between the *purātana* or *pracīna* and the *navya* or *nūtana*.

The other, the 'absolute' use of the term, is a new western coinage. It is based on a new world-view and imparts a heavily meaning-loaded sense to what was, traditionally, a simple, innocuous word. It has no analogue in Sanskrit. The word, '*ādhunika*' has been coined for it in many Indian languages. The world-view it is rooted in, is an all-embracing vision about man, his Destiny, and the nature of history and change. There are differing strands within the world-view, but that does not disturb the over-all picture. The spread of westernisation over the globe has made this world-view a near-dogma, turning 'modern' in its new sense, into a global cultural catch-word.

There is according to this view, a clear 'axial' break in history between the old, the traditional, and the 'modern'. With the 'modern', history has moved into a new, higher gear, arriving at a new categorically advanced civilisation which is no less than a quantum leap forward from the old and traditional. The spirit of the new 'modern' is not limited to a particular discipline or pursuit, but constitutes a total cultural quality that pervades every aspect of man: his institutions as well as his consciousness. The roots of the 'modern' may lie in the phenomenal advances in science and technology, but it pervades human life in all its aspects, encompassing social, political and economic institutions as well as art and thought and the very stuff of our experience. It is a completely new civilisation.

There are said to be certain deep-rooted historical reasons due to which the new 'modern' was born in the west, where to use a metaphor from ancient Indian cosmogony, a 'womb' was ready and waiting for it. Historical forces are complex things but if one were to look for a single cause for the emergence of the 'modern' in the west, it would not be difficult to point at it: the new 'modern' is the fruition of the rational, critical spirit, a unique gift of the Greeks to the west.

But though born in the west, the 'modern' civilisation is universal in essence and intent. It is, as it should only be, an evangelical civilisation. Like the 'universal' Roman empire, or a true messianic religion, it has spread beyond its boundaries, first through violence and conquest; but now its violent phase is over. The seed has spread over the world and every country must nurture it on its own. The 'modern' has become a truly 'international' civilisation, the first in history; though being a produce of the west, the leadership, the inspiration, the very form of this 'international' civilisation naturally remains western. The 'international' is, in other words equivalent to the 'modern'.

Though, of course, the *word* 'international' could be more acceptable to those self-respecting non-western people who find 'modern' too western and alien.

The rootedness of the 'modern' in the west results in what might seem a paradoxical situation: for though the modern is a categorical break from the tradition, it is yet a vital part of the western tradition; the continuity between the 'modern' and the 'traditional' remains intact in the west. But this is not possible anywhere else. Given the historical circumstances, the situation is only natural, though it might seem strange and parochial. The 'modern' is, after all, a break from the western past out of which it has emerged and with which it has dynamic links.

As a result, the 'modern', though an absolutely new civilisation for the rest of the world, is only relatively new to the west itself, since the west has a continuity of tradition. This continuity perhaps appears more evident in certain areas, like art and thought, but it is, in truth, all-pervasive. Indeed, one major task of history is to reveal the vital links between the old and the new in the west, showing how the 'modern' is a *pariṇāma*, a transformation of the tradition itself.

Other civilisations may also have had a development of their own; that is to say, they may have their own traditions, but however rich these traditions may be, they could not have produced the 'modern'; they were not impregnated with it. Such civilisations, such as that of India, are, therefore, essentially 'traditional'. Except, of course, in areas where the new 'modern' from the west has replaced the tradition. The 'modern', for this reason, in essentially 'traditional' civilisations means a categorical break with the past, the giving up of tradition.

Like all historical processes, 'modernity' takes time to set in. The old takes time to die and be entirely replaced by the new. As a result, 'traditional' civilisations are condemned to harbour two disparate streams of development for some time: one, their own, the 'traditional' and the other, the 'modern', till they become entirely 'modernised'.

We, in India, have certainly become 'modernised' in the

primary sense that we have accepted the new absolute meaning of 'modern' as the true meaning of the word. This implies the ingestion of the historical picture too, which the meaning is embedded in. The proofs of this lie in every field of our life. We make a distinction, which we consider very significant, between a 'traditional' and a 'modern' in what we do, the 'traditional' being the Indian and the 'modern', the western or western-inspired. In fact, we live in two civilisations, the 'modern' and the 'traditional', as we march bravely towards complete 'modernisation'.

But meanwhile we must bear with a 'traditional' along with a 'modern' in almost everything. This is only to be expected. Let us take the arts. The 'traditional' exists with the 'modern' in most of the arts: painting, sculpture and architecture, for example. We have a well-entrenched, western-inspired 'modern' in these arts, though the 'traditional' also persists, But the 'traditional' has been put in its place. It is on the way out. We are preserving it as a relic of the past, even sometimes as a living relic, but its value is that of something in a museum. And this is how it should be.

What is perturbing, however, is the fact that we have no 'modern' in music and dance. All we have is 'traditional'. And what is more, there seems to be no real prospect of having a 'modern' in these arts. Our sensibilities fail to respond to 'modern', that is, western music, except, may be, in forms that cannot be called the deepest expressions of the musical sensibilities of the west. How, then, can we have a 'modern' in music?

The question does bother us 'moderns' sometimes and leaves us perplexed. We can, of course, dismiss the question saying that a taste in music like our taste in food is traditional; this need not cause us much concern as long as we are 'modern' in what really matters. This, plainly, is too facile to satisfy anyone with any sensibility. And the 'modern', moreover, is a total civilisation, on what ground can we exclude music from it, especially since we do have a 'modern' in the other arts. We cannot but be worried for our failure to have a 'modern' in music, blaming this lapse, perhaps, on our love for 'traditional' music, a stubborn hangover from a past which still clouds our consciousness.

But let us reflect. Is not our perplexity a result of a confusion of categories, a verbal *moha*? We are prepared to grant that within its own tradition, our music has been growing as vitally as western music within *its* own tradition, yet we never even consider calling it 'modern'. We have accepted the new, western, absolute meaning of 'modern' as the true meaning of the term along with the historical myth which makes this meaning so overwhelmingly momentous. We fail to notice the significance of the fact that the west, in its own case, persists in using the original relative meaning of the word 'modern' and its historians are busy looking for the seeds for everything new in the old.

The reason is not difficult to comprehend. The word 'modern' does not mean something created out of the void. It presupposes a cultural framework, human activity with an organised continuity, in other words, a tradition. The modern is a new transformation of this tradition; without it the word itself would be meaningless. Cultural traditions are many and they have nurtured many 'moderns' and unless we allow the 'international' to triumph, there is no reason why there should not be a multiplicity of them in the future: different 'moderns' in different cultures. The new western 'modern' claims a special, unique, monolithic status, which its historical destiny has granted it — and which we, too, gullibly seem to be granting it — of being global in intent, even though its tradition is localised in the west. Anything not linked with the west cannot be 'modern' in this scheme, by definition.

It is not strange, therefore, that in whatever we have become 'modern', in painting, sculpture, architecture — and even thought — the tradition which we belong to is no longer our own, but the western tradition. The history of modern painting, sculpture, architecture or thought in India has hardly anything to do with India beyond a short period, after which it has to jump to the west, its real home. And, conversely — or rather perversely — anything which cannot trace its history to the west, like Indian music, dance or — the continuities in our thought — remains 'traditional'. Now the 'traditional by virtue of the meaning of the term is lacking in true appropriate vitality — even though it might be doing new things in its own way — which only the 'modern' has. This is what perturbs us about Indian music. The cause, plainly, is a verbal *moha.*

There are other undesirable consequences of this *moha.* Having equated the 'traditional' with the 'dead' or the 'dying', we have condemned our traditions in painting, sculpture, architecture and thought as devoid of vitality. And having made this judgement, we feel justified in allowing them a kind of secondary existence, till they really breathe their last.

Yet the 'modern' too disturbs many of us. For we have lost our own identity in whatever we are 'modern'. Calling the 'modern' international, does perhaps provide a face-saving device for some, but these do not care for an identity in any case. Those who do, feel that though we have lost an identity and given up a whole rich and long tradition, all we have gained in return is the status of a cultural province of the west. A status which does not deserve serious attention in itself; its life-sources, its mainsprings lie elsewhere. It has nothing really of its own to offer. It may have some individuality, but all provincial growth has it. India, perhaps, has a little more of it; it has had, after all, a long tradition of its own, a tradition which still flows inertly along as a parallel civilisation. This is what gives India its individuality, but this is not something necessarily good. For the tradition, truly, is a hurdle in India's path to modernity which would have been straighter without such a complex, cumbersome tradition.

One major reason why India's tradition, indeed, all that is 'traditional', is a hurdle to modernity, is its lack of the critical spirit. Tradition is accepted and perpetuated largely through faith or unthinking convention.

This is tradition as modernity sees it. But let us see how the tradition understands itself. For, tradition, thus understood, is *not* synonymous with the Indian notion of *paramparā*, the Indian equivalent of 'tradition'. Accepted uncritically, preserved only through blind faith and repetitive, or only continued as mere convention, *paramparā* is known by another name; it is called *rūḍhi*. True, *paramparā* also seeks continuance, as all meaningful human activity must, but what it seeks to preserve and continue is the essence and spirit of an activity, not every detail of its content. Criticism is an essential part of *paramparā*, in the light of which it can be changed and transformed. *Paramparā* is even willing to ask deeper questions such as, what is the essence and spirit of an activity, implying, in principle, the acceptance of far-reaching modifications and transformations.

Really foundational thinking in India regarding the nature of a *paramparā* in the arts was carried out in the field of literature and theatre, though it has a universality which makes it relevant to music or any other creative conscious human activity — a relevance which did not go unrecognised. Thinking in literature influenced thinking in general. Some of India's most profound literary theorists and critics have reflected on the requisites of a *paramparā* and their analysis is worth a look. There seems nothing quite as articulate in the west.

A *paramparā,* according to these thinkers, consists of three elements:

1. The *kavi*, that is, the poet, the playwright, or in other words, the artist.
2. *Kavikarma*, what the poet or artist does and the produce of this activity, the poem or the work of art.
3. The *sahṛdaya,* the sensitive recipient, the critic.

These elements constantly interact; one, moulding, modifying and transforming the other. The artist works with the forms that he or she inherits, continuing or transforming it in the light of *vyutpatti* and *pratibhā*, two notions central to the Indian understanding of the manner in which the artist works upon the forms he receives. *Vyutpatti* means an understanding and grasp of inherited material and recreating it with the little amount of modification, any true preservation necessarily calls for. *Vyutpatti*, plainly, is the key to the preservation and continuity of any tradition. *Pratibhā*, parallel to 'genius' and a similarly hallowed word, is understood as that faculty of the mind (*buddhi*) which introduces innovations, opening new vistas.[1] *Pratibhā* is not limited to the artist. The *sahṛdaya*, the sensitive critic can also have it, though of course, *vyutpatti* is as important for him, or perhaps even more so than it is to the artist. The *sahṛdaya's pratibhā* is, naturally, different from that of the *kavi*. The *sahṛdaya's* role is to comprehend, compare and evaluate. It is he, who among other things, evaluates whether a creation is a product of *vyutpatti* or of *pratibhā* and assigns it a place in the *paramparā*. The *kavi's pratibhā* is appropriately called the *kārayitrī pratibhā*, the capacity to create something new. The *sahṛdaya's pratibhā* is the *bhāvayitrī*, the reflective, the cogitative *pratibhā*.

The two *pratibhās* complement each other and, ideally, creative persons have them both. Together they form a single whole. 'The single truth of imagination expresses itself in the dual roles of the poet and the critic', said Abhinavagupta (10th-11th centuries), one of the most *pratibhāvāna* and influential critics India has produced. Uttuṅgodaya, a later Kerala critic, commenting on these remarks from Abhinava, who was from Kashmir, was in favour of granting a greater role to the critic than the poet: it is the judgement of a critic, he says, which, in the first place, makes the distinction between what is a poem and what is not.[2] Given this ideal one would expect a large body of critical literature. This one does find. Its tenor is not the same as what we know as literary criticism from the west. It is more

---

[1] *Navanavonmeṣaśālinī buddhiḥ pratibhā*, is an almost universally accepted 'definition' of *pratibhā*. The word '*unmeṣa*' in this pithy definition literally means, 'the opening of the eyes', suggesting new horizons.

[2] The words we have quoted from Abhinava are from the verse with which he opens his renowned commentary, the *Locana* on the *Dhvanyāloka*: *kramātprakhyopākhyāpra-sarasubhagaṁ bhāsayati tat/ sarasvatyāstattvaṁ kavisahṛdayākhyaṁ vijayate//* Uttuṅgodaya, in his *Kaumudī* on the *Locana*, comments: '*sahṛdayakartṛkaviśiṣṭavicāra-kriyāgocarībhūtasyaiva kāvyasya mukhyatayā kāvyarūpatvāditi brūmaḥ*. See *Dhvanyāloka* with *Locana* and *Kaumudī*, Kuppuswami Sastri, Ramacandra Diksitar and T.R. Chintamani (eds.); Kuppuswami Sastri Research Institute, Madras, 1944, pp. 3-4.

theoretical and philosophical. It does not cognise what the west knows as the 'history of literature', a central concern of the critic in the west, though it is aware in its own way of its own *paramparā*. The processes by which a poet transforms the works of older poets to create something new is spoken of, but is not strung together into a history. Moreover, the historical context of an artist, his individual personality, has not been considered too important in India, though his individual *kavikarma* and his *pratibhā* has been.

What we know as criticism from the west consists largely in the impressionistic, imaginative reactions of an individual *sahṛdaya* to works of art seen in their context. Such criticism is not unknown in India and there have been some great exponents of it such as Kuntaka (11th century) and Mahimabhaṭṭa (also 11th century), but this was an exception rather than the rule. Generally, critics in India were interested in larger aesthetic questions and matters of theory. They spoke of their subject matter from a distance as it were. Their great discussions, continuing over centuries into our own times are stimulatingly rich and varied, but they only occasionally provide personal reactions to specific artists or their works. Yet they do give us a powerful vocabulary for criticism of a more individualistic tenor. There is, moreover, evidence to believe that such individual criticism was not only potentially present, but was practised to a greater extent than the more respectable mainstream, critical literature testifies to. The practise of it was oral. Its pronouncements, being considered more ephemeral, relevant to individual works of art rather that art in general, were not written down. Still, vestiges of this oral tradition consisting of pithy judgements by individual critics concerning individual poets and their merits were sometimes encapsulated into striking verses and are to be found in the numerous anthologies of Sanskrit poetry compiled between the 12th and the 20th centuries.

Theoretical literature on music, too, has a long history going back to Vedic times. Moreover, there is no break here between the 'modern' and the 'traditional' as in most contemporary thinking concerning literature and the other arts. However, the principal focus of the literature on music has been musical structure. Aesthetics was a comparatively minor consideration. It never acquired the vigour and depth that it did in literature. Keeping largely aloof from the philosophical mainstream of Indian thought, it never raised probing questions that could have given it the intellectual spine which literary aesthetics had. But this is not to deny its strength and presence. Musical texts speak of desirable and undesirable musical qualities (*guṇas* and *doṣas*), much in the manner of early literary critics. They also speak of styles though not very discursively; greater detail, however, is found in their delineation of kinds of musicians and what makes one more creative and greater than the other. They also speak of the importance of critics and the knowledge a good critic should possess. Besides, they speak of a host of things that can be identified as part of the complex scheme of ideas which we call the aesthetic aspect of a musical culture, even though they do not make musical aesthetics a major theoretical concern of their discourse. Criticism of actual music, of individual musicians, is even more rare in musical texts than is the criticism of poems and poets in the works on literary criticism. In search for examples, we must look to non-musical writings, where, needless to say, their occurrence is quite incidental. These provide us, however, with glimpses of an activity, which like literary criticism of a similar kind, remained largely oral. We might quote here an interesting example from a famous play, the *Mṛcchakaṭikam* of Śūdraka (between 2nd and 5th centuries). Cārudatta, the cultured protagonist, praises the singing of a friend, a professional musician, in the following words, after listening to him for a whole night till the early hours of the morning:

'He is not singing any more, but I can still hear his music. His soft voice, clinging harmoniously to the accompanying strings, while it moved over a succession of notes, still rings in my ears. His control was effortless, his music delicate, with phrases repeated out of passionate intensity. When the movement of the melody, called for a high note, the effect was still gentle.'[3] This interesting example is quite general in its judgement — one notes its relevance to certain contemporary styles of singing, too — but it is, perhaps, deliberately so. It is an example from a work where speaking in greater descriptive or critical detail about a work of art would itself have been an aesthetic fault, distracting the audience from the play itself. But criticism as practised within musical circles of the kind assumed in the play must have been much more richer in detail. Yet, however thin it might be, it does give us a glimpse of the kind of music criticism practised in urbane circles during the Gupta age. After the 12th-13th century, musical culture came to harbour certain ideas which looked at music not so much as an art but as a species of magic. The roots of the ideas were perhaps old, but their preponderance was new. They found entrance into formal musical texts. This was a development which has no parallel in literature as an art.

One of these new ideas was the association of a *rāga* with a time of the day or night or with a season. The idea began with the notion that certain musical forms were more *auspicious* when performed at a certain period of the daily or yearly cycle. Later, around the 16th century, the association was raised to an aesthetic principle: it was believed that a *rāga* was more beautiful, more effective as a piece of music, only in association with a certain time. The belief became part of musical practice, the repertoire of *rāgas* was more and more strictly distributed over the major periods of the day and night. In more recent times, this principle was gradually given up in the south. But in the north, it found a strong 'modern' champion. Pandit Bhatkhande, a major influence in contemporary Hindustani music, defended the practice on the basis of what he thought was

---

[3] *taṁ tasya svarasaṁkramaṁ mṛdugiraḥ śliṣṭaṁ ca tantrīsvanaṁ varṇānāmapi mūrchanāntaragataṁ tāraṁ virāme mṛdum/ helāsaṁyamitaṁ punaśca lalitaṁ rāga-dviruccāritaṁ yatsatyaṁ virate'pi gītasamaye gacchāmi śṛṇvannival/ Mṛcchakaṭikam,* Act 3, verse 5; p. 70 of the Nirṇayasāgara press edition, third printing, Bombay, 1909.

a 'scientific' ground. He argued that there was a psychophysical connection between the tonal structure of a *rāga* and specific periods of the day and night. He never really demonstrated this connection, but his assertion gave life to a curious practice which might otherwise have died a natural death as it did in the south.

Another, a more magically oriented idea was the notion of the miraculous effect of a *rāga* when correctly sung by a master — indeed, the proof of his being a master lay in the miracle he could create. *Rāga malhār,* it was believed, could cause rain, *rāga dīpak* could cause fire, *rāga śrī* could bring a dead tree to life and *gūjarī* could attract deer from the far-off forests. And great musicians could demonstrate this. True, not all *rāgas* were to be judged by such effects, nor did the idea find room in the texts on music, except marginally. Yet, it had a great hold over musical culture. It still continues to haunt us, though in a milder, more rationalised manner. I remember friends remarking that when they heard Allaudin Khan play *malhār* on his *sarod*, they could hear the sounds of rain falling outside the hall; if they closed their eyes.

The miraculous legends of *gūjarī* attracting deer is perhaps connected with another idea which took deep roots in the musical culture after the 12th century. This was the idea of *rāga-dhyāna*, resulting in thousands of *rāga* paintings, very popular among painters and their patrons till the 19th century and still much admired. One recurring motif in these paintings is the association of *rāga gūjarī* with deers: the *rāga* is shown as a beautiful woman playing a *viṇā* in a forest, with deer flocking around her.

The notion of the *rāga-dhyāna* seems to have come into vogue around the 13th century. It began with conceiving and painting a *rāga* as a deity, a kind of minor god or goddess. Later, in the 16th century, the gods and goddesses were mostly secularised and transformed into men and women. They were painted in more dramatic and attractively human contexts and *rāga*-paintings became a very popular genre. *Rāgas* as deities could never become quite as popular. We must add, however, that the idea of a *rāga* as a man or a woman in a dramatic situation was taken more seriously by painters and their patrons rather than musicians and their audience, despite the fact that music theorists were quite taken with the idea and almost every text written between the 14th and the 19th centuries, includes a section on *rāga-dhyāna;* besides, there were numerous little treatises called *Rāga-mālas* in Sanskrit and the vernacular devoted exclusively to *rāga-dhyānas.*

There is nothing particularly odd in such ideas having found vogue in musical circles. In trying to react to a formal, abstract art, such as music, we seem naturally to seek a more tangible and corporeal basis for our judgements. This is what the *rāga*-time notions do or what the *rāga-dhyāna* ideas seek. They try to assimilate music to something we can see. Giving miraculous powers to *rāgas*, makes them even more 'visible' in their effects, if not in themselves. Earlier critical vocabulary, though it was not assimilated to ambitious aesthetic theories regarding the musical art, such as the critical vocabulary in literature was, by and large avoided giving it a representative nature, a content as well as a form, if we take Carudatta's criticism of his musician friend as a typical example. Yet earlier musical aesthetics, too, was not able to avoid the enticement of the *rasa* theory, which had almost become *the* universal aesthetic theory in India. A fertile notion, propounded for understanding the aesthetics of theatre, it was taken over by literary theorists and such was their influence on aesthetic thinking in general, that it became synonymous with the experience of any art. The notion had become a dominant cultural ideal, rather than just an idea, and writers on music, too, adopted it. But they did so quite unthinkingly, without *adapting* it to the special needs of music where a distinction cannot be made between form and content as it can be in theatre and literature.

Music, for the last few centuries in India, has had no lack of *kārayitrī pratibhā*, but the *bhāvayitrī pratibhā* of the *sahṛdayas* has lagged behind, even more so in matters of aesthetics than in musical theory. The art was willing to change, experiment and grow, without losing the spirit of its *paramparā*, musical theory was incapable of keeping pace: more so, it appears, in the north than in the south; for these were the centuries when the *paramparā* bifurcated into Hindustani and Karnatic.

In the north, the situation in musical theory is now much livelier. Ever since Pandit Bhatkhande, whose career spanned the late 19th and early 20th centuries, there has been a growing interest in musical theory and musical textual history. Bhatkhande was also, to a great extent, responsible in introducing a more modern, institutionalised, tradition of transmission and patronage in music, without losing the strength of the old and a continuity with it, such as has *not* happened in the arts of painting, sculpture and architecture.

But an analogous renewal in music criticism and aesthetics has yet to take place. It had potentialities and still has them. The *oral* tradition of music criticism as carried on among artists and sensitive listeners has a rich vocabulary based on tradition though it lacks a systematics. The systematics can come only if the oral becomes written. This is not to say that there is no written tradition of criticism. Newspapers have necessitated one. But it has all the weakness of something nurtured purely by journalism. It has no touch with the oral vocabulary of the tradition, though there are some critics who are beginning to dabble in one. Using English, and a modern vocabulary, it is like a lost soul unable to find itself, though growing in power. The written tradition which is now, acknowledgedly, a must, can only acquire strength and spine from an intellectual effort that must not be limited to newspaper writings and becomes rooted in more serious reflection, not limited to effervescent musings, to be forgotten the next day. For this, it must look to the rich aesthetic thought of the past, albeit with a critical eye, for Indian aesthetics is not always *directly* concerned with music though it bears seeds of possibilities. It must also learn from the western experience. Though greater caution must be exercised here. For Indian music is not western music.

What a modern music critic in India can learn from the west

is an approach, forging a history of the art. History of art, indeed history itself, is a new way of looking at things in India. Many of the other arts, especially literature, have good histories now. But not music. Old music does not survive unchanged, so central is the role of improvisation and individual genius in India. The little notation that does survive, gives only a skeletal idea of the music and still has problems of decoding. But while a larger history of music in concrete terms is elusive at present — though interesting attempts are being made at a reconstruction — yet a history of arts approach to the music of our own century is possible. A great deal is present in recordings as well as notations. An in-depth study in palpable formal terms of various musicians, their individual style and development, the currents and cross-currents influencing the art, its changes and its continuities, is possible today. And it would be extremely interesting for both the artist and the listener and the critic to become aware of this. But the needed intellectual effort to make such studies still remains largely a mere possibility, though one feels that the musical community as a whole will welcome it and feel enriched by it.

CHAPTER – TWO

Transformation as Creation

(A notion of imagination as Creative Transformation envisaged by certain ancient Indian literary critics and its application in the field of music.)

The idea of creative imagination naturally suggests artistic activity. Activity such as that of the writer, the painter, the sculptor, the musician, the dancer, the architect and the like. This, we generally think, is the homeground of creative imagination, though as has been justly pointed out, every human endeavour, whether of thought or action, presupposes it, or, at least, needs it in order to be significant. The writer comes first on my list because we who deal in words tend to think of literature before any other art. But I have another, a more important reason for listing him first. Reflections over the writer's art, that is, literature, has a longer history and a greater depth of critical self-awareness in India than thinking about any other art, a fact which is perhaps true of most cultures.

Indian literary criticism, however, gives great attention to form and this makes some of its concepts and formulations relevant not only to literature, where the content is as important as the form, but also to the more "formal" arts such as music, dance and architecture. In talking about the relation of art to society, we need to discuss these arts, too, and relate the creative activity in them to the changing social milieu to the extent that this is feasible. As I am more familiar with music, most of my comments in this direction will relate to music and particularly Hindustani music and its history. What I have to say is rather exploratory and I hope it will be imaginative enough to save it from being merely fanciful.

The first part of my paper will be devoted to presenting in outline a concept of literary creativity as conceived by

Ānandavardhana and treated in detail by Rājaśekhara, in which the idea of transformation plays a key role. The new, according to these ancient Indian critics, is born through imaginatively restructuring the old. This, one may point out, has always been true of all arts everywhere. Artists, be they poets, painters, sculptors, architects, or musicians, work within a tradition. They are heirs to a body of forms, that is, of "given" creations, which guide and shape their own endeavours. Transformation, in other words, is manifestly an inherent process in any artistic creation. Artists learn by copying and create by transmuting. This is even more obvious in cultures, where tradition is not a bad word and a new work is deliberately modelled on the old.

The importance of Ānandavardhana and, following him, Rājaśekhara lies in the fact that they have conceptually articulated the role and significance of the transformatory function in artistic creativity. These Indian critics, so far as I know, are the only ones who have consciously *theorised* about this function, even though its *use* has been common enough in all arts everywhere. They distinguish between kinds and modes of transformation, and Rājaśekhara categorizes them in detail, analysing the various processes involved at some length. They also distinguish between creative and non-creative trasformations. Their discussion is worth recording in itself, but for me what they have done in the field of poetry will serve as a prelude for a similar attempt in analysing the creative process in music, a formal, non-representational art where creation more obviously involves transforming the given.

Alaṁkāraśāstra, the name given in India to the literature of critical thinking concerning *kāvya* — the general term for imaginative writing — produced some of its most penetrating works over a period of two to three centuries between the 9th and the 12th, mostly in Kashmir. A few of the questions which occupied the critics were: What is *kāvya* ? How is it distinct from other writings ? What is its purpose ? What is *rasa* ? How is *rasa* aroused ? In whom ? These were hotly debated issues and many insightful ideas and theories came up as a result of prolonged discussions lasting over numerous generations. Related to these were the questions regarding the nature of creative imagination and how it operates.

Interesting in our context, I believe, is the answer given by Ānandavardhana to the last question as to how creative imagination operates. Ānandavardhana discusses it in the last section of his remarkable work, the *Dhvanyālokā*, written sometime towards the end of the 9th century. It became one of the most influential critical works in India concerning *kāvya*. A century after its composition, the celebrated Abhinava Gupta wrote an equally influential commentary on it which he named the *Dhvanyālokalocana,* renderable, perhaps, as "The eye-opener to the *Dhvanyāloka.*"

The critical thinking of the period we are speaking of, was pursued in an ambience of general philosophical theories and debates. This, I think, lends it a lasting depth and universality, even though this character has also been responsible for disparaging comments by historians oriented towards the impressionistic criticism of the 19th-century West. To them, Indian critical thinking was too general, too distant from the phenomenon it dealt with. Moreover, in this view, even where it came close to what it dealt with, it was much too formalistic. But it is just this formal character which makes it significant for me here.

Before getting on to what interests me in the *Dhvanyāloka*, let me briefly introduce it in the perspective of Indian poetics. The idea of *rasa*, one of the central, or perhaps *the* central, concept in Indian aesthetic thinking was initially outlined by Bharata, the semi-mythical author of the *Nāṭyaśāstra*, a work on theatre belonging in its present form to the beginning of the Christian era. Translating the term *rasa* is a tricky problem, as has been pointed out countless times. It is not only difficult to think of a simple, single equivalent word or phrase, such as, "dominant mood", "feeling", "basic emotions", "sentiments", "ethos" or the like, but futile to think of any. Anything but a long discursive explanation can only oversimplify, and thus distort, a complex concept which, as it stands, is definitive of the aesthetic realm in general as well as of emotions savoured through the experience of *kāvya,* emotion thus rendered as being in some sense "trans" or "extra" normal. My intention, in this paper, is not to discuss *rasa*, except indirectly. I will assume in my readers a familiarity with the concept.

Bharata, writing on theatre, had outlined the notion of *rasa* in connection with drama. More complex issues concerning the nature of *rasa*, the number of *rasas*, how distinguished, how aroused, how emotion in the *rasa*-state differs from ordinary experience and the like, were taken up much later mostly by the Kashmiri theorists of the period we have spoken of. It was argued that *kāvya* in general, of which drama, termed *dṛśya kāvya*, was but a species, gave rise to *rasa* in ways analogous to drama. Semantic issues were also involved in discussing *kāvya,* for *kāvya* uses words as its medium. The moot problem here posed before the *ālaṅkārikas* was: what distinguished the use of this medium in *kāvya* since words are also used in scientific, injunctive and other writings. It is in this area that Ānandavardhana's chief contribution lies. The semantic theories he had inherited argued for what may be called a pragmatic, common-sensical or "literal" concept of meaning. Ānandavardhana contended that words have meaning in many expressive, emotive ways not envisaged in this semantic scheme which took only the denotative sense into account.[1] Words, he said, do not only depict, they also evoke. Their power cannot really be understood within any semantic

[1] Before Ānandavardhana, Indian semantics, or what may be called its main strand, postulated a *śakti*, "a power" in words termed *abhidhā* through which they directly denoted their objects. *Abhidhā,* it was believed, was aided by another "power" termed *lakśaṇā* which came into play when *abhidhā* landed into obvious absurdities. As in common usages like, "I drank five glasses", "He passed through hell", "John is a rat". The function of *lakśaṇā* in such cases was to restore the denotative *abhidhā* sense through simple "logical" connections or associations. Thus "glasses" = "What they contain", "hell" = "suffering" and "rat" = "unpleasant habits or properties of a rat". Here the function of *lakśaṇā* ended. It merely came to the rescue of *abhidhā* when usage showed such waywardness. It did no more. One can see, however, that "hell" and "rat" in these sentences cannot be reduced to any simple denotative meaning. They have a suggestive aura which cannot be tied down to *abhidhā* and this is one reason which led Ānandavardhana to argue for *dhvani*, an evocative "power" in words, beyond *abhidhā* and *lakśaṇā*.

scheme which takes only logical relations into account. They have a large nimbus or aura of multiple meanings which they express through psychological, rather than logical, relations. He called this aura of meaning or "meaningfulness" — if one may use this word — *dhvani,* which I think can be best translated as "echo". Abhinava, in explaining it, speaks of *anuraṇana* or "resonance".[2] The *kāvya*-ness of *kāvya* lies in its powerful use of the potency of *dhvani* in words. It is, Ānandavardhana further argued, through the transliteral, often multivalent and multi-splendoured echo of meanings in words that *kāvya* generates the experience of *rasa.*

Ānandavardhana's *Dhvanyāloka,* which literally means "light on *dhvani",* is divided into four chapters called *udyotas,* literally, "illuminators". He believed that in *dhvani* he had discovered a new, revolutionary principle, which could illuminatingly transform all previous theorising concerning *kāvya.* In the first three *udyotas* of his work Ānandavardhana occupies himself in demonstrating that linguistic usage cannot be fully comprehended without accepting *dhvani.* He explores the various modes and ways of its operation showing how all that is fruitful in previous theorising can be more meaningfully subsumed under its workings.

In the fourth *udyota* Ānandavardhana speaks of how an awareness of the working of *dhvani* can give us — meaning the poet and his audience, *kavi* and *sahṛdaya* — an insight into the process of creation. The *udyota* begins with the proclamation that imagination is capable of infinite novelty (*pratibhānantyam*). Interestingly, however, the capability of creating something new is defined as the capacity to renew, that is, to give an "old" established theme, motif, image or expression a new freshness by restating it with a richer nuance. The creative use of *dhvani,* says Ānandavardhana, can impart newness to a poetic statement though it be a restatement of older, "given" material (*vāṇī purātanakavinibaddhārthasaṁsparśavatyapi navatvamāyāti*). He gives a few instances to illustrate his

---

[2] Abhinava on *Dhavanyāloka, udyota* I, *kārikā,* 13: see p. 241, vol. 1 of Dr. Ramasagara Tripathi's edition of *Dhavanyāloka* (Motilal Banaridass, 1973).

contention. The illustrations show how an established *mazmūn*, to give a familiar term from Urdu-Persian literature, signifying poetic theme or substance, becomes enriched in the hands of a greater poet who can wield his words with a greater suggestive power. An old poem in the hands of a creative poet is transformed into a new work.

It would be helpful here to take an example given by Ānandavardhana himself. Quoting a well-known verse from Amaru, he places against it a newer poem on the same theme or *mazmūn*. The freshness or the originality of the new poem, he says, cannot be denied, despite the force of the original.

Amaru's poem is:

Śūnyaṁ vāsagṛhaṁ vilokya śayanādutthāya kiñcicchanaiḥ
nidrāvyājamupāgatasya suciraṁ nirvarṇya patyurmukham/
viśrabdhaṁ paricumbya jātapulakāmālokya gaṇḍasthalīṁ
lajjānamramukhī priyeṇa hasatā bālā ciraṁ cūṁbitā//

[Certain that they were alone in the room, the young bride slowly raised herself a little on the bed. She gazed long at her husband's face as he lay feigning sleep. Thinking that he was really asleep, she planted a kiss on his cheek. No sooner than she did this, she saw the soft hair on his face bristle with pleasure. Overcome with shyness, she at once hid her face. Laughingly, her lover hugged her and gave her a long kiss.]

It is a masterly poem in the original Sanskrit, chiselled in its artistry, painting a dramatic, evocative scene. None would easily dare to tinker with it. Yet a later poet modelled his own poem on it and produced perhaps a greater masterpiece. What he did was to rearrange the same scene, infusing it with a greater depth and inwardness. The author of the newer poem is unknown. Perhaps Ānandavardhana knew the name but does not mention it.

I would like to put in a remark here by way of parenthesis before quoting the newer poem. The notion of *rasa*, I have said, was conceived by Bharata in the context of theatre. The dramatic manner of depicting *rasa* tended to become normative and a marked dramatic element is present in much Sanskrit poetry.

Amaru's poem pictures a scene not unlike a dramatic tableau which, though not entirely frozen or static, has a situational quality easily seen as an intense moment of heightened drama. My translation aims at outlining the dramatic scene described, the rich poetic nuances are, of course, lost.

The newer poem in Sanskrit reads:

nidrākaitavinaḥ priyasya vadanairvinyasya vaktraṁ vadhūḥ
bodhābhāsaniruddhacumbanarasāpyābhogalolaṁ sthitā/
vailakṣyādvimukhībhavediti punastasyāpyanārambhiṇaḥ
sākāṅkṣapratipatti nāma hṛdayaṁ yātaṁ tu pāraṁ rateḥ//

[As her husband lay feigning sleep, the young bride placed her cheek softly against his, forcibly restraining herself from the bliss *(rasa)* of kissing him passionately. And yet she throbbed with joy (*ābhoga*). He, too, remained unmoving lest she move away, embarrassed. Thus holding themselves back from what they intensely desired to do, their hearts were yet transported beyond the summit of eros.]

The playful movement of the earlier scene here becomes totally still, the outer movement transfigured into a vibration within. The action is so internalised, it transcends the realm of drama, becoming pure poetry: it can no longer be rendered on the stage. The poet certainly succeeds in handling his model imaginatively, metamorphosing his given material into something new and original. Such transformation, in Ānandavardhana's view, was nothing short of creation.[3]

[3] Significantly, this verse, unlike the earlier one, uses purely verbal, "poetic" devices to great effect. It has two instances of the figure called contradiction or paradox: (1) the girl is described as *niruddhacumbanarasā,* "deprived of the bliss of kissing" and yet *ābhogalolaṁ sthitā*, "vibrating with joy" *rasa* and *ābhoga* acting as synonyms here. (2) The other instance, occurring in the last line is obvious enough. Its effect is heightened by a subtle *double entendre* on the phrase *sākāṅkṣapratipatti* which means literally "unfulfilled desire" but also, as a technical term in grammar, "an incompletely formulated sentence", which "wants" something before it can make sense: a sentence left hanging in the middle of sense and nonsense as it were. An utterance such as, "Fortunately I... ", for example, which demands additional phrases such as, "was there" or "had money", or "could hang on to the cliff" or the like, to make sense.

He cites, in this connection, an interesting opinion held by some critics who denied the very possibility of original creation in poetry. These critics argued that the purpose of poetry was to express universals of experience (*anubhāvyānubhavasāmānyam*). Such universals were finite in number and common to all men at all times, past or present. And, as such, they had already been expressed by earlier poets leaving nothing for modern poets to say. If, nevertheless, a new poet felt that he was making an original utterance, this was just make-belief, a subjective opinion (*mānamātram*). Ānandavardhana rejoins that if this view were true we would have had no original poetry after Vālmīki's *Rāmāyaṇa*, the epic considered the *ādikāvya,* the primal poem in Sanskrit literature. For one would be inclined to assert that Vālmīki, the archetypal, paradigmatic poet, had already expressed the universals of experience. But this is patently absurd. It goes against the overwhelming judgement of *sahṛdayas,* discerning lovers of poetry, who recognise great poetry and poets after Vālmīki.

The *pūrvapakṣa,* the view which denies the possibility of new creation, argues, in reply, that all that is new in a so-called new poem is the use of new expressions for the same old things. In answer, Ānandavardhana asserts that a new word inevitably implies a new meaning, a new content (*vācya*), because words are inextricably (*avinābhāvena*) linked with their meaning or content. New expressions cannot but imply a new content.

Ānandavardhana admits that resemblances — *saṁvādāḥ,* 'conformances' he calls them — do exist between the creations of poets, between the old and the new. Some may be involuntary since, as he says, minds of men work in similar ways.

However, this is not to deny the possibility of entirely original poetic creation. Just as nature, he remarks, can always create a new object[4] in spite of the endless variety of what it already has, so can a poet. But having said this he exhorts poets not to be afraid of *saṁvādas,* not to desist from a deliberate model-oriented practice

[4] *Dhvanyāloka, udyota* 4, *vṛtti* on *kārikā* 10.

and reliance on handling existing material. For this can be done creatively, resulting in new, "original" poems.

Saṁvādas between poems can be, according to him, of three kinds: 1. *Pratibimbavat,* that between a man and his mirror image; 2. *ālekhyavat*, that between a man and his representation in painting: a painting necessarily transforms what it paints. (The kind of painting which Ānandavardhana and his contemporaries would have known, such as that of Ajanta, transforms quite palpably); 3. *tulyadehivat*, that between two men similar in looks but with distinct identities of their own.

Only the third kind of *saṁvāda* is really creative: a poem reconstituted with the same elements as those of its model, but infused with a new self or spirit. Ānandavardhana does not go into the details of how the three types of *saṁvādas* he speaks of are to be distinguished in actual poetic practice. He leaves this to the judgement of his reader, assuming that one who had studied the rest of his work would be able to arrive at the details on his own. The example we have quoted from him earlier is certainly, in his view, an instance of creative transformation, that is the *tulyadehivat.*

Inspired perhaps by Ānandavardhana, another theorist, Rājaśekhara, whose career followed soon after that of Ānandavardhana, used a similar scheme for analysing poetic creativity.[5] His work, or what survives of it, the *Kāvyamīmāṁsā* is a manual for poets, intended as advice concerning how best to develop their art. It is in the context of plagiarism, *parārathaharaṇa,* that Rājaśekhara discusses ways of handling older material. He goes into much greater detail in discussing the matter than Ānandavardhana. For, unlike his predecessor, he was talking to poets about the techniques of their craft —

[5] Rājaśekhara quotes Ānandavardhana at the beginning of the 5th chapter of his *Kāvyamimāṁsā.* Also in a stray verse attributed to him, he praises Ānandavardhana's concept of *dhvani:* See *op. cit.,* G.O.S. ed., edited by Dalal and Shastri, Baroda, 1934, p. 156. It is not unlikely that Rājaśekhara was not directly inspired by Ānandavardhana in this matter, but that both were drawing from a common tradition current among critics and poets.

kavikarma — not only delving into principles.

Rājaśekhara uses the phrase *parārthahaharaṇa* to mean appropriating something written by another. Yet *haraṇa* if creatively done, he says, is not *haraṇa* but *svīkaraṇa*, "assimilation", a legitimate, indeed, commendable poetic practice. *Svīkaraṇa* operates through creatively transforming given material.

Rājaśekhara classifies various ways of handling older material on the basis of what he calls *yoni:* source. He has three basic categories of *yoni*: (1) *anyayoni*, a new poem of which the source is transparent, where one can easily make out the model on which it is based. (2) *nihnutayoni,* "concealed *yoni"*, where the older poem is transformed beyond recognition into a new work. (3) *ayoni,* a poem without a source, an entirely original, non-model-oriented creation. Rājaśekhara further subdivides the first and the second of these categories into sub-classes. But the third, *ayoni*, has no subclass; it is not really a way of handling older material but a category in itself. It cannot be further classified, for how can one prefabricate categories for the entirely original ?[6]

Rājaśekhara subdivides *anyayoni* into two broad classes: (1) *pratibimbakalpa* and (2) *ālekhyakalpa.* These parallel the first two classes in Ānandavardhana (the suffix *kalpa* here is synonymous with *vat* of the earlier classification). Rājaśekhara describes the *pratibimbakalpa* — what may be called the mirror-image class — as no more than rewording an older poem in newer terms, thus making a change which does not alterzthe *paramārtha,* the "essential meaning" of the given.[7] This is an uncreative category, as in Anandavardhana. But unlike

[6] Rājaśekhara does speak of three very broad "kinds" of *ayoni* poems, making a distinction on the basis of subject-matter: *laukika,* "this-worldly" concerned with things of this world; *alaukika* "trans-worldly" concerned with the gods and *miśra*, "mixed", concerned with a combination of the two: *Kāvyamimāṁsā,* chapter 12. But this classification is radically different from the others in principles; its basis is not how the new transforms the old. Any corpus whatsoever of poems can, in fact be classified as *laukika, alaukika* and *miśra.*

[7] *Kāvyamimāṁsā,* Chapter 12.

Ānandavardhana, Rājaśekhara grants some creativity to the next class, namely the *ālekhyaprakhya* (*prakhya* in also synonymous with *vat*) — he was after all writing for the poet who is also a craftsman and could not keep his standards too stringent. He defines *ālekhyaprakhya* as: "making a given theme or subject matter seem different through somewhat touching it up, refining it, making it more elegant (*saṁskārakarma*)."[8] The example he gives is illuminating. He quotes an old verse which describes the black snakes twined around Śiva's neck, with their hoods raised, as sprouts emerging from the dark, world-destroying poison stored in Śiva's throat — the poison having sprouted due to the life-giving waters of the close-by Gaṅgā dripping on them. This verse became the model for another which makes a minor variation in the metaphor. The new verse describes the white snakes twined around Siva's locks as sprouts emerging from the root-like half-moon which the god wears in his matted locks, watered by the nearby Gaṅgā. The language of the second verse closely follows the first and is obviously modelled on it. We have here a clear case of a variation on a theme, though admittedly a minor one.[9]

The two categories which Rājaśekhara considers really creative are the *tulyadehitulya* and the *parapurapraveśatulya* (*tulya* is an other synonym of *vat*) — he commends them with the words: *so yaṁ ullekhavānanugrāhyo mārgaḥ:* "This is a recommended path worthy of its name"; though in recommending *ālekhya*, he does not use the extra adjective, "worthy of its name".

Ānandavardhana had spoken of *tulyadehivat* as an apparent outward similarity but a marked inner difference between two poems. Rājaśekhara inverts the definition: he defines *tulyadehitulya* as a poem apparently differing from its model in content yet having a clearly-felt inner resemblance.[10] He gives two examples, each differently expressing a theme, common in Sanskrit poetry: "an extraordinary object needs an extraordinary

[8] Ibid., Chapter 12.

[9] Ibid., Chapter 12.

[10] Rājaśekhara, *op. cit.*, Chapter 12.

home." The first poem expresses the idea thus: horses are common objects and can live in any home, but only a king's palace is a proper home for an elephant, or else it should be left in the forest. The second, a purportedly derivative poem, expresses the same idea through a change of metaphor: a diamond, it says, deserves a royal home or it had better not be taken out of the mine where it belongs.

Rājaśekhara's examples are not as inspired as those of Ānandavardhana or Kuntaka, to mention another theorist. They are not convincing as good examples of creative writing. But we are not here concerned with Rājaśekhara's critical judgement of poetry, but rather with his analytical categories which remain formally valuable, whatever the aesthetic value of the illustrations he gives to demonstrate them.

The *parapurapraveśa,* the other broad sub-class under *nihnutayoni*, is not found in Ānandavardhana. The word literally means: "A person who has entered an alien town". He would look different, transformed by the new surroundings. Rājaśekhara defines this suggestive term more discursively as: "keeping the root idea or motif of the model but changing its context," its "entourage", he calls it, using another evocative word.[11]

Each of the four categories recorded above has eight sub-classes. It is interesting to see how Rājaśekhara makes his sub-divisions, illustrating each with a verse. He has a very formal approach; he gives us quite a structural analysis of the ways and techniques by which a given poem may be transposed or transmuted. He sounds startlingly like a musician recounting the different ways in which given musical pieces or themes may be varied. Each variation bears a name, some are colourfully figurative, and given, it would appear, by practising poets.

I would like to list here some of these variations — without quoting the examples Rājaśekhara cites as illustrations — mainly to project more vividly his formal approach, suggestive of the practice of musicians.

---

[11] Rājaśekhara, *op. cit.,* Chapter 12.

I will begin by listing a few of the eight sub-species he classifies under *pratibimbakalpa*, which in his view was a transformation not deserving to be called "creative". I will mainly list those which rely on structural change. The very first is termed *vyatyastaka* — a name which may be rendered as "scattering the sequence". It is defined as "changing the order of parts without affecting the whole." The second is *khaṇḍa* — meaning "a segment". This consisted of using part of a larger theme turning it into a complete poem. The third is *tailabindu* — literally "a drop of oil" — defined as enlarging or rather spreading out a brief idea in a manner resembling the spread of a drop of oil on water: considered an ugly shapeless spread. Another is *naṭanepathya* — "an actor's costume" — a transformation which merely translates a poem into another language, like an actor changing his dress. In music this could mean changing the words of a tune without making a change in the music.[12] These, I think, are enough to indicate what Rājaśekhara is trying to do. He adds that making variations of the above kind only stamps a poet as a non-poet, revealing a lack of creativity (*kaverakavitvadāyī*).

Ālekhyaprakhya, which Rājaśekhara allows to be a creative mode of transformation, also has eight sub-species. Many of these, significantly, are structurally similar to those of the earlier non-creative mode. *Vyutkrama,* defined as the reversal of a given manner of stating a theme (*krameṇābhihitasyārthasya viparītābhidhānam)*, is really no different from *vyatyastaka,* where the change consisted of a rearrangement of parts.

Another variation, *navanepathya* — "new costume" — is the same as *naṭanepathya,* — "an actor changing his costume" — of the earlier category. Similarly, *uttaṁsa,* — "an earring" — defined as "giving importance to a subsidiary idea" can be

---

[12] Śārṅgadeva, the author of the famous 13th-century epitome on music, *Saṅgitaratnākara,* categorizes *vāggeyakāras* (composers), into three classes. The best are those who compose both the music and the words in a song. The lesser ones are those who borrow another's music, merely composing new words for it.

equated with the earlier, *khaṇḍa* — "a segment" — that is, that using part of given theme.[13]

The difference is the addition of a new dimension, namely, creativity, which cannot be totally reduced to structure. What was just a transformation becomes here a creative transformation. Rājaśekhara quotes a verse from an earlier critic to express this idea. The entire range of available matter, says this critic, is given to the poet for transformation, which can be effected as an actor uses colour to transform himself through make-up.[14] The simile of the actor has been used again, but notable is the phrase used for expressing the idea of the kind of change effected, *anyathātvamivārcchati:* "achieves a distinctive identity". Creative handling makes it a *felt* qualitative change, though the structural process remains the same.

There are some interesting sub-divisions of the remaining two categories, the *tulyadehitulya* and *parapurapraveśasadṛśa* which could be listed and discussed here. But I think we have had enough of Rājaśekhara. What I have in mind is not to discuss him but draw from him some cues in understanding creativity in music.

I need not stress, to begin with, the key role of improvisation in Indian music, or in other words, the basic transformational approach towards the given material. In poetry, at least sophisticated *kāvya* poetry, the same verse is, ideally speaking, handed over exactly as it was composed. If distortions have taken place, the reason is that the transmission process has not been quite as ideal as one could wish. Two different copies of the same poem are — or should be — identical. A Kālidāsa cannot be changed, though a *new* poem may take him as a model. In Indian music there are few genres where such an ideal is even sought for. In Ravīndra Saṅgīta or in film songs one does seek to make different renderings replicas of the original. But these are recent, non-'Traditional', genres.

---

[13] For sub-species of the *ālekhyaprakhya,* see chapter 13 of the *Kāvyamīmāṁsā.*

[14] Ibid. *loc. cit.*

The attempt at exact replication is a recent ideal in music, introduced from the west, where transformation is the prerogative of the composer. He alone may transform given material to create something new, as in the Sanskrit tradition of art-poetry. But once a composition is given final shape it has to be rendered, ideally at least, exactly as given. Some transformational role is allowed to the conductor who may "interpret" a work in his way. But this is, in many cases, because of ambiguities in the scores of given compositions.[15] And even so, the transformation that does take place remains much below even the level of Rājaśekhara's first category, the *pratibimbakalpa*. The performance of a western symphony is an attempt to produce a mirror image of the original. Rājaśekhara's *pratibimbakalpa,* despite its name — "mirror-image" — is more than producing a replica, a copy, of a given work. It is, we have seen, a transformational category, however insignificant one may judge the *quality* of the transformation to be. It, grantedly, does not produce a *new* work. In Hindustani music, a transformation that may be fittingly termed *pratibimbakalpa,* is certain to creep in between all traditional musical genres whether light or classical, whether a *ghazal*, a *qawwali* or a *ṭhumri,* a *khyāl* or a *dhrupad.* No two renderings of a piece in these forms, even by the same musician, are exact replicas. If we still speak of the "same" piece it is because we judge the transformation to be insignificant, or in other words, *pratibimbakalpa*. A transformation there is bound to be, its quality or degree depending on the genre; its total absence would be a rare thing,

[15] In music, as in many other arts, a degree of what may be termed "interpretation" is involved in even faithfully copying a work. A copy in music can never be a mechanical copy in the sense that two copies of the same poem are. Such copies can only be produced on a gramophone or a similar device. A musician reproducing an original cannot do so mechanically. For reproduction itself is an art, a process which is bound to leave some imprint of the artist on the work he copies. He cannot but interpret, in other words, as he copies. But interpretation, in a significant sense, comes in only when the original is uncertain, not given in its entirety, and thus having parts or aspects capable of alternate renderings.

needing, indeed, an unusual, out-of-the-ordinary effort.

The reason is that musical education itself consists of training in the techniques and norms of improvisation. True, a musician is also taught certain more or less pre-set forms, but the handling of these has to be essentially improvisational. The more *śāstrīya,* "classical", the form, the greater, one might think, paradoxically, the role of improvisation in it. Thus, improvisation, is central to *ṭhumrī, ṭappā, khyāl* and *dhrupad.* Transformation in other words, is built into the very making of any particular performance in any of these forms.

In analysing and judging such music, transformational categories such as those of Rājaśekhara can plainly be of great help. When we speak of two performances or renderings of a *ghazal, ṭhumrī* or *khyāl* being the "same", the identity in such cases can be meaningfully understood only in terms of a *pratibimbakalpa* likeness. A later rendering is never exactly a replica of the earlier one. There is bound to be some rearrangement of parts. We speak of the two as being the same because we feel no real change has taken place — there is no *anyathā-bhāva,* to use an earlier phrase quoted from Rājaśekhara.

This raises a question. Can we delineate the structural details of what I have, following Rājaśekhara, called the *pratibimbakalpa* in music ? His model, I should think, will not serve as more than an analogy: music does not use words in which form and content can be analytically sifted with convenient ease. Music is form alone, or at least, the content in it is inseparable from form. The distinction of word and meaning so essential in poetry is meaningless in music. Analytical categories applying to poetry, however structural, cannot be used for music without important modifications and alternations. Details will have to be worked out, though I must confess, I have as yet not made a move in that direction.

But if we have to work out any details at all we must first seek to answer two crucial questions: What is the "given" in music that the musician seeks to transform and how and with what does he do it ?

In seeking to answer these questions, I shall be speaking of the "classical" forms alone, though what I have to say may be seen at the end of my analysis to apply also to the relatively lighter forms of Hindustani music. The answer to the first question is obviously: a *rāga*. In classical music what a musician is taught are *rāgas* which are his "given". But the "given" in this case is a peculiar "given". It is not a pre-formed structure which a musician has simply to reproduce. A *rāga* is a generalised form. Take the description of any *rāga* and what you will have is a general description of its form: rules and norms concerning the total path the *rāga* should traverse. Its *antaramārga,* as the ancients aptly called it: the scale (*thāṭ*) to be used, notes to be emphasized, weakened, dropped, jumped over, to be more significantly interlinked, to be used in ascending or descending, obligatory bends or twists to be made between them and so on. Given this, any *rāga* can in principle be realised or given concrete form in a number of different ways. But this is true only in principle. In practice certain crystalisations have taken place, crystalisations made by generations of creative musicians, to which a new practitioner becomes heir. These crystalisations are a musician's "given". They are not, however, fixed or frozen entities. They cannot be reproduced as replicas: though, of course, they have elements which are relatively more stable, such as the *bandish.*[16] But a large part of their form remains fluid and malleable.

These crystalisations, I think, can best be described as styles. We have in Hindustani music four major styles of rendering a *rāga* (not to speak of sub-styles — *gharānās* — within these): the *dhrupad* style, the *khyāl* style, the *ṭhumrī* style and the *ṭappā* style. I believe that in order to seek an answer to the second question I had asked earlier, namely, how and with what does a musician create and transform a *rāga* (for every creation itself involves transformation, using improvisation as it does), we must

[16] A composition "fixed" in its melodic contours, set to a certain rhythmic cycle (*tāla*) and often forming the nexus around which improvisation takes place.

look for the structural basis of musical style.

But before I analyse further, I must deal with an objection that is bound to arise concerning what I have just said. I have spoken of four styles in which a *rāga* can be rendered, implying that any *rāga* can be rendered in any of these styles. The immediate objection would be that this is simply not true. *Ṭhumrī* is sung in only a handful of *rāgas*; so is *ṭappā.* There are *rāgas* of more recent origin in which *dhrupad* is not sung,[17] others such as *Khamāj* and *Bhairavī* in which *khyāl* is not sung. Yet *dhrupad* and *khyāl* are the two encompassing, inclusive styles in Hindustani music: most *rāgas* can be sung in both and almost all *rāgas* can be sung in either of them. We should, therefore, it may be argued, speak of only two styles of rendering *rāgas.* The other two are not truly universal styles, being limited to a few *rāgas.*

I would, in reply, like to argue two points. One: it is true that presently the *ṭhumrī* and *ṭappā* styles are confined to a very few *rāgas* and are in this sense lame styles. But this is a relatively recent development. Earlier these styles were as broad-based as the *khyāl.* There existed *ṭhumrīs* in all the *rāgas* in which *khyāls* were sung. Tradition bears this out. And if one needs documentary evidence, one has only to pick up the two collections of Lucknow *ṭhumrī* published by the University Press of the Sangita Nataka Akademi, U.P., and look at the list of *rāgas* in which Lallan Piyā and other equally famous singers had composed *ṭhumrīs.* One of these two collections is devoted entirely to Lallan Piyā, a singer who lived into the twentieth century.[18]

---

[17] When I say "sung", I also imply "played", for the musical styles I am speaking of apply to the manner of rendering a *rāga* irrespective of whether this is done in singing or playing.

[18] *Ṭhumrī Saṅgraha* compiled and notated by Gangadhar Rao Telang, Lucknow, 1977. *Lallan Piyā Kī Ṭhumrīyāṁ,* compiled and notated by Bharatendu Bajpai, Lucknow 1977. We gather from the introduction of the latter work that a direct disciple of Lallan Piyā died in 1950. It is not unlikely, therefore, that Lallan Piyā himself was alive at the beginning of the twentieth century.

This might at once prompt a question: why has *ṭhumrī* declined, and so speedily ? I will not let this question distract me here and move on to my second point which, in fact, follows from the first. The fact that the *ṭhumrī*, *could* mould any *rāga* to its stylistic needs, just as *khyāl* does today, certainly proves that it is *capable* of being an encompassing, universal style like *khyāl*, even though it no longer is so. One can quite possibly envisage a resurgence of *ṭhumrī* and its extension to more and more *rāgas* once again (the *ghazal*, a form somewhat similar to the *ṭhumrī*, is witnessing such an extension) though the possibility seems to me remote. But the very fact that such a possibility can be visualised is enough for my purposes. It shows that the *ṭhumrī* is a possible universal style like *khyāl*.

The same can be said of *ṭappā* which is almost on the brink of total disappearance. It is today a style without any vitality. There are very few *ṭappā* singers and the total number of *ṭappās* one hears may be counted on one's fingers. Yet there was a time when *ṭappās* were sung in a so-called serious *rāga* like *Pūriyā*:[19] and I would maintain that even if this were not true, the possibility of its becoming so would still be undeniable. Indeed, if there is any style which deserves resurgence it is the *ṭappā*.

Before I take any further step in speculating on the structural basis of musical style, I would like to point out that style relates not only to structure but also to sensibility. A change in style is an index of a change in sensibility. And sensibility is related to milieu in however tenuous, not-exactly-definable a manner that the relation may have and hence to history and transformations in society. Consider the four major musical styles we have been speaking of. Their marked difference in musical idiom and hence the different sensibilities they express needs no comment. The severe, sombre *dhrupad* with its austere lines and curves is a

---

[19] Dr. Prem Lata Sharma, Head of the Dept. of Musicology, at Banaras Hindu University, recently told me that she heard a musician from Bihar sing a most intricate *ṭappā* in *Pūriyā*, properly maintaining the *rāga* form. Apparently a tradition of *ṭappā* singing, which has disappeared from the rest of North India, survives in a remote corner of Bihar.

world removed from the mellifluous *khyāl* of which it is the parent. The "effeminate" eighteenth century social milieu of the court of Muhammad Shah, known as *rangile,* "the colourful one", in which *khyāls* as we know them took shape, was far removed from the more "heroic", war-like, rough period between the fourteenth and the sixteenth centuries when *dhrupad* emerged out of the earlier *prabandha* form. *Ṭhumrī,* lighter in feel and approach than the *khyāl,* emerged out of *khyāl* in the nineteenth century. The *ṭappā* was born of *ṭhumrī.*[20] The genius behind this intricate filigree-like form was a Punjab musician named Shorī Miyān, said to have been trained in the *ṭhumrī,* style. Other influences moulding the classical *ṭappā* are not very clear. It does not seem to have much more than its name in common with the popular folk *ṭappā* of Punjab.

The historical aspect of the emergence of these styles is certainly suggestive of some connection between the successive transformations in music and something "akin" in the emergent social milieux which nurtured them. But with a formal art like music it is difficult to pinpoint the nature of this connection: to speak concretely of what was "akin" in the social structure. In music, where form and content are inextricably merged, the style *is* the sensibility. We cannot separate the expression from what it expresses. We cannot, consequently, speak of any concrete factor in a social structure which music represents or mirrors.

To return to the question of style, I find the category of *tulyadehivat* quite illuminating in understanding the relation between *rāga* and different styles of rendering it. The *tulyadehivat* according to Ānandavardhana occurs when two poems are similar in appearance but different in spirit. What happens to a *rāga* rendered in different styles is analogous. The tonal structure of a *rāga,* its *antaramārga,* remains recognisably the same even with a change of style (otherwise we would not be

[20] It is not, however, certain whether the *ṭhumrī* came before the *ṭappā* or after it. It should also be remarked here that be plainly, to make any connection between *ṭappā* and the social milieu is much more difficult than is the case with the other three styles.

speaking of the same *rāga*), yet a great difference can be felt in spirit. We can recognise, say, *rāga Bihāg*, in a *dhrupad*, a *khyāl*, a *ṭhumrī* or a *ṭappā* as the same *rāga* but the *Bihāg* in each of these cases is expressive of a very different ethos.

Conversely, the *tulyadehivat* can also help us to form a criterion for judging if a new style has been achieved. Today it is the *khyāl* alone where significantly new and exciting experiments are being made in style. The similarities in two *dhrupad* renderings of any *rāga* by two different musicians can, I feel, be more often than not appropriately termed *pratibimbavat*. At best with a more sensitive, creative musician, it does not move beyond the *ālekhyavat*. The reason is that *dhrupad* is a closed, confined style. Transformations are strictly circumscribed and not allowed to stray beyond prescribed limits. This is what allows *dhrupad* to retain its strength and character. But it also prevents it from producing such different styles as we have in the *khyāls* of Amir Khan and Kumar Gandharva, to take two tellingly extreme examples. The difference between two *khyāl* styles is surely in the *tulyadehivat* class.

Though I am tempted here to speculate on the sensibility, or rather the gamut of sensibilities, that modern *khyāl* embodies and their relations with today's milieu, I must now turn to the analysis of the structural components of musical style, the raw material with which it is constituted.

At this point I would like to introduce a rather unfamiliar technical term, the *sthāya*, which I find promising in making the analytical attempt I am aiming at. Śarṅgadeva defines *sthāya* as: "*rāgasya avayavāḥ sthāyāḥ*": "*sthāyas* are the limbs of a *rāga*." The actual music of Śārṅgadeva's days, that is, the early thirteenth century, is no longer available to us, except in imaginative reconstruction: our own music is in many essentials a legacy from it. However, it is clear from Śārṅgadeva's descriptions that in speaking of *sathāya* he has in mind musical phrases, idioms, melodic figures and the like, in other words, organic structural units of a kind a musician would use to "build" any *rāga*. He gives a long list of *sthāyas* which he apparently considers the basic limbs, organic "building blocks" for constructing a *rāga*; any *rāga*. The *sthāyas* — from the root "*sthā*", "to remain" — are the "constants" which a musician handles in order to make his improvisations.[21]

Modifying Śārṅgadeva a little, I would like to speak of *sthāyas* as the smallest organically meaningful structural units into which the totality of melodic movements in a *style* may be reduced. Following Bharata, I would like to call *sthāyas, geya-mātṛkās.* Let me explain. In speaking of dance, ancient theorists distinguish between two basic categories of dance: the *nṛtya* and the *nṛtta.* The *nṛtya* was mimic in purport; one could not speak of *nṛtya* without *abhinaya*, mime. But *nṛtta* was purely formal. Bharata calls it a dance which has no connection with the meaning of any text[22] whereas expressing textual meanings was central to *nṛtya.* In analysing the structure of *nṛtta*, Bharata speaks of basic units of movements which he terms *karaṇas.*

He also calls them *nṛtta-mātṛkās:* literally, the "mothers of dance", so named because these in larger clusters constituted the dance as a whole.[23] Abhinava Gupta's comments in explaining the meaning of *karaṇa* are significant. Abhinava describes *karaṇa* as a body movement which has the quality of grace *(gātrāṇāṁ vilāsakṣepa).* He further qualifies it as the smallest movement which is nonpragmatic, not made with a utilitarian purpose, and yet having the sense of a single

---

[21] In fact, interestingly, Śārṅgadeva has a short but remarkable section on how a musician can transform given material to make new creations. This can be done in an uncreative way by changing the words or the *rāga* of on old song. But if the musician wishes to retain the *rāga* the path of transformation to follow would be to make a creative change in the *sthāyas: rāgaḥ sthāyāntarairnava (Saṅgītaratnākara, 4, 362).*

[22] *Nāṭyaśāstra* (G.O.S. ed.) Vol. 1. 4, 262. *Nṛtta* is here spoken of as: "*na gītakārthasambaddhaṁ na cāpyarthasya bhāvakam.*"

[23] See, however, the article, in this collection entitled *Taṇḍu: The First Theoretician of Dance,* where the analysis is more complete and truer to Bharata's text. The *mātṛkas* were, as it emerges there, units smaller than the *karaṇas*. Yet the purport of the point made here remains undisturbed, whether we take the *karaṇa* as the smallest unit or the *mātṛkā*.

unit.[24] A *karaṇa* is, in other words, the smallest aesthetic block into which *nṛtta* may be analysed. Clearly, *sthāya*, as I have spoken of it, is a notion analogous to *karaṇa*. This is why I have also called it *geya-mātṛkā*, "the mother of song". *Sthāya* in my sense is the smallest unit into which a musical style may be broken.

Even in common musical parlance we do speak of different *sthāya*s in connection with different musical styles, though we do so loosely. Expressions like *ṭhumrī kā aṅga, khyāl ka aṅga, dhrupad kā aṅga, ṭappe ka aṅga,* (the *aṅga* of *ṭhumrī,* of *khyāl*, of *dhrupad,* of *ṭappā*) are common among musicians. *Aṅga* in such usage is neither unambiguous nor precise. But an important aspect of the meaning of *aṅga* in such contexts is plainly structural. *Dhrupad kā aṅga* means melodic movements typical of the *dhrupad* style, such as *gamak*, the *sūt* and the like. Listed together and further analysed such movements can yield typical *sthāya* units of the style.

Though I have not made the necessary detailed analysis for identifying and listing typical *sthāyas* of various styles, I believe the exercise will yield fruitful results. The *sthāya* approach can be helpful not only in understanding style, but it may also be valuable for understanding the transformation of one style into another. For if *sthāya* can be seen as the basis of style, the transmutation of *sthāya* can be shown to be an important basis of the emergence of a new style. We, in fact, do speak of such a process when we say, for example, "*dhrupad ke aṅga ko khyāl meṁ ḍhāl liyā*": "the *aṅga* of *dhrupad* has been moulded into that of *khyāl*". Mutating a *dhrupad aṅga* to render it into a *khyāl aṅga* is common among musicians, a fact which can easily be demonstrated. The word *aṅga* in such usages stands for certain *types* of *sthayas* which can be meaningfully differentiated.

---

[24] Abhinava on *Nāṭyāśāstra* 4, 28-33: "A (graceful) movement distinct from those made in connection with avoiding the undesirable (*heya*) and achieving the desired (*upādeya*) is *karaṇa*... a single movement from one point to another appropriate point is *karaṇa*". *kriyā karaṇam. kasya kriyā. nṛttasya. gātrāṇāṁ vilasakṣepasya. heyopādeyaviṣayakriyādibhyo vyatirikta yā tatkriyā karaṇamityarthaḥ.*

CHAPTER – THREE

Ancient Indian Music and the Concept of Man

Music does not embody concepts. It cannot. Only language embodies concepts. Yet we are surely tempted to ask: How is change in musical form related to change in the concept of man from one epoch to another ? Or in other words: Do changes in musical forms bear any intimate relation with changes in ideas concerning man: his nature, his place in the world, his goals ?

Before we can attempt any answer to this question, a tricky problem intrudes: How are we to correlate change in musical forms with change in concepts ? Can there be a yard-stick that can gauge relative change with any right and fair degree of dispassion ? Let me put the question in another way: Can we on hearing a piece of music, or a corpus of musical forms, have an idea of the concept of man that the music implies or assumes ? The answer, I think, cannot really be given in the positive unless we do so in a loose sense and take extra-musical factors like sung-words or the lore surrounding music into account. Conversely, can we on becoming familiar with the concept of man, held by certain musicians, or even certain cultures or epochs, come to know the forms of music they might have created ? I doubt if this is possible. Let me take an example: Renaissance in Europe was an age when the entire spirit of the times, both in thought and art was profoudly influenced by classical ideals. A student who knew the general character of the Renaissance but not its music, might expect a similar manifestation in music too. Yet Renaissance musical forms, unlike, painting, sculpture and thought, show no Greek trait. They are basically different. For Greek music was melodic while Renaissance music is polyphonic and harmonic. Let us take another example that is closer to most of us and therefore perhaps more telling: Concepts of man have certainly undergone many changes in India over the last two centuries within which period a whole new epoch has dawned. Yet do we see a similar tranformation in music ? We do not. Many people, indeed, complain that music unlike painting, sculpture, architecture and even literature has not changed to suit the modern outlook and ethos.

Let us also look at the matter from another angle. Let us see if profound changes in music are accompanied by analogous changes in concepts and *weltanschauung*. Polyphony was introduced in Europe in the 9th century and it gradually replaced the earlier monodic music by the 12th-13th centuries. No change could be more profound in musical history. But do we perceive a similar change in the concept of man ? We do not. The great change from pagan to the Christian ethos had already taken place centuries earlier and Europe from the 5th to the 9th centuries continued to create music within the monodic system it had inherited. No doubt there were transformations: the introduction of new forms and a new spirit, but these were minor compared to the fundamental change that came with polyphony. One can see no change in the European world of thought and ethos that can be associated with this basic change in music.

Now let us take an example from India. During the 14th to 16th centuries, a great change in Indian music took place with the introduction of the *thāṭ-melakartā* system which superseded the earlier *grāma-mūrchanā* scheme. Accompanying this change in theory was the introduction of the *tānpūrā* as the drone.[1] The historical outlines of this change remains vague in comparison with

---

[1] The exact date, or even century, when the *tānpūrā* was introduced is still a matter of debate and conjecture. *Tānpūrā* was certainly present in the 17th century, as miniature paintings show. It may have been introduced earlier. However, even if its actual use came after the 16th century, the new music, within which its use became so crucial and almost 'logical' was a product of the period between the 14th and 16th centuries. See also my Hindi article entitled, 'Saṅgīta Ke Itihāsa meṁ Śilpa Kī Bhūmikā', *Saṅgīta meṅ Anusandhān Kī Samasyāyeṅ aur Kṣetra,* ed. Subhadra Chaudhury, pub. Krishna Brothers, Ajmer, 1988, pp, 111-134 (also included in the volume devoted to Hindi of the present collection) for further reflection on the history of the *tānpūrā*.

what we know from Europe, because music-history in India is hazy in comparison with music-history in Europe. Yet the occurrence of a major change is beyond doubt. But it is difficult to think of a parallel change in the concept of man or in the concepts held by man during that period that can in a relevant sense be said to have accompanied the change in music. True, this was a period of great political upheaval, when the old order was being shattered and was giving place to a new set-up. But the moot point is with what, in this change, can we connect a change in music. I cannot think of any element or conjunction of elements to which one can relevantly point. Islam certainly brought with it many new movements of thought and culture and art. The influence of these on poetry, painting, architecture and social institutions are explicit enough. But the new influence hardly provides any perspective for understanding the change in music. Even the fact that there was a great infusion of new forms in the wake of the conquest does not really afford a satisfactory explanation for the change. For Islamic music is not drone-dominated. Moreover, the change that occurred was nowhere as drastic as the change from monody to polyphony: what happened can, I think, be best characterised as a rearrangement of old forms around a new fulcrum, the drone. No amount of infusion of new forms, let alone a change in *weltanschauung* can explain this phenomenon. A greater change in *weltanschauung* occurred in Indian history with the introduction of British rule, European ideas and ideals; yet all this left music unaffected in its basic forms.

What I have said was intended as a brief cautionary preface to any attempt at understanding music in relation to concepts. I do not mean to deny that many major, enduring movements and currents in music may to some relevant degree be fruitfully understood in the perspective of major movements in ideas and cultural ethos. But this is true of our *attitude* to music rather than its form and the relation between these two remain weak, slender and ambiguous. Let me illustrate this in relation to *sāma* and some later currents in musical culture. We cannot really explain the *forms* which *sāma* and later music took from what we know of the Vedic and later concepts of man and his place in the world.[2] But the ideas held about music, the lore surrounding it, can certainly be understood illuminatingly in the light of a larger *weltanschauung*. It can help us understand concepts and attitudes *about* music, even if it does not really explain its forms. Attitudes to music, the concepts we hold about its value and nature create the ethos and audience in which music is made. Understanding these is important for an understanding of the musical culture within which forms are created, cherished and preserved, if not the forms themselves.

The Vedic world view was dominated by the concept of the *yajña*. For the Vedic people *sāma* music like the Vedic *mantra* was not created but revealed, *dṛṣṭa*; also like the Vedic *mantra* it was immutable: not a syllable could be changed in a *mantra* and not a note in a *sāma*. Like the *mantra*, *sāma* was associated with *yajña*. Inherent in the Vedic concept of *yajña* was an idea of cosmic cofunctioning and reciprocation: through *yajña*, gods and men entered into a relation of give and take.

The image of the cosmos that emerges from Vedic concepts is that of an organic whole consisting of discrete parts functioning reciprocally in unison. I would like in this context to relate a story from a *Brāhmaṇa* text, the *Jaiminīya-Upaniṣad-Brāhmaṇa*, belonging to the *Jaiminīya śākhā* of the *Sāmaveda*.[3] The story concerns a dispute for supremacy among six gods: Agni, Vāyu, Āditya, Prāṇa, Anna and Vāk. Each stakes his claims with arguments. Agni says: 'I am the mouth of the

[2] The major reason lies in the fact that Ancient *sāma* is not known to us in its ancient form; a great deal of *sāma* survives but we cannot be sure of its authencity. Vedic music has certainly changed much more in transmission than the Vedic texts.

[3] In what follows I rely almost exclusively on the *Jaiminīya Upaniṣad Brāhmaṇa*, for my thoughts regarding *sāma* and Vedic views in general. What I have said can, I believe, be corroborated from other sources. But I have not done so here. One reason for my exclusive attention to the *Jaiminīya Upaniṣad Brāhmaṇa* is to project the importance of this text in music history, an importance hardly, as yet, noticed. My references are to the Tirupati edition of the text; *Jaiminīyārṣeya-Jaiminīyopniṣadbrāhmaṇe*, Kendrīya Sanskrit Vidyāpītha, Tirupati, 1967.

gods. And of men. To me are given the *yajña* offerings. I distribute foods to the gods and men. Without me gods and men would remain without a mouth with which to feed themselves. There would be no *yajña* offerings and consequently no food for gods or men. The whole purpose of existence will be defeated. Nothing will remain." All gave assent to Agni's words. Without him, they all agreed, nothing will remain. Then Vāyu spoke: "I am the *prāṇa*, the breath of life in the gods. And in men. If I go away, life, too, shall be washed away. Without me all will be defeated and nothing will remain". All gave assent to Vāyu's words, too. Without him, they agreed, nothing will remain.

The other gods argued in a similar vein till each saw the truth of the others claim. They saw that each was dependent on the other (*ekaikāmevānu smaḥ*) and without anyone of them the whole will be defeated (*yannu naḥ sarvāsāṁ devatānāmekācana na syāt tata idaṁ sarvaṁ parābhavet*).[4]

This mode of reciprocal functioning, with each part performing its innate function was in the Vedic view what made the whole cosmos exist and move. The true, inherent rhythm of this movement, a rhythm which made everything fall into its proper place and season (*ṛtu*), was *ṛta*. Man was as much part of *ṛta* as were the gods: both interdependent on each other, acting as it were, as counterpoints to each other. Indeed, the Vedic conception of the cosmos, readily brings to mind the image of an orchestra playing different melodies to produce a single harmony.

This conception was reflected in the performance of the *yajña* ritual, too. It was a ritual performed by a group of priests with different functions, acting in unison. Part of the ritual in the more important *yajñas* was the singing of hymns to the gods. This was done by the *sāma* preists, who sung *ṛcas* from the *Ṛgveda* to music, which like the *ṛcas* themselves, was revealed and transcendental. *Sāma* itself was sung by a group of three singers, the *prastotā,* the *pratihartā* and the *udgātṛ* often aided by a number of subsidiary singers, the *upagātṛs*. To each of the

---

[4] *Jaiminīya-Upaniṣad-Brāhmaṇa*, 4, 8, 1-3.

three main singers was assigned a different part of the five or seven part *sāma*-structure. One of the parts was sung by two musicians seperately. The finale was sung by all together.

Connected with the Vedic concept of *ṛta* was the notion of what has been termed cosmic correspondences. Everything in this world, however, seemingly disparate had an inner mystic correspondence with other things, a correspondence which is often spoken of as a relation of identity. Every part of the *yajña* ritual had a cosmic correspondent which often also provided its *raison d'etre*. Similarly, every element in the human microcosm had its correspondent in the macrocosm. The *Brāhmaṇa* and *Āraṇyaka* texts are full of such correspondences. I would like to quote here an example that concerns *sāma*. A *sāma* we have said, could be sung in seven parts, these were the seven *bhaktis*, named:

1. *hiṅkāra* 2. *prastāva* 3. *ādi* (or *praṇava*) 4. *udgītha*
5. *Pratihāra* 6. *upadrava* 7. *nidhana*

The *Jaiminīya-Upaniṣad-Brāhmaṇa* speaks of a relation of identity between these *bhaktis* and various aspects of the cosmos. Thus each *bhakti* is said to correspond to a different quarter in the space: *hiṅkāra* is the east, *prastāva,* the south, *ādi,* the west, *udgītha,* the north, *pratihāra* is *that* quarter, *upadrava* is the *antarikṣa* and *nidhana* is *this* quarter.[5] Another passage says: *Hiṅkāra* is mind, *prastāva* is Speech, *udgītha is prāṇa*, the life-breath; *hiṅkāra* is the Moon, *prastāva* is Fire, *udgītha* is Āditya, the Sun, and so on.[6] At another place we find: *hiṅkāra* is the season of spring, *prastāva* summer, *udgītha* is the season of rain, *pratihāra* autumn and *nidhana,* winter. It is worth mentioning in parenthesis that this ancient feeling for correspondence has echos in our own assigning of different seasons to different *rāgas.* The idea that different musical forms could correspond to different hours of the day, has also an ancient parallel, for another passage reads: *hiṅkāra* is the hour before sunrise, *prastāva* is the hour of

[5] *Jaiminīya-Upaniṣad-Brāhmaṇa*, 1, 10, 1.
[6] Ibid. 1, 11, 1.

the half-risen sun, *ādi* is the hour when cows set forth for pasture, the midday is *udgītha, pratihāra* is the afternoon, *upadrava,* the hour of dusk when the sky becomes red and *nidhana* the hour when the sun has set.[7]

The ancient Vedic concept of man and his relation to gods and the world was clearly a concept of mutuality and innate inter-relationships. It was a concept, given which one would reasonably expect its expression in music to be in the form of polyphony. There was even the presence of group singing. And yet from all accounts and evidence the music was monodic. Indeed, all subsequent music history in India, which avowedly begins with *sāma*, is a history of monodic music. But music could quite conceivably have taken an entirely different form right from the Vedic period.

Perhaps even more than the forms of *sāma,* the Vedic *attitude* to *sāma* has played a crucial role in subsequent musical history. The Vedic regard for *sāma* shines out bright and clear from all their deliberations. It shines out even from the little we have quoted and that from a single text. *Sāma* for the ancients was an essential element in the ritual process and consequently an essential element in the total harmony of the world. Through *sāma* one could participate in *ṛta*.

Through it one could also attain *amṛta*, supreme immortal being. It could lead one to *brahma*, the highest transcendental truth and knowledge; and it could be the source of *rasa*, the greatest bliss on this earth here and now. In *Jaiminīya-Upaniṣad-Brāhmaṇa*, the *gāyatra sāma* is identified with the mystic syllable *Om*, which is identified with supreme *brahma.*[8] *Om* is the foundation on which the world stands. A legend related in this *Brāhmaṇa*, reports a question which Pṛthu, son of Vena, asked of the divine *vrātyas*: the heavens, he said in a verse, rest on Sūrya, the Sūrya on Pṛthvī and the Pṛthvī on Āpaḥ, the primal waters, on what, he asked, do

[7] Ibid. 1, 12, 1. For quite another, more analytic view of the contemporary *rāga*-time relation prevalent in Hindustani music see: 'An Enquiry Into the Rāga-Time Association In The Light of History', in this volume.

[8] *Jaiminīya-Upaniṣad-Brāhmaṇa*, 1, 1, 1,; 1, 11, 6; 1, 2, 2.

these waters rest? *Om* was the answer.[9] This *gāyatra sāma* is elsewhere in the *Brāhmaṇa* identified with *amṛta*: "*tadetadamṛtaṁ gāyatram/ etena vai prajāpatiramṛtatvamagacchat/ etena devāḥ. etena ṛṣayaḥ.*"[10] *Gāyatra* is the instrument by which the noose of death can be loosened.[11]

Sāma is, therefore, an *upāsanā*: a path to ultimate realization. Āruṇi asked Vāsiṣṭha Caikitāneya as to which god he worshipped. "We worship *sāma*", was the proud answer: Agni, Pṛthvī, the primal waters (Āpaḥ), the Antarikṣa, the heavens, he added were all but aspects of *sāma* (*Jaiminīya-Upaniṣad-Brāhmaṇa* 1, 14, 1).

Sāma, then, was cherished with the greatest esteem that the Vedic people harboured for what they valued. One could, however, object here that *sāma* was prized not for its music but for the *ṛk mantras*, the really cherished possessions of which the *sāma* music was no more than a vehicle. This was not so, for *sāma* was a revealed form in its own right, just as the *ṛcās*. Further in many cases *sāma* was plainly valued for music alone. An example is that of the *anṛca sāma. Anṛca sāma* was a form of *sāma* that had no *ṛk* base and was sung to meaningless syllables.[12] A story speaks of its transcendental powers. The gods coveted heaven. But try as they might, they could not attain their goal. Frustrated, they went to Prajāpati for his advice. Prajāpati told them that they could attain, *svarga*, the heavenly world of light, through *anṛca sāma*. The gods, therefore, emptied the *sāma* of its *mantra* content and through it attained *svarga.*[13]

Aśarīra sāma was perhaps another name for *anṛca sāma* (for the *ṛk* has been called the *śarīra* of *sāma* in the above story).[14] A legend, seemingly historical, tells of the great occult powers of

---

[9] Ibid. 1, 2, 3.

[10] Ibid. 3, 7, 3.

[11] Ibid. 4, 7, 1. *Yajña* is here identified with *Puruṣa*: *Puruṣa* with *udgītha.* The singing of *udgitha* loosens all the knots with which death binds the *yajamāna.*

[12] For a more detailed discussion see the essay, collected here, entitled, 'The Search For the *Apauruṣeya* or Absolute in Music', especially pp. 286-305.

[13] Ibid. 1, 4, 1.

[14] Ibid. 1, 4, 1.

aśarīra sāma. Kaupyeya Uccaiḥśravā, the king of Kurus, was a close and dear friend of Keśī Dārbhya, the king of Pāñcāla. Uccaiḥśravā died, leaving Dārbhya sad and sorrowful. Once when Dārbhya had gone out hunting, he saw Uccaiḥśravā in the woods. Dārbhya tried to embrace his friend. But Uccaiḥśravā was like empty space or the insubstantial wind, he was disembodied. Dārbhya could not touch him. 'What has happened to your body and form?' he asked his friend. In reply Uccaiḥśravā spoke of the *āśarīrī sāma,* The power of the *sāma,* he said, had removed from him the dross of flesh and he was now a disembodied spirit. Through *aśarīrī sāma*, he said, a man could attain the abode of gods. He asked Dārbhya to look for a *brāhmaṇa* who knew this *sāma.* Since it was through this *sāma* that the gods themselves had become disembodied spirits. Dārbhya searched everywhere in his kingdom but found none who knew this *sāma*. Then one day he met a *brāhmaṇa* named Pratṛda Bhalla who lived in a *śmasāna* (a cemetery). Pratṛda Bhalla was an expert in *aśarīra-sāma*. The *śarīra-sāma,* the *sāma* sung to *ṛcās*, he said, was within the reach of Death, but *aśarīra-sāma* was *amṛta* (*atha yadaśarīraṁ tadamṛtam*). Finally, through the power of this *sāma*, Bhalla turned Dārbhya into a disembodied god.[15]

The story illustrates the ancients' belief in the power of music alone in certain of its forms. Music was for them capable of magical transcendental powers. It was perhaps practised in this capacity within certain esoteric circles as the association of Pratṛda Bhalla with the *śmasāna* suggests. This suggestion is strengthened by the fact that Bhalla, according to the story, was opposed by the more 'regular' *sāma*-singers of Dārbhya's kingdom. I would here like to note, in passing, that this legend is the earliest precursor that I know of, of the later stories about occult powers that certain musicians, such as Tānsen possessed and similar powers inherent in certain musical forms, such as *rāga Dīpaka.*

[15] Ibid. 3, 6, 1 to 3, 7, 1.

I have tried to stress the Vedic people's regard for music at some length because this early attitude struck deep roots in the Indian psyche and kept the impulse to music alive under certain overwhelming attacks that hit at the very base of the impulse. The attacks came from what may be called the *sanyāsic weltanschauung* that had its source in a very ancient *muni* or *śramaṇa* tradition, but which grew to overpower the Indian mind in the epoch which produced great *sanyāsīs* like the Buddha, Mahavīra and a host of lesser, though cumulatively very influential, teachers. The Vedic fold itself was moved by the *sanyāsic* ideal, and the older ideal of *yajña* and *ṛta* lost its vigour and vitality. This ideal was now on the defensive and was being metamorphosed by the incorporation of new elements, many of which were quite alien to its former spirit.

Music had no place in the *sanyāsic weltanschauung*. The world in this view was nothing but misery, *duḥkha*. Man was bound to the world by desire and he was bound to suffer in an endless cycle of births as long as this bondage lasted. Liberation lay in transcending the world to *nirvāṇa* or *mokṣa*, where alone was bliss. The road to *nirvāṇa* led away from the allure of the senses and its objects which tied man to the world through desire. All that tempted man to the world was to be shunned. This included music, for music fed the sensual fire. The ban on music encompassed all music, for music was an intoxicant by nature.

In practice, however, music in some of its forms was accepted. No ideal however austere and music-shunning ever totally rejects music when translated into a large cultural movement. But the only function that music could rightly have was to act as a vehicle for words which expressed the *sanyāsic* ideal and the *sanyāsic* experience. Music in its pure forms, too, was certainly tolerated, and many who were moved by the *sanyāsic* ideal were, no doubt, moved by music, too; but music was, in the ultimate analysis, an alien intruder in this world. To the Vedic people music could be an *upāsanā*, a path divine; now it was fuel for *vāsanā*, the path of eternal misery.

It is easy to see why we hear of no distinctive Buddhist or Jain music. There was no true impulse for music in the Buddhist or Jain ethos. Yet this world-view had consequential ramifications in music history. For like the Vedic *weltanschauung*, the *sanyāsic* ethos too exercised a deep influence on the Indian mind. The presence of these two contrary attitudes was bound to produce a tension and ambivalence that has left its stamp in the history of all subsequent musical culture.[16]

After the age of *sāma*, music found its next great creative impulse in the theistic cults of Vaiṣṇavism and Śaivism. These cults had grown from small beginnings in the Vedic age, and had imbibed and amalgamated much from different strands of worship and thought current in the subsequent period of spiritual and intellectual ferment through which they grew. These cults claimed to embody the essence of the Vedas. This could be questioned, for there was much that was new in them and what there was of the old was much transformed. Yet much of the Vedic spirit did abide in them though in new garbs. Just as for the Vedic people, ritual in these cults was a vital element of religious life, and music was vital for ritual. But the ritual had much that was new in form and ethos. So had the music.

The new sacred form or corpus of music, created in the devotional atmosphere of the cults, was *gāndharva,* it was dedicated to the worship of gods, especially Śiva. *Gāndharva*, the ancient texts say, was metamorphosed from the *sāmic* gamut of forms. It was also cherished and valued in an analogous manner both as ritual and as a form spiritual. Like *sāma,*

---

[16] We thus find a defence of music in later saṅgīta texts, prompted, no doubt, by the strictures in the *Smṛtis*, which are deprecative of music, especially musicians, who are in some, passages even forbidden to enter cities, and live *with* the citizens. This is, obviously intended as a device to save the citizens from the musician's immoral influence. Music itself is, however, not forbidden. In fact, some forms of music are extolled by *Smṛtis* and *Purāṇas* (which are often bracketed with *Smṛtis* as texts and *dharma*) themselves as divine. The *Yājñavalkya Smṛti* extols the singing and playing of musical forms such as the *gītakas* of *gāndharva* (for *gitakas*, see my *A Study of Dattilam,* Impex India, Delhi, 1978). In *bhakti*, music was included as part of *sādhanā.*

gāndharva is important in later musical history not only as a form which was the fountain-head of much later development but also the spirit behind it and the attitude towards music it presented.

CHAPTER – FOUR

Words and Music

It is not uncommon to hear people complain against classical singing that words sung are so distorted that they can hardly be understood. Another complaint, which often goes with this, is that lyrics sung by classical musicians are of an inferior poetic quality. Those who voice these complaints are often persons who have a greater rapport with poetry than with music. It is not difficult to answer them back. A number of poets who give public recitations sing their poems. It is certainly reasonable to demand that they should pay proper attention to the quality of the music. This they rarely do. It is common to hear a poet publicly sing his poem full-throatedly to a poor piece of music in a bad voice quite out of tune.

Bickering, however, can get one nowhere. Moreover, complaints against the use and quality of words in classical music are voiced not only by indifferent music lovers but also by some musicians themselves. It will, I think, be more fruitful to try and understand the question of the way or ways in which words may relate to music.

Music and poetry, it will be generally admitted, are quite capable of great power on their own. Yet singing always has to make use of words. It seems, therefore, legitimate to complain that since words are necessary in music they should be used with taste and proper aesthetic care towards the poetic meaning being conveyed.

But when I say words are necessary in singing, what I mean, strictly, is that syllables or vocables are necessary for singing. This can be done without using meaningful words. Since ancient times — at least since the days of Bharata — musicians have been able to get across the problem of using syllables without using words. They have been using nonsense syllables: *stobhākṣaras*, or as Bharata calls them, *śuṣkākṣaras*. Current music has its own corpus of nonsense syllables which are used in singing *taranā* and in *ālāpa*.

It will seem an insignificant truism to assert that in making music musical values dominate. But we tend to forget this when we complain that classical singers distort the words they sing. A classical singer is intent upon building melodic wealth so as to give form to a *rāga*. Words obviously cannot create a *rāga*; the singer thus feels free to distort them if the melodic line so demands. One should remember that singers have been distorting words since the days of Vedic *sāma* music, in which a number of distortions were accorded due sanction and were termed *sāma-vikāras*. These *vikāras* were various ways in which words were distorted and twisted in singing *sāma*. Classical singers then, have the strength of 'divine' sanction behind them. In complaining against them, I feel, one should rather complain that in paying overmeticulous attention towards proper intonation of words, a musician has impoverished a *rāga* or has deprived us of melodic riches.

In what I have said above, I have perhaps been too extreme in defending the musical autonomy of classical singing. This, I think, is needed. But one can still ask the question: Are music and poetry forms that can never be significantly associated? It would certainly be absurd to assert this. The association between music and poetry is an old one and this alone is proof enough that they go well together.

Meaningful association between two or more art-forms which can be said to be autonomous in themselves, is a common fact of aesthetic experience. There are a number of composite art-forms in which 'independent' arts are combined to create a meaningful and homogenous aesthetic whole. Drama is one such art, so is film. Drama uses quite different arts and skills to create the total effect that it does. The same is the case with film. Dance, too, as we know it, is a composite art; for it is always associated with music (a dance performance was in ancient times also known as *saṅgītaka*).

Music has similarly been associated with poetry. The association is and has been of a very varied kind. In forms like the *khyāl* words can become pegs on which to hang the music. There are also forms in which a tune becomes the peg on which to hang words. Yet there are other forms in which the two are more evenly associated, where the blend is so balanced that the one enriches the other and still creates a total whole — *Ṭhumrī* can be cited as an example, though in *ṭhumrī,* I feel, music has the upper hand, in spite of the fact that words play a greater role than in *khyāl*. An example of a more balanced association would be that of *ghazal*, especially as sung by certain great *ghazal* singers like Begum Akhtar. Her music has grace, charm, finesse and melodic wealth; but it is nevertheless, enriched in its total effect by the poetic content, to which it likewise, adds a new aesthetic dimension. Her music is certainly enjoyable on its own, but it does not form as profound a musical experience as does the *khyāl* when rendered by a master such as, for example, Amir Khan.

Another form, in which, to my mind, music and poetry are beautifully wedded, is the traditional *padāvalī kīrtan* of Bengal. Here a great tradition of music as well as of poetry combine to create a deep and moving experience. Each art enhances the power of the other and for those who have experienced the effect, they become virtually inseparable.

There are other approaches to singing in which music or poetry become more or less dominant. Indeed one criterion which may be broadly said to demarcate more 'classical' from 'lighter' forms of sung music is the lesser or greater dominance of the word content. Bharata, too, had evidently recognised this criterion when distinguishing between the more 'classical' *gāndharva* music of his age and contemporary theatrical songs (*gāna*), he stated that the approach to *pada*, or sung words was radically different in the two. In *gāndharva*, words were subservient to the music whereas in theatrical songs, words naturally formed the dominant element.

Our music has a rich repertoire of varied forms. Not all forms seek the same kind of effect. Our insistence that all singing should seek to express the feelings of the sung poem is really a demand for introducing a single goal in all music-making and denying to music the autonomy it has cherished for centuries. Such a demand would put unnecessary boundaries to our own aesthetic experience.

CHAPTER – FIVE

Why Study Ancient Musical Texts ?

I

The question that forms the title of this essay is not intended to be rhetorical or just a verbal device to catch attention. The value of studying ancient musical texts is by no means generally granted, even by those who are seriously involved in the pursuit of music. It is common enough to be accosted with the question: Of what use is the study of old texts for an understanding of our musical art as we practise it today ?

As a student of ancient musical texts, I would like to ponder over this question and enter into some of its ramifications in order to seek answers.

There is often a curious paradox in our attitude to the past. Although in a certain mood of denunciation, we cast doubt on the value of studying old texts, yet, in a different frame of mind, we proudly proclaim and extol our music as age-old, rooted in time immemorial. More often than not, however, this latter sentiment hardly amounts to anything more than paying lip-service to the past; the purpose, at times, being just to add value to the present, hike up the price of what we have by calling it an antique.

The truth remains that an understanding and appreciation of the historical dimension has never been a major aspect of our musical culture, or, for that matter, culture in general. It was common enough to praise the past, as it still is, or emulate it. But this attitude never gave rise to any concerted effort to study the forms and achievements of the past in any kind of a historical perspective. No real attempt was made to perceive forms of the past as points in a process of change, a process itself worthy of serious study.

Early writers on music have, no doubt, described and even, in a skeletal form, notated older music as it was current during their time, or as they found it outlined in earlier texts. But they hardly ever asked themselves the historian's questions: How, through what process, have forms changed ? How did newer forms come out of the old and in the shape they did ? Why did change take place, what was its character, what were the factors that led to it ? Even if the old texts do sometimes speak of these matters, they do so indirectly, in the course of speaking of other things, or in a very cursory, superficial manner. Such questions were never uppermost in their mind. Certain writers of the older texts were so indifferent to chronology that in describing or naming forms, they did not bother to keep the old and the new apart. Modern scholars have remarked on the frustrating difficulties of historically sifting the forms described in a number of musical texts.

Compared to the past, history today receives far more serious thought in musical circles. Historical questions engage our minds and provide an impulse for earnest enquiry. A direct access to a greater range of forms (created over a relatively larger span of time) is also now available to us, thanks to the invention of recording devices. We can now actually hear a musician of the past, even if only of the recent past, on recordings. Our experience remains fragmentary, limited to bits and scraps which were recorded — and that, too, quite indifferently by more modern standards; yet to be able to actually hear an Abdul Karim, a musician separated from us by two generations, would have been unimaginable in earlier times. This extension in our range certainly adds to the total quality of our experience and widens our response.

But though, more responsive, in some ways, to history, a historical awareness has not quite become ingrained in our general outlook. A non-chalant disregard for history shows itself, for example, in the interminable quarrels over the 'purity' of the *rāga*. The notion of 'purity' is, in such contexts, admittedly complex; but it has an aspect that is certainly historical. To elucidate this point, I would like to examine some of the assumptions which we tacitly make when we discuss the 'purity' of a *rāga*. One assumption is that a *rāga* was created once and for all at a certain point in time, and every individual rendering of it is an attempt at a true copy of the original, pristine form. The more successful the attempt, the 'purer' the *rāga*. Variants occur because of 'impure' copies multiplied over time, and against these one must be on guard. Implied clearly are two further assumptions: one, that we always have direct access to the original blue-print of a *rāga*, for otherwise we cannot speak of true copies; two, that *rāga*-s are conceived as immutable forms to be transmitted in every specific detail.

Now, to decide whether these assumptions are justified or not surely calls for a probe into the manner in which *rāga*-s are conceived and transmitted in our tradition and how good our chances are of reaching back to the original form of a *rāga*, especially if it is an old *rāga*. What is called for is, in short, a historical probe. But though we are often quick in passing judgements with respect to 'purity', we hardly undertake the necessary enquiry.

The truth is that quarrels over 'purity' usually boil down to quarrels over favourites. These are, more often than not, battles between partisans supporting different artists or loyal to certain *gharanā*-s, battles in which 'purity' is bandied about as a weapon. The interest is not really in discovering this 'purity' whose roots lie in the past, but in championing a cause.

In the Indian poetic tradition, a discerning *sahṛdaya* — a man who could aesthetically respond to a poetic utterance — had before him a large body of literature, spread over centuries. The nature of a *sahṛdaya's* response, however, hardly took the historical factor into account; it was largely aesthetic. In evaluating poems, questions like when it was written, how it was historically connected with prior works, how it reflected its own period of time, were rarely taken into consideration. Much thought was expended on certain problems; What distinguished a poetic utterance from utterances in general ? What constituted poetic merits and blemishes ? What were the distinguishing characteristics of the aesthetic experience which poetry aroused ? The almost unanimous answer to this last question was: *rasa*, understood as a conglomerate of factors that differentiated the aesthetic from other experiences. *Rasa*, interestingly enough, was placed in a realm beyond time, like the mystic experience. No wonder, then, that poets separated by centuries were evaluated without really taking these intervening centuries into account. The attitude, to use the terminology of linguistics and social science, was synchronic, rather than diachronic. The history of Sanskrit literature was not born, understandably enough, till modern times.

Our musical culture today, is, in its aesthetic attitude, similar to the ancient poetic culture; a historical interest has come to be a part of it but this interest is still peripheral. We value forms for themselves, for the wealth and variety of aesthetic experience they can afford us. We are not really interested in probing into how forms are linked over time, how they change, how one leads to another or moves away from another. We respond to what appeals, without caring much for how it is embedded in time and history. The fact that the notion of *rasa* looms so large in our evaluation of music is also to a degree indicative of its ahistorical character: the *rasa* mode of aesthetic perception cannot take history into account.

My purpose here is not to deny that art can transcend time. On the contrary, I quite share the view that art is nothing if it does not have something to say to us here and now, whenever it may have been created. Greek sculpture, the ancient Indian temples, the Ajanta murals, Renaissance painting, to name only a few random examples, are great creations of art, not merely because of their historical importance, but because they have a quality of being more than-contemporary; we can respond to them across time, in spite of time. They all belong to a realm of *rasa* which is beyond time.

Yet, if the purpose of art is to enrich experience, then viewing objects of art with some understanding of their history, undoubtedly, adds a new magnitude to our awareness of their nature. History gives a perspective to our consciousness by placing objects in a total cultural milieu both horizontally and vertically. Horizontally, as an object placed alongside many others at a certain moment of time; vertically, as an object viewed in company with those that came before and followed across time. This perspective helps us to understand the dynamic inter-connections between forms, how they interact with each other as well as with the general human situation of which they are a part. We learn how and in what aspect they change or remain constant.

II

The sole reason why the history of music in India remains neglected or weak as part of our way of looking at our creations is not because of any disinclination to study its development. There are also certain other problems inherent in any exploration of this kind. History can be studied only through the traces left by the past. In studying art-history, the major traces or data are the art-objects themselves. For social, economic, and political history, the historian does not need to have a direct observation of those events, people, movements and forces which he seeks to study. He can derive the knowledge he needs from other kinds of evidence: documents, records, literature and similar other traces of the past and these are often enough for his purposes; such data, indeed, are the standard grist for the historian's mill. One need not directly perceive an event or an act in order to understand it.

But art by its very nature, imposes a different demand. In art, the palpable particular, the form as it was created, is of supreme importance. For the secret of art lies in the actual object of art, something that can be directly, sensuously, apprehended

This is where the historian of music in India faces an insurmountable hurdle. Beyond a certain period, and a period which hardly extends beyond the very recent past, direct experience of music as actually rendered becomes almost an impossibility. In the field of plastic arts and of literature, forms have survived from the distant past, though with greater or lesser abundance for different periods. These forms, moreover, can be arranged more or less securely within demarkable epochs and often within fairly narrow limits of chronology. We actually have architecture, sculpture and painting dating back to two thousand years and more which can be viewed in this manner. But can we say the same for music or the other performing arts for that matter?

Many, it is sure, would assert that we do indeed have ancient musical forms even today. Our contemporary classical music, they would say, embodies forms which are, in truth, age-old. But how old our forms are, and in what exact sense 'old', is a moot question. A look at the nature of the tradition in which they have been preserved and are handed over will, I believe, throw some light on the matter.

In the west, music going back from the nineteenth and eighteenth centuries to the Renaissance, and even to some extent to the Middle Ages, has been preserved more or less in the shape it was originally created. This has been done through a sophisticated system of notation and an endeavour, rooted in western musical culture, to preserve compositions intact (an endeavour, which today has become more than ever refined through research, resulting in attempts by learned bodies to recapture the very tone of old music through, for example, instruments reconstructed as they were in the past). True, we listen to the early western composers only through renderings by modern conductors and performers and it is well-known that a conductor or performer will impart his own interpretative nuance to a work, even if unconsciously. Yet a contemporary interpretation of earlier music is never allowed to stray too far from the original, notations of which can always be referred back to. Any performance of Bach remains unmistakably Bach despite differences in approach.

Things are quite different in Indian classical music, more markedly perhaps in its Hindustani form. When we hear a Bhimsen Joshi or a Kumar Gandharva, or any other great contemporary, singing *khyāl*-s by the eighteenth century composers, Sadāraṅg or Adāraṅg, it is impossible in priciple to tell how much of the music to which we are listening is truly eighteenth century music.

One reason is that though we clamour for 'purity' and wage battles over it, yet, paradoxically enough, we consider no artist an *ustād,* a master, if he is not truly original. What we cherish in an artist is his individual creative genius, his unique musical vision. Even older masters, with whom we are still closely familiar, Faiyaz Khan, Abdul Karim Khan, Amir Khan, were all prized for this quality. An *ustād,* moreover, is not expected to show creative ganius merely through composing new pieces and developing a new style and idiom in which he renders these new pieces. What is really expected of him is that his own unique imagination and artistic conception should be writ large on whatever he is performing, whether it is a Sadāraṅg *khyāl* or his own composition. A sensitive western performer or conductor, too, may have a unique style, an individual flavour that enters into whatever he renders, but never do we mistake Bach's creation for another's. On the other hand, a great Hindustani performer is more akin to a creative Renaissance sculptor, who, in copying a Greek or Roman model, transformed it into something quite his own.

The value placed by modern Hindustani music culture on uniqueness of vision in rendering *khyāl* is not an accidental or contingent matter. It is not a new and sudden growth, entirely different in spirit from Indian musical culture and tradition as a whole. Even a little reflection will show that the factor which accounts for the Hindustani musician's cultivation of uniqueness is a factor which evidently has been inherent in Indian music for centuries. I have in mind the central role we have assigned to improvisation.

Improvisation is woven into the very fabric of our music-making. In teaching forms, what is transmitted is not only a corpus of music but also a manner and technique of improvisation, the two elements being inextricably interwoven. Hindustani music, in its *khyāl* and allied forms, perhaps places more stress on improvisation, but in this, it only errs on the right side and does not introduce a totally new element uncharacteristic of our music. Evidently, it was always the practice in our music that a *śiṣya* could become a master not merely through being able to reproduce forms, however skilfully and expressively, but by succeeding in handling forms he had learnt in such a manner as to transform them creatively. A man of towering genius could even gloriously transfigure them.

The role of improvisation seems however to have varied in degree and extent. It could be subjected to greater or lesser constraints. Thus compared to the Hindustani tradition, Karnatic music has been exercising more controls on improvisation by limiting it more strictly, at least in certain areas such as the rendering of *kṛti-s*. Compositions of old masters like Tyāgrāja are carefully guarded from the mutating encroachment of improvisation. Consequently, we have a more secure assurance that *kṛti*-s have been handed down undistorted. In the North, on the other hand, an old *chīz* (composition) can have as many sharply distinct variations as *gharānā*-s, or even musicians; since within a *gharānā*, too, individual variations are not uncommon.

But improvisation, though confined, is still given a major role in Karnatic music. A *kṛti* within a *rāga* may be carefully guarded from mutation but the totality of a *rāga*-presentation does allow plenty of room for improvisation. How much of this has slowly crept into the *kṛti*-s themselves poses a genuine question.

The basic problem for a historian, in this context, is how to measure the extent of variation in an old form. Seeking an answer is a frustrating exercise because there was no sophisticated system of notation subtle enough to record all the contours of a *kṛti* or a *chīz* before recent times, against which a check may be made. We are, perforce, left to intelligent guesses on the basis of known musical practice and tradition.

But even if we grant that in the *kṛti*-s we have truly been able to preserve old music in the original, how far back does this take us ? Hardly more than two centuries.

Dhrupad, one may say, takes us further back. And it is certainly true that *dhrupad* as a form and style goes back to the fifteenth century and perhaps earlier. But the pertinent question again surely is: how old are the *dhrupad*-s that we have ? No exact answer can be given. Many *dhrupad*-s are certainly older than the current *khyāls*, and *dhrupad*, in general, undoubtedly, preserves an earlier musical idiom. Also, relative to the *khyāl, dhrupad* is guarded with greater caution against mutating influences. Still, it is difficult to get rid of the feeling that this care to preserve *dhrupad*-s has acquired greater favour only after the ascendency of the *khyāl*. Earlier *dhrupad*-s too seem to have been in a similar state of flux: witness, for example, the great variations to be found in the same *dhrupad* as sung in different *gharānā*-s. The element that varies sometimes is not only a pattern here and there, within the same *rāga*, but the *rāga* itself. We find that the same Tānsen *dhrupad* is sung to one *rāga* in the Dagar *gharānā,* but to a different *rāga* in Vishnupur. A further complexity is added by the presence in the past of four *bānis*, four different modes of rendering *dhrupad,* which must also have multiplied mutations.[1]

Here, again, in the absence of a proper notation system before recent times, it is impossible to gauge the extent to which improvisation has transformed forms. A search for the original can turn out to be, as the proverb goes, like a hunt for the primal trunk of an ancient, overgrown banyan tree. Unlike in the west, no need was felt in India to develop a sophisticated system of notation for recording music with exactitude. A notation system has been in existence for some centuries, at least since the *Bṛhaddeśī* (*circa* 7th century AD), but it was too crude to be an appropriate vehicle for the music it was meant to record. The little that has been recorded is moreover, skeletal and minimal, besides being, for us, enigmatic. It cannot convey a true picture of the totality of music that obtained. The reason why so little was recorded was that, as is the case today, what was conveyed from one generation to another consisted not only of a collection of forms, but also of modes and principles of improvisation by which to develop them; notation could be of no more than rudimentary or secondary use for this purpose. Before the introduction of recording devices like the gramophone disc and

---

[1] On this matter of the historical relation between the *dhrupad* as we have it and the *khyāl*, I would like to refer the reader to my Hindi article, 'Dhrupad Kā itihās: ek naī dṛṣṭi kā āgrah', vol. II of this collection (in preparation); also the journal '*Dhrupad*' *Vārsikī*, 1987, pp. 16-30.

the tape-recorder, a full-fledged musical structure, such as that of a *rāga*, could never be captured in its entirety.

Given the material that we have and the nature of the tradition, an attempt to reconstruct the music of the past in any palpable form does not appear to be a promising venture. Yet attempts are certainly worth making and perhaps with more research and greater knowledge in depth, the notation preserved in works like the *Bṛhaddeśī* (*circa* 7th century AD). the *Saṅgīta Ratnākara* (13th century AD) will begin acquiring a breath of life instead of remaining mere signs to puzzle over.

It would be interesting here to note that Rāṇā Kumbha, the famous Mewar King, had in the fifteenth century made an attempt to recapture old forms. In introducing his monumental *Saṅgītarāja*, he asserts that he had not only read descriptions of ancient forms in ancient texts, he had also tried to experience these forms directly (*'anubhūyārthataḥ:' Saṅgītarāja*, 1, 1, 1, 37). Later in his work he even gives his own reconstruction of *jātis, kambala gāna* and the like, forms which in his days were no longer extant. The attempt seems to have been, in many essentials, a failure, as I have elsewhere tried to show (*A Study of Dattilam*, pp. 180-181). But it was certainly an attempt worth making. Also for his times, it was a rare endeavour. Again in his commentary on the *Gītagovinda*, Jayadeva's celebrated poem composed in the twelfth century, Rāṇā Kumbha tells us that he had searched for a commentary on the work that could reveal the music to which it was set. Finding none, he set Jayadeva's *aṣṭapadīs* to his own music (*Rasikapriyā*, 1, 15, 16: the entire work is full of musical details; also *Saṅgītarāja* 2, 4, 2, 28-29). For us, *his* music, too, remains a closed book as it is not recorded in notation, but in terms of hints that could have aided a contemporary musician to improvise.

III

But if we have no music from ancient times, we have a reasonably large and continuous array of musical texts and manuals. Another major source of information is the huge corpus of sculpture, painting and imaginative literature from different periods. This latter body of evidence reveals a great deal about the context in which music was made, its social cultural paraphernalia and its apparatus. Sculpture has many portrayals of musical instruments and sculptural history can project a picture of how they have changed over time. So can painting, which has, in addition, preserved pictures of music and dance concerts in a more vivid, realistic manner than sculpture. Literature is a still richer source. It provides us with insights into the role of music in general culture. It reflects details of the social, human, background into which music was integrated, presenting us with a lively idea of the diversity of musical practice, the varied functions of musical forms and the complexity of attitudes towards them. Literary works also contain helpful details concerning technical terms of music, since many poets and imaginative writers were men groomed in a many-sided culture, and well-grounded in the techniques of music.

The texts and manuals, however, remain the primary data. They are all that we have on music as such. Other evidence can be corroborative or augmentative, the texts are foundational. A student of musical history is perforce led to get as much out of them as he can.

The earliest textual material on music we have is the large though often scattered body of writings in Vedic literature. This material contains very interesting reflections on music and mirrors an ethos, echoes of which are present in our music culture to this day. But music in this literature is not an object of analytic and descriptive study.

We do not know when the study began to assume such a character. Perhaps at the time when the study of the Vedic language was emerging as a methodical science in the three *Vedāṅgas*: *Nirukta, Vyākaraṇa* and *Śikṣā*. Yāska's *Nirukta* goes back to the seventh century BC, Pāṇini's *Vyākaraṇa* is two or three centuries later, *Śikṣā* works are later still. The tradition of these *Vedāṅgas*, devoted to analysing language semantically, grammatically and phonetically, is older and goes back at least to the eighth and ninth centuries BC.

The impetus for these *Vedāṅga* texts was provided by the need to conserve and understand *mantra,* the Vedic speech. *Sāma,* the Vedic song, was as sacred as the *mantra*. It is reasonable to suppose that the study of *sāma* music began at the same time as the *Vedāṅga*-studies devoted to *mantra,* and with a parallel intention. The earliest work of this nature that we have is, however, a relatively later work, the *Nāradī Śikṣā*, which like other works of the *Śikṣā* genre, belongs to the beginning of the Christian era and is not quite free from even later interpolations. But *Śikṣā,* as a branch of study, is as old as the other *Vedāṅgas*. A *Śikṣā*, when concerned with *mantra* was a phonetic study; devoted to *sama*, it was a study of music. No other *Śikṣā* on *sāma*, besides the *Naradī,* survives.

The *Naradi Śikṣā*, along with the richer and more organised *Dattilam* and the *Nāṭya śastra*, can perhaps be placed in roughly the same chronological bracket. Somewhat later, more scattered material is to be found in the small sections on music in the Jain canonic *Ṭhaṇaṁga Sutta*[2] and the older *Purāṇa-s.*

These are all works antedating the *Bṛhaddeśī,* usually placed in the seventh century. With this work we come to a new group of texts, which, while borrowing the old conceptual framework and material, are yet devoted to newer interests and forms. This is a fairly large group; representative works being the *Bharata Bhāṣya,* the musical section in the *Mānasollāsa, Saṅgīta Cintāmaṇi, Saṅgīta-Samaya-Sāra* and, above all, the *Saṅgīta Ratnākara* (early 13th century AD).

With the thirteenth century there appears a lull in textual activity which begins anew with newer interests in the fifteenth century. Many old traditions continue, earlier material is still incorporated, but there is a sharp change in the conceptual framework, reflecting a major upheaval in music. Many old terms acquire a new content. Some new terms and concepts

---

[2] A translation and a study of the *Ṭhāṇaṁga Sutta* forms a part of this collection of essays. See, 'Music in the *Ṭhāṇaṅga Sutta*'.

become consequential. Also, now begins a division of the large material we have into Hindustani and Karnatic.

IV

The above brief, and even perhaps at places controversial, survey is meant to convey some idea of the range of material spread over time. A few words now concerning the character of this literature, what we can learn from it and what we cannot.

Texts from the *Nāradī Śikṣā* onwards contain a rich vocabulary for analysing and describing musical forms. But, as we have noted earlier, before, the *Bṛhaddeśī* there is no attempt at mapping structures precisely or, in other words, to notate them. In fact, it is in this text that we first meet with the syllables, *sa, ri ga ma,* as abbreviated signs for musical notes. *Dattilam*, written some centuries earlier, evinces great effort at brevity and some very ingenious formula-like descriptive devices. But the *sa, ri, ga, ma* syllables are not used. In this text, as in the *Nāṭya Śāstra* and the *Nāradī Śikṣā*, the name of a note is always fully spelt out: *ṣaḍja*, *ṛṣabha*, *gāndhara* and so forth. Abbreviations must have developed sometime after these texts, which were written in the first or second centuries AD and before the seventh century, the probable date of the *Bṛhaddeśī*.

Not only was a notation system not quite paid attention to,[3] no method of measuring tones through string-lengths or a similar precise manner was developed. Musicians tuned by the ear, even as today. In fact, it is not till the sixteenth or seventeenth centuries that we find tones being given in string-lengths. This fact further compounds the difficulty of reaching at ancient forms with any exactitude.

The texts, it appears, were written and studied within a well-established *sampradāya*, a tradition of musical culture in which a

---

[3] However, for a discussion as to *why* the notation system remained undeveloped, and the importance of notation in earlier Vedic music, see 'Reflections on the Logos of Music', the last eassy in this collection especially pp. 315-316. The reader might also see the author's *Saṅgita Evaṁ Cintan*, Prabhat Prakashan, Delhi, 1994, Chapter 1.

basic knowledge of forms, a training of the ear, and a general understanding of the framework of music was already assumed in a student. Details about forms in ancient texts abound, but they only concern general features, individual details are left to the knowledgeable students to fill in.

The reason for this lies not only in the fact that these were advanced manuals, but also, evidently, in the forms themselves. The ancient *jāti*-s were *rāga*-like structures and have been proclaimed as the progenitors of *rāga*-s. Like the *rāga*-s, the *jāti*-s were forms which could only be described in their general formal features, through stating the principle of their structural formation, because they allowed room for free movement or improvisation. This freedom was extremely restricted and hedged round by numerous limits, because *jāti*-s were sacred structures, similar in this aspect to Vedic *sāma*. Every movement in them, like ritual action in the *yajña*, was determined through rules. Yet, unlike *sāma*, they did allow freedom. With them an entirely new element was introduced into Indian music: the nucleus for our *rāga*-s was born. *Jāti*-s gave rise to other forms in which the principles governing melodic movement were gradually loosened, modified, transformed, reduced in number and importance. It is this line of development to which *rāga*-s belong.

A study of ancient texts can, therefore, help us form a picture of how the principles of improvisation have changed over time and come to be what they are today. And here we have an example of the kind of history which the texts can help to formulate. In respect to exact form, however, the texts present a picture somewhat analogous to an archaeological site, revealing bare ground-plans or sometimes only clues to these, the rest of the structure being left to the imagination. We do, however, have the present forms, embodying many ancient principles of construction, to help the imagination.

Besides forms, music has a conceptual framework with multiple functions: analysing forms, describing them, commenting on them aesthetically, spiritually, metaphysically, scientifically and in other ways in which we do talk about music and relate it to the rest of our experience. This framework itself has a history which reflects the history of forms themselves. Here the texts offer a rich fare to the historian of musicology, and the student of music in general.

The texts can also be instructive to us as practising musicologists. Today we have gained in being able to describe forms with greater quantitative accuracy. But we have lost much in the richness, width and penetration of analysis found in the best of the earlier text. Often when we grope for a suitable method of analysis or an appropriate category with which to classify and name a phenomenon, we find ourselves at a loss. A sensitive study of the earlier texts can be helpful here.

The texts can also have a clarifying role. Earlier I had spoken of quarrels over the 'purity' of *rāga*. An historical understanding of the character of *rāga*, as a form, will surely help us to see the issue in a clearer light and the fight over it will be less dogmatic.

Many musical terms such as *śruti*, *svara, mūrchanā, tāna, varṇa* among others, have been with us for centuries. Their meaning-content has been changing with change in music. But the constancy of the use of the terms themselves tends to create the false impression that meanings too, have remained unchanged. Consequently, layers of meaning, which have become mixed up, create confusion or bewilderment when we apply these terms today. A historical study of these terms, to use an archaeological analogy again, can help us separate various strata of meaning and perhaps dispel some confusion.

CHAPTER – SIX

Taṇḍu: The First Theoretician of Dance

Speaking of theoretical activity in India, we proudly single out the glories of Yāska (7th century BC), Pāṇini (6th–5th century BC) and their predecessors, who were the first thinkers in the world to subject language to a theoretical analysis, semantic and grammatical. We forget certain others who are equally ancient. One of them is Taṇḍu. Taṇḍu was the first theoretician in the world to analyse dance.

Taṇḍu wrote, or perhaps, like some ancient theoreticians, orally composed a *śāstra* on dance which has not come down to us in its original form. The *śāstra*, however, is incorporated in Bharata's *Nāṭyaśāstra* and it is on this that we shall base our account of his endeavour. We shall be aided in this by the *Abhinava Bhāratī*, the insightful commentary which the renowned Abhinavagupta wrote on the *Nāṭyaśāstra* in the 10-11th centuries.

How old is Taṇḍu ? There is no way we can give an answer. He is certainly older than Bharata, who used many existing *śāstras* including Taṇḍu's *śāstra* on *Tāṇḍava* to compile his own *Nāṭyaśāstra* around the beginning of the Christian era. Bharata presents Taṇḍu's *śāstra* in his own way, as he does many other of the *śāstras* that he uses. Yet we can reasonably expect a good many of Taṇḍu's own words to have been preserved in Bharata's reformulation, for this would only be natural in reproducing a tightly-knit technical work, such as a *śāstra* usually was.

But the *śāstra* as a whole has, however, suffered a distortion in Bharata's hands, as we shall attempt to show. Bharata has split it into two parts, assimilating one of them into his own text in such a manner as to almost obliterate its separate identity. We shall try to show how.

But we are more interested in Taṇḍu's approach to his material, the *Tāṇḍava*. As we have already pointed out, *śāstric* or theoretical activity concerning the performing arts seem to have begun as early in India as theoretical activity concerning language. Pāṇini was familiar, with a *Naṭasūtra* which he ascribes to an *ācārya* named Śilālin. Nothing is known of this *sūtra* or of Śilālin beyond Pāṇini's reference to them. But the very fact that Śilālin's work is called a *sūtra* indicates that it was a systematic, organised enterprise. Did the word *'naṭa'* in the *Naṭasūtra* stand for a dancer or a play-actor ? We have no way to know. Some have suggested that the *'naṭa'* here stands for a juggler. But that seems unlikely, since composing a *sūtra* was considered a serious activity. Juggling was certainly not a serious enough activity to call for a *sūtra* to be written on it. But if Śilālin's *Naṭasūtra* was either on dancing or playacting, it is surprising that Bharata seems unaware of it. Bharata has named many authorities who taught or wrote on the performing arts, yet nowhere does he mention Śilālin. Nevertheless, we must not forget that many old works have been genuinely forgotten. We know the authors of some through their mention by later theoreticians, who have, however, not mentioned everyone. *Śāstric* works are not histories, except incidentally, we would not have known of Śilālin and his *Naṭasūtra* except for Pāṇini's incidental mention of him.[1]

Taṇḍu may have been as ancient as Śilālin, though we can never be sure. But we can be sure of the fact that his endeavour was connected with ancient Śaivism, which took the performing arts very seriously, creating forms that continue to live with us. In music it produced the *gāndharva*, which through transformations provided the basis for our *rāgas*. It also produced the *Gāndharva-śāstra*, which, likewise, remains the basic framework behind our theorising about *rāgas*.

Tāṇḍava was the dance counterpart of *gāndharva*. It was the dance Śiva himself created and danced. This, indeed, makes *Tāṇḍava* more central to Śaivism than *gāndharva*. *Gāndharva*

---

[1] It may be noted here, however, that the *Amarakośa* does list *śilālin* as a synonym of '*naṭa*' and '*bharata*', obviously meaning an 'actor'; See *Amarakośa*, *kāṇḍa* 2, *śloka* 12. See also *Bhāratīya Saṅgīta kā Itihāsa*, Thakur Jaidev Singh, Sangeet Research Academy, Calcutta, 1994, p. 280.

was not *created* by Śiva, nor performed by him, as *Tāṇḍava* was. It was only *addressed* to him.[2]

The story goes that Taṇḍu formulated his *śāstra* when Śiva asked him to teach the *Tāṇḍava* to Bharata. What Taṇḍu did was to create the first known theoretical analysis of dance as a form, which became a model for subsequent Indian enterprise in the field.

It is a model worth understanding on its own. For what Taṇḍu created can be characterised as one of the earliest systems for constructing, or generating complex forms out of simple entities through certain rules for transformation. What is extremely interesting is the fact — something which is pointedly brought out by Abhinava — that the simple units of which the dance was constituted as well as the complex whole they formed were self-contained entities. Unlike language on which Pāṇini theorised, the structure of Tāṇḍu's dance did not refer to, or mean, anything beyond itself. The dance was form alone — a significant form, being beautiful, joy-giving and created by Śiva himself — but its significance was not acquired through any *meaning* outside itself such as language essentially has.

Thus from the view-point of theory, Taṇḍu's discourse upon dance is one of the earliest attempts at building what might be called a generative system of pure forms *without any content.* It should be of great interest to theorists who think that creating such systems is one of the supreme goals of theorising.

Taṇḍu's system can be likened to that of Pāṇini. Except that Pāṇini's system is not a system for generating pure forms. The complex linguistic whole which Pāṇini was interested in analysing was the *pada,* a usable unit in a sentence. Pāṇini broke up *padas* — Sanskrit *padas*, which were his concern — into smaller units.

---

[2] The *Nāṭyaśāstra* is, in truth, somewhat ambivalent in speaking of Śiva's creation of *Tāṇḍava.* In verse, 4, 13, Śiva says, "*mayāpīdaṁ smṛtaṁ nṛtyam*". Abhinava understands '*smṛtam*' to imply that the dance was without a beginning, ever-created: "*smṛtamityanāditvamasya darśayati*". Later in the chapter Bharata, however, says," *sṛṣṭvā bhagavatā dattāstaṇḍave*" — where Bharata speaks of the various parts and formations of *Tāṇḍava*, their creation by Śiva and then Śiva's teaching of them to Taṇḍu. (For this latter passage, see, 4, 259-260: all references are to be G.O.S. edition of the *Nāṭyaśāstra*.)

These units of *dhātu, pratyaya, upasarga*, were analytic in the sense that they were not usable on their own. But they were not units of pure structure. They were meaningful units. They could be variously combined by rules of formation which Pāṇini meticulously notes. Any number of *padas* could be generated by them, provided the rules were observed. But there was always an outside constraint. Whether a *pada* was acceptable or not depended on whether it had meaning or not.[3] Taṇḍu's system, on the other hand, had no such constraint. It was not a system for *abhinaya*, which like language has to have a meaning outside itself. It was a system meant for generating pure dance which was form alone. The *Nāṭyaśāstra* is aware of this central distinction and Bharata expresses it through an interesting story.

After Bharata had created the *nāṭya*, he presented a play before the Devas and the Asuras who enjoyed it immensely. The art, Bharata then thought, should be presented before Śiva — with the idea, perhaps, that Śiva was the ideal *sahṛdaya*, the quintessential discerning, sensitive critic. He approached Śiva with a play called the *Tripura-dāha*, a dramatised version of an episode from Śiva's own life. Śiva was pleased with Bharata's *nāṭya* and praised it. But he also asked Bharata to add something to it which it did not have. This was the *Tāṇḍava* dance, which Śiva himself was fond of dancing. But could this really be done ? The very idea of adding a pure, non-representative form to *nāṭya*, which like language inherently depended on a world of meaning outside itself, raised an aesthetic problem. This was voiced by the Ṛṣis to whom Bharata related his story. The very soul of *nāṭya*, the Ṛṣis said, was *abhinaya,* which was a means for representing the happenings of the world on the stage; how could *Tāṇḍava* fit into such a representation, since it had no concern for meanings nor could it represent a happening. Bharata agreed

---

[3] It may also very well be doubted whether Pāṇini *intended* to create a *generative* system, even though his analysis may be *used* for this end. Taṇḍu, however, clearly intended to *design* a generative system. For a more extended argument on this line, see my *Saṅgit Evaṁ Cintan*, Prabhat Prakashan, Delhi, 1994, Chapter I.

with the Ṛṣis. He was aware that *Tāṇḍava* was a pure, non-representational form. *Tāṇḍava*, he agreed, was quite unrelated to anything that happens in the world. It was, he said, beautiful in itself, a source of joy on its own, without depending on anything beyond itself.[4] Yet he did incorporate, it into his *nāṭya*. We shall see how he did it. We shall discuss the principle he adopted to adapt the alien *Tāṇḍava* into the *nāṭya*. One thing which made this possible was Taṇḍu's analysis of *Tāṇḍava* into smaller units. The *Tāṇḍava* as a whole could not be incorporated into the *nāṭya*, but it was possible to incorporate its parts, using them to a different end.

The *Tāṇḍava* consisted basically of complex formations called *aṅgahāras* which could be strung together into larger wholes. The *Tāṇḍava* that Śiva danced had a repertoire of 32 *aṅgahāras*. Taṇḍu's goal as a *śāstrakāra* was to describe these *aṅgahāras*. The method he chose was to analyse them into smaller building-blocks. His analysis follows two stages. At the first stage, Taṇḍu analyses *aṅgahāras* into what he calls *karaṇas*. These are 108 in number. Different combinations of *karaṇas*, Taṇḍu says, produce different *aṅgahāras*. A combination of two *karaṇas* gives rise to what he terms *nṛtta-mātṛkā*. Though obviously more complex than a *karaṇa*, the *nṛtta-mātṛkā* is not yet an *aṅgahāra*. For the *aṅgahāra*, Bharata says, consists of two, three or four *nṛtta-mātṛkās*. Bharata, however, goes on to say:

> "Three *karaṇas* form *aṅgahāras* called *kalāpaka*; four of them form *ṣaṇḍakas* and combinations of five *karaṇas* are known as *saṅghātakas*. *Aṅgahāras* can also be formed by combining six, seven, eight or nine *karaṇas* together."[5]

One thing is clear at this stage. Given a set of 108 *karaṇas*

---

[4] *Ṛṣaya ūcuḥ* : *yadā prāptyarthamarthānāṁ tajñairabhinayaḥ kṛtaḥ/ kasmānnṛttaṁ kṛtaṁ hyetat kaṁ svabhāvamapekṣate/ na gītakārthasambaddhaṁ na cāpyarthasya bhāvakam/*
Bharataḥ : *artrocyate na khalvarthaṁ kaṁcnnṛttamapekṣate// kiṁ tu śobhāṁ prajanayediti nṛttaṁ pravartitam/ prāyeṇa sarvalokasya nṛttamiṣṭaṁ svabhāvataḥ//*
Nāṭyaśāstra : 4, 261-264.

[5] *Nāṭyaśāstra*, 4, 30-33. The translated portion comprises verses 32 and 33.

and the rule that a combination of three to nine of these could make an *aṅgahāra*, it is possible to produce innumerably more *aṅgahāras* than the 32 which Śiva's repertoire consisted of. The result of Taṇḍu's analysis was thus to enlarge the possibilities inherent within Siva's dance. Taṇḍu uses the *karaṇas* (or so it appears from the text we have) only to describe 32 *aṅgahāras*, presumably those danced by Śiva and no more. But given his simple rule of forming *aṅgahāras* out of a combination of three to nine *karaṇas,* other *aṅgahāras* could easily be formed though he has not actually described them. Indeed, given the rule, his actual detailed descriptions of *aṅgahāras* seems quite unnecessary.

Later theorists were aware of the fact that Taṇḍu's formulation contains the possibilities of many more *aṅgahāras* than the 32 which Śiva employed in his dance. Performers made use of these possibilities in their own compositions. Abhinava, therefore, says that there is no end of *aṅgahāras* that can be performed, but the 32 danced by Śiva are especially sacred.[6] Taṇḍu's *śāstra*, in effect, opened up the restricted *Tāṇḍava* of Śiva without diverging from it in form and conception. This is, remarkably, the character of many Indian *śāstras* including Pāṇini's grammar. Many would argue that Pāṇini has, indeed, been the central influence behind much Indian *śāstric* thought because his grammar became the model for other writers: his

---

[6] "*aṣṭottare karaṇaśate jñāte catuḥśaṣṭikaraṇayojanayā truṭitāṅgarityā yadyapyānantyamaṅgahārāṇāṁ tathāpi prādhānyādadṛṣṭaphalaṁ pratyādhikoparaktatayā dvātriṁśannāmato nirdiṣṭāḥ*" — Abhinava on *Nāṭyaśāstra*, 4, 27. This may be translated as: "Once the 108 *karaṇas* are known, they can be combined to form endless *aṅgahāras* through the application of the 64 *yojanās* (the *yojanā* is not a part of Taṇḍu's vocabulary. It seems to refer to techniques and modes of putting *karaṇas* together employed by dancers during Abhinava's times) and the *atruṭitāṅga* method (another term not found in Taṇḍu). Yet only 32 *aṅgahāras* are of greater importance in the creation of *adṛṣṭa* (the ritual effect that leads to *svarga*); therefore only these have been described by individual names."

For *yojanā* and the *atruṭitāṅga* method, see below. The word *atrutstāngarityā* reads *tratitāṅgarityā*, an obviously incorrect reading as will become evident later in the discussion.

fascinating analysis of language became the paradigm for other analyses. To me it seems more likely that Pāṇini's own exercise was not a cause but itself an outcome of a general cultural and intellectual approach — or one might call it 'style' — that delights in creating new forms out of a set of given units, varying, transforming and sometimes even transfiguring, certain basic patterns. Certainly, no historical links with Pāṇini can be traced in the various *śāstras* which are impregnated with the same intent of opening up latent possibilities.

A *karaṇa*, however, was itself a complex unit and quite obviously so. Even a simple glance at the description of *karaṇas* will not fail to impress this fact upon us. Taṇḍu, too defines a *karaṇa* as a 'combination of the movements of the hand and feet'— *hastapādasamāyogo nṛtyasya karaṇaṁ bhavet* (4, 30). The words 'hand' and 'feet' here are — as Abhinava points out (see fn 10 on p. 6) — short-hand for the various limbs of the upper and the lower parts of the body; this is clear also from Taṇḍu's own description of the *karaṇas,* where a *karaṇa* is defined as a combination of the movements of the different parts of the upper and lower limbs of the body. I shall return to this below.

Let us take a couple of examples of *karaṇas*. The *karaṇa* named *maṇḍala-svastika* (the eighth in the list) is described as follows:

> With the body in the still position (*sthāna*) called *maṇḍala*, bring the two hands to the *svastika* position in such a manner that they remain equipoised with the palms raised and facing inwards. Such is *maṇḍala-svastika*.[7]

The *karaṇa, kaṭicchinna* (eleventh in the list) is:

> The hands should have a *pallava* formation and placed near the head. The waist should be turned first to one side

[7] *Svastikau tu karau kṛtvā prāṅmukhordhvatalau samau/ tathā ca maṇḍalaṁ sthānaṁ maṇḍalasvastikaṁ tu tat// Nāṭyaśāstra,* 4, 68-69. See also Abhinava's comments here. He also speaks of a *yojanā* in connection with this formation, though the word does not occur in the original. This was, evidently, an addition to the description made by Taṇḍu. The purpose apparently was to incorporate into the description certain techniques and modes of movement which had become parts of a dancers performance and which were thought to be important enough to figure in *śāstric* descriptions.

and then the other and this should be done repeatedly. Such is *kaṭicchinna.*[8]

Even these two examples, rather randomly chosen, are sufficient to reveal the complexity of the *karaṇas*. Each of them can be plainly analysed into smaller, more atomic, units. Such an analysis was, indeed, made by Taṇḍu; it is, in fact, assumed in his description of the *karaṇas;* mark his use of phrases like 'the *svastika* position' or 'the *pallava* formation', which are obviously *parts* of *karaṇas*. These smaller units are also named *mātṛkās*.

Taṇḍu introduces his description of the *karaṇas* with these words:

Listen to me, I shall now describe (the *karaṇas*) making a note of the movements of the hands, the feet, the hips, the thighs, the breast and the back. (I shall also describe) the *sthānas*, the *cārīs* and the position and the movements of the hands needed in *nṛtta* (i.e. *Tāṇḍava*) known as the *mātṛkās*. Combinations of *mātṛkās* produce the *karaṇas*.[9]

Clearly, the *karaṇa* is a combination of many discrete positions and movements of the various parts of the body, and each of the *karaṇas* can be broken into these smaller 'units'. Indeed, as Taṇḍu unequivocally says, the *karaṇas* are nothing but assemblages of these smaller parts. The words '*sthāna*' and '*cārī*' are also worth noticing here. '*Sthāna*' stands for a stationary position and '*cārī*' for a movement. All dance, as Abhinava says, is stillness coupled with movement (*avasthānaṁ gatiśceti*). Thus every smaller part into which a *karaṇa* was analysed could itself be characterised in two distinct ways: still or moving. However, the term *mātṛkā* which recurs here can cause confusion. Earlier, Taṇḍu had told us that a *mātṛkā* was a much larger building block in the dance: two *karaṇas*,

---

[8] *Nāṭyaśāstra, 4, 71-72.*

[9] *hastapadapracārantu kaṭipārśvorusaṁyutam//*
uraḥpṛṣṭhodaropetaṁ vakṣyamānaṁ nibodhata/
yāni sthānāni yāścāryo nṛttahastastathaiva ca//
sā mātṛketi vijñeyā tadyogātkaraṇaṁ bhavet/
Nāṭyaśāstra, 4, 58-60

he had said, made a *mātṛkā*. Yet now he tells us that *mātṛkas* are smaller units in the formation of the *karaṇas* themselves. No justification is provided for this puzzling use of the same term in two very different, palpably contradictory, senses: *Mātṛkās* cannot both form a *karaṇa* and be formed by them. Fortunately, we have Abhinava whose comments help us to sort out the confusion. *Mātṛkās*, Abhinava says, are of two sorts: (1) the *nṛtta-mātṛkā* which was formed *through karaṇas* and (2) the *karaṇa-mātṛkā*, the smallest units in a dance which *form* the *karaṇas*. The different uses of the term *mātṛkā,* it would seem, indicates the two stages of Taṇḍu's analysis of the *aṇgahāras* that Śiva employed in his dance. At the first stage Taṇḍu analysed the *aṅgahāras* into *karaṇas*, asserting that these smaller building blocks could, through a simple rule of formation, give rise to *aṅgahāras*. But since the *karaṇa* is itself a complex figure, Taṇḍu in the second stage of his analysis breaks it into yet smaller building-blocks, which are not further analysable, and names these the *mātṛkās*. This appears reasonable enough, yet a confusion remains. Taṇḍu had said earlier that *two karaṇas* formed a *nṛtta-mātṛkā*; he had not equated the *karaṇa* itself with a *nṛtta-mātṛkā*. But if the *nṛtta-mātṛkā* consists of two *karaṇas*, one fails to see how it can be an essential building-block in the formation of *aṅgahāras*. The *aṅgahāras* are *not* combinations of *pairs* of *karanas*. One fails, indeed to see the purpose in Taṇḍu's *śāstra* of the concept of *nṛtta-mātṛkā*. Abhinava does try to give a justification, but it can hardly convince. He argues that only after *two karaṇas* have been shown to us is it possible to perceive the activity before us as part of a dance and not as part of another, an entirely different sort of activity.[10] This raises the interesting

[10] Abhinava's text here is obviously corrupt. Ramakrishna Kavi, the editor, has tried to repair it, and as in many such cases, with some success. The text reads : *karaṇadvayaprayogena ca vinivṛttābhimāno nāsti,* which Kavi emends to *karaṇadvayaprayogena ca vinirvṛttanṛttābhimāno nāsti*. Abhinava goes on to say: *tataḥ paraṁ tu nṛtyatītyabhimānātka-raṇadvayaṁ nṛttamātṛketyuktam*. This may be translated as: Even till two *karaṇas* are performed one does not understand it (*abhimāna*) as a dance; after that, however, the perception (*abhimāna*) is clearly that of a dance and this is the reason why a pair of *karaṇas* are called a *nṛtta-mātṛkā*. (See Abhinava on *Nāṭyaśāstra* 4, 28-33).

question of when do we begin to identify an activity as that particular activity and not any other, but it clearly offers no cogent justification for considering the *nṛtta-mātṛkā* as a building block in the formation of *aṅgahāras*, a notion that Abhinava seems to entertain; he defines *nṛtta-mātṛkā* as: *nṛttasyāṅgahārātmano mātṛkā utpattikaraṇam* (4, 28-33). It is the *karana* which can be really called the '*utpattikaraṇa*', 'the generative material', of the *aṅgahāra*, for the *aṅgahāra*, as we have seen, was made up of sets of *karaṇas* — three to nine — and not of *pairs* of *karaṇas*. Moreover, a single *karaṇa* should on its own have been sufficient to convince anyone that what was happening was a dance: the examples described above are sufficient to impress this upon us. Abhinava like a loyal commentator was trying to justify the text of a *śāstrakāra* even though there was no justification. If we, too, want to be generous towards the *śāstrakāra* — as in all intellectual honesty we should be — a better justification, I think, would be to say that the text here is perhaps corrupt.

The term *nṛtta-mātṛkā* is, then, redundant. It has no role in the *śāstra* properly speaking and can be replaced by the *karaṇa*. *Mātṛkā* should be taken to mean only what Abhinava calls, *karaṇa-mātṛkā*, the smallest unit to which dance could be analysed.

How can we define the smallest unit in pure dance ? Taṇḍu does not raise this question, which his analysis inevitably demands. Abhinava too does not raise it, but his definition of a *karaṇa* is very suggestive in this regard. A *karaṇa*, he says, is a movement. Of what, one might ask. It is, he replies, a movement of pure dance, of gracefully stirring one's limbs; moving them in an act which is not directed towards any utilitarian aim of getting something or of getting away from something. It is a movement, he continues, of the upper and lower parts of the body, made in such a way that it forms a coordinated whole (*saṅgatatayā 'truṭitatvena)*. A movement of this kind when made from a previous position to another appropriate position, constitutes a single movement. And this is the *karaṇa : kriyā karaṇam, kasya kriyā ? nṛttasya, gātrāṇāṁ vilāsakṣepasya. heyopādeyaviṣaya-kriyādibhyo vyatiriktā yā tatkriyā karaṇamityartham ... tasyāḥ kriyāyāḥ svarūpamāha — 'hastapādasamāyogaḥ'. hastopalakṣi-tasya pūrvakāyā-vartiśākhāṅgopāṅgādeḥ pādopalakṣitasya cāparakāyāgatapār-śvakaṭyūrujaṅghācaraṇādeḥ saṅgatatayā 'truṭitatvena vṛttiyojane. pūrvakṣetrasaṁyogatyāgena samucita-kṣetrāntaraprāptiparyantatayā ekā kriyā tatkaraṇamityarthaḥ. (Nāṭyaśāstra*, Vol. I, GOS ed. p. 90). Abhinava adds that the concept of such a unit of a single movement exists in *loka* (ordinary behaviour of men and women), except that in dance the central thing is the grace and beauty of the movement and not its purposiveness. Obviously, this definition of a single unit in a dance is too large to form the smallest unit or *mātṛkā*. But if we modify the definition to mean the single movement of a single limb, we can come much closer to what we want. Problems would still remain. What is a single limb ? for example. On what grounds do we say that the movement is not the same but different, especially in the case of movements that might resemble each other. A related and more important question is: can we ever make a complete inventory of the units of smallest movements that the body can make and make with grace ? And what is grace after all ? There would have to be some arbitrariness in what would be called the unit of a movement — an arbitrariness, mitigated, however, by the limits of the *śāstra* itself: the *śāstra*, after all, is concerned with a specific form of dance, the *Tāṇḍava*, and not all non-representative dance in general. The *mātṛkās* of Taṇḍu, therefore, are a set of more or less definitely innumerable atomic units of movement in the *Tāṇḍava*: units that can be arrived at by analysing the *karaṇas*.

However there is still a problem on which Abhinava does not seem to have pondered at all. *Tāṇḍava* is not only *gati* but also *avasthiti,* as Abhinava himself says. So our atomic units must comprise not only of units of movement — in terms of which Abhinava defines a *karaṇa* — but also units of stationary poses. These, perhaps, can be defined as the end result of a movement which can then be frozen into an *avasthiti*.

The outline of Taṇḍu's *śāstra* that we have had so far was based, as we said, on the fourth chapter of the *Nāṭyaśāstra*. We find Taṇḍu speaking of the *mātṛkās*, but unlike the *karaṇas*, these are not described in detail, though their knowledge is *assumed* in the description of the *karaṇas*. The reason why it has been possible for Tāṇḍu to describe complex formations such as *karaṇas* in single, short, succinct verses is that his description has a very technical tenor. And this comes from the fact that smaller movements comprising a *karaṇa* — namely the *mātṛkās* — have been referred to through single epithets or short phrases with a precise but detailed meaning. Let us take examples from the two *karaṇas* we had described earlier. In describing *maṇḍala-svastika*, the text says (I quote from my translation earlier) :"with the body in the still position called *maṇḍala...*" The reference here is to a *sthānaka* (or *sthāna*) with the technical name *maṇḍala* the form of which is taken as understood through the term. The term is obviously what we would call a technical term. Further in the description of the same *karaṇa*, we find the description: "bring the two hands to the *svastika* position ..." *Svastika* is plainly another technical descriptive term, a short-hand for a more detailed description of a bodily position. Even a quick look will show that such technical terms are quite central to the description of the *karaṇas*. Like all technical terms they need to be explained and elaborated. And this is a necessary part of the function of any *śāstra*. The *śāstra* would be largely unintelligible without it. But the fourth chapter of the *Nāṭyaśāstra*, which purportedly contains the entire description of the *Tāṇḍava*, *does not* explain the technical terms it so profusely uses. Has Taṇḍu failed in his function as a *śāstrakāra*? His *śāstra* clearly appears to be essentially incomplete.

But this is not really the case. What has happened is that Bharata has taken Taṇḍu's description of the *mātṛkās* out of its proper and appropriate place and removed it elsewhere using it for his own purposes. Taṇḍu's description now forms part of a larger, much more ambitious, repertory of the units of atomic movements and positions of the various parts of the body that could be used in *nāṭya,* and is to be found in chapters eight to eleven of the *Nāṭyaśāstra,* where technical terms like the ones named above have been explained. If we look at Abhinava's *ṭīkā* on the *karaṇas* in chapter 4, we discover that he quotes relevant passages from chapters 8-10 in order to provide details and expound the terms used in Taṇḍu's description of the *karaṇas*. Clearly, matter which belonged to chapter 4 has been taken to these later chapters. Any number of examples can be given. But for our purposes here, the two terms noted above should be indicative enough. The *sthāna* termed *maṇḍala* is described among other *sthānas*, which also figure in the description of the *karaṇas,* at *Nāṭyaśāstra* 10, 65-66.[11] The *svastika* is described at 9, 186-187.[12]

Taṇḍu's *śāstra* must have contained a description of just those *mātṛkās* which were needed for his *Tāṇḍava*. Bharata has many more. What is even more distinctive is the fact that Bharata has appended a *viniyoga* — a *karma*, as Bharata calls it — after every individual *mātṛkā* that he describes. The *karma* was of central importance for Bharata, for it tells of the use or uses to which a movement could be put in the context of *nāṭya*, which was Bharata's prime concern.

But it was also Bharata's way of incorporating the pure form of *Tāṇḍava* into his own *abhinaya*-oriented *nāṭya*. For *abhinaya* can *make use* of any bodily movement whatsoever towards some representative end. It can *impart* a meaning to a movement or gesture *within* a *nāṭya* context even though the movement may not have a meaning in itself. One way of giving a movement a meaning can be through a convention by stipulating that a certain movement will refer to such a thing. Another is through its

---

[11] The *maṇḍala* was also known as *aindra*, 'related to Indra' and is described as follows:

aindre tu maṇḍale pādau catustālāntarasthitau//
tryasrau pakṣasthitau caiva kaṭijānū samau tathā

[12] *caturasrasthitau hastau haṁsapakṣakṛtau tathā*
tiryaksthitau cābhimukhau jñeyau talamukhāviti
tāveva maṇibandhānte svastikākṛtisaṁsthitau
svastikāviti vikhyātau ...

semblance to *loka* that is, meaningful gestures found in ordinary behaviour.

'There is no gesture or position of the hand which cannot be used meaningfully in the *abhinaya* of *nāṭya*', says Bharata.[13] What he says of the hand is true of any gesture whatever. Abhinava says this in a more discursive language in the beginning of chapter 9, where speaking of the *karma* or *viniyoga* of various gestures he comments that *abhinaya* can be accomplished with gestures, in two distinct modes: the *lokadharmī* and the *nāṭyadharmī.* The *lokadharmī* are gestures taken from *loka,* the actual behaviour of men. The *nāṭyadharmī* is stylised. It uses the gestures of *nṛtta* in various ways to enhance the evocative power of *abhinaya.* It can consist of the use of *karaṇas* to create an atmosphere of grace and beauty especially in situations of love. It can employ those *nṛtta* gestures, which being similar to gestures in actual use, are suggestive of them, and it can even incorporate elements that mean nothing by giving them a meaning through a convention (*naṭasamaya*).[14]

At one place Bharata does make a distinction between gestures of *nāṭya* and of pure dance or *Tāṇḍava.* He does so in speaking of the gestures of the hands where he has a separate section for 64 kinds of *nṛtta-hastas*: see *Nāṭyaśāstra,* 9, verses following 10. The names of these *nṛtta-hastas* were obviously taken from Taṇḍu who uses them in his description of the *karaṇas*. For Bharata, however, these *nṛtta-hastas* were to be used in *abhinaya*. After naming them, Bharata says: "now listen

---

[13] *nāsti kaścidahastastu nāṭye 'rtho 'bhinayaṁ prati*

Nāṭyaśāstra 9, 162.

[14] *abhinayasya dvividhā itikartavyatā lokadharmī nāṭyadharmī ca ... nāṭyadharmasyāpi dvidhā - nāṭyopayogamūlabhūtakaiśikīsampādanocitalaukika-śobhāhetuḥ yathā - āveṣṭitādicaturvidhakaraṇarūpā. kācittvaṁśena lokamupajīvati, yathā-varṇāturena hastena tatra vyavahitena loka upajīvyate. loke hyanirdeśyatāśeṣaṁ vastu nirdidikṣuridṛśaṁ tādṛṣamitthambhūtamityavasare prayuktameva caturaiḥ. evaṁ janāntikādau vācyam. naṭasamayamātrarupā nāṭyadharmī samayasyākiñcitkarasya kalpane prayojanābhāvāt.*

Abhinava on *Nāṭyaśāstra* 9, 1-3.

to their description and their *use* (in theatre) — *yathālakṣaṇame-teṣāṁ karmāṇi ca nibodhata*" (*Nāṭyaśāstra* 9, 17). And this is what he proceeds to do.

Despite the fact that Taṇḍu's *karaṇa-mātṛkās* have become mixed with extraneous material in Bharata's repository of gestures and positions, it is yet, I think, possible to sift and segregate them on the basis of their names. Bharata has not changed the names given to them by Taṇḍu.

It is not our aim here to attempt such a sifting, though anyone who desires to detach Taṇḍu's *śāstra* from its *Nāṭyaśāstra* context must undertake this exercise. But what would be more interesting in getting to know Taṇḍu as a *śāstrī* would be to ask the question: how did he relate the *karaṇa mātṛkās* to the *karaṇas ?* Did he formulate any set of rules by which *mātṛkas* could be combined to from the *karaṇas* ? We do not know. But clearly a rule as simple as one he has for combining *karaṇas* into an *aṅgahāra* would not have done in this case. It does not work even in the case of *aṅgahāras* if Taṇḍu's purpose was to *deduce* only the 32 *aṅgahāras* which Śiva danced from his set of 108 *karaṇas*. Indeed, it is difficult to see how *any* set of general rules for putting the *mātṛkās* together can be formulated which will yield just the needed 108 *karaṇas*, no more and no less.

The only rule, or rather principle, which Taṇḍu does voice is that every *karaṇa* had at least two distinct sets of *mātṛkās*: (1) those consisting of hand movements and positions and (2) those consisting of the movements and positions of the feet (or perhaps the lower position of the body as a whole); for he defines *karaṇa* as *hastapādasamāyogaḥ.*[15] Further, in initiating his description of the *karaṇas*, he says, before listing them, "I shall describe how the *hasta* and the *pāda* are to be formed in them (that is, in the *karaṇas*) — *eteṣāmeva vakṣyāmi hastapādavikalpanam*" (*Nāṭyaśāstra* 4, 34). But plainly this is not enough, for if this were the only rule to be followed we will

---

[15] *hastapādasamāyogo nṛtyasya karaṇaṁ bhavet.* *Nāṭyaśāstra* 4, 30.

have innumerably more than 108 *karaṇas*.

Abhinava, indeed observes that since a *karaṇa* is a combination of a set of bodily movements, (*gati*) and positions (*sthiti*), there is really speaking no limit to the number of *karaṇas* that can be formed. What Taṇḍu wanted was to limit the number of such possible formations. It is for this reason, Abhinava adds, that Taṇḍu has listed certain *specific* movements and positions for the purpose of *karaṇa*-formation.[16] Yet it is obvious that even the *specific* movements and positions which Taṇḍu lists can give rise to an infinity of combinations. Taṇḍu does not seem to have devoted attention to building a system by which the combination of the atomic *karaṇa - mātṛkās* could be limited to the formation of only a favoured set of figures. His *karaṇa-mātṛkās* aimed only at providing a list of movements and positions into which his 108 *karaṇas* could be conveniently broken down.

In explaining Taṇḍu's *śāstra* Abhinava uses certain concept which are not to be found in Taṇḍu himself. Two such concepts stand out: the concepts of *yojanā* (See fn. 7) and of *vartanā*. Abhinava obviously considered these to be important concepts since they are central to his descriptions of the *karaṇas*. Every *karaṇa*, as we have seen, consisted of a number of movements and positions, the *karaṇa-mātṛkās*. The *karaṇa* was a whole built out of these smaller building-blocks. It was, obviously, not a mere juxtaposition of these smaller movements, but a graceful arrangement of them. This called for *yojanā*, an appropriate putting-together or 'arranging', and *vartanā* a proper *manner* in which to do this. (A parallel can be found for *vartanā* in the word *barat* of a *rāga*, that is, the 'right' way of moving over the notes in it). Both these terms clearly have an aesthetic intent. *Yojanā* and *vartanā* aimed at associating the different positions and movements of the different limbs — namely, the various *mātṛkās* of the upper and the lower parts of the body — in such a

---

[16] *tena gatisthitisammilitaṁ karaṇamityānantyaṁ yadyapi karaṇānāṁ taṭhāpyaṅgahāro-payogitvādetāvaduktamiti ślokasya tātparyam.* Abhinava on *Nāṭyaśāstra* 4, 59-60. 4, 59-60, which occasions this observation; it has been translated earlier by us: see fn 9.

way that the whole had a smooth fit, with nothing hanging loose or disjoined (*saṅgatatayā'truṭitatvena vṛttiyojane*, as Abhinava puts it; '*vṛtti*' here is a synonym of *vartanā*). Yet these were not purely aesthetic terms. They also had a descriptive content. Abhinava *describes* the *yojanā* and *vartanā* for almost all the 108 *karaṇas*. He also speaks of the proper *vartanā* for moving into one *karaṇa* from another, adding that these are matters which the practising dance *ācāryas* are conversant with.[17] They appear indeed to be matters more intimately connected with *prayoga* than *śāstra*.

Yet *yojanā* and *vartanā* seemed to have entered organised *śāstric* discourse, much before Abhinava, who was not *introducing* these terms but using them in a manner that assumes their currency in organised discourse. Thus he speaks of *karaṇa-yojanās* as sixty four in number.[18]

The *yojanās*, evidently, formed a organised scheme. We do not know how the scheme was articulated in discourse. But here, certainly, was a possibility of formulating a system by which the *mātṛkās* could be associated through a set of rules. There is no way to tell if the possibility was actualised. From the post-Taṇḍu

---

[17] Commenting on the first *karaṇa*, the *talapuṣpapuṭam*, he says: *yadā tu karaṇāntarasanniveśanantaramidaṁ karaṇaṁ prayujyate tadā tyakta-vyatadīyahastapādāpekṣayā ādātavyakaraṇagatahastapādādyapekṣayā ca yathā vartanākrameṇa svayameva tyāgopādāne atruṭitatayā vā sampadyate tathā kartavyamityalaṁ nṛttācāryagopita (ryopayogi) nā'nena etacca yathāvasaraṁ darśayitvā sarvaṁ nirūpayiṣyāmaḥ.*

Abhinava on *Nāṭyaśāstra* 4, 60-62.

This may be translated: "When this *karaṇa* is formed after the formation of another *karaṇa,* then the transition between the *hasta* and *pāda* gestures of the earlier *karaṇa* to those of the present one is to be made through such a series of *vartanās* that the whole process of giving up the earlier *karaṇa* and taking up the new one should be spontaneous or smooth (*svayameva tyāgopadāne atruṭitatayā vā sampadyate*); but these are practical matters more relevant for *ācāryas* of dance and we need not go into them. In any case I shall speak of them at the right place." The reading *nṛttācāryagopita...*, changed to *nṛttācā(ryopayogi)* by Ramakrishna Kavi, suggests another meaning:... 'but these are matters which the *ācāryas* wish to keep secret, and we need not go into them...'

[18] See Abhinava on *Nāṭyaśāstra* 4, 19-27.

texts on dance that we have, it is evident that it was the notion of *vartanā* that was given more attention than that of *yojanā*. Kallinātha commenting on the dance section of the *Saṅgītaratnākara*, where *vartanā* is an important concept (See Kallinātha on *Saṅgītaratnākara* 7, 348-349) speaks of an earlier text ascribed to Kohala where 24 *vartanās* have been described. He quotes the entire section concerned with these *vartanās* from this text. This text in fact states that the 24 *vartanās* were described by Taṇḍu himself.[19] Two of the *vartanās* are however, ascribed to *ācārya* Kīrtidhara, who may have been one of the first *ācāryas* to have articulated the concept of *vartanā* in the *śāstra*.

The *tāṇḍava* grew also as an art in later times. Later theorists speak of *mātṛkās* both of *sthiti* and *gati*, i.e. of both the *sthānaka* and the *cārī* kinds, which were not part of Taṇḍu's scheme. Clearly, the *tāṇḍava* was flexible not only *within* the system of *karaṇa* and *mātṛkās* formulated by Taṇḍu on the basis of *Śiva's aṅgahāras*, but could also borrow and adopt new movements and gestures without losing its central character. The new *sthānakas* and *cārīs* were called *deśī*. The process of ever new *deśī* formations is in principle an endless process. There is no reason why it should stop, though it seems to have done so at present.

---

[19] *caturviṁśatirityuktā vartanā bhaṭṭataṇḍunā* — the *Kalānidhi* of Kallinātha on *Saṅgītaratnākara* 7, 348-349.

CHAPTER – SEVEN

Improvisation in Indian Music*

When an Indian musician sings or plays he does not "improvise", at least not in the sense in which the word "improvisation" is commonly used in Western musical terminology. His aim is to build the structural character of a particular modal form which is called a *rāga*. In this elaboration his "improvisation" does not merely consist in the technical development of a "theme" which can neither contain the extensible quality of a *rāga*, nor could it ever have the many-sided potentiality inherent in the structure of a *rāga*. In fact, varied "themes" with many improvisations can be introduced in a *rāga*, each one of them with the intention of revealing different facets of the *rāga*. Confusion will, indeed, arise if a *rāga* is equated with a theme.

A *rāga* holds in itself elements that are fixed as well as those that are malleable; in its elaboration neither of them can be ignored. One of the mysteries of a fertile and unbroken tradition is that in it contraries are reconciled. Nothing in it can be overtly stated as rigidly fixed, and yet its archetypal forms, which continue over the ages to be the source of inspiration and of creative expression, remain inviolable. A *rāga*, in its final description, is, perhaps, such an archetypal musical form.[1]

The scale of a *rāga*, its particular ascent and descent, the significant notes and phrases which highlight its distinctive form, the process of its unfoldment or elaboration are handed down to a musician by his teacher. He also learns the basic patterns and the ways of attacking notes or phrases in a particular *rāga*, the

---

* Written in Co-authorship with Shri Vivek Dutt.

[1] A *rāga* is perhaps closer to an idea or a concept, and not an archetype, since new *rāgas* can be created and old *rāgas* can undergo crucial changes. For a development of *this* thought or idea see my *Saṅgīt Evaṁ Cintan* (Hindi), Prabhat Prakashan, New Delhi, 1994.

shades in which notes are effectively used and their characteristic movements (*calan*). Normally he conforms to certain more or less fixed formulas and to the sequence in which basic patterns of elaboration are used, as also to many other techniques of style and ornamentation. His education sharpens his awareness and he starts to evaluate effective phrases as well as meaningful approaches to a *rāga* crystallised by his contemporaries and by the great masters of the past. With this rigorous training complemented by a rich heritage, a classical Indian musician begins his career. It is only after he has mastered the formal or fixed elements in a *rāga,* that he feels confident to handle those that are flexible and spontaneous. The insight of a great master, which adds new features to the elaboration of a *rāga*, tends to become an established rule for his pupils and for many of his contemporaries. This phenomenon gives birth to a specific school or *gharanā* as it is called. A great musician is in this sense somewhat like a master craftsman who, while belonging to a tradition, simultaneously moulds it according to his genius. He not only imparts his peculiar sensitivity to the already existing patterns but also presents his own vision of them. And if his vision be original, intense and comprehensive enough, a great musician can create radically new styles. This was the case for styles of singing called *khyāl, ṭhumrī, ṭappā*, etc., developed between the seventeenth and the nineteenth century, and which are considered more brilliant than the older and more solemn *dhrupad.*

To obtain a clearer picture of what may be called "improvisation" in northern Indian Music, we shall try to sketch, though in their barest outlines, some of the methods adopted in the elaboration of a *rāga*. In typical *dhrupad* singing, for example, where the rules are comparatively rigid, the basic structural plan proceeds from the establishment of the scale and mood of a *rāga* in a slow non-rhythmic development. This long prelude is called the *alāpa.* The entire structure of the *rāga* is virtually established through the *alāpa*. In *dhrupad* singing the *alāpa* is without words, utilizing conventional syllables which have no meaning. The *alāpa* is followed by the singing of a poetic text of a few words — usually four lines — in rhythmic cycles of measured beats. *dhrupad*, properly speaking, is this part, which is elaborated by means of various patterns improvised upon the note structure in different tempos. This, naturally, leaves ample scope for a musician to display his virtuosity. The *dhrupad* is usually followed by a lighter composition called *dhamār* built on a rhythm of 14 time-units (divided into 3+2+3+2+2+2). This provides the musician with another occasion to display his virtuosity in rhythmic forms. The unfoldment, in all the three stages, moves from the severe to the joyful, from sheerness to richness and from a slow to a gradually increasing tempo.

The *alāpa* begins with a sober movement revealing the elemental form (*rūpa*) and establishing the basic mood (*rasa*) of a *rāga*.[2] It is first treated with a few essential notes around the middle tonic (the *madhyama sā*) unless the structure of the *rāga*, for example Bahār, Sohini or Deshkār, demands a different treatment. The musician then develops the *alāpa* in the lower octave which brings out the more solemn aspects of the *rāga*. With each step a new facet of the *rāga* emerges, opening up new possibilities of expression and nuance. Seizing upon these possibilities, the musician freely plays with them, yet without ever disfiguring either the process of unfoldment or the basic form of a *rāga*. The logic of unfoldment leads him to the next higher note or step in a *rāga* till the musician reaches the higher tonic (*tāra sā*). This marks the completion of one stage which according to some schools is termed the *alāpa* of the basic development. Next he, or she, explores the inherent possibilities of the higher octave. This is the *alāpa* in the second development. After he has established the widest possible uses of the notes (*svaras*) in the three octaves he then begins to play with the structure as a whole. All this takes place without definite

---

[2] For a critical discussion of the cogency of the concept of *rasa* to music, see my Hindi article in volume two, entitled, 'Saṅgīta aur Rasa-siddhānta: ek Samasyā.' The article is also included in *Bhāratīya Kalā-dṛṣṭi*, ed. Sachhidanand Vatsyayan, Prabhat Prakashan, Delhi, 1985.

rhythm patterns, in a free and flowing tempo undergoing a subtle and gradual acceleration. The rhythm becomes distinctly marked, assuming the form of a *tāla*, or a patterned cycle of beats, after the unfoldment reaches a climax encompassing all the movements of the low, the middle and the high octaves. When the musician feels that he has brought the *rāga* to an apex, he ends it usually by singing a characteristic phrase in slow tempo ending on the middle tonic, thus bringing back the *rāga* to the place from where its unfoldment had started.

The *alāpa* is followed by the *dhrupad*. *Dhrupad* is a composed song developed in four distinct musical parts: a basic form (*sthāyi*), a development in the higher octave (*antarā*), an overall movement (*sañcārī*) and the final section (*ābhoga*). There have been many celebrated *dhrupad* composers in north India; among the earliest whose compositions are still available, although with changes and modifications made by numerous later generations, is Nāyak Baiju (C. 14th century AD). A composition or *bandish* as it is called, is an aesthetic epitome of a *rāga*, with all its salient features as captured by the vision of a master musician. It is set to a particular rhythm-structure (*tāla*) and is first rendered in its basic tempo (*laya*) which may differ from one school to another or from musician to musician. The role of *tāla* in a *bandish* is equally important, for a *rāga* moulded to the form of a specific *tāla*, acquires the distinct movements of that *tāla*, which affect the mood and the complexion of the *rāga*. This obviously is the reason why no one ever thinks of rendering a comparatively serene *rāga* like Mālakosha in the lively *dādrā* rhythm (3+3), though theoretically speaking such a feat would not be impossible.[3]

The development of the melodic form and of the rhythmic variations begins after the *bandish* has been rendered in its basic tempo. With the basic tempo as the background, returning to it from time to time after an important new movement, the

---

[3] See, however, the essay in this collection entitled, 'Transformation As Creation,' pp. 33-34.

artist now takes the liberty of creating new patterns in rhythm and new melodic variation. Only through this freedom can he reveal different shapes and undertones of feelings latent in the mood of a *rāga*.

This, in brief, is the usual plan of elaboration of a *rāga* in the *dhrupad* style, yet is not compulsory. The "step-like" plan of elaboration, though considered to be a more elegant and complete way of unfoldment, is by no means a binding rule. Many artists, especially in the *khyāl* style, follow a different plan. Bade Ghulām Ali, for example, often chooses to sketch out a *rāga*,[4] first in its broad outlines with a few grouped and well measured melodic figures. The details, the colours, the improvised elaborations are filled in gradually. There are certain *rāgas*, such as Bahār, Deshi Todi, Kāmod, Paraj, Vasanta, etc., where to create the individual form and flavour of the *rāga* this more condensed treatment is far more necessary. The plan in such cases has only two phases: the development in the *sthāyi* and that in the *antarā*. All the other elements are absorbed and integrated within these two.

Thus we see that a North Indian musician while rendering a *rāga* constructs or builds it. Such a construction necessarily involves techniques of which we could only indicate the barest outline. A musician sets himself a general plan and follows it, yet at each step he puts in his own creative interpretation in formulating, enriching and giving meaning to the patterns he employs. An artist, though confined to adhere to the accepted forms of *rāgas*, is still free to exercise his creative insight and imagination, improvising — if this can be called improvisation — at every step of the elaboration. It was once pointedly expressed by a traditional musician that an artist's individual imagination and the rigid laws to which he has to conform are like the two wheels of a chariot, both of them being equally indispensable for its movement.

---

[4] Bade Ghulam Ali was alive when this essay was written (in the mid sixties).

CHAPTER – EIGHT

Bharata and the Fine Art of Mixing Structures

Bharata, with whose work I shall be concerned in the present paper, is the purported author of the *Nāṭyaśāstra*, an ancient text on dramatics. I speak of him as "the purported author" because modern scholarship doubts his authorship of the text. It questions whether this huge tome of about 6000 verses was written by a single author. What I have to say about the text may tend to favour the traditional belief that the *Nāṭyaśāstra* does, indeed, have a single author. Tradition calls this author, Bharata.

My purpose here is not to discuss the authorship of the *Nāṭyaśāstra*, though my discussion may be seen to have a tacit bearing on the question. What I propose to do in this paper is to study the *Nāṭyaśāstra* in the light of the three concepts we have decided to reflect upon,[1] namely, "system", "structure", and "discourse." A significant way of doing this, I think, would be to try and understand Bharata's enterprise as an interesting answer to two related questions. One, "What happens to structures which are parts of different, distinct wholes — we could say systems — when these structures are amalgamated to form quite another whole or system ?" And secondly, "How to formulate a *śāstra*, that is a theoretical scheme of discourse, for this new resultant whole, given a context where the different structures transposed into this new whole are already formulated into systems with well-defined *śāstras* of their own ?" These somewhat long-winded, obscure-sounding questions will, I hope, become clear as I proceed to discuss the answers to them that we can deduce from Bharata: as we begin to discern, that is, Bharata's formal and conceptual moves towards formulating a

[1] The essay began as a paper written for a seminar devoted to these three concepts. It was subsequently enlarged and modified.

śāstra concerning *nāṭya* or theatre, and the framework of ideas and forms within which he makes his moves.

Let me begin with *rasa* – with which all aesthetics in India ends. We have become used to thinking of *rasa* as a master concept which demarcates the field of all aesthetic experience and discourse. This was a later understanding of *rasa*, which though founded on Bharata, who was the first man to use the term for aesthetic discourse,[2] differed markedly from his use of the notion. *Rasa* for Bharata, was not a conceptual tool for demarcating and discoursing about aesthetics as a sphere of experience distinct from others. This was a move made a thousand years after him by Ānandavardhana and especially Abhinavagupta. For Bharata, *rasa* was a principle through which different, discrete fields of aesthetic activity, each with its own separate canons, goals and conceptual schemes of discourse, could be combined into a single composite, unified whole. *Rasa*, moreover, was not one but many — Bharata always speaks of *rasas*, in the plural — meaning that different fields could be differently combined to form different wholes with distinct flavours, that is, distinct *rasas*. A *rasa* was what made a whole hang together as a composite body combining disparate parts, and this could be successfully done in more than one way, hence the many *rasas*.

The task Bharata set himself was unusual. The modern analogy that comes to my mind is to think of his task as an

---

[2] The *Nāṭyaśāstra* speaks of *rasas* in terms that seem to indicate that the idea of *rasa* and of the various distinct *rasas* was an already established one. See *Nāṭyaśāstra* (henceforth also sometimes referred to as N.S.) 6, 15-16: all our references to the N.S. will be to the Gaekwad Oriental Series, Baroda, edition of the text with the only extant commentary on it, the *Abhinavabhāratī* of Abhinavagupta. The *rasas*, this passage says, were taught by Druhiṇa. This could be the name of a pre-Bharata *ācārya,* but is in some likelihood used as a synonym for 'Brahmā', the creator, who is also the creator of *nāṭya.* The name Druhiṇa is used for Brahmā in the N.S. more than once: see, for example, N.S. 1, 81-82 and 1, 127.

Yet, even though Bharata may have inherited the idea of *rasa* from predecessors, all later thinkers consider him the first *ācārya* in this matter, taking his formulations as the basis for their own theorising.

endeavour to discourse on the film as an art. Most of us would grant that the film is a distinct art-form. Yet, it is obviously a composite art. It has carved a separate niche for itself by combining different arts, skills and techniques into a single separate whole. And, importantly, it is a *new* art that combines arts and skills, such as music, literature, acting, which not only constitute independent arts with established aesthetic fields of their own, but they are also arts with their own distinct frameworks of consciously articulated discourse and aesthetic canons. The film, for these reasons, provides a better analogy for understanding Bharata's task than does drama. We have become used to taking the script of the drama for the drama itself, as we constantly do, for example, in the class-room. Aristotle, the prime guru of western aesthetics may be regarded as partly responsible for this. He considered the plot as the main element of a drama. The various aspects of performance were, for him dispensable.[3] The plot can be expressed in a script, not the performance. For Bharata *nāṭya* without *prayoga* — performance — would have been *kāvya* or literature, not drama. This, for us, is true of the film, which we hardly ever confuse with its script. Furthermore, Bharata was writing of theatre as a *new* art, created by combining already existing art such as the film palpably is.

For anyone who might want to construct a distinct framework of concepts for discoursing on film, both its newness and its palpable composite quality, will present special problems, and he can, I think, benefit from Bharata's model. For Bharata, too, was talking of a composite art, newly created, and in a

[3] Although Aristotle speaks of six distinct constituents of tragic drama - plot, character, diction, thought, spectacle and song - he picks out one element as the central element, plot. And so he could say: "the power of tragedy is independent both of performance and of actors, and besides, the production of spectacular effects is more the province of the property-man than the playwright". (On *the Art of Poetry*, tr. T.S. Dorsch in Penguin Books, 1965, p. 41). Indeed, Aristotle treats drama chiefly as a playwright's art and thus could assert: "tragedy fulfils its own special function even without the help of action, and just in the same way as epic, for its quality can be seen from reading it" (ibid, p. 74).

context where the different arts that his *nāṭya* combined were sophisticated arts in their own right, accorded independent aesthetic status and formulated through independent analytical frameworks. This posed for Bharata a special set of problems and gave a special texture to his conceptual framework suited to a truly new and composite art.

Rasa, we have seen, was for Bharata the principle through which different arts could be successfully combined into a single whole. Another comparison with Aristotle might throw more light on the nature of *rasa* and its aesthetic intent. Like Bharata, Aristotle's major concern in his *Poetics* is with drama. Aristotle also talks of drama, mainly tragedy, as a composite art, speaking of the different media it combines. Mark, further, the parallel in Aristotle's concept of "mimesis" - imitation - and Bharata's concept of "*anukaraṇa*" which may also be translated as "imitation." But Aristotle has nothing parallel to *rasa*. The reason is that for Aristotle all art, and not just drama, is imitation — imitation of human action. Thus, though drama is composite, it is composed of similar entities, all aiming at imitation. This is also the reason why Aristotle could pick one of the elements — the plot in the case of drama — as the most characteristic, the most "essential" part of drama. For Bharata, however, not all art was *anukaraṇa*. The most prestigious forms of dance and music that he had inherited, structures from which he transposed into his theatre, were acknowledgedly non-representational arts; they did not aim at *anukaraṇa* of *lokasvabhāva* (the human condition). The problem for Bharata rather was, how were different arts, which do not share the goal of *anukaraṇa* with drama, to be so associated with it as to become an integral part of it — to become *uparañjaka* (aesthetic aid) to it, to use Abhinavagupta's expressive term. *Rasa* was the principle for constructing and judging the 'rightness' of such associations.

Consider the metaphor Bharata uses for explicating the notion of *rasa*. "How can one suitably illustrate the concept of *rasa* through an example ?", he asks. And then answers: "*rasa* should be compared to drinks like *ṣāḍava* (literally, "a mixture of six") produced by combining *guḍa* with different *vyañjanas* and spices." *Rasa* for Bharata was clearly an art of making a good mixture, a smooth cocktail, mixing different drinks — as the word *vyañjana*, translated by Abhinavagupta as "liquid," clearly suggests. In his gloss on the word *ṣāḍava,* Abhinava points out that its flavour is quite distinct from the flavours it combines, *madhura* (sweet), *tikta* (sharp), *amla* (sour), *lavaṇa* (salt), *kaṭu* (bitter) and *kaṣāya* (astringent), taken singly or in a mechanical mixture.[4]

Bharata repeatedly speaks of the mixed character of *nāṭya.* The very first chapter contains the following statement: "There is no field of knowledge, no craft, no art, no application, no activity which is not to be seen in *nāṭya*."[5] He voices the same idea towards the end of his work, just before he begins to speak of music and the forms it takes in theatre. He speaks here of *nāṭya* as *vividhāśraya*, "that which depends on many." The whole verse where this phrase occurs is pertinent to his notion of theatre as a composite art. He says: "Song, instrumental playing and *nāṭya* which is

---

[4] *ko dṛṣṭāntaḥ. atrāha – yathā hi nānāvyañjanauṣadhidravyasaṁyogādrasaniṣpattiḥ. yathā hi – guḍādibhirdravyairvyañjanairauṣadhibhiśca ṣāḍāvādayo rasā nirvartyante tathā nānābhāvopagatā api sthāyino bhāvā rasatvamāpnuvantīti :* N.S. 6, prose passage following verse 31. Abhinava commenting on the word '*ṣāḍava*', remarks, "*ṣāḍavādayā iti lokaprasiddhebhyaḥ parasparaviviktebhyo madhuratiktāmlalavaṇakaṭuka-ṣāyebhyo miśrebhyaśca vilakṣaṇaḥ ṣāḍavaśabdavācyāḥ*".
In this passage Bharata speaks of *rasa* as an admixture of *bhāvas* alone, but *nāṭya* was a much more varied mixture, a combination of different objects not only of the same kind but of different categories altogether. In a later passage, as we shall see, Bharata uses the metaphor of an *alāta-cakra* (a firebrand) to speak of *nāṭya* as a combination of objects very different in nature. The present metaphor can also serve the same purpose, perhaps more aptly.

[5] *na tajjñānaṁ na tacchilpaṁ na sā vidyā na sā kalā/*
nasau yogo na tatkarma nāṭyesmin yanna dṛśyate//
N.S. 1, 116. We translate '*yoga*' as 'application', following Abhinava who cogently explains '*yoga*' in this passage as '*yojanā*', that is, 'application'. The various skills and knowledges, he adds, are to be applied in *nāṭya* in various combinations. The combination can be simple, as of different things from the same field (of *bhāvas*, for example: see footnote above) or complex, that is of different things from distinct fields of activity and knowledge: "*yogo yojanaṁ teṣāmeva jñānādināṁ kalāntānaṃ svabhedairan-yonyasvabhedaiḥ*".

vividhāśraya should be rendered like an *alāta-cakra* (a flaming torch so rotated as to appear like an unbroken circle of fire)."[6]

Abhinava again has an interesting gloss. "To call *nāṭya vividhāśraya* — depending on many — he says, is to say that *nāṭya* is a mixture of many distinct activities so distinct that they need to be apprehended through different sense-organs.[7] These have to be carefully combined into a single whole so that to the mind of the audience they appear as one single object. The flame of a torch in an *alāta-cakra* does not simultaneously appear at different points of space: skill alone makes it appear so through the achievement of an equilibrium. Similarly a theatric performance consists of different activities that have to be skillfully brought together into a single equilibrium *(sāmyāpādana)*."[8]

Bharata was aware that the different activities he was combining into a single *alāta-cakra* was each a world in itself with a distinct universe of discourse. He begins talking about the *nāṭya* proper in the sixth chapter of the *Nāṭyaśāstra*. Earlier chapters were introductory, both to the idea of the *nāṭya* and the

---

[6] *evaṁ gānaṁ ca vādyaṁ ca nāṭyaṁ ca vividhāśrayam/*
alātacakrapratimaṁ kartavyaṁ nāṭyayoktṛbhiḥ// N.S. 28, 7.

Here the use of '*nāṭya*' as distinct from '*gāna*' and '*vādya*' implies that in the admixture of things that produced *nāṭya*, song and music could be dispensed with: there could be *nāṭya* without them. Some theorists, as Abhinava points out, had on the strength of this passage opined that *nāṭya* could be viably formed without song and dance: '*anye tu manyante – gītātodyavihīnādapi prayogādpāthyamānādapi daśarūpakād bhavati siddhirityanena sūcitam.*" This seems a reasonable interpretation. Yet Bharata gave great importance to song and music in his scheme, treating them at an extensive length. This justifies Abhinava in commenting that *nāṭya* in Bharata's scheme remains incomplete without song and music : "*tāvati hyaparipūrṇatā nāṭyasya paripūrṇaṁ ca sarvānugrāhi nāṭyasvarūpamabhidhitsitaṁ muneḥ*" (on the N.S. passage quoted above).

[7] *yasmādvividhāśrayaṁ bhinnendriyagrāhyavividhakriyārūpaṁ tasmādyatnenāsyaikatātatsampādyā yenaikabuddhiviṣayatā sāmājikasya gacchet.* Abhinava on N.S. 28, 7.

[8] *alātatejaḥkaṇo na hi vastuto yugapadanekadeśasambandhi lāghavayatnena tu tathā sāmyamāpāditam:*

Abhinava on N.S. 28, 7.

actual *nāṭya*, which began with a ritual-like *pūrvaraṅga* (literally, "that which precedes the staging"), described in chapters four and five. With the sixth chapter begins the formal *śāstra* of the *nāṭya*. A *śāstra* formally began with a catalogue of the major concepts and categories that together described and articulated the field to be surveyed. Such a catalogue, a conceptual itinerary of what was to follow, was often termed '*uddeśa*'. Bharata calls it *saṅgraha* – "a collection." Introducing the *saṅgraha*, he says: "It is difficult to say every thing about *nāṭya* in its entirety. Why ? Because it consists of many fields of knowledge (*jñāna*) and an infinite variety of skills (*śilpa*). Even a single field of knowledge is like an ocean in itself, difficult to cover in all its essentials (*arthatattvataḥ),* what to speak of many.[9] Not only was Bharata aware of different "oceans of knowledge," to use his own phrase, he was also aware of their theoretical formulations. He deals at various lengths with a great variety of subjects all of which were together needed to build up *nāṭya*.

He begins with architecture, in the sense that the second chapter of the *Nāṭyaśāstra* contains an expert description of the *nāṭya-gṛha*, the theatre-hall. I have called it an expert description because it is couched in technical language and shows awareness of architecture as a *śāstra*, an organised scheme of discourse.[10] He describes a number of possible structures of various sizes and shapes, recommending those with the best acoustics and the best view of the stage for all viewers.[11] More integral to the theatre

---

[9] *na śakyamasya nāṭyasya gantumantaṁ kathañcana/*
kasmādbahutvājjñānānāṁ śilpānāṁ vāpyanantataḥ//
ekasyāpi na vai śakyastvanto jñānārṇavasya hi/
gantum kiṁ punaranyeṣāṁ jñānānāmarthatattvataḥ//
N.S. 6, 6-7.

[10] Thus Bharata speaks of 'three different out-lays for the theatre hall conceived in accordance with the *śāstra*': *trividhaḥ sanniveśaśca śāstrataḥ parikalpitaḥ*. *Śāstra* here obviously refers to *vāstuśāstra*, the science of architecture. His entire treatment of the subject shows his knowledge of the science.

[11] *prekṣāgṛhāṇāṁ sarveṣāṁ tasmānmadhyamamiṣyate/*
yāvatpāṭhyaṁ ca geyaṁ ca tatra śravyataraṁ bhavet//
N.S. 2, 21.

itself was the division of the stage-space into separate sections, known as the *kakṣyā-vibhāga* (described in chapter 13). *Nāṭya* for Bharata was a representation of *triloka*: all three worlds, of gods, men and demons. The *kakṣyā-vibhāga* divisions symbolically transformed the stage into the cosmos, alloting separate space to separate *lokas*; and since it was the world of men that was to be mostly represented, the *kakṣyā-vibhāga* divided the stage into different geographic categories such as the city, the village, the forest, the mountain, the river and the like.

More interesting for my purpose, however, are the transformations that were needed to make the arts of performance, music, dance and the arts of language, — speech, poetry, narrative, — integral to *nāṭya* and how these transformations have been conceptualised. Let me take up three of these to illustrate three different ways in which Bharata orchestrates the given material into forming the *nāṭya* and the conceptual tools he uses for the purpose.

I will begin with what Bharata calls the *pāṭhya*. *Pāṭhya* may be translated as "dramatic speech." Bharata includes it in his *saṅgraha* list as an essential element and concept in theatre,[12] which it obviously is. The literal meaning of *pāṭhya* is "that which is to be

---

[12] Bharata's *saṅgraha* is contained in the following
kārikā: rasā bhāvā hyabhinayāḥ dharmī vṛttipravṛttayaḥ/
siddhiḥ svarastathātodyaṁ gānaṁ raṅgaśca saṅgrahaḥ//
N.S. 6, 10.

Pāṭhya is not named here but indicated by the term *svara.* Earlier, in chapter one, Bharata names *pāṭhya* as an essential element in *nāṭya* : *jagrāha pāṭhyamṛgvedāt*. (N.S. 1, 17). Later in chapter 17, where the matter is taken up for detailed description, it is indeed, described under *pāṭhya*. This makes the use of another term for it in the *saṅgraha* puzzling and incongruous, a serious fault in a *śāstric* treatise. Such faults in the *Nāṭyaśāstra* are not uncommon, – the *Nāṭyaśāstra* was not only a *śāstra* but also a canon and Abhinava who tries to justify them in many cases sometimes gives up exasperatingly. In this case the use of *svara* for *pāṭhya* in the *saṅgraha* though not justified and even confusing – for *svara* would more naturally point at music rather than speech- yet seems significant. *Svara* distinguished ordinary *pāṭhya* from dramatic *pāṭhya*. The notion of *kāku*, central to understanding *pāṭhya* as dramatic speech, cannot be understood without bringing in *svara*, as Abhinava points out: *iha kākuṣu svarā eva vastutaḥ upakāriṇaḥ* (Abhinava on N.S. 17, prose passage following verse 102 a).

read out". The reference is to the script, to be spoken by the actors performing a play. The science of speech, that is, phonetics as a discipline concerned with the articulation of the sounds produced in uttering a language was already a sophisticated science in India centuries before Bharata, who is placed in the beginning of the Christian era. This science, known as *Śikṣā*, grew out of the need of properly pronouncing Vedic *mantras*, and had become commonplace in any study of language. Pāṇini writing his grammar in the sixth or fifth century BC assumes this science as given. The science analysed speech sounds, *varṇas*, into vowels, consonants, semivowels and sifted these on the basis of the physiology of speech production – such as the different places the tongue moves to in articulating different sounds (called *sthāna*) – and the different kinds of respiratory effort needed for pronouncing them (termed *prayatna*). These have now become commonplaces of modern linguistics too, and, indeed, the modern science was inspired in this by the ancient when the west took up the study of Sanskrit. This science deals, however, only with the right articulation of speech-sounds. What theatre requires is more. It requires *evocative* articulation of speech. Dramatic speech cannot be, to use a phrase from Abhinava again, "like reading out from a book." It rises and falls, bellows, whispers, whimpers, whines, soothes, pleads and does a hundred other things which cannot be understood in terms of phonetic categories alone. Bharata, therefore, added a new category to those he had inherited. This was the concept of *kāku*. *Kāku* may be compared to the notion of *dhvani*, propounded by Ānandavardhana to speak about language as evocation as distinct from language as information, command or analysis. Bharata, unlike Ānandavardhana, does not debate or argue his point. He merely enunciates the notion of *kāku*, borrowing the musical concepts of *svara* and *sthāna* in order to explicate it and to talk of its various modes and types. *Sthāna*, in this context, means the various registers, — low, medium, high, – over which the voice ranges in affective speaking as much as in singing. *Svara* stands for musical notes or tones, Speech, inevitably, uses these too. Unlike song, *svaras* in speech remain vague approxmations to musical tones, unclear and subsidiary to linguistic communication.[13] Yet, an actor should remain aware of *sthāna* and *svara* if he wants to command expressive speech and wield it as an art.

Music, too, was an integral part of theatre as it is in the film today. Bharata's theatre used music both as background effect, as is common to all film-making, and as songs as in Hindi films. The śāstrically articulated form of music in Bharata's days was the form known as *gāndharva*. It was an ancient form, born out of the still more ancient *sāma*, and is said to be the progenitor of contemporary forms. Its thorough, and analytically rich *śāstra*, was the basic framework within which all later forms were understood and analysed.[14] Like the *śāstrīya* music of today, *gāndharva* was a very formal art. It was non-representational while the soul of drama is *anukaraṇa*. To become an *uparañjaka* of drama, to lose its own individual voice in the totality of forms that constituted drama (to echo Abhinava once more who uses in this context the phrase: *nāṭya-sāmagri-madhyanimajjitani-jasvara*),[15] it was necessary that *gāndharva* be modified both in its form and conception. Phonetics became *pāṭhya* by the addition of an extra element, *kāku*. To turn

---

[13] *udāttānudāttasvaritakaṁpitarūpatayā svarāṇāṁ yadraktipradhāna-tvamanuraṇanamayaṁ tattyāgenoccanīcamadhyamasthānasparśitvamātraṁ pāṭhyopayogīti darśitam. yadi hi svaragatā raktiḥ pāṭhye prādhanyena lambyeta tadā gānakriyāsau syāt na pāṭhah.* (Abhinava on N.S. 17, prose passge following verse 102 a).

This may be rendered in English as follows: "In *pāṭhya*, *svaras* lose their own specific savour, their ringing quality, their function being only to raise the pitch of the voice or to lower it, to accentuate (a word) or shake it: the movement of the voice over the various registers is all that is needed for this purpose (and not a clear enunciation of musical tones). If the savouring of tonal values in themselves were to become important in *pāṭhya*, it would become song; no longer remaining speech."

[14] For more details on this question see my, *A Study of Dattilam*, New Delhi, 1978, p. 126.

[15] Distinguishing *gāna*, that is, theatrical music, from the pure form, *gāndharva*, Abhinava remarks : *gānaṁ tu nāṭyasāmagrīmadhyanimajjitanija-svaraṁ sāphhalyāya iti svarūpabhedo'pi* : Abhinava on N.S. 33, 1, a long passage which seeks to describe and analyse the distinction between *gāna* and *gāndharva*. The passage has been discussed in detail in *A Study of Dattilam*, mentioned in the footnote above.

gāndharva into *gāna* or *dhruvā* - terms in the *Nāṭyaśāstra* for theatrical songs – Bharata, in a manner of speaking, stands it on its head, that is, inverts it. *Gāndharva* was defined as: *svara-tāla-padātmakam-* "consisting of patterns of *svara,* associated with *tāla* and *sung* to *padas*, words." *Pada* was, in this group, a partner only in name. It could be dispensed with, as in the instrumental playing of *gāndharva* or become a string of nonsense syllables — such as *jhaṇṭuṃ, diṅgle, titijhala, kucajhala,* parallel to the modern *nom-tom.*[16] Even meaningful words, were in *gāndharva,* mere pegs to hang the music on. *Gāndharva* was, obviously, analogous to modern *dhrupad* or *khyāl*. It could not be used in *nāṭya* as such. Imagine a Hindi film hero singing a love song to his beloved in *dhrupad.* Bharata's theatre did, indeed, use song in ways that the Hindi film uses them. The genealogy of Hindi films, in fact, goes back to Bharata in more ways than this. However, to return to *gāndharva,* it was used in *nāṭya* through *dhruvā*, Bharata's name for *nāṭya*-songs. *Dhruvā* transmuted *gāndharva* totally, in spirit and form.

This could only be done by letting *svara* and *tāla* be dominated by *pada*, that is, the sung text. This, in fact, is how Bharata defines *dhruvā*: "*A dhruvā*," he says, "should be so composed that its music has an affinity with the meaning (of the sung text); it should be able to project the meaning".[17] In *dhruvā*, as opposed to *gāndharva, svara* and *tāla* were at the service of *pada*, they were there to lend the power of melody and rhythm to the sentiments expressed in the sung text. To change the independent spirit of *gāndharva* in this manner, and make it an *uparañjaka* of *nāṭya*, called for basic structural changes in *gāndharva*; it called for an entirely different approach to form. Bharata has a fairly long section on how

---

[16] Bharata notes the following 'words' for *gāndharva* with the remark that they were sung by Brahmā himself:

tānyakṣarāṇi vakṣye yāni purā brahmagitāni /
jhaṇṭuṁ jagatiya diginigi jhaṇṭuṁ prathame layāntare cāpi/
titijhala kucajhala madhye titikucavṛddhaṁ bhavejjyeṣthe //

N.S. 31, 104.

[17] *yasmādarthānurūpā hi dhruvā kāryārthadarśikā/*

N.S. 29, 29.

gāndharva forms are to be converted to *dhruvā*.[18] He gives us certain rules to be followed. I will speak of the more important ones that reveal his approach. There were, to begin with, two important negative rules: one, *varṇa-prakarṣa* was to be avoided in *dhruvā*. two, certain *alaṅkāras* were not be used.[19] Let me explain: *varṇa-prakarṣa* means, "stretching a syllable inordinately." This is common enough in *dhrupad* and *khyāl* and was evidently, common in *gāndharva,* too. It is a typically music-oriented approach to a sung text. In singing a word, say "*rāma*", the singer will often start weaving a melodic pattern on the vowel "*ā*," thus stretching it, prologing its duration to an incordinate extent before coming to "*ma*" – the dominant impression on the listener's ears, resultingly, is that of a musical movement and not of the *word* "*rāma*". If this process is repeated on many syllables of longer passages, such as, to take a random example, *"ban calat rāma raghurāi"* ("Rāma, the king of the dynasty of Raghu, goes to the forest"), the musical content will tend to overpower the linguistic purport totally. This is not usually to be desired in songs which are embedded within a dramatic action, whose main intent is to convey evocative meanings.

Another thing that could "distort" a syllable was the use of certain kinds of melodic figures – *alaṅkāras*. Bharata names those *alaṅkāras* which were not to be used in *dhruvā*, or at least, not to be used with their full force.[20] Besides these negative rules – they were clearly more like rules of the thumb — Bharata also hints at certain positive ones. One such was that *gāndharva svara*-forms (which were strict, inflexible, hieratic forms known as *jātis*) were to be used only through their more popular, more flexible derivatives (such as

---

[18] N.S. 32, 1-46.

[19] *saptarūpagatā jñyeyā alaṅkārā budhaistvime /*
naite (sarve) dhruvāsviṣṭāḥ śruti (śrotṛ) varṇaprakarṣaṇāt//
na hi varṇaprakarṣastu dhruvāṇāṁ siddhiriṣyate/
N.S. 29, 26-27.

The readings in brackets are suggested by the editor, apparently, on the basis of Abhinava's comments.

[20] *śyeno vāpyathavā bindurye cānye'ti (tu) prakarṣiṇaḥ/*
te dhruvāṇāṁ prayogeṣu na kāryā svapramāṇataḥ//
N.S. 29, 27-28.

the *grāma-rāgas,* to which are own *rāgas* are historically related). Another was that *gāndharva-tālas* which were as strict and inflexible, and as purely "musical" as the *gāndharva svara*-forms, were to be so moulded for the purposes of *dhruvā,* that the contours of *tāla* were to follow the *chanda* – the metre – of a sung poem.[21] All the rules, in fact, boiled down to a single principle: to get the right tune to suit the song in the given context; or in other words, to use the phrase Bharata himself uses in many contexts about different arts, to compose "*yathā-rasa*", as the *rasa* dictates.[22] To make music, in Abhinava's words, *uparañjaka* to the theatrical whole.

In *dhruvā* or *gāna* we have a small composite unit where two different arts, in this case poetry and music, become fused into one, in order to form what might be called a sub-system within the totality of *nāṭya*. I call *dhruvā* a sub-system because it was geared towards a larger totality. All fusions of music and poetry where both these arts yet retain their individuality (unlike *gāndharva* or *khyāl* or *dhrupad*) as in certain *ghazal* forms (here Begum Akhtar comes to my mind) or the great *Vaiṣṇava padāvalī kīrtan* of Bengal are not sub-systems but wholes in their own right. Abhinava, indeed, remarks that a *dhruvā* was not quite satisfactory outside the *nāṭya*.[23]

---

[21] The *tāla*-structure of *gāndharva* was based on an extraordinarily large time unit. Its forms had, besides, little in common with metres of popular verses, which were sung as *dhruvās*. Thus both the *gāndharva tāla*-measure and its *tāla*-structure had to be modified and moulded to current metrics for the purpose of *dhruvā:*

yānyaṅgāni kalāścaiva gītakāntaragatāni tu/
tāni chandogatairvṛttairvibhāvyante dhruvāsvatha// N.S. 29, 14.

[22] He says this about *dhruvā,* for example:

tathā rasakṛtā nityam dhruvāḥ prakaraṇāśritāḥ/
nakṣatrāṇīva gaganaṁ nāṭyamudyotayanti tāḥ // N.S. 32, 430.

Meaning : "*Dhruvās* designed according to *rasa* in dramas and depending upon them, make them resplendent like the stars make the sky". See also N.S. 32, 427; N.S. 34, 65, which says about *vādya:*

rasasatvabhāva (bhāvasatva) yogān (gaṁ) dṛṣṭvābhinayaṁ gatipracāraṁśca /
vādyaṁ nityaṁ kāryaṁ yathākramaṁ (yathaṁ) vādya (vṛtta) yogajñaiḥ//

[23] *na hi nāṭyadbahirlayabhaṅga (ṅgyā)pi dhruvāgānaṁ gīyamānasukhamutpādayati* Abhinava on N.S. 33, 1. The printed edition has '*gīyamānamukhaṁ*' instead of '*gīyamānṃ sukhaṁ*', a meaningless reading which we have amended. Abhinava says: "Outside the context of drama a *dhruvā* song gives

A contemporary example may bring the point home better. Take a Hindi film song. We may like it on its own, but if we watch it on the T.V. with the film-scene into which it was woven we do feel that something is "added" to it, making it richer. Hence the popularity of T.V. programmes such as *Citrahāra*. A good Begum Akhtar *ghazal*, however, forms a fused whole in itself, not needing anything more to enrich or "complete" it.

Dance was another important ingredient in *nāṭya*. It was so in the form of *nṛtta*, an ancient well-schematised art, similar in this respect to *gāndharva*. Also like *gāndharva*, it was a formal, non-representational art. It presented the same problem to Bharata: How was it to be made integral to *nāṭya* which, unlike it, was *anukaraṇa*-oriented ? Indeed, in the case of *nṛtta*, Bharata is more articulately aware of this basic aesthetic problem. We find him expressing the problem at the end of a charming little story, a myth, related at the beginning of the fourth chapter. Bharata having created a specific *nāṭya*, a *samavakāra* called *Amṛtamanthana*, showed it to the gods and demons who enjoyed it greatly (partly because it was an enactment of a great deed of their own doing). Satisfied, Brahmā proposed that a *nāṭya* should now be shown to *Śiva*, the great critic. So Brahmā, Bharata and his troup, all went to the beautiful Himalayas where Śiva has his home. A *ḍima*, another form of *nāṭya*, called *Tripuradāha* (with a story from Śiva's own deeds) was presented before him. Śiva was pleased. But he made a suggestion. He said that he had created a dance which should be incorporated into *nāṭya* as part of its prologue called *pūrvaraṅga* where it could be associated with *gītaka*-songs.[24] This would, he adds, lend colour

---

no pleasure even through sung in style". He compares it to a spoilt child (*lālita*) away from the company of his doting kin and elders about whom no one is any longer bothered when the parents are not there: *so'yamatra lālita iva gurusaṅghasevāvaikalyādanusandhivarjastathāpi na smaryate. Dhruvā* then appeals only to immature minds (*sukumāra-mati*): *sukumāramatimeva hi prati prāya idaṁ pravṛtāt.* Abhinava on N.S. 33, 1.

[24] *mayapidaṁ smṛtaṁ nṛtyaṁ sandhyākāleṣu nṛtyatā/*
nānākaraṇasaṁyuktairaṅgahārairvibhūṣitam//
pūrvaraṅgavidhāvasmiṁstvayā samyakprayojyatām /
N.S. 4, 13-14.

to the proceedings and the meanings of the songs, too, could thus be represented through *abhinaya* gesture and mime.[25] He then asks his disciple Taṇḍu to describe this dance and teach it to Bharata. A long manual on this dance, termed *nṛtta* and also *tāṇḍava* (since it was taught by Taṇḍu), follows — Chapter 4, verses 19 to 260. At the end of the description, from which it is clear that what is being described is a pure, non-representational art form, the *ṛṣis* to whom Bharata was relating his *śāstra*, put to him these questions: "*Abhinaya* was created by the wise so that meanings may be grasped; why was the *nṛtta* created? what condition does it depend upon? For it has no connection with the meaning of a *gītaka*-song nor does it evoke or represent (*bhāvayati*) any meaning whatsoever."[26] The *ṛṣis* were quick to discern that *abhinaya* and *nṛtta* were quite different in intent and this for two reasons. Firstly, *abhinaya* was intimately connected with meanings, that is, textual meanings of a song (or a script) which it conveyed or rendered through gestures and mime; *nṛtta* had no such connections with any text, it created an independent aesthetic world through body-movements and gestures. Secondly, *abhinaya,* like *nāṭya* itself, was an *anukaraṇa*, it imitated *lokasvabhāva*, the human condition; it depended on this *anukaraṇa*, for without *anukaraṇa* there could be no such category as *abhinaya*. What condition, what *svabhāva*, the *ṛṣis* ask, does *nṛtta* depend upon? The implication is clear: *nṛtta* creates its own "condition," it does not depend upon any other.

The *ṛṣis* had asked these questions in the context of the *purvaraṅga* where the aim of the performance was ritualistic, not *anukaraṇa*- oriented. The forms employed were *gāndharva* and *nṛtta*. *Nṛtta,* as the story we have related earlier suggests, was introduced later: Śiva asked Bharata to *add* it to the *pūrvaraṅga*.

---

[25] *vardhamānakayogeṣu gīteṣvāsāriteṣu ca //*
mahāgīteṣu caivārthānsamyagevābhineṣyasi/
N.S. 4, 15.

[26] *ṛṣaya ūcuḥ: yadā prāptyarthamarthānāṁ tajjñairabhinayaḥ kṛtaḥ //*
kasmānnṛttaṁ kṛtaṁ hyetatkaṁ svabhāvamapekṣate/
na gītakārthasambaddhaṁ na cāpyarthasya bhāvakam //
N.S. 4, 261-262.

The *ṛṣis* failed to see the logic of this addition. How was *nṛtta*, an art as independent and non-representational as *gāndharva* to be associated integrally with *gāndharva* ? Bharata really gives no answer to this question. Abhinava denies any integral relation. He speaks of the association of these two independent arts through an interesting metaphor: They are, he says, like two kings who happen to march together, with their independent armies towards a common enemy.[27]

Nṛtta, then could not even be fused with *gāndharva,* another purely formal art like itself. How was it, then, to be orchestrated into *nāṭya* ? In order to understand how *nṛtta* became *nāṭya-sāmagrī,* a part of the dramatic whole, it would, I think, be helpful to become acquainted with Bharata's concept of the *nāṭya-dharmī Nāṭya* was an *anukaraṇa* of the world, especially, the human condition, *lokasvabhāva.*[28] But it made no attempt to replicate the world. What it presented was a world transformed through imagination, the artistry and devices that playwrights and directors of plays could command. This transformed world, and the means by which the transformation was made, were both called *nāṭya-dharmī*, "having traits peculiar to *nāṭya*". *Nāṭya-dharmī* was based on *loka-dharma*, "traits belonging to the world of men," yet it created a world of its own.[29]

---

[27] *svapratiṣṭhite'pi dvaye yena yatsammelanayogyaṁ tattatra prayujyata ityetāvānaṅgāṅgibhāvaḥ. evaṁ śatrujvalanapravṛttāmarṣā(ttasā)bhimānanara-patidvitayavat* - Abhinava on N.S. 4, 252. (Volume 1, page 126 of the edition we are quoting).

[28] *nānābhāvopasampannaṁ nānāvasthāntarātmakam/*
lokavṛttānukaraṇaṁ nāṭyametatmayā kṛtam//

N.S. 1, 112.

This idea is repeated many times in the *Nāṭyaśāstra*.

[29] *yo'yaṁ svabhāvo lokasya sukhaduḥkhakriyātmkaḥ/*
so'ṅgābhinayasaṁyukto nāṭyadharmī prakīrtitaḥ//

N.S. 13, 81.

For a more detailed exposition of this important concept, see my article entitled' The Nāṭya as Conceived by Bharata', the *New Quest*, March-April, 1984. Also, published in *Indias Intellectual Traditions,* ed. Prof. Daya Krishna, ICPR and Motilal Banarasidass, 1987, pp. 104-114. Bharata's drama was an imaginative recreation of reality. Music and dance were integral to it. The action shown had to be designed in a particular way, leading always to success in

It was an idealised world presented in a stylised form. Ordinary gestures were heightened and rendered with the grace of dance.[30] This opened the door for *nṛtta* to enter into the realm of *abhinaya*. Bharata counts *nṛtta* as one of the three elements (*vastus*) of *abhinaya*.[31] *Nṛtta* was amalgamated into *abhinaya* not only indirectly, by imparting extra grace to the bodily actions and expressions needed by actors on the stage, thus making the whole *abhinaya*, the entire tone of presentation *nāṭyadharmī*. It was also used to enrich what might be termed the "language of gestures", used as part of *abhinaya*. *Abhinaya* has many aspects. Some are more strictly *anukaraṇa*-based than others. Projecting human feelings, emotions, states of mind, through the exacting art of reproducing the physical signs, facial expressions, almost involuntry bodily movements or gestures that normally accompany them, is a major part of *abhinaya,* and is patently *anukaraṇa*-based. So is the art of the mime, the reproduction of the actions of specific characters or types of characters. Apart from these, *abhinaya* also includes that gamut of gestures, borrowed or reproduced from *loka*, that are like language, fixed conventional symbols given a certain meaning. Raising the thumb as an indication of victory for example. This is a *conventional* gesture, rooted in a particular culture, and is symbolic of victory; it *means* "victory." It may mean nothing in another culture or might convey quite another meaning. In many parts of India, thus, the same raised thumb, especially if also moved from left to right, might mean "look how I have duped you." Such gestures are, obviously, very different from those that

---

an undertaking and a happy consummation. In this way Bharata's idealised world was *nāṭyadharmī* in a specific sense peculiar to it. Bharata was aware of this but he was also aware that all theatre, in as much as it is a recreation of the world and not its replica, was bound to be *nāṭyadharmī* in some essential way.

[30] *ativākyakriyopetamatisattvātibhāvakam/*
līlāṅgahārābhinayaṁ nāṭyalakṣaṇalakṣitam//
N.S. 13, 73.

[31] *asya śākhā ca nṛttaṁ ca tathaivāṅkura eva ca/*
vastūnyabhinayasyeha vijñeyāni prayoktṛbhiḥ//
N.S. 8, 15.

imitate an *action* or those that imitate *signs* of mental states. All *abhinaya* uses such gestures in the form that they are available from *loka*. Bharata's *abhinaya* added to the available vocabulary of the language of gestures by incorporating into it many *nṛtta*-gestures and assigning them meanings.[32] We are familiar with such usages from the Bharata-inspired *abhinaya* of *Bharata Nāṭyam* or *Oḍḍisī*. In fact, in these styles of dance, we may see the same gestures in a purely *nṛtta* context as well as in *abhinaya*, where they are used to project the meanings of words in a song. Such a usage should be regarded as a part of the *nāṭya-dharmī,* since the function of *nāṭya-dharmī* was not only to idealise and stylise, but also to incorporate all such devices and conventions which any theatre must use, if it aims at representing the *loka* on a stage. Thus the *nāṭya-dharmī*

---

[32] Compare Abhinava: *abhinayasya dvividhā itikartavyatā lokadharmī nāṭyadharmī ca. ādyā dvividhā – cittavṛttyarpakatvenānubhāvasya, yathā – "garve'pyahamiti tajjñair-lalāṭadeśocchritā" (N.S. 9, 19) iti. kevalabāhyāva–yavarūpa vā yathā padmakośasya kamapi nirūpaṇe. naṭyadharmyapi dvidhā – nāṭyopayogamūlabhūtakaiśikīsampādanoc–italaukikaśobhāhetuḥ yathā – āveṣṭitādicaturvidhakaraṇarūpā. kācittvaṁśena lokamupajīvati yathā varṇātureṇa hastena tatra vyavahitena loka upajīvyate. loke hyanirdeśya–tāśeṣaṁ vastu nirdidikṣurīdṛśaṃ tādṛśamitthambhūtamityavasare prayukta–meva caturaiḥ. evaṁ janāntikādau vācyam. naṭasamayamātrarūpā nāṭyadharmī samayasyākiñcitkarasya kalpane prayojanābhāvāt.*

This remarkable passage may be rendered as following:

"*Abhinaya* may be accomplished in two different modes, *lokadharmī* and *nāṭyadharmi. Lokadharmī* is of two kinds. The first consists of *anubhavās* – bodily positions, gestures or actions – that indicate a state of mind: like the lifting up one's head in pride (N.S. 9, 19). The second consists of only an outward showing, as when one indicates a lotus flower (through one's palms and fingers). *Nāṭyadharmī* is also of two kinds. The first consists of movements of pure dance such as the *āveṣṭita*, movements which are used to impart an ethos of more than ordinary beauty and joy in rendering the *kaiśikī vṛtti*. Some (stylised gestures) depend partly upon *loka*, such as the use of the hand gesture called the *varṇātura* which depends indirectly upon *loka:* for in real life, too, a similar gesture is used when one has not been able to explain something quite fully and wants to show what it is like exactly (*tādṛśamitthambhūtam*). The same (kind of part–dependence on *loka*) is to be found in convetions such as the *janāntika* (the aside). The *nāṭyadharmī* here is nothing but the set of conventions (*samaya*) used by actors, and these certainly serve a useful purpose (in *nāṭya*), for there is no point in having a convention that is redundant."

comprised the use of "theatrical" devices such as *svagata* (something said loudly to oneself which other characters do not hear but the audience does); *ākāśabhāṣita* (in which a character speaks to someone off the stage, speaking both his own words and that of the other); *kakṣyāvibhāga* which we have described earlier and the like. To these were *added* conventional meanings imparted to certain *nṛtta*-gestures which otherwise had no meaning of their own. This was done sometimes on the basis of a slight similarity with something in the *loka*.

In *nṛtta*, body movements had nothing to *say*. Incorporated in *abhinaya*, which is essentially *anukaraṇa*-dependent, they acquired or were given a meaning beyond themselves. *Nṛtta* thus became an *uparañjaka* of *nāṭya*, helping to render it *nāṭya-dharmī*, acquiring, in the process, a new, transformed significance.

Nāṭya-dharmī in theatre employed not only *nṛtta*, but, understandably, also music. Music, indeed, is a normally accepted *uparañjaka* of all theatre, even the most *loka-dharmī*, such as the "realistic" theatre of the modern west. In Bharata's theatre, music was employed in the form of *dhruvā* or *gāna* and *vādya* - terms Bharata uses in his *saṅgraha*. *Dhruvā*, or *gāna*, we have already discussed. It was something we might today consider as extremely *nāṭya-dharmī*, oriented as we are to western theatric practice. *Vādya* was instrumental music played as back-ground accompaniment.[33] We have seen how *dhruvā* could be considered a sub-whole within the

---

[33] One of the first things that the stage director did in making the stage ready for a show was to seat the musicians on it. This is a practice still followed in classical dancing. Bharata calls it *kutapa-vinyāsa*. The instruments used, besides the voice, were flutes, harps and drums. Music was used to accompany *dhruvā*, some modes of accompaniment being very different from what we today know as *saṅgat* (for details see, *A Study of Dattilam*, p. 257-259). Music also served as accompaniment to *nāṭya* itself, independent of *dhruvā* songs. It was in itself a major *nāṭya-sāmagrī*, and it was expected of musicians that they would mould it and flex it to suit the ethos of the moment. Some rules of the thumb were established for the purpose, and a list made of which *rāga* to use when; these lists grew to great lengths with post-Bharata *ācāryas*.

nāṭya totality. Another sub-whole was *abhinaya*. *Abhinaya* included *nṛtta* as well as *pāṭhya*, which we discussed when speaking of Bharata's notion of *kāku*. *Abhinaya, dhruvā, vādya* and *pāṭhya* together formed a larger whole for which Bharata uses the term *vṛtti*.[34]

Vṛtti (literally, "the manner of being or doing") is thus a central concept in the *Nāṭyaśāstra*. The word *vṛtti*, indeed, is as difficult to translate as *rasa*. There is no equivalent term in western languages for this important concept. There was a large collection of organically associated forms which together comprised the *performance* of a play, the total manner and style of stage presentation, its overall weave and texture. Bharata, unlike Aristotle, considered performance, or *prayoga* as he called it, essential to drama. Achieving the right *vṛtti* was the soul of *prayoga*. Bharata recognises four distinct *vṛttis*, relating each to appropriate *rasas*. Though clearly a mix, a *vṛtti* had a character, a temper, a savour of its own. Like all good aesthetic wholes, it was not just a sum of its parts but something

---

[34] A concept seemingly related to *vṛtti* is that of *pravṛtti* , which Bharata treats at some length (N.S. 13, 36-86). *Pravṛtti* meant the different usages regarding language, dress, custom, behaviour and the like of people from different regions of India. Bharata also speaks of their differences in terms of temper and taste. These had to be borne in mind while representing different regional types. *Vṛtti*, however, is a more universal notion. It is not concerned with representing regional life-styles but the human condition as such. It is also, clearly, more intimately related to theatre as an art: it is a *nāṭya-dharmī* concept being central to the very idea of *nāṭya*. *Vṛtti* can be formed only in *nāṭya* with the various means at the disposal of the *prayoktṛ* (the stage director). It is something to be imaginatively created, while *pravṛtti* is something out there in the *loka*, a raw material for *anukaraṇa*, which *vṛtti* uses and puts together with other things to create theatre. Thus we find that the *pravṛttis* have been subsumed by Bharata himself under *vṛtti*: *nānādeśaveṣabhāṣācāro loka iti kṛtvā lokānumatena vṛttisaṁṣritasya nāṭyasya mayā cāturvidhatvamabhihitaṁ bhāratyārabhaṭī sāttvatī kaiśikī ceti* (N.S. 13, prose passage following verse 37). Bharata says, "People live in different lands and follow different usages of language, dress and customary behaviour, and, therefore, in conformity with *loka* itself, I have spoken of *nāṭya*, which however depends on *vṛtti*, as being of four kinds, *bhāratī, ārabhaṭī, sāttvatī* and *kaiśikī* (these being the names of the four *vṛttis* described by Bharata)".

more, something quite magically more. No wonder then that Bharata has a myth about how *vṛttis* were created in divine action and *līlā*.[35]

Let me give you an example of *vṛtti*, for, fortunately, we can still experience a Bharata-like *vṛtti* in performance. A *Bharata Nāṭyam* or an *Oḍḍisi* piece in the *abhinaya*-form displays a composite art parallel to *vṛtti*. It is a mix containing music, song, *nṛtta*, mime, gestures and its aim is to depict *lokasvabhāva*, human sentiment and emotion. Witness, for example, an *Oḍḍisi* piece rendered to a Jayadeva *aṣṭapadī*, the one, let us say which sings of Radha's tryst with *Kṛṣṇa*, her futile, frustrating wait, her anger, her *viraha*, and what we have in the total presentation is a *vṛtti*. But we still do not have *nātya* as conceived in Bharata's scheme. What is lacking is an adequate plot, a story depicting human *action,* not just human sentiment. *Vṛtti*, in Bharata's vision, though conceivable without a proper story, needs the backbone of *itivṛtta* for completion.

Itivṛtta, literally, "this is what happened", was Bharata's

---

[35] It is noteworthy that after giving us a myth about the origin of *nāṭya* as a whole, right at the beginning of the *Nāṭyaśāstra*, Bharata gives us a separate myth about the origin of *vṛtti* in the 20th chapter of his work as he takes the topic up for a detailed treatment. The *vṛttis*, according to Bharata's story, were inspired by the very first deed that Lord Viṣṇu Himself undertook when he awoke from his divine sleep. After having taken creation back into himself (during *pralaya*), the Lord slept on the primal serpent Śeṣa, floating on the undifferntiated Cosmic Ocean (*ekārṇava*). He was rudely awakened by two demons, Madhu and Kaiṭabha who wanted a battle with him. A fierce fight ensued, and as the three fought, they exchanged rude and angry words, their bodies quickened with a turmoil of fierce and frenzied emotions. Thus were born the three *vṛttis, bhāratī, ārabhaṭī* and *sāttvatī* dominated respectively by speech, physical action and a display of emotion. The graceful, *śṛṅgāra*-oriented *kaiśikī* was born of the movement of Lakṣmī as she looked on at her husband Viṣṇu, and began to tie her loosened hair with delicate dance-like movements. N.S. 20, 1-24.

The *Nāṭya*, Bharata says in chapter one, was created out of the four Vedas. The *vṛttis,* too, were important enough to have been provided a similar origin independently of *nāṭya*:

ṛgvedādbhāratī kṣiptā yajurvedācca sāttvatī/
kaiśikī sāmavedācca śeṣa cātharvaṇādapi//

N.S. 20, 25.

name for the dramatic plot, which was to be enacted through one or more *vṛttis.* The final success of a *prayoga* – a performance – lay in the achievement of the adequate *vṛtti*, which would suit an *itivṛtta.*

An adequate *itivṛtta* demanded adequate action. It had to be conceived as a story of human effort directed towards a desirable goal.[36] In the best of plays, namely, in the types known as *nāṭaka* and *prakaraṇa*, in which the *nāṭya* of Bharata revealed its full powers, displaying all its various elements, the action progressed from seed to fruition in five stages growing from small beginnings to great results as in the *Śākuntalam,* where the casual love and dalliance of a king matures into a profound inner awakening and the birth of a great emperor who ruled over the whole of India, and gave it its name, Bharata. The *itivṛtta* was as *nāṭya-dharmī* as its *prayoga*. One major *nāṭyadharmī* element in *itivṛtta* was the rule that an action must end with the attainment of its goal. All plots were to be success stories. There could be hurdles, sorrow and pain, but no failures; tragedy was not accepted as a form of *itivṛtta.*

Plotting an action was central to *nāṭya*, but *nāṭya* was also affective *evocation* of *lokasvabhāva*, not merely its depiction through action. It aimed at producing *rasa*. In this the *vṛttis,* as pure *prayoga,* were more important than the action and plot, though naturally the *vṛttis* had to function with the plot, as related to it. The *vṛttis* could, yet, be sufficient in themselves to evoke *rasa*. The *Oḍḍisi abhinaya*-piece, danced to Jayadeva's *aṣṭapadī* that I mentioned earlier, clearly evokes *rasa; śṛṅgāra* in this case, but it is not *nāṭya*. For it is miserably lacking in action and plot. The *Bharata Nāṭyam*, too, is for the same reason not Bharata's *nāṭya*, though it similarly employs *vṛtti* and evokes *rasa. Rasa*, therefore, cannot be really said to be definitive of Bharata's *nāṭya;* a *nāṭaka* or a *prakaraṇa* or a similar form (Bharata names ten types) rich both in *prayoga* and *itivṛtta* was what Bharata truly meant by *nāṭya*.

[36] S.N. 19, 1-20.

Yet *vṛtti*, though insufficient by itself, singly or in combination, to form *nāṭya* was sufficient to evoke *rasa*. It was the smallest unit into which *nāṭya* — in its *prayoga* aspect — could be analysed. It also fulfilled the other requirement essential for *nāṭya*, namely, a *nāṭya-dharmī* recreation of the human condition. Consequently, a major part of Bharata's effort in the *Nāṭyaśāstra* concentrates on the making of *vṛttis*: he first describes its discrete building-blocks, the various arts with which it was built up, and the aesthetic and affective principles for putting them together into the composite whole that constituted a *vṛtti*.[37] Indeed Bharata's *śāstra* as a *prayoga-śāstra* may be characterised as a system for putting together different arts in order to form viable *vṛttis*.

Bharata speaks of only four *vṛttis*, but this was a prescriptive limitation, almost a fiat. The theatric usage he had in mind evidently did not need any more *vṛttis*. His system, however, is a system of infinite possibilities. He does not give us specific forms but general ways of achieving them. He explores rules and principles for forming *vṛttis*. Instructively, even the four *vṛttis* he describes in some detail, are described in general terms. Concrete formations were left to the judgement and creative skill of the *prayoktṛ*, the director: though in this process, actually crystallised forms handed down from tradition must have played a great formative role, as they do in classical music today. But as in classical music to-day, the *system* within which forms are made and understood is, essentially, a system of possibilities. However, the various arts with which a *vṛtti* was built up were each, as we have seen, a realm into itself. Many of these were not *anukaraṇa*-oriented, in fact, they had no relation to

[37] The affective principle is described by Bharata in what can be meaningfully termed his theory of *bhāvas*, which is an essential part of his *rasa*-theory. I, too, have described the theory in my own way in my, 'The Path that Bharata did not take' an article to be published by the Saṅgita Nāṭaka Akademi, New Delhi; see also my review article, 'Sanskrit Criticism, by V.K. Chari, published in the *Journal of the Indian Council for Philosophical Research,* Vol. X, no. 3, 123-138.

lokasvābhava, and thus, as we have argued above, they could not aim at evoking *rasa*, because *rasa*, in Bharata's definition, cannot be aroused by a non-representational art form. Hence the occasion for the question asked by the *ṛṣis* concerning the relevance of *nṛtta* to *nāṭya*. And hence, also, Bharata's efforts at *incorporating* the non-representational *within* a representational scheme.

Significantly, the analytical approach Bharata adopts in describing *nṛtta* is, in a crucial sense, very different from the one adopted in describing *nāṭya*. The approach to the analysis of *nāṭya* is fundamentally "holistic": *Vṛtti,* the smallest viable structural unit constituting *nāṭya*, was itself a whole composed of smaller wholes such as the *dhruvā*; *vṛtti* was a composite structure *made up* of structures borrowed from different 'independent' realms. Also, a *vṛtti* was outward-looking in the sense that it could not be viable, could not even be comprehended as a *vṛtti*, unless it could be related to *rasa* and the *anukaraṇa* of *lokasvabhāva*. *Nṛtta*, on the otherhand, has been analysed by Bharata through, what may be characterised as a *māṭṛkā* approach. A *nṛtta-māṭṛkā*, a term Bharata himself uses, was the name given to the smallest "atomic" structure to which *nṛtta* forms could be analytically reduced. Bharata delineates a repertoire of such atomic structures which could be combined to form larger formations known as *karaṇa* and *aṅgahāra*. *Aṅgahāras* were formed with *karaṇas* and were more "complete" forms, which in combinations produced *nṛtta* wholes. Various such wholes were possible, since *nṛtta,* as much as *nāṭya,* was a system of possibilities. This idea comes out explicitly in Abhinava who comments that *karaṇas* could, in principles, be infinite, even though Bharata deliberately restricted their number to 108 as he wanted to describe only certain specific *aṅgahāras*.[38] These were the

---

[38] *ayaṁ bhāvaḥ-aṣṭottare karaṇaśate catuṣṣaṣṭikaraṇayojanayā truṭitāṅgagatyā (ṅgagatarītya) yadyapyānantyamaṅgahārāṇāṁ tathāpi pradhānādṛṣṭa phalaṁ pratyadhikoparaktatayā dvātriṁśannāmato nirdiṣṭāḥ.* Abhinava on N.S. 19-27. For a more detailed description and discussion of this matter, see the essay, 'Taṇḍu: The First Theoretician of Dance', in this collection.

aṅgahāras necessary for the *nṛtta* rendered in the *pūrvaraṅga*, which was both a dance and a ritual, and as ritual its forms were fixed and determinate.

Vṛtti, being a representational device, could not be understood without being related to *rasa* and *anukaraṇa*. But *nṛtta* was non-representational, it needed no reference outside of itself in order to be viable, and to make artistic "sense". A *nṛtta-mātṛkā*, therefore, had to be understood as a self-contained atomic structure, a unit of significance in itself. Consequently this is how Abhinava defines a *karaṇa,* another term for the *nṛtta-mātṛkā*:[39] "*Karaṇa* is an act. But of what is it an act? It is an act of *nṛtta*, of the body in movements executed gracefully (*vilāsakṣepa)*. (Hence) *karaṇa* is an act different from those made with the utilitarian intention to acquire something beneficial or discard something harmful.... One unitary act (*ekā kriyā*) executed from one point of space to another "appropriate" (*samucita*) point, is a *karaṇa*."[40] We clearly have here the concept of an atomic *nṛtta* movement which, being a non-utilitarian "dance" movement, has no reference

[39] There is confusion in the use of the terms *karaṇa* and *nṛttamātṛkā*. Bharata says, in a passage, that *aṅgahāras* - complex *nṛtta* wholes - are made up of *karaṇa* units: *sarveṣāmaṅgahārāṇāṁ niṣpattiḥ karaṇairyataḥ* (N.S. 4, 29). In a later passage he says: *yāni sthānāni yāścāryo nṛttahastās tathaiva ca/ sā mātṛketi vijñeyā tadyogātkaraṇaṁ bhavet/* (N.S. 4, 59-60).

This suggests that *karaṇas* themselves were made up of *mātṛkās*, which, one would suppose, were still smaller units. And, yet Bharata emphatically states that the *nṛtta-mātṛka* was a relatively complex unit consisting of two *karaṇas*: *dve nṛttakaraṇe caiva bhavato nṛttamātṛkā* (N.S. 4, 31).

This is a confusion concerning the proper use and definition of terms. The *Nāṭya-śāstra* does sometimes make such a confusion. The text as we have it has not passed through a very clean and clear process of transmission. However, the *concept* of an atomic *nṛtta* unit is clear enough, whatever we may choose to call it, *karaṇa* or *nṛtta-mātṛkā*. The issue is discussed at some length in the earlier essay, 'Taṇḍu: The First Theoretician of Dance.'

[40] *kriyā karaṇam. kasya kriyā? nṛttasya. gātrāṇāṁ vilāsakṣepasya. heyopādeyaviṣay-akriyādibhyo vyatiriktā yā tatkriyā karaṇamityarthaḥ... pūrvakṣetrasaṁyogatyāgena samucitakṣetrāntaraprāptiparyantatayā ekā kriyā tatkaraṇamityarthaḥ.*

Abhinava on N.S. 4, 28-30.

outside of itself. Unlike *abhinaya*, it has no reference to *lokasvabhāva*.

The *mātṛkā* or *karaṇa* – approach to analysing structure within a system was not limited to *nṛtta*. It was also used in phonetics, which analysed all speech sounds into a finite number of atomic phonemes, the *varṇa-mātṛkā*, capable, in principle, of infinite combinations. A similar analysis was made by Bharata (and his is the earliest example we have) of percussion playing (*puṣkara vādya*), an art which, apparently, was as sophisticated and as "independent" an art in Bharata's days as it is today. Bharata speaks of sixteen *vāk-karaṇas* — *bols* we call them in Hindustani music today – which are "basic" sounds indicative of sounds played an drums: *ka kha ga gha ta tha da dha ṭa ṭha ḍa ḍha ma ra la ha*, these in various combinations, on the basis of *tāla, laya, yati* resulted in infinite patterns.[41]

I must now end; yet I can not resist the temptation to add a few remarks, make some brief reflections and raise a question or two inspired by Bharata's endeavour. His formulation of *nāṭya*, or rather *nāṭyas* – since his conception has ample room for alternate formations – is itself an example of the *vṛtti* approach practised in a grand manner. Whatever he describes, he relates integrally to *nāṭya*. We have discussed a few examples, but there are others: imaginative literature and psychology, to speak of two more. In discussing *kāvya* – imaginative writing – used in composing the script of a play, Bharata keeps constantly advising the *kavi*, the poet, to design his narrative, plot, style, diction even his versification in such a way as to make it appropriate for *nāṭya*. He did not want the poet to be carried away by the demands of his own art. He tells him to beware of getting lost in the play of language or

[41] These sounds could themselves have various formulations, apparantly through different ways of producing them on a drum. Thus '*ka*' could have the forms '*ke*' '*ko*' '*kaṁ*' as well as '*kra*' '*kla*' '*kle*' and '*klaṁ*'. Other "basic" sounds had similar multiple formulations as Bharata notes at N.S. 34, 43-44. Bharata speaks of various combinations of these sounds made not only on the basis of *laya, tāla* and *yati* but also *mārga, lepa, pracāra* etc. (N.S. 34, 40).

imagery or *alankāras*, for their own sake.[42] His interesting thoughts on psychology, as reflected in his discussion of *bhāvas* and their role in *rasas*, deserve close attention on their own. But, significantly, in his description, *bhāva is inseparable from abhinaya* (and thus *nāṭya*). Even his explanation of the meaning of the word *bhāva* (otherwise meaning, "feeling", "emotion", "sentiment" and the like) reflects this dual understanding. He explains *bhāva* less as a manner of *being* than a manner of *showing* or representation. In fact, his definition of *bhāva* could also be a definition of *abhinaya*.[43]

---

[42] Bharata says: *suśliṣṭasandhisaṁyogaṁ suprayogaṁ sukhāśrayam/ mṛduśabdābhidhānaṁ ca kaviḥ kuryāttu nāṭakam//*

N.S. 19, 141.

Meaning: "A poet should take care to compose a *nāṭaka* in such a way as to properly knit its various *dramatic* sequences together (the *sandhis*) so that it can result in a good stage-production (*suprayoga*). It should use a lucid language so that it is easy to perform.' Elsewhere he reiterates:

Cekṛḍitaprabhṛtibhirvikṛtaiśca śabdairyuktā
na bhānti lalitā bharataprayogāḥ/
yajñakriyeva rurucarmadharairghṛtāktairveśyā
dvijairiva kamaṇḍaludaṇḍahastaiḥ//

N.S. 16, 127.

It is often forgotten, that Bharata's entire treatment of *kāvya* is geared, like his treatment of all else, towards *nāṭya*. His work is, by historical accident, the earliest available *śāstric* work on *alankāra*, but it is not perhaps representative of the state of the *śāstra* as such during his days as modern historians of *alankāra śāstra* tend to think of it. His whole treatment is so plainly *nāṭya*-oriented that many of his rhetorical categories do not make sense without keeping *nāṭya* in mind: his scheme of 36 *kāvya-guṇas* (chapter 16) are palpably related to *kāvya* as designed for theatre. He has obviously made a *selection* from available categories, inventing new ones for his own specific purpose.

[43] N.S. chapter 7 begins thus: *bhāvānidanim vyākhyāsyāmaḥ. atrāha bhāvā iti kasmāt. kiṁ bhavantīti bhāvā, kiṁ vā bhāvayantīti bhāvāḥ? ucyate-vāgaṅgasattvo-petān kāvyārthān bhāvayantīti bhāvāḥ.*

That is to say: "Now we shall delineate *bhāvas*. Here it may be asked: how are they *bhāvas*? Are they *bhāvas* because they *are* or are they *bhāvas* because they reveal (what is)? The answer is, they are *bhāvas* because they *reveal* (or project) the plot and sentiments (*arthāḥ*) of a *kāvya* through such modes of (*abhinaya*) as the *vācika* (speech), the *aṅga* (body movements and gestures) and the *sattva* ('involuntary' physical states indicative of emotion where there is no movement or gesture, but conditions such as sweating, flow of tears, horripilation or 'goose flesh' and the like are projected by the actor in order to reveal a conscious state).

Nāṭya, formulated as a grand *vṛtti* was also a grand *anukaraṇa*, the grandest possible representation of the world in art, providing in its own *nāṭya-dharmi* way an experience almost as direct as of the world itself (Abhinava therefore calls *sākṣātkalpa* "direct-like"). Yet, in this representation were orchestrated many arts which were non-representational. They acquired a representational meaning only as part of a *vṛtti*. Structures of pure music and dance, woven into systems of their own, had not only to be carefully selected, but even transformed before they could become parts of a *vṛtti*-whole. Bharata tells us how "pure" structures were transformed for this purpose. He describes only one side of what must have been a two-way process as we know, for example, from the history of music. A structural transformation in art, though made for the sake of transference into quite another art with a different aesthetic goal, is yet bound to have a moulding effect on the original art itself, even if it does not effect its non-representational intent. The addition of new "*deśī*" *karaṇas* and *mudrās* to the pure *tāṇḍava,* as reported in later texts such as the *Saṅgītaratnākara* of the 13th century, appear to have followed this path.

The very possibility of the transference of a structure from a system of pure art into an *anukaraṇa*-oriented *vṛtti* might, however, accost us with a fundamental question: "how can pure non-representational structures acquire any representational meaning at all?" True, the same structure as part of a different *vṛtti* could acquire different "meanings", since different *vṛttis* were connected with different *rasas,* yet even allowing room for such ambiguity, the question we have posed still remains relevant, for not any structure could become part of any *vṛtti*. A

In this passage the word '*abhinaya*' is not actually used, but immediately after it, having stated that the verb '*bhū*' in his use of *bhāva* is to be understood as used in an instrumental sense, Bharata defines *bhāva* more unambiguously as:

vibhāvenāhṛto yo'rtho hyanubhāvaistu gamyate/
vāgaṅgasattvābhinayaiḥ sa bhāva iti saṁjñitaḥ//
vāgaṅgamukharāgeṇa sattvenābhinayena ca/
kaverantaragataṁ bhāvaṁ bhāvayan bhāva ucyate//

N.S. 7, 1-2.

structure, clearly, had to have some "affinity" with the *vṛtti* into which it was transposed or else there could be no justification for choosing one structure rather than another as more "appropriate." But on what principle can one gauge the "affinity" between forms of very different character? Bharata forces us to ask this question without suggesting an answer. I too, shall not attempt any answer here (which, of course, is not to say that I can).

I must remark, though, that the question is not limited to the attmept made in the *Nāṭyaśāstra* — which, however must be thanked for suggesting it clearly — or even to aesthetics in general. It has larger ramifications. Many of our own modern *śāstras* also aim at a *vṛtti*-like approach: such disciplines from the social sciences as history, sociology or anthropology for example. These are meaning-oriented "human" disciplines that amalgamate the results of many others, pressing them to their own cognitive aims. A historian takes pride in being the master *sūtradhāra* who can envision the whole range of disparate human activities within a single *vṛtti*-like amalgamated meaningful whole.

He speaks, for example, of the 'spirit of an age'. An 'age', in his notion, is a *vṛtti*-like whole produced by the combination of multifarious human activities and pursuits. The 'spirit' of an 'age' like the *rasa* of a *vṛtti,* ties different realms together into a meaningful whole, infusing into each part the character of the whole.

Yet though analogous to *rasa* and *vṛtti*, the idea of the spirit of an age is much more ambitious. An age is an all-subsuming whole engulfing every single human activity in every detail, without, ideally, a residue. The spirit of an age should be perceivable in every limb of this cosmic entity, and, if, perchance, something is admitted to have remained untouched by this omnipresent 'spirit', it also remains unexplained and not quite understood in a historian's scheme of things, an embarrasment to his vision. The question of the basic affinity between different realms is not really raised. Affinity is taken for granted before it is discovered with the assumption that if things are together they must have an affinity.

Rasa in Bharata's framework is in an important sense different from such a conception of 'spirit'. And this is because *vṛtti* is not an all-subsuming whole like 'age'. The different, discrete activities with which a *vṛtti* is constructed do not lose themselves entirely in a *vṛtti*. In order to fit into a *vṛtti*, an activity, in Bharata's scheme, has to be transformed in significant ways, thus creating a new entity out of the old, a new entity with a new goal, modified rules of formation, and a new "affinity": something designed not as an independent activity, but as a part of another, in many ways, an alien thing. Meaningful discourse about this new entity needs new concepts that must focus upon it as part of an alien whole. Activities that merge into a *vṛtti* thus yet retain their separate identity. What merges into a *vṛtti* is something carved out of an autonomous realm which continues to have its independent existence, with its own, independent structures and its own separate world of discourse. Thus, for example, when *dhruvā* is carved out of *gāndharva* and moulded to fit the *nāṭya, gāndharva* continues in its own character, holding its own distinct sway. Bharata never lets us forget this. Therefore, the universality of *rasa* in his framework is something confined and limited, because the territory of *vṛtti*, too, is limited. The idea of *rasa* can apply to an activity only in as much as it is part of a *vṛtti*. It can, thus, be used to understand *dhruvā* but not *gāndharva* (or music as such). Later theorists made *rasa* into a much more cosmic concept, a defining trait of the entire realm of the aesthetic, embracing all the arts equally in this entirety. Constructing unifying concepts that embrace whole gamuts of human activities or entire realms of knowledge is a natural temptation. A concept, after all, has to be general in essence. One tends to make it more and more so, weaving a totally universal system around it. There is no denying the appeal of such universal concepts and systems that tie up a whole range of diversity into a single monolithic bundle. But this does injustice to the complexity of phenomena, glossing over what does not fit, and distorting others to squeeze them into a straitjacket. Such system-building is a great temptation for thinkers today, not only in science but also the 'human' disciplines.

Bharata's approach is refreshingly distinct in this respect. In amalgamating different realms he remained aware that what was achieved was just another realm, a *vṛtti*, which though seeking to envision human reality in a 'holistic' manner, yet did not unify different realms into a larger all-inclusive whole but only created one more realm among others. Therefore, he conceived of a multiplicity of such combinations: *vṛtti* is not one but many. Reality could be recreated in many ways. Moreover, the *vṛtti*-scheme of forming new wholes and discoursing about them was relevant only to realms carved out of other realms combined into a *vṛtti*. There remained other realms where a *mātṛkā* scheme of discourse was more germaine. These were 'formal' realms that could be significantly analysed into 'atomic' units. These were realms that did not reflect the world, they were not meant to recreate reality; and thus they resisted assimilation into another realm. It is possible for a *vṛtti*, in Bharata's scheme, to assimilate *mātṛkā*-oriented structures, but never an entire *mātṛkā*-oriented realm, that is, a formal realm, where the analytical *mātṛkā* approach is significant to discourse.

CHAPTER – NINE

Bhārata Muni and Hindi Films[1]

Seeing films is certainly one of the most popular pastimes in India. Consequently, films-making is one of our largest industries. Scores of films are produced every year in all the major Indian languages. By far the largest number of films produced are Hindi films. These have a magnetic mass-appeal even in non-Hindi-speaking regions. Hindi films can, indeed, be said to typify all popular films made in any Indian language. General observations about their form or content will apply, on the whole, to all Indian films.

My endeavour here will be to make some observations regarding one of the most neoticeable formal peculiarity of the Hindi film: the preponderance of song and dance interludes in its narratives. I will attempt to show that the roots of this practice lie in the centuries-old theatrical traditions of India. This will also throw some light on the rationale of the practice.

Songs and dances in Hindi films are so woven into the story as to be integral to its development. They are as important to the totality of the film-narrative as the plot, and the skills and techniques of cinematography and character-acting.

On the popular Hindi screen, it is not an occasional film or any specific narrative genre that employs songs and dances; they are part of every film, whatever the narrative. Songs and dances are put in as a rule; it is the exceptional film that does not employ them.

Hindi films have a rich gamut of stories. Many genres or narrative-types can be distinguished. Distinctions, no doubt, tend to merge into each other, yet one can meaningfully classify and talk of them. Two broad divisions are obvious: we have, firstly,

---

[1] An essay in investigating some formal continuities from ancient Indian theatre to the popular modern medium.

what are called 'mythological' films in which the narratives are based on popular versions of tales from the *Purāṇas,* the *Rāmāyaṇa* and the *Mahābhārata,* as well as currently popular mythic legends. Secondly, there is the broad category of what may be termed 'human drama'. This includes narratives of a great variety, ranging from love-stories, tales of patriotism, humour, issues relating social rights, to crime-thrillers and 'westerns'. Many of these stories are certainly cliche-ridden, making 'formula' films. But there are also simple human tales told in a convincing, simple human manner.

But whatever the film's narrative, whether 'mythological, or 'human', it is certain to contain a good amount of songs and dances. This is quite unlike the practice in the west where only the 'musical' integrally incorporates songs into the plot. In a Hindi film, songs and dances are an inevitable part of the aesthetic means employed, whether the film is an intense human drama or a pure fantasy. Songs and dances are not something superimposed upon a film's narrative: something appended from time to time in order to lend colour or spectacle to the show. They are inseparable from the Hindi film's very mode of story-telling. The principal characters themselves make use of songs and dances at crucial moments in the film.

To many of us, who have acquired a taste for films from the west, the effect of such song-dance interludes, boxed within the action as part of the action, can often seem to be very unsettling and incongrous. All the more, because when not dancing or singing, the characters usually behave in a natural, normal enough manner. Whole scenes can take place as if in real life amidst natural situations and surroundings, with the characters acting in a realistic, more or less unaffected style. But, then, suddenly, a transformation occurs, and the spectacle turns into something like a ballet or an opera. Characters who had been behaving in a natural way break into a song or a dance or both. And after this sudden song-dance interlude is over, they revert back to normal, till such a time when a similar interlude may follow again.

Many of us feel bewildered at these trransformations. We never quite understand the rationale behind the odd coupling of such disparate modes. It is, I think, a combination which is not consciously produced. We cannot understand it in terms of any properly thought-out aesthetic principles. Formal influences dominating the Hindi film remain at a largely unconscious level or at least at a level where they are not resolved into a well-assimilated and self-aware scheme or design.

The roots of this curious mixture of two different modes of narration or theatric presentation found in the Hindi films can, I think, be traced to the influence of two quite disparate traditions. One is the cinema of the west and its dominant trends of natural presentations. The other is indigenous Indian theatre where stylized presentation was the rule.

The cinema as a medium was developed in the west, where, from its inception, it fostered the goal of recording events as they occur. The very first films to be made were short, one minute documentaries recording every-day occurrences.[2] Early narrative feature films, too, had a strong realistic intent, though other influences, mainly of various kinds of popular theatre and shows were also at work. Yet, in spite of other influences, realism — an attempt at recording the feel of lived life — has always been a major thrust in all cinema making. The medium itself has a built-in propensity for such a naturalism. More than any other method of representation, the cinema has the potential to give us an illusion of happenings actually taking place before us in the panoramic surroundings of life. It is the only medium in which the making of a documentary — an audio-visual record of actual events — is possible. The movie camera, in truth, acts as a documenting instrument even when filming a fantasy.

Film-making in India came from the west. Indian film

---

[2] Roy Armes, *Film and Reality*, p. 23 (Pelican Books, 1974). The first films to be shown, records Armes, were made by the Frenchman Lumiere who gave his premier show in December 1895. Earlier, Edison had commercially exploited what he called the kinetoscope, but this equipment could not project an image on a screen; only one viewer could see a film at a time *op.cit.*, pp. 90-92.

makers borrowed their technique and much of their cinematic style from the west. They still keep doing so. A strongly naturalistic mode of representation thus is a part of their approach. Consequently, the narrative in a Hindi film often moves as if the viewer was conducted through scenes taking place in real life. The plot unfolds amidst surroundings containing all the signs of actuality. Much of the film is, indeed, shot on actual locales. A Hindi film, even when a fantasy at its core, has a surface aura of actuality, except, perhaps, in purely mythological films.

The other major influence in moulding narrative feature films has been the indigenous theatre. The very first ambitious narrative feature films to be made in India were, in fact, filmed theatre shows. In May 1912, R.G. Torane released his *Puṇḍalīka*, a film on the famous saint from Maharastra. *Puṇḍalīka* was based on a Marathi drama of the same name.[3] The film was an immediate success. In 1913, the famous film *Rājā Hariścandra* by D.G. Falke was released. This, too, was influenced by the theatre of the day. In 1917, J.F. Madan produced and released a film called *Satyavādī Rājā Hariścandra* in Calcutta. The Victoria Theatrical Company which staged Hindi and Urdu plays was actively associated with its production.[4]

In the thirties, sound was introduced into Indian films. Theatre, with its songs, dances and music, now came into full play in the cinema. Many stage hits were made into films, popular songs from the stage became film hits, stage actors became film heroes and stage producers became film directors.[5] Thus songs and dances came into the films from popular theatre, and have since remained a constant feature through changing modes and fashions of narrative genres, motifs and cinematic styles.

It is a well-known aesthetic maxim that a suspension of

---

[3] Feroz Rangoonwala, *Bhāratīya Calacitra kā Itihāsa*, pp. 26-27. (Atma Ram and Sons, Delhi. 1975).

[4] Ibid., pp. 29-36.

[5] Feroz Rangoonwala, *op. cit.*, See chapter 5, where the facts noted above are borne out.

disbelief is necessary in the viewer for him to establish a rapport with the narrative being unfolded. Abhinava Gupta, the renowned aesthetician (writing in the 10th-11th centuries), has remarked that if an action being staged lacks in plausibility, the mind of the spectator will never be able to immerse itself in it.[6] And certainly if one begins to question or doubt the plausibility of any major aspect of the action being shown one's emotional involvement with the narrative is bound to be hampered.

In Hindi films, the disturbing yet inveterate habit of characters to transform themselves, as if by magic, into songsters or dancers at regular intervals, is surely a feature that may tax one's sense of plausibility. But, curiously enough, the general Indian viewer faces no credibility problems. He finds nothing odd or unnatural in characters suddenly taking to a song or moving into a dance amidst otherwise normal action. The truth, on the contrary, is that in certain situations and emotional contexts, the viewer actually expects a song or a dance. He considers these to be appropriate means of dramatic expression at the right moment. He considers them as appropriate not only in situations where they might be plausibly expected in real life but also in contexts where people do not normally give vent to feelings through such means.

There are critics like Dilip Padgaonkar, who have looked for a naturalistic explanation for songs and dances on the Hindi screen. Padgaonkar, in one of his columns contributed to the *Times of India,* remarks that Hindi films are full of song and dance because life in India is itself full of song and dance.[7] Such a view is taken by many who would like to seek a convincing 'naturalistic' justification for the practice. But this explanation is not really convincing. In reply to it, it may be observed that India may well be full of song and dance — and, indeed which country or culture lacks them ? — but songs or dances certainly do not occur in situations where

---

[6] '*saṁvedyamasambhāvyamānāḥ saṁvedye saṁvidaṁ viniveśayantumeva na śaknoti*', *Abhinavava Bhāratī* on ch. 6, *Nāṭyaśāstra,* p. 280. (All reference are to the Gaekwad Oriental Series edition of the *Nāṭyaśāstra,* unless otherwise stated).

[7] I am unable to recollect the date on which this column was published.

they are common in films. Where in real life do we find jilted lovers singing away songs such as '*Jāyen to jāyen kahān*' on a footpath in front of their beloved's house ? Such a scene, if it were to occur in real life, would create bathos instead of pathos.[8] Yet, similar scenes are quite common in the films. Courtship in a Hindi film can rarely progress without the boy and the girl singing and dancing away to glory. But how many couples can we think of who court in the manner of the films ? In fact, dance along with music plays a much larger part in western courtship: though films made in the west hardly ever make use of songs or dances to depict love. In parenthesis it may also be added that on the Hindi screen couples dancing western style to western music are usually shown as dissipating, not expressing sincere love.[9]

The use of song and dance interludes cannot, I think, be explained on the premise of naturalism. The key to the matter

---

[8] Apparently, in ancient times, too, there were critics who thought on the same lines as Padgaonkar. Music played a major part in ancient drama. A school of critics argued that this was in imitation of real life. Abhinava has combatted this idea. He observes that drama is not a replica *(anukaraṇa)* of real life. True, he says, critics of the imitation school may argue that in real life, too, music accompanies such common and diverse activities as dining, bathing, being put to sleep, being woken up and the like (as was not uncommon with those who could afford it), but such a use of music did not take the same form nor did it have the same purpose as music in theatre. In theatre, Abhinava remarks, songs of a specific kind were used. They were not replicas or reproductions of music used in common situations of life. Theatric music was, moreover, used as integral to drama, whereas music in real life when accompanying the activities mentioned above, was only something that imparted a kind of auspiciousness to the occasion; it was nothing more.
ataścedaṁ nānukaraṇaṁ tato yatkaiściccoditaṁ tadanavakāśam. na ca gītavādyayuktaḥ sarvāvasthāsu kaścidanukārya iti, na tvanukāryatvena gītādaya ityuktam. pariharo'pi ya uktaḥ aśanagamanasnānasvāpapratibodha-bhojanādyāsu gītavādyaṁ ceṣṭāsvatiprathitaṁ ityādi tadapyanupannam. na hi gamanādautaddhruvātālādirūpeṇa gītādi loke'sti maṅgalamātratvādṛte. (Abhinava on *Nāṭyaśāstra* 1, 107).
Dhruvā, it should be borne in mind here, was the name given to specially designed theatric songs. See Abhinava's introduction chapter 33 of the *Nāṭyaśāstra*, Abhinava calls *dhruvā: nāṭysāmagrīmadhyanimajjitanijasvara*: in other words, integral to drama as an art.

[9] This was true of films which the author was familiar with when he wrote this piece in the mid-seventies. Things seem to have changed.

will be found elsewhere. Songs and dances in Hindi films are used as theatric devices for narration; their source should be looked for in the established conventions of the dramatic art in India.

Any film which aims at narrating a story, has to do much more than merely record surface events. It has to transcend the simple documentary and reveal not only how people move and behave but also what they feel and think. The narrative film has to convey the inner felt aspect of human situations, and convey it in an aesthetically evocative and acceptable manner. The art of the theatre has developed with just such a goal. It has perfected many techniques, devices and stylistic motifs for communicating the unseen, inner life of men.

The film as a medium has grown by exploring the immense possibilities of its own specific form. But it has also adapted — in however transformed a manner — many *mores* of artistic expression developed in the theatre.

Like other arts, theatre has developed differently in different cultures. In different traditions, drama has come to acquire certain distinct sets of aesthetic conventions and devices. The conventions of any dramatic culture appear as 'natural' to viewers belonging to that culture; their responses become conditioned to accept them as *normal in drama.*

Films in India have, perhaps, greater ties with the theatre than films made in other countries. The Hindi movie has direct links with popular Marathi, Bengali and 'Parasi' theatre, and with traditional Indian theatre in general. In fact, the Hindi film is basically a theatric show, albeit presented on an immense stage as large as life itself, thanks to the possibilities of the cinematic medium. It has, however, few touches of the pure cinema that we find in the work of great western directors or their Indian counterparts.

The use of song and dance as an integral formal element in theatric presentation is a factor running through all traditional Indian dramatic shows. The roots of this theatre go back to a remote period. Many characteristic elements of this theatre, and through it of Hindi films, reach back to Bharata, the Master of dramaturgy. Hindi films follow the footsteps of that ancient *ācārya* in many matters of form and spirit.

Bharata composed his epitome on theatre, the *Nāṭyaśāstra,* almost two millenium ago. Bharata himself was the spokesman of a theatric tradition which had become well-entrenched by his age and antedates him by at least a few centuries. This tradition continues in popular indigenous theatre.

It continues also in the films, although few of us are conscious of the roots of our film-making in Bharata, least of all the film-makers.

Though an unconscious influence, Bharata yet remains a potent influence. The dramatic tradition of Bharata has entered deep into our culture and still unconsciously shapes and conditions the theatric responses of our audiences. It also shapes and conditions many formal elements in the so-called 'formula' films of Bombay.

Bharata's own theatre was a consciously and meticulously cultivated art. He analyses every factor and technique of this art in detail. What is more important, he also discusses the rationale of his theatre-making. Bharata's theatre was cultivated as a demanding and refined art for centuries after the Master, before passing into popular vernacular theatre as a moulding influence.

The principles of Bharata's theatre were further analysed by commentators on the *Nāṭyaśāstra* and later writers on the art of drama. No commentaries survive except that of Abhinavagupta. His is a significant and stimulating work. Abhinava was alive to the subtleties of the theatre, and speaks as one who had a direct and vital experience of the art. He was also a great theorist, alive to the nuances of significant analysis. We can take him as our guide.

Two concepts of Bharata are especially pertinent in this context: the concepts of *lokadharmī* and *nāṭyadharmī.* These are related to the mode of translating human reality into theatre. They denote the two elements of the natural and the theatrical (the latter including conventions and devices adopted by theatre as an art) which are present in all dramatic representations. *Lokadharmī* means 'taken from the actual behaviour of people'. *Nāṭyadharmī* means 'factors or elements peculiar to drama, and which drama uses to translate human reality into theatre'.

The purpose of drama, says Bharata, is to recreate the human condition in all its complexities and richness of experience.[10] But the recreation of human situations through the medium of theatre

---

[10] *nānābhāvopasampannaṁ nānāvastvantarātmakam/lokavṛttānukaraṇaṁ nāṭyametanmayā kṛtam. Nāṭyaśāstra* 1, 112. The following is also worthy of note: *yo'yaṁ syabhāvo lokasya sukhaduḥkhasamanvitaḥ/so' ṅgābhinayopeto nāṭyamityabhi dhīyate. Nāṭyaśāstra* 1. 119.

Bharata conceives of drama as aiming to represent not merely the human condition, but also the trans-human actions of gods and titanic demons (see *Nāṭyaśāstra* 1, 118). However, the main dramatic forms, *nāṭaka, prakaraṇa, nāṭikā, prahasana, bhāṇa* — dealt mainly with a human story, though gods could enter as minor characters. Abhinava speaking of *nāṭaka,* the paradigmatic form of all drama, brings this point out when he says: '*na ca sarvathā devacaritaṁ tathā' varṇanīyam kintu divyānāmāśrayatvena prakarīpatākānāyakādirupeṇa...*' (on *Nāṭyaśāstra* 18, 10).

In certain dramatic forms, such as the *samavakāra, īhāmṛga* and *ḍima,* gods and titans predominated. But these were minor dramatic forms, being mainly spectacular shows.

Bharata, significantly enough, says that drama acquires interest and intensity only through a human narrative depicting both joy and sorrows (*Nāṭyaśāstra* 18, 12). Gods, by nature, are incapable of sorrow. They could not be leading characters in the true dramatie sense. In presenting them as dramatic characters it was necessary to humanise them. But this, if carried too far, could controvert the divine character of a god, and adversely effect a spectator's sense of credulity. One had thus to be careful when introducing a god as a dramatic character. Abhinava remarks: *yadi tu mukhyatvenaiva devacaritaṁ varṇyate tattāvadvipralambhakaruṇādbhutabhayānakarasocitaṁ cennibadhyate tanmānuṣacaritameva sampadyate pratyuta devānambhidhayādhānaṁ prasiddhivi-ghātakam. tatra cokto doṣaḥ; vipralambhādyabhāve tu tatra kā vicitratā rañjānāyā etatpramāṇatvāt. ata eva hṛdayasaṁvādo'pi devacarite durlabhaṁ na ca teṣām duḥkhamasti.* (Abhinava on *Nāṭyaśāstra* 18, 10). This may be translated as: "If one were to present a god as the chief character [in a play], and if he were to be shown in situations evolving the *rasas,* (the emotional ethos) of love in separation, pathos (felt for the character), wonder (at his deeds) or fear (for him), then this will amount to turning the god into a human being, resulting in incredulity and thus hampering the desired effect, especially if the god is also given a well-known name. This is indeed, the reason why a god as a [dramatic] character fails to arouse sympathy in a viewer, since the gods do not suffer."

It is here also worth quoting Bhārata's seemingly strange maxim that, gods when shown were to be shown in the background of the land of Bhārata and not in their own godly abodes. The reason Bharata gives is that in celestial abodes there is no sorrow or unhapiness (*Nāṭyaśāstra* 18, 98-99). Bharata obviously aimed at giving some semblance of suffering humanity to gods when presenting them on the stage.

obviously poses many problems at both the technical as well as aesthetic levels. There is, firstly, the problem of space: the panoramic human world has to be staged on a very much reduced area, a tiny platform. There is also the problem of time: years have to be shown within hours. There is, above all, the problem of recreating emotions and feelings, the inner life of man which is the greater part of the human condition.

Drama attempts to solve these problems in different ways. Some of the more tricky problems involve the use of theatric devices and conventions. These Bharata includes within the *nāṭyadharmī*. *Nāṭyadharmī* in Bharata thus embraces a host of things. It is the name given to the proper deployment of stage space, the use of stage props, of costume and make-up, and the like. It also denotes such stage conventions as the 'aside'*(svagata),* the stage whisper *(janāntika)* and what was known in Sanskrit drama as the *akāśa-bhāṣita:* this was used by a character when conversing with someone not present on the stage. The character in such a situation, uttered both parts of the dialogue himself.

Theatre is a composite art. It uses for a dramatic purpose many arts which are in themselves quite independent. It makes use of poetry or poetic speech (apart from the more normal prose dialogue), dance or stylised dance-like gestures and music. These are deployed in drama to express feelings and to create the intended atmosphere, mood or ethos. Their use is also *nāṭyadharmī,* and may be called the more 'inner' aspect of the *nāṭyadharmī*.

Bharata gives a long list of items that he calls *nāṭyadharmī (Nāṭyaśāstra* 13, 70-86). I quote a few verses from a passage where he speaks of the use of music, poetry and dance:

"When characters, utterances and feelings are shown as over-reaching the normal, when the mode of acting breaks out into graceful dance-like movements... then we have the characteristics of *nāṭyadharma.*[11]

"When speech is intoned in a song-like manner, when

[11] *ativākyakriyopetamatisattvātibhāvakam/līlāṅgahārābhinayaṁ nāṭyalakṣaṇalakṣitam* (*Nāṭyaśāstra* 13/73).

language adopts poetic graces and when a man does not appear as himself, then we have the *nāṭyadharmī* mode.[12]

"When the natural condition of man in sorrow or in joy is expressed through the use of music (*aṅga)* and (heightened) acting, then we have *nāṭyadharmī.* A drama should always be performed in the *nāṭyadharmī* mode because the desired evocative effect cannot be achieved without music and (heightened) acting".[13]

In introducing the notions of *lokadharmī* and *nāṭyadharmī,* Abhinava makes interesting observations: Drama, he says, employs both these modes of representation with the aim to recreate human condition and experience (*lokasvabhāvamevānuvartamānaṁ dharmidvayam*). Man is variously motivated and to show him as he is on the stage is the equal concern of both *lokadharmī* and *nāṭyadharmī.* That is why, says Abhinava, Bharata speaks of them in context of play-acting. There is, he adds, nothing in drama that is outside the scope of the human mode of being (*laukikadharma)*; *nāṭyadharmī* occurs wherever

---

[12] *ṣvarālaṅkārasaṁyuktamasvasthapuruṣāśrayaṁ yadīdṛśaṁ bhavennāṭyaṁ nāṭyadharmī tu sā smṛtā* ibid 13, 74.
In using the phrase '*asvathapuruṣāśrayam*' Bharata may have been referring to the transfiguration of a character in certain situations — as of Vikrama in the fourth act of *Vikramovarśīyam* - and the resulting change in the mode of acting, which then becomes more dominated by song and dance. Abhinava says that the phrase refers to women assuming the garb of men: '*yatra puruṣo na svarūpe tiṣṭhati api tu strībalamāśritya; prayojyaḥ puruṣa yatra na svarūpasthaḥ api tu striyā prayuiyate tannāṭyadharmī'*. In ancient drama men characters were sometimes acted by women. The *Kuṭṭanīmatam* for example, speaks of an all-women performance of *Ratnāvalī* (see verse 801, where women are said to have assumed the role of the hero and his friend). This was *nāṭyadharmī*, also in the sense of being a theatrical convertion, for the audience was aware of the male characters being actually women.

[13] *yo'yaṁ svabhāvo lokasya sukhaduḥkhakriyātmakaḥ/so'ṅgābhinayasaṁyukto nāṭyadharmī prakīrtitā// nāṭyadharmī pravṛttaṁ hi sadā nāṭyaṁ prayojayet/na hi aṅgābhinayātkiñcidṛte rāgaḥ pravartate// Nāṭyaśāstra* 13, 81 and 84.
In the first verse above Abhinava explains *aṅga* as: *aṅgairātodyādibiḥ.* Commenting on the second verse, he makes a similar statement: *aṅgāni ca gitātodyāni. Aṅga* clearly refers to the musical content of a dramatic performance.

ordinary human behaviour is raised to a higher pitch for producing greater dramatic effect (*rañjanādhikyaprādhānya-madhirohayitum*) through the multifarious artistry of the poet and the actor.[14] However, though dependent on *loka*, and employing the 'natural' mode of representation, the space created by *nāṭya*, or drama, is, in a basic sense, *nāṭyadharmī*. Abhinava explains the relation between the *lokadharmī* and the *nāṭyadharmī* through the analogy of a sculptural frieze: *lokadharmī* is the ground, the well (*bhitti*) upon which the *nāṭyadharmī* is chiselled like a frieze.[15]

From what has been said of the *nāṭyadharmī*, it should, I think, be evident that this is not an element peculiar to Bharata's theatre alone. All theatre empolys it in some form or the other. It is also employed in films in ways analogous to theatre, and, indeed, in ways borrowed from the theatre.

Music has always been one of the chief *nāṭyadharmī* elements in all theatre and dramatic tradition everywhere. It plays a large part in films, too, and pervades even the most realistic film in the form of background music. In India it is introduced *within* the dramatic action itself and made integral to the plot and narrative. This is, so to say, taking a kind of logical step and bringing that which is evocative in the background into the foreground.

Ancient Indian theatre made use of music, both as background accompaniment as well as in the form of songs

---

[14] *tathā hi loksvabhāvamevānuvartamānaṁ dharmidvayam, loko nāma janapadavāsī janaḥ. sa ca pravṛttikrameṇa prapañcitaḥ. tatprasaṅgenaiva tāvaddharmyāyātā, sā cāṅgikaśeṣatayā vaktavyā... sā ca dvedhā. yadyapi laukikadharmavyatirekeṇa nāṭye na kaściddharmo'sti tathāpi sa yatra lokagataprakriyākramo rañjanādhikyaprādhānyama-dhirohayituṁ kavina-ṭavyāpāre vaicitryaṁ svīkurvan nāṭyadharmītyucyate.* Abhinava on *Nāṭya-śāstra* 13, 70.

[15] *laukikasya dharmasya mūlabhūtatvānnāṭyadharmaṁ vaicitrollekhya-bhittisthānat-vāditi.* Abhinava. ibid.
The word *ullekhya* in this passage has clearly been used in the sense of a frieze. The verb *ullikh* has the sense of 'to chisel', 'to chip' and the like, besides other denotations: see Monier-Williams' *Sanskrit-English Dictionary*.

within the plot itself. Theatric songs were called *dhruvā*. Abhinava, in an expressive phrase, describes the *dhruvā* as: *nāṭyasāmagrīmadhyanimajjitanijasvaram'*,[16] meaning that the *dhruvā* had a distinct voice in the totality of the diverse elements that together created a dramatic whole.

Bharata observes that drama without songs is bound to remain ineffective and unevocative just as a painting devoid of colour.[17] He further says that songs should be used not only to lend colour to a dramatic show, they should rather be interwoven into the very fabric of the drama. Commencing his section on music, Bharata begins by speaking of the integral relation between song and drama. He conveys this point through a metaphor: "song, instrumental music and *nāṭya* (i.e. such elements of theatre as play-acting) are disparate factors which are produced through quite different skills. But they should be so brought together as to create a single, undivided *alātacakra*'[18] *Alāta* means a torch, a fire-brand. An *alātacakra,* was a fiery circle, produced when a fire-brand was skilfully rotated.

Abhinava, too, speaks of the intimate relation between songs and drama as a whole. He explains the relation as that obtaining between the *uparañjaka* and the *uparañjanīya.* Drama was the aesthetic whole, the *uparañjanīya,* to which songs provided

---

[16] Abhinava uses this phrase for characterising the function of the *dhruvā*, in his introductory comments on chapter 33 of the *Nāṭyaśāstra.*

[17] *yathā varṇādṛte citraṁ na shobhotpādanaṁ bhavet/evameva vinā gānaṁ nāṭyaṁ na gacchati sukham//Nāṭyaśāstra 32, 425.*

[18] *evaṁ gānaṁ ca vādyaṁ ca nāṭyaṁ ca vividhāśrayam/alātacakrapratimaṁ kartavyaṁ nāṭyayoktṛbhiḥ//. Nāṭyaśāstra* 28, 7.
Commenting on the phrase *vividhāśrayam,* Abhinava observes that various different skills need to be combined to produce a drama through quite distinct artistic endeavours. Moreover, they were apprehended differently, through different sense organs. They were to be carefully brought together to form a whole: *yasmādvividhāsrayaṁ bhinnendriyagrāhyavividhakriyārūpaṁ tasmādyatnenāsyaikatā tatsampādyā, yenaikabudhiviṣayatā sāmājikasya gacchet.* For a more detailed discussion concerning this important insight of Bharata, the reader may like to see, 'Bharata and the Art of Mixing Structures', an earlier essay in this collection. The essay was actually written much later than the present one.

aesthetic aid, *uparañjana.*[19]

Occasions for the use of theatric songs, or *dhruvā,* were numerous in ancient drama. They had as many occasions as there are human moods and emotions. *Dhruvās* were, however, categorised into five types on the basis of their role and function in the theatre. These types were: *prāveśikī, niṣkrāmikī, prāsādikī, ākṣepikī* and *antarā.*

Ancient theatre was saturated with *dhruvās.* Even exits and entrances of characters were heralded through a *dhruvā*: *prāveśiki*, as the name indicates, announced an entrance; *niṣkrāmikī* announced exits. *Prāsādikī* and *ākṣepikī* were more integrated within the dramatic action and were deployed to depict ethos and sentiment essential to the plot.

Bharata lays down that appropriate *dhruvās* should be sung

---

[19] *evaṁ gānaṁ ceti nāṭyaṁ tāvaduparañjanīyam... ata eva hi gītavādyanāṭyakṛta-siddhirityukteti kiṁ pradhānam kimaṅgamiti bhāge saṁśayyate. pūrvameva tu siddhinirūpaṇe etāvatā prayogatvamiti parijñātam. tasyoparañjanīyatoktā bhavati madhyāvasthitena ca siddhinirūpaṇe ākāṅkṣivaduparañjakvargo'pi spaṣṭa eva bhavati.. kiṁ caivaṁ sati siddhyādhyāye gītavādyavaiṣamyādi kimartha-mucyate. prāktana eva samādhānavargo yuktaḥ. uparañjakopaskṛtasya nāṭyasya naṭyateti bhedyatvāttatpaścā-dupāttam.* This may translated as: 'And thus should music function, (acting as an aid) to theatre, which is intended as the main aesthetic goal (*uparañjanīya*). With this in mind, the success of a performance (*siddhi)* has been seen as a (mixed) rendering of song, instrumental music and *nāṭya* (the actor's art in rendering a script). A question (however,) could arise as to which of these three is really the main aesthetic goal (intended by Bharata). This has been made clear in the preceding chapter (no. 27) concerning '*siddhi*' ('success'), where the nature of how a performance (should fit together) has been spoken of. There (in that chapter) its (i.e. *nāṭya)* being the main aesthetic goal (*uparañjanīya*) has been articulated; (*nāṭya*) occupies the centre of attention. What is required as aesthetic aid in order to complete a (*nāṭya*) performance (*ākāṅksivat*), has also been clearly spoken of there. But if this is so (one might ask,) why does the chapter on *siddhi* include a (separate) description of what makes for error, disorder or disharmony (*vaiṣamya*) in the use of song and instruments? The answer to this has already been given (in what is said above). A *nāṭya*, indeed, becomes a *nāṭya* only in association with its aesthetic aids (such as music); this is the reason why (music) is spoken of *afterwards* (in chapter 28 and the following chapters); this is done in order to distinguish its (function, which is a subsidiary one).' Abhinava on *Nāṭyaśāstra* 28, 7.

during a performance with an eye to dramatic intention (*arthavidhi*): time, place, season, character and the sentiment that is to be conveyed.[20] He lists a whole gamut of emotions, moods and situations where appropriate *dhruvās* could be sung. There seems to be hardly any shade of human feeling or nuance of a sentiment where a *dhruvā* could not be used. An appropriate *dhruvā* could be employed in situations of anxiety, zeal or longing (*autsukya*), or even in situations where a character dissimulated his real feelings (*avahittha*). *Dhruvās* could express moods of reflection (*cintā*), lamentation (*paridevita)*, dejection (*dainya)* or misery (*viṣāda)*. They could be sung in situations pregnant with turbulent emotions, whether of the pleasant or unpleasant sort: they could be used to express extreme joy or feeling of awe and wonder as well as violent anger, agitation (*āvega*) or perplexity (*sambhrama*). They could be sung in a mood of quiet happiness (*prasāda*) or one of remembering things past (*anusmaraṇa)* or at the first joyful meeting of lovers (*navasaṅgama*), or, indeed, in any mood of love (*śṛṅgāra*).[21]

The parallel with Hindi films is, I think, palpable. Any lover of film music will be able to name a number of song-hits expressive of the different moods listed in Bharata's prescription. The prescription, clearly, continues to hold sway.

Hindi film-makers are, however, hardly aware of their roots in Bharata. They do not expend much thought on why they use songs. They do not seek aesthetic explanations or vindications. Songs are used because they make a hit both on the screen and off it. The more thoughtful of the film directors who are busy making popular films perhaps consider songs as an anomaly, but for them, too, it is an anomaly which has yet to be made use of to please the masses

---

[20] *evamarthavidhiṁ jñātvā deśakālamṛtuṁ tathālprakṛtiṁ bhāvaliṅgaṁ tu tato yojyā dhruvā budhaiḥ//* *Nāṭyaśāstra* 32, 328.

[21] *Nāṭyaśāstra* 32, 319-329.

Abhinava, commenting on *Nāṭyaśāstra* 29, 13, quotes a fairly long passage from a treatise attributed by him to Kaśyapa who has given a much longer list than Bharata of sentiments and situations where a *dhruvā* could be effective. Kaśyapa also names the melodic forms appropriate for *dhruvās* expressing different feelings.

(filmdom's ultimate justification for everything). Better directors try to make use of songs with greater dramatic sensitivity. Still, I feel that they are never really happy with the idea of inserting songs in every film. The ordinary viewer has no such qualms; he thinks of the songs as natural and essential.

In ancient times songs were accepted as a part of drama not only by ordinary viewers but also by the thoughtful and the aesthetically discerning. Ancient theorists have not only prescribed the use of songs they have also tried to formulate an aesthetic rationale for this convention.

Kaśyapa, an old theorist, quoted by Abhinava, makes an elucidating remark: "The impact of the *dhruvā* song", he says "frees the viewers from their normal egotistic preoccupations (*nijāveśa*) and produces a state of consciousness devoid of the dross of self-interest upon which the dramatic ethos of the moment (*prastuto rasaḥ*) can be readily stamped".[22] Abhinava himself makes a similar observation in commenting upon the dramatic effect of the *prāsādikī dhruvā* upon the viewer. He says that the poetic impact of a lyric blended with the spell of subtle and graceful melody brings the audience round to a receptive state of mind in which a rapport with the dramatic mood is quickly established.[23]

That music has great powers for creating a desired ethos or mood, is realised by all theatre producers and their counterparts, the movie-makers. We see that music is a potent tool in the hands of a skilful stage director or a modern movie-maker. He makes use of music not only within the play or the film-narrative proper, but even before the play begins. The aim is to create the right atmosphere and transport the audience away from their normal every-day concerns. We thus have music even when the film titles are being shown; indeed, music of some kind is played to us right from the moment we enter the cinema hall, even before any image is projected on

---

[22] *dhruvāgānānnijāveśe tyakte niṣkaladhījuṣām/sāmājikānāṁ hṛdaye niṣkrāmet prastuto rasaḥ//* See *Abhinava Bhāratī* on *Nāṭyaśāstra 29, 13.*

[23] *Kāvyagatenotkarṣeṇa rāgaprasādasya jātyaṁśakagītivarṇālaṅkārasya saubhāgya-kṛtasya sāmājikahṛdayaṁ tanmayībhāvāpattiyogyatāmātmano jananamiti gītiśobhayā vā prasādayojanaḥ. Abhinava Bhāratī* on *Nāṭyaśāstra* 32, 314.

the screen. Ancient stage directors, too, realized the importance of music in this respect. Kālidāsa has noted the effectiveness of music in winning over the attentiveness of the audience to the play being staged. In the staged prelude (*āmukha*) to his *Abhijñāna Śākuntalam*, the stage manager (*sūtradhāra*) asks his wife, the *naṭī* to entertain the audience with a song and after her song remarks: "Well sung, Lady. Your melody has so enrapt and stilled the audience that they seem like people painted on a canvas. Tell me now which play should we entertain them with."[24]

Abhinava speaks of the same effect in more general terms. In the context of discussing the aesthetic process through which theatre creates *rasa* (relish), Abhinava talks of the ancient auditorium and the atmosphere pervading the auditorium before the play began. The auditorium, says Abhinava, is full of delightful objects, of beautiful sights, sounds, smells and lovely sophisticated women. This was enough to charm the mind of even the aesthetically untutored *(ahṛdaya)* viewers away from their usual preoccupations and prepare them for the dramatic spectacle. Music and songs were two major factors responsible for creating this 'trans-normal' atmosphere of the auditorium.[25]

Songs employed within the play proper were *dhruvā* songs. Two of these, *prāsādiki* and *ākṣepikī*, we have said, played a great dramatic role within the plot.

The purpose of the *prāsādikī* (from *prasāda,* to clarify, make glow or brighten) was to heighten or intensify the ethos of a situation or a sentiment. Abhinava gives an illustration from a typical scene. Rāma's sorrow after the abduction of Sītā could be expressed through a *prāsadikī,* which would deepen the pathos of the moment. *Prāsādikī* could be used in any similar

---

[24] *sūtradhāraḥ: ārye, sādhu gītam. aho rāgabaddhacitavṛttirālikhita iva sarvato raṅgaḥ. tadidānīṁ katamatprakaraṇamāśrityainamārādhyāmaḥ. Abhijñāna Śākuntalam,* Act. 1.

[25] *nijasukhādivivaśībhūtasya kathaṁ vastvantare saṁvidaṁ viśrāmayediti tatpratyūhavyapohanāya pratipadārthaniṣṭhaiḥ sādhāraṇyamahimnā sakala bhogyatvasahiṣṇubhiḥ śabdādiviṣayamayimi (mayai) rātodyagānavicitra-maṇḍapapadavidagdhagaṇkādibhiruparañjanaṁ samāśritam. yenāhṛdayo'pi hṛdayavaimalyaprāptyā sahṛdayīkṛyate. Abhinava Bhāratī* on *Nāṭyaśāstra* 6, 31.

situation.[26] It could also be used to re-establish a mood which had become disturbed through the introduction of an adverse element.[27]

The function of *ākṣepikī* was more complex and dramatic. Through *ākṣepikī* a prevalent mood or sentiment could be abruptly and violently altered by the *'ākṣepa'* or sudden intrusion of a contrary element. Abhinava gives two telling examples. One is from a play called *Udāttarāghava.* The play is not available but the script was based on the familiar Rāma-story and Abhinava's point can be understood without difficulty. There was a scene in the play where Rāma and Sītā were shown in a tender loving mood; suddenly an angry Rāvaṇa enters, and sings a song expressing his anger and violent design towards Rāma who had disfigured his sister and killed his kinsmen. He sings:

"Stop, wretched hermit,
where are you off to?
you have humiliated my sister,
and given me extreme pain.
The fire of my fury
is further fanned by yet another tormenting wind:
for you have destroyed
my kinsmen, such as Khara.
I will quench this fire now
through the torrent of blood
gushing from your mutilated body
and your cleaved heart."

This song, Abhinava aptly adds, was to be sung in a fast turbulent tempo. The prevalent soft mood of the scene was thus utterly shattered by this sudden intrusion of impending violence.[28]

---

[26] cf. *Abhinava Bhāratī* on *Nāṭyaśāstra* 32, 31.

[27] *yā ca rasāntaramupagatamākṣepavaśāt kṛtā prasādayati. rāga-prasādajananīṁ vidyāt prāsādikīṁ tāṁ tu. Nāṭyaśāstra,* 32, 314.

[28] *tatrākṣipyamānarasā yā dīptatayā drutā. tathā udāttarāghave rāmasya prastutaśṛṅgārakramollaṅghanena: "are tāpasa sthiri(ro) bhava kvedānīṁ gamyate. svasurmama parābhavaprasava ekadattavyatha. kharaprabhṛi-bāndhavodvalanavāta-sandhukṣitaḥ. taveha vidarībhavattanusamucalacchoṇi-takṣarācchuritavakṣasaḥ prasamametu kopānalaḥ." ityādinā (rāvaṇavākyena). Abhinava Bhāratī* on *Nāṭyaśāstra* 32, 313.

The second example of the *āksepikī* is from the *Veṇīsaṁhāra* by Bhaṭṭa Nārāyaṇa. Aṣvatthāmā, the son of Droṇa, is ready for battle. He hears a great uproar from the battlefield and imagines that this is the outcome of his father's war-like deeds. He is full of elation and sets out to meet his father. Suddenly from the background someone sings a plaintive song in an appropriately slow, pensive tempo: 'O where now is your father". Aśvatthāmā was thus being told of the death of his father. The prevailing mood is controverted totally.[29]

These instances are interesting in themselves. But what is more interesting is that they reveal how even in matters of detail, the tradition of using song in theatre, and thence into films, has continued almost intact. Like Bharata's theatre, Hindi films too, have their *prāsādikī* and their *ākṣepikī dhruvās.* Instances of *prāsādikī,* where the ethos of the moment is intensified through song are so numerous and obvious that they need not be exemplified: lovers sing of their joys or sorrows; brothers and sisters express their mutual love through songs; mothers, daughters and sons do likewise, and so on and on. There is hardly any sentiment which cannot be accentuated through a song.

The use of *ākṣepikī,* too, is common enough. An example or two might bring the point home. In an early episode of the film *Johny Merā Nām* we are shown a scene where a man (played by Devanand) clandestinely meets a woman (played by Hemā Mālinī) for the purpose of exchanging stolen valuables. The meeting takes place at the small railway station of Nalanda, and an atmosphere of suspense and mystery pervades the whole scene. Police officers on the trail of the girl suddenly appear and advance towards her. For a moment the girl and her companion can see no way of escape; tension mounts, when with an unexpected abruptness, the man and the girl start singing a love song (*'vādā to nibhāyā'*), pretending that they are lovers on a

---

[29] *yathā vākyākarṇanena mūlarasasyāykṣepyasya tu raysya māsṛṇye. sthiteti vilambitā, yathāśvatthāmno yuddhavīre kramolaṅghanena: 'kuto' dyāpi te tātaḥ' iti nepathyaśra-vaṇādi tasya karuṇarasasya. Abhinava Bhāratī* on *Nāṭyaśāstra* 32, 313.

rendezvous. The tense mood falls apart and is superseded by a mood of playful love.

In another recent film, *Bobby,* we again come across an *ākṣepikī* like use of song. An estrangement occurs between the young lovers, around whom the story is woven, in the second part of the film. The girl is angry with the boy who pursues her to Kashmir. She is irreconcilable and the boy suffers mental and physical torments. At last when the boy is about to give up and go away after making a final attempt at bringing her around, we see him moving away from her tent. Suddenly, the silence of the night is broken by a group of Kashmiris singing a *sūfi*-like song about the greatness of love (*ḍholnā main ni bolnā*). The hero stops in his steps; the girl, too, comes out of her tent and slowly, as the effect of the song seeps in, we see her mood changing from that of sultriness into tenderness.

There is also the famous scene in the film *Tere Mere Sapne,* where we see the hero going away dejected from the home of the heroine after she has rejected his proposal of marriage. Suddenly the heroine sings a song of love and acceptance to him through a window (*jaise rādhā ne mālā japī)* and slowly but surely the whole mood changes.[30] Film goers will, we are sure, recall many similar episodes where a song plays a decisive role in effecting a dramatic transition from one mood to another.

Another remarkable parallel shows that the link between Bharata's drama and Hindi films is even more intimate. A *dhruvā*, Bharata says, could be either *ātmasaṁstha* (sung by one self) or *para-saṁstha* (sung by another).[31] Abhinava explains the difference through an examaple. Rāma's sorrow at Sītā's abduction could be expressed through a song in two ways: either Rāma could himself sing of his sorrow: this would be *ātmasaṁstha,* or Lakṣmaṇa could sing a song expressing the

[30] I owe a note of gratitude to friends and colleagues in the Department of History And Indian Culture, University of Rajasthan, especially to Dr. G.S.P. Misra, for suggesting these examples.

[31] *dvividhaṁ tu smṛtaṁ sthānaṁ parasṁthātmasaṁśrayam. Nāṭyaśāstra* 32, 317.

pathos of the situation: this was *para-saṁstha.* The aim in either case was to express Rāma's feeling.[32]

We come across the *ātma-saṁstha* and *para-saṁstha* in Hindi films also. The *ātma-saṁstha* is common enough. The instance quoted above from *Bobby* provides and example of *para-saṁstha.* The *para-saṁstha* sometimes assumes strange modern disguises. For example a heroine may not sing of her sorrow herself, but might switch on the radio where a song will express her feelings. Songs sung by wandering *sādhus,* or by boatmen often serve a similar purpose. The song *sun mere bandhu re* in *Sujātā*, sung by a boatman, for instance, is employed to express the unexpressed longings of the heroine.

Music in film-songs has certain marked characteristics. One basic principle of composition followed is that the musical content should remain subservient to the dramatic purpose. This entails some limitations upon music making. The poetic content of a film song (except in some rare cases) is its primary content. The aim of the song's musical content is to play up or highlight the poetic content and give it additional effectivity. The musical content cannot break loose of the poem as it does in classical music where the musical form dominates. Therefore in film music great care is taken to keep the words of a song undistorted in order that the meaning is not lost in the intricacies of pure music as often happens in classical forms. This is quite natural, for music here is a tool serving dramatic ends.

Bharata has articulated this point in terms of a rule: 'melodic

---

[32] *yathā rāmasya sītādiprayuktavipralambhe tadāśrayameva kadācit pātrāntarāśra-yaṇena. yathā tasyaiva vipralambhe lakṣamanāśraye nitarāmāhurityatra, tadāha. paras-aṁsthātmasaṁśrayamiti. parasthagataṁ lakṣamaṇasya. ātmāśrayaṁ rāmasya. nanu vā parasyāsau karuṇa eva bhavati. na hi rāme vipralabdhe lakṣamaṇasya vipralambhaḥ. kevalaṁ tadduḥkha-duḥkhitasyāsya karuṇa... etaduktaṁ bhavati. laksamaṇasya karuṇe vinayocite masṛṇa manthare gāne prayuktepi tu rāmavipralambha eva prayojakībhavati. Abhinava Bhāratī* on *Nāṭyaśāstra* 32, 317. The point Abhinava is making is that although the *rasa* evoked by Lakṣamaṇa's singing is *karuṇa* and not *viraha śṛṅgāra,* the *karuṇa* in such an instance is occasioned by *viraha* and helps to heighten it.

figures which tend to put too great a distance between sung syllables should be avoided in a *dhruvā,* or else the meaning of the song will be lost to the audience and the very purpose of a *dhruvā* will be defeated".[33] This rule holds good in films too.

We notice, that music in films is quite unrestricted by many of the rules of melodic formation that the high-art forms of classical music have come to acquire. Film songs aim to create a programmatic, theatric effect rather than a sustained musical one. Composers feel free to use and mould any form into any shape provided they can produce the desired effect and elicit audience response.

Ancient composers, too, were similarly given a relatively free-hand in composing music for *dhruvā* songs: the true measure of success for a *dhruvā* was its dramatic effectiveness (though *dhruvās* had come to acquire certain formal rules or guiding patterns which Bharata and other theorists have noted). Abhinava has, in a long passage, given a list of formal rules that were binding in the ancient high-art form of classical liturgic music called *gāndharva;* these were either flaunted or loosely handled in the *dhruvā*.[34]

Dance too was an essential element in Bharata's theatre. Much of the acting itself was stylized, hence dance-like. Dance-proper also had its recognised dramatic use. A significant section of the *Nāṭyaśāstra* is, therefore, devoted to dance-techniques.

A major use of dance was in the *kaiśikī vṛtti.* The notion of *vṛtti* is an important notion in Bharata's concept of the theatre. The term is often roughly translated as 'a mode of acting'. But it denoted more, for it signified the over-all dramatic tenor of a particular situation, of which the mode of acting was just one

---

[33] *saptarūpagatā jñeyā alaṅkārā budhaistvime/ naite sarve dhruvāsviṣṭāḥ śruti (śrotṛ) varṇaprakarṣaṇāt. na hi varṇaprakarṣastu dhruvāṇāṁ siddhiriṣyāte... yasmādarthānu-rūpā hi dhruvā kāryārthadarśibhiḥ. Nāṭyaśāstra* 29, 26-27 and 29. Abhinava comments: *'nanu vā(cā) rthasyaiva hi tatra prādhānyam. varṇe vā (cā)laṅkārabalena prakalpyamānārthapratītivighaṭite'* pyatīteṣvakṣareśvanusandhānamasambhāvi.

[34] *Abhinava Bhārati* on *Nāṭyaśāstra* 33, 1.

constituent, though a major one. Bharata speaks of four *vṛttis*. *Kaiśikī* was one of these. It has been described as a mode of presentation where actors and actresses appear on the stage in pleasing and colourful dresses, women predominate, and the atmosphere is full of song and dance: the whole mood and action is such as to arouse feelings of love and eros.[35] *Kaiśikī* was, in general, the name given to any dramatic action that had grace, colour or softness.[36] The aim was to create an atmosphere of flirtation and light-hearted gaiety. Conversation was dominated by playful banter or *narma*; and dance with music helped to set the right dramatic tone. *Kaiśikī* often served as the setting in which love was born and grew. The *Kaiśikī* mode was thus important in any play with love as a major theme.[37]

The opening scene of Harṣa's *Ratnāvali* provides a good example of *kaiśikī*. King Udayana, the hero, is shown in a carefree mood; it is spring and the whole town rejoices in the festivities of the season. People dance and sing on the streets. The king watches from atop his palace with his friend, the jester (*vidūṣaka*). Two young maid-servants approach him, dancing a mirthful dance and singing a song of spring and love. Playfully, the jester, too, joins them in the dance. His comical artlessness adds broad humour to the spirit of mirth. The stage is set for the unfolding of the story of love between Udayana and Ratnāvali.

Damodara Gupta (8th century AD) in his *Kuṭṭanīmatam* describes the above scene from *Ratnāvali* as it was actually rendered in performance. The scene opens with Udayana

---

[35] *yā ślakṣṇanaipathyaviśeṣacitrā strīsaṁyutā yā bahunṛttagitā/ kāmopabhogapra-bhavopacārā tāṁ kaiśikīṁ vṛttimudāharanti. Nāṭyaśāstra* 20, 53. For a more detailed discussion of the concept of *vṛtti* see, 'Bharata And The Fine Art of Mixing Structures', in this collection.

[36] Cf.: *raudrādirasābhivyaktāvapi kartavyaṁ yo'bhinaya upādīyate so'pyanuprā-savalanāvartanādyātmakasundaravaicitryasyāśraṇayā, duḥśliṣto 'śliṣta eva vā na rasābhivyaktiheturbhavatīti sarvatraiva kaiśikī prāṇāḥ. Abhinava Bhāratī* on *Nāṭya-śāstra* 1, 44.

[37] Commenting on '*Nāṭyaśāstra* 1, 44 where *kaiśikī* is described as: "*nṛttāṅgahārasampannā rasabhāvakriyātmikā*; Abhinava makes the following general remarks about this *vṛtti: "sṛṅgārarasasya tu nāmagrahaṇamapi na tayā vinā śakyam."*

watching the townsfolk, men and women, young and old, all dancing the joyous, erotic dances of spring and singing songs to match the bacchic mood. They dance uninhibitedly to the accompaniment of music and revel in an exchange of coarse, bawdy remarks.[38] They sing festive songs, their breath short with the exertion of the dance.[39] An old man breaks into a solo dance to the accompaniment of loud music, claping his hands to the rythm.[40] A young woman, intoxicated with wine, sings: 'May it ever be spring, when one can freely embrace the man one desires', and she proceeds to do so.[41]

These details of bacchic revelry that were shown on stage are missing from the script of the play. Harṣa only hints at them without giving any detailed stage-directions for their performance. From his script one could even get the impression that the revelry was not to be actually performed but only suggested poetically. But actual productions evidently deployed stage actions as described by Dāmodara. It was through such action, exuding an atmosphere of mirth, song, dance and eros, that the *kaiśikī* mode was realized.

The scene as drawn by Dāmodara Gupta, reminds us of scenes similar in intent (though perhaps not quite as broad in tone) which are common enough on the Hindi screen. One can think of a number of films where the action opens with a picnic scene: where the mood is playful, mirth and music rule the day and, inevitably, there is song and dance. The stage is set for love; and, indeed, the picnic scene is often the scene where boy meets girl and the two become enamoured of each other. Besides a picnic-setting for song and dance and love, we have other similar settings in village-fairs or rustic dances or even (as in the

---

[38] *nṛtyati paurajanaughe provāca vayasya paśya paśyeti/ tulya-śiśutaruṇavṛddhaṁ samaguptāguptayuvatipraceṣṭam/agaṇitavācyāvācyaṁ krīḍanti janāḥ pravṛddhaharṣāḥ. Kuṭṭanīmatam,* 882-883.

[39] *gātrāyāsasamutthitabahuniḥśvāsaprakīrṇapadagītam. ibid.* 889.

[40] *tūryaravavyāmiśritakaratalatāloddhūtaṁ pranṛtyantam/muhurupi jātaskhalanaṁ sandarśitadārḍhyasauṣṭhave sthaviram.* ibid., 890.

[41] *astu vasantaḥ satataṁ svādhīnābhiṣṭajanasamāśleṣaḥ iti/gāyanti rabhasādāliṅgati madavaśāttaruṇī* ibid. 891.

Ratnāvali) the festivities of spring itself. These certainly provide examples of the *kaiśikī* as presented on the Hindi screen. Their occurrence is not due to any conscious adaptation of old forms, but as in the case of songs, these modern versions of ancient forms are informed and moulded by a continuing tradition which works at a level beyond conscious design.

Besides serving to create a prelude for love, *kaiśikī* was also employed to express love itself. Sequences in films where lovers express their love, singing and dancing with much mirth and gusto should, I think, be also counted among examples of *kaiśikī.* Bharata indeed, seems to prescribe such expressions of love in enjoining that 'joyful dance should be used to express love between man and woman'.[42]

Indeed, in Hindi films, lovers dance only when expressing a joyous, triumphant love. Separated lovers or lovers who have fallen apart do not dance, though they may sing. Curiously enough, Bharata has a dictum: 'dance should not be employed in situations showing a girl who has been jilted by her lover or is away from him or has quarelled with him'.[43]

In movies dance is also presented as a kind of show within the show. Often the heroine is an accomplished dancer, and she is made to appear in a stage show. The hero is among the viewers and love dawns. Such scenes also have their prototypes in ancient plays. The most well-known instance is Mālavikā's dance before Agnimitra in the second Act of Kālidāsa's *Mālavikāgnimitram.*

---

[42] *yattu saṁdṛśyate kiñciddāmptyarmadanāśrayam/nṛttaṁ tatra prayoktavyaṁ praharṣārthaguṇodbhavam. Nāṭyaśāstra* 4, 306.

[43] *khaṇḍitā vipralabdhā vā kalahāntaritāpi vā/ yasminnaṅge tu yuvatirna nṛttaṁ tatra yojayet. Nāṭyaśāstra* 4, 308.

It must be noted, however, that the purport of this verse- and of the one quoted in the last footnote – within the context of dramatic action is not clear. Only *nṛtta,* pure dance, is fobidden unless the situation is one of joy. This does not rule out *nṛtya* or dance with *abhinaya* which seeks to express poetic meanings though dance-gestures. Dance in an ancient play was certainly not always expressive of a joyous mood. The fourth act of *Vikramorvāśīyam* is an obvious instance. A similar use of dance must have been made in other plays, too.

Such a show within a show was technically known as *nāṭyāyita*. Abhinava Gupta explains *nāṭyāyita* as an occasion in the play where some of the protagonists themselves become audience to some action or spectacle within the play itself, The analogy Abhinava gives is that of a dream within a dream.[44]

Nāṭyāyita, thus defined, is a broad category. Mālavikā's dance in the *Mālavikāgnimitram* or the staged dances shown in Hindi films clearly form one class of *nāṭyāyita.* The scene in *Ratnāvali,* described above, with Udayana watching the festivities of the townsfolk, also falls within the definition of *nāṭyāyita.*

In Hindi films dance performances also assume other forms of *nāṭyāyita.* Because dances presented as shows in films are not always stage dances, they are presented in other ways, too. We have street dances or group dances or festive dances or just *impromptu* dances, with one or more of the main protagonists dancing, others watching, or in an inversion of this theme, with one or more of the main characters dancing to an audience of casual observers, not otherwise figuring in the story. These are all dances that may be said to fall within the category of the *nāṭyāyita.*

Dances presented in this manner are sometimes nothing more than spectacles, their connection with the narrative being extremely thin. Often, however, they are integral to the action. Cabaret shows, for instance, are almost a must in Hindi films. They are brought in whether they fit in or not. But at times they serve a dramatic function. They help lure the 'good' hero into a life of crime and dissipation. Dance as seduction, which such a dance may be called, is sometimes woven even more firmly into

---

[44] *tasmāditthametad vyākhyātvyam: iha yadā svapnopyekaghano dṛśyate tanmadhyata eva ca kiṁ dṛśyamānaṁ parasya svapna eva jāgradrūpatāmāpādite svapno'yaṁ mayā dṛṣṭa iti varṇayate, tadā jāgradapekṣayā svapnavyavahrārah, na tatra pāramārthika ityaupacārikaṁ tadapekṣaṁ tasya svapnatvamiti tasya svapnāyitavyavaharo dṛṣṭaḥ. evamihāpi nāṭya ekaghanasvabhāve hi sthite tatraivāsatyanāṭyānupraveśānnāṭyapātreṣu sāmājikibhūteṣu tadapekṣayā yadanyaṁ nāṭyaṁ tasya tadapekṣayā nāṭyarūpatvaṁ pārmārthikamiti nāṭyāyitamucyate. tacca dvividhaṁ nāṭyarūpakaniṣṭhameva vā kāryāntaraniṣṭhaṁ vā. Abhinava Bhārati* on *Nāṭyaśāstra,* 22, 48.

the fabric of the plot. The scene in *Victoria No. 203* where the heroine (acted by Saira Bano), playing for time, dances an erotically suggestive dance, wearing nothing more than a towel — to the one-man audience of the villain (played by Ranjit), is one instance of such a use of the dance. Here the dance is clearly an integral part of the action, for without it the heroine would not have been saved from the prurient intentions of the villain and the story could not have taken the turn it did. A similar scene is the scene in *Johny Merā Nām* where the well-meaning lady-friend (Padmā Khannā) of the hero (Devanand), dances a seductive dance in the villain's (Premnath's) hideout in order to save the hero. In the film *Loafer* there is a scene where the heroine (Mumtaz), who has been forced to act as a ploy for a gang of criminals, walks coolly into the hero's (Dharmendra's) room, and without wasting a single word, begins a dance soliciting his love. She succeeds, the hero falls in love with her, and this is a crucial event in the narrative. Instances of this sort can be multiplied *ad infinitum.*

It is difficult to say whether such a use of the dance was made in ancient theatre, too. Surviving scripts do not provide examples. Yet it is not difficult to see that the use of *nāṭyāyita* as integral to the plot was not totally absent. Consider Mālavikā's dance in the *Mālavikāgnimitram.* It was the dance of a girl offering herself in love to her lover (the accompanying song has the phrase 'I pine for you my lord'). Agnimitra's friend, the *vidūṣaka*, rightly, interprets the dance as Mālavikā's offer of love to the king.[45]

We see thus that Hindi films use song and dance in a manner analogous to ancient theatric practice. We usually do not think of *Johny Merā Nām* and *Mālavikāgnimitram* as being connected in any way. But once we begin to see the connections, we can have a better understanding of much that strikes us as incongruous in Hindi films.

---

[45] *'bho vayasya catuṣpadavastukaṁ dvārīkṛtya apyupasthāpita ātmā tatrabhavatyā' Mālavakignimitram,* Act II.

CHAPTER – TEN

Bharata and the Hindi Film Revisited

I had argued in an earlier paper[1] that the so-called popular formula-oriented or *masālā* Hindi film uses — though perhaps without conscious purport — theatric devices, which may be understood as constituting a kind of culturally-rooted narrative grammar, articulated much more self-consciously in the *Nāṭyaśāstra*. My concern in that paper was to demonstrate, through examples from various films, that the use of song and dance as an integral element in a film — both in unfolding its action as well as its sentiment or ethos (*rasa*) — was part of an ancient practice, the roots of which could, in fact, be traced back to Bharata's famous treatise on theatre.

The present paper seeks to re-examine the earlier paper: to extend its scope, criticise it, question it, offer comments on it, in short to reformulate it in the light of what I have thought on the subject since I wrote it. But before I do that, let me sum it up in brief. The paper begins by asking a question which was born of an uneasy, unsettling feeling I have had — and I presume other have had it too — watching certain kinds of scenes in a typical Hindi film, where the mode of narration undergoes a strange and sudden change, and as we move through an action which is realistic enough, flowing naturally in surroundings presented in a natural, lifelike mode, when suddenly as through the force of a magic mantra, the whole thing is transported to another plane. The characters who had been behaving naturally suddenly swing into a song and dance, the language of speech changes from prose to poetry, the whole action seems to move out of reality

---

[1] "Bharata Muni and Hindi Films" published in *Jijñāsā: A Journal of the History of Ideas and Culture*, the University of Rajasthan, Jaipur, vol. 2, No. 2, April 1975, pp. 84-106. The essay has been printed here just before the present one.

into a kind of trance-like, dream-world. And there it remains suspended till the song and dance sequence ends, and we switch back again to a natural mode.

The transformation from the natural to the dream-like song and dance mode, was what appeared as strange and unsettling to me. But most Indian viewers take it in their stride. To them there is nothing strange about such a switch in the narrative mode from the natural to the dream-like. In fact, such switches are quite expected, and people would readily point out when they are appropriate. Their nonoccurrence when they should have been there, is what might strike the ordinary viewer as strange. How does this happen, and why do Indian viewers accept such switches in the very flow of the story as quite in order ? This was the question I had asked myself. The answer, I thought, lay in the ancient roots of the Indian theatrical tradition, roots which still sustain the popular Indian theatre, of which the film is in its central intent only a modified form. This led me to Bharata and his *Nāṭyaśāstra*.

Drama, Bharata says, imitates the world, But this imitation, he adds, is a *nāṭyadharmī* imitatiton; that is to say, it is essentially theatrical in nature. It transforms as it imitates. Because it must. It is just not possible to imitate the world on the stage without filtering it, mediating it, hence modifying it, through the use of certain conventions and devices which belong not to the world but to theatre as a medium of representing the world. Creating this 'imitation' world, — or perhaps a more appropriate description would be a 'virtual' world — moreover, is not an arbitrary activity. It must be communicated to a large audience, making them feel that what is being represented is indeed an evocative spectacle drawn from the world. This is patently not possible unless the devices which theatre uses to project the world on the stage are accepted as 'natural', that is, 'natural' to the world of theatre.

Translating reality on to the stage presents many problems. First, there is the problem of framing: the vast, literally limitless world has to be imitated on a stage, infinitesimally small by comparison. Different theatrical traditions adopt somewhat different conventions to overcome this problem. Bharata's stage used the device of *kakṣyā-vibhāga* for the purpose. The stage was divided into different sections or segments representing different parts of the world, land, water, forest, city and the like. Another device, that of the *janāntika* was necessary because the theatre not only imitates the world but seeks to communicate this 'imitation' to others. *Janāntika* was the 'aside', where two persons converse without being heared by others present on the stage, but, of course, by every one in the audience. This a device found not only in the Indian but also the western theatrical tradition. Other devices included the use of props', costumes, make-up and the like which Bharata's theatre — indeed most theatre — uses for the purpose of recreating the world on the stage.

Such devices, in Bharata's conceptual scheme, were included under what he called the *nāṭyadharmī*, the mode of presentation peculiar to theatre as theatre. Such devices are an essential part of what can be meaningfully called the formal grammar of theatre, which like the grammar of a language that we converse in, must become second nature to us, in order that we may use it with spontaneous ease. *Nāṭyadharmī* devices must, in other words, become accepted *samayas,* or in other words conventions internalised by author, producer and audience alike, if they are to work at all.

The *nāṭyadharmī* devices, noted above, were geared towards the imitation of the outer world. It is more difficult, and also more important for theatre to represent the inner world of feeling and thought. For this is what theatre is really about. Bharata includes devices and conventions under the *nāṭyadharmī* which aim at representing the inner world of feeling and thought on the stage. The *nāṭyadharmī* for this purpose takes recourse to music, dance and what Bharata has called the 'heightened' language of poetry. Most theatrical traditions use such *nāṭyadharmīs*. But the mode of employ is not always the same. The theatre of the west and following it the film — uses music as a *nāṭyadharmī*;

but it uses it in the background, except for such, special prodcutions as the 'opera' and the 'musical'. In traditional Indian theatre — and following it in the Hindi film — music is used not only in the background, but also in the foreground, as song, and this is done not in a special genre but in all films whatever its theme: mythological, fantastic or realistic.

The use of song and dance as a part of the very fabric of theatric representation has been accepted as an internalised *samaya* — convention — in the Indian tradition. It has even been canonised by Bharata who was revered as a more than a human authority. It has thus become part of the very grammar of theatric form for centuries, through Bharata to modern times, being employed in both classical and folk forms. It is internalised as part of the *natural* language of theatre, and hence of the Hindi film. Its use, therefore, causes no unease, except to those of us who have become alienated from the tradition, and to whom the traditional theatric language seems 'unrealistic'. We are ready to accept music in the background — since the west accepts this, though this is hardly realism — but music as song in the foreground, as a part of the action itself, seems to us unnatural and upsetting.

This was the thrust of my argument in the paper which I propose to revisit here. In order to demonstrate how rooted in Bharata the use of song and dance is as a *nāṭyadharmī*, I had put forward examples from the film that matched Bharata's precepts not only in principle but also in the details of theatric usage. The examples were meant to illustrate two ways in which songs and dances are, I think, integral to the narratives presented in Hindi films : (1) as means for expressing emotions and (2) as an essential part of the action itself, forming a crucial element in its very narrative movement.

Examples illustrating the use of song and dance for illustrating emotions or sentiments are so common and pervasive in the Hindi films that it should not be necessary to cite exampels. There are hardly any emotions for which one cannot find a number of songs, or song and dance sequences, though some emotions, as is only to be expected, engage greater attention than others. One might even be able to work out an interesting history of the changing taste in emotions and sentiments over the last few decades as reflected in the films — a reliable mirror for the popular psyche — if one were to take the trouble.

Examples of songs and dances as integral to the action itself do perhaps need to be illustrated. I had given some illustrations in my earlier article. But I would like to give here a few new ones to show that the practice is deeply ingrained, and by no means given up in more recent films. I do not think that I need to give more than two or three examples, for these should be indicators enough and suggest others to the reader, who might be able to think of even more telling ones. My first example is from *Namak Halāl*, quite a box office hit in the recent years.

A cabaret dancer (Parveen Babi) is hired to kill a rich hotel owner (Shashi Kapoor). But being a Hindi film heroine and so essentially good by nature, she undergoes a change of heart, helped in the change by the attraction she feels for the hero, Shashi Kapoor. Her change of heart is obviously important for the story, and is projected through a song which she sings to the accompaniment of a dance she performs in Shashi's hotel. "The hunter has fallen in love with the prey, a target of her own arrow", she sings[2] and the viewer can now be assured, that despite all appearance to the contrary, no harm can come to Shashi from her. Later in the story, we have another song and dance by her, even more intimately woven into the action. After Parveen's feelings for Shashi - and his for her - have been more overtly established in the story, she invites him to a party on her yacht where she is celebrating her birthday. She sings and dances for his benefit when he arrives, but the performance is being used by the villain as a cover for a plot to kill him, a plot in which she is forced to become a party. Her purported object is to

---

[2] *shikārī khud yahāṁ shikār ho gayā/calāyā tīr jo mujhī pe cal gayā/saiyyād ko bulbul se pyār ho gayā.*

lure him to a spot where a latch will open by the weight of his body and swallow him into the sea where a killer, impressively dressed up in a scuba diver's costume, awaits him. The plot goes awry because of the timely intervention of Amitabh Bachchan, the other hero in the film, but the moot point is that the song and dance are a *part* of the plot.

Let me give you yet another example, this time from a film named *Pyārī Behnā.* There is a scene in the film, a typical enough scene, where the hero (Miṭhun Chakravarti) and the heroine (Padmini Kolhapure) — a poor but good looking, and rather earthy, girl whom Miṭhun's sister, dearer to him than his life (the *pyārī behnā),* had invited to live with them — express their love for each other for the first time. The scene is set in a charmingly green, inviting landscape, traditionally considered the best suited for such activity, as part of the *uddīpana vibhāva*, a condition for the arousal of the mood of love, *śṛṅgāra rasa.* Miṭhun, an electrician with the Railways, is sitting idle in a trolley, when Padmini comes and joins him. They had obviously been in love for some time, but it is now that they express it, singing and dancing and frolicking in the love-arousing landscape, leaving the trolley unattended. Suddenly, there is an emergency somewhere along the railway track. Miṭhun is needed immediately. A bell begins to ring insistently in the trolley. But Miṭhun is busy making a louder noise nearby, singing, the now famous song, '*tum na batāo*' with his beloved. He cannot hear the bell. His failure to do so is a turning point in the story, resulting in all kinds of disasters and complications.

These examples should be enough, but here is an another, this time from a farce entitled *Bīwī O Bīwī.* The story is a comedy of errors with two look-alikes, both played by Sanjiv Kumar. One of the two Sanjivs is a retired army officer, a widowed middle-aged man with an only daughter. He is played as an exaggeratedly comical disciplinarian, a civilian-hating officer, who is yet afraid of his mother like an over-grown child. The other Sanjiv is a rogue, a cheat living by his wits. The hero, a young civilian (Randhir Kapoor), falls in love with colonel

Sanjiv's daughter, and she, as is to be expected, with him. The marriage is fiercely opposed by her father, who will have nothing to do with a civilian, but it has the blessings of the girl's domineering grandmother. Meanwhile, Sanjiv, the cheat, an expert in impersonation, comes to know about the colonel, who is a rich man, and being a look-alike, should be easy to impersonate. He enters the colonel's house dressed as the colonel, and asks for the keys of the safe from the colonel's mother, and then proceeds to rob his look-alike, making away with a big loot. A curious and startled Randhir Kapoor spies Sanjiv during the act. It strikes him as not being quite in character, and secretly follows the false colonel to the park where the cheat has a tryst with his 'Molly'. The false colonel proceeds to sing and dance with her with great gusto, happy over his success. This song and dance also acts as the trigger for a series of the kind of confusions we associate with a comedy of errors that the film is. It forms an important link in the narrative. For the now completely baffled, astounded and enraged Randhir Kapoor, not knowing that the cheat is not the colonel himself, takes the colonel to be a double-dealer with a concealed personality quite at odds with the one he assumes in public. Randhir denounces the colonel to his mother, initiating a series of humorous confusions.

These examples, from different kinds of films, will, I hope, suffice to illustrate that song and dance play an important role in the action itself. I will, however, also like to add here quite another use of song and dance strongly reminiscent of Bharata's usage. I had not spoken of it in my earlier paper, since I had not been able to see the parallel then. But recently, on watching an old movie, *Boy Friend* (made perhaps in the fifties with Shammi Kapoor and Madhubala in the lead), and half a dozen new ones, I could not miss it.

Every important character on Bharata's stage was introduced with a song called the *prāveśikī dhruvā*, an 'entrance song'. The song served the purpose of letting the audience know the kind of person who is being introduced into the story. The character came on the stage accompanied by appropriate words set to suitable music, as he moved and danced around the stage with befitting gestures and gait, before entering into the story and the action. In Hindi films not every important character is introduced to us with such a song. But the hero very often is. I will give a few examples. Let me begin with the old movie *Boy Friend.* The story opens with Shammi Kapoor, the personable hero, the good man at heart, imprisoned for petty theft, coming out of jail. And then with a song we get to know him, his temperament, his desires, as he sings and prances and dances atop a moving train, travelling to Bombay. The song he sings reveals his heart for us. He is clearly not a thief. Circumstances have made him wayward, but if he can find the right girl who will love him and cherish him, he will return to the 'world', the social world of upright people, a good and worthy citizen (*mujhe apnā yār banā le, main ho jāūṅ sansār kā*). The song, and especially the dance, also introduce to us his likeable, but impetuous, non-chalant, devil-may-care character. Immediately after the song, we find the stage set for the hero to meet the woman (Madhubala) who will turn him to the path of virtue. After a series of misadventures, this, as expected, is exactly what happens.

This is neither an isolated nor a dated example. Such *prāveśikī dhruvās* still continue to be an important element in many Hindi films. Consider *Namak Halāl* of which we had spoken earlier, too. Amitabh Bacchan is the real leading character. He grows up in the village with his grandfather, becoming as a young man, a stupid, country bumpkin. His disappointed grandfather sends him off to Bombay so that experience might teach him a thing or two about life, and also to stand on his own two feet (as the old man puts it). In Bombay, a friend takes him to a very urbane and posh hotel, hoping to get him a job there. It is with this incongruous event that the action really begins. We see Amitabh now in his true colours. We get to know him as he really is, and as he is going to be throughout the movie. In the very 'modern' and rich surroundings of the hotel, he sings the immensely popular song, *pag ghunghrū bāndh mīrā nācī thī,* and good-naturedly dances to it with great gusto like a dizzy *bhāṇḍa*. We get to know his clownish character, his commitment to an 'old-world' sense of moral values and his yearning for love and life. This prepares us for what to expect of him in the action to follow. We find Smita Patil eying him with fond indulgence, he dances, as and moves into one odd antic after another, and we know who the heroine is; expectations are aroused in us of pleasant love encounters, again, of course, through song and dance. And as the narrative moves our expectations are fulfilled.

In *Bīwī O Bīwī* we are introduced to the hero, Randhir Kapoor, in the very first scene as the movie opens, and he is seen dancing and singing on the steps of a temple. He is desperate in his desire to get married, and pleads to God to find him a wife, just any girl, so desperate is he (*bīwī dilā do gorī ho kālī ho* and so forth). This, as it turns out, is an introduction both to him and his story. In *Sharābī*, where Amitabh is again in the lead, an altruistic young man, addicted to alcohol (to which he was introduced almost in his cradle by his own widowed, extremely pre-occupied father), we are introduced to him through a song and a drunken dance. It gives us a glimpse into his friendly, philanthropic soul and his yearning for an all-consuming true love which will rid him of his unwanted addiction to alcohol (*pyār agar mile to har nashā hai bekār*). One is reminded of Shammi Kapoor's opening song in *Boy Friend.*

The *prāveśikī* is sometimes sung by two characters if both are in the lead. In an old film, *Victoria Number 203,* Ashok Kumar and Pran play two thieves with hearts of gold, and are virtually the heroes of the film. They are also introduced with a song, which sets the theme for the plot. In a more recent film, *Īmān Dharam*, two young men, Amitabh Bachchan and Shashi Kapoor, who too are well-meaning rogues, appear for the first time singing a song, *ham jhuṭh bolte hain, mānate hain/ log jhuṭh bolte hain, mānate nahīn* (We are liars but we accept that we are liars, other people lie, but they do not accept that they lie).

I had argued in the earlier paper that the reason why the effect of the song and dance sequences jar on our sensibilities is because the Hindi film juxtaposes a stylised, theatrical, *nāṭyadharmī* mode with scenes which are more natural and realistic. This is, I had said, an unconvincing and odd mixture of two disparate tradititions which does not quite succeed with a more sophisticated audience, and, further, the juxtaposition is made rather crudely and mechanically. The reason for this, I had argued, was that the Hindi film works consciously with western realism and unconsciously with Bharatan stylisation without the vision to fuse them into a single satisfactory whole. The camera as a medium, I had stressed is geared to realism by its very nature. It is the most efficient instrument ever invented for recording life in its panoramic setting. No other medium approaches it in this. This gives the film a greater capacity to imitate life, at least in its outer appearances than theatre ever could. In Hindi films, too, the camera works as an instrument for realism. And this makes the dream-like song and dance sequences even more unsettling.

But I now have misgivings about this view. It seems to me to be too facile. If the Hindi film really combines two radically different modes of theatre in a mechanical manner, then it should jar on most of its viewers. But a question remains. If to explain why an average Indian viewer accepts the film mode of presentation as natural, we must look into the tradition, where in the tradition do we find the kind of clashing juxtaposition that we find in the films?

What I have just said can be put in Bharata's words also. How can a Hindi film succeed if it fails to build up a *vṛtti*? The term *vṛtti*, in Bharata's conceptual scheme, was the term used for a total theatrical whole, a right, aesthetically satisfactory combination of the various elements that theatre as an art puts together, into a distinct whole: acting, music, dance, language and narrative be mutually complementary and compatible. *Vṛtti* is obviously multiple in principle, and each can be achieved in many ways. But surely one way to spoil a *vṛtti* would be to mix two entirely disparate modes of presentations : the realistic and the stylised. And to spoil a *vṛtti* is to spoil ones chance for *siddhi*, the success of a play with its viewers. But the Hindi film does succeed.

The truth, I think, is that the Hindi film does not aim at realism at all, except very superficially. It aims at creating a world of its own, a narrow, simplistic world painted only in certain primary colours, eschewing all mixed hues, the complexities of real life. The narrative and the action of the film moves entirely within this specially created hot-house world. It is an ideal moral world governed by elemental, wish-fulfilling laws. No character oversteps the boundaries of this confined world. What appear as switches in the mode of presentation from the realistic to the stylised are not really switches at all. They follow and fit into the motif-governed character of this world. They make theatrically appropriate sense within it. A character swinging into song and dance is not being suddenly transported into a new dream-world. He is already within one. All he is doing is adopting a more appropriate mode for properly expressing feelings and emotions. Within the world in which he moves, this, indeed, is expected of him. The audience can predict such switches in modes. It is no sudden, startling or jarring affair.

It is not right to say that the Hindi film *juxtaposes* some *nāṭyadharmī* elements which are a heritage from traditional Bharatan theatre and mixes it incongruously with elements from quite a different way of doing theatre. Indeed, the Hindi film has much more of Bharata than a peculiar use of song and dance. Its entire narrative or plot is also Bharatan in spirit. It is out and out *nāṭyadharmī* in intent and design, reflecting old Bharatan narrative ideals as much as the mode of presentation. The *itivṛtta*, Bharata's term for a plot or narrative, was fable-like, it was invariably conceived as a success story. In Bharata's organic metaphor, the *itivṛtta* was to grow from seed to fruition, the final fruit being moral and desirable. The goal-oriented movement of the story was, however, not to follow a straight forward path for that would make it dull. The path was made purposely crooked. It swerves away from the goal in order to make its realisation all the more exciting and wonder-arousing. But this is merely to add spice to the fable, and not to introduce real conflict or evil in it. Right in the middle of the story, says Bharata, the seed that has taken roots and is growing should disappear from our view, there should be an attempt to put things right again, the end should seem to be in sight only to elude us, and it is only in the end that things should work out satisfactorily, and, of course wonderously.[3] It was in the carving of this deliciously circuitous route, and bringing it to life that the genius of the writers and producers of plays lay. The attempt of the writers and producers of the typical Hindi film is patently similar. The world they create may be poorer and less sophisticated in many ways than that of Bharata, but it certainly reflects the same theatric spirit, not only in parts, but as a whole. Let me quote Bharata to end with : "(The first stage in the *itivṛtta*, the plot) is *mukha* where a seed is sown and it takes roots; along with it arise a variety of (suitable) *rasas* (moods, sentiments), and meaningful situations. This is how the *mukha* is to be presented (on the stage) in a narrative. *Pratimukha* in all plays (is the second stage) where the seed sown in the *mukha* becomes manifest. But as it appears it also disappears. (In the third stage), namely, *garbha*, the seed grows. It attains its end, and yet it does not. It has to be ferreted out again. (In the fourth stage) *vimarśa,* temptation or anger or a calamity (seems) to uproot whatever had been attained upto the *garbha*. (But in the final stage) *nirvahaṇa,* the meaningful events of the *mukha*, where the seeds of the action were sown, and

---

[3] This is my own summary of what Bharata says in *Nāṭyaśāstra*, 19, 39-43: I give the original:

yatra bījasamutpattirnānārasārthasambhavā / kāvye śarīrānugatā tanmukhaṁ parikīrtitam // bījasyodghāṭanaṁ yatra dṛṣṭanaṣṭamivakvacit / mukhanyastasya sarvatra tadvai pratimukhaṁ smṛtam // udbhedastasya bījasya prāptīraprāptireva vā / punascānveṣaṇaṁ yatra sa garbha iti saṁjñitam // garbhanirabhinnabījārtho vilobhanakṛto' thavā / krodhavyasanajo vāpi sa vimarśa iti smṛtaḥ // samānayanamarthānāṁ mukhādyānāṁ sabījinām / nānābhāvottarāṇāṁ yadbhavennirvahaṇaṁ tu tat//

which had given rise to different situations and moods (*bhāva*) are brought to (fruition)."

The ideal here is the creation of an emotionally satisfactory world of fulfilment; adversity due to negative sentiments or deeds was so arranged as to *add* to the ultimate sense of flowering and fruition, without detracting from it.

It is not difficult to see why the dominating *rasa* in the *nirvahaṇa,* the finale, was *adbhuta,* wonder: *nirvahaṇe, kartavyo nityaṁ hi raso'dbhutaḥ* (N.S.18,43). Events leading towards a negative or tragic end were somehow to be brought around to a satisfactory consummation, through 'strange' turns or quirks in the plot, or the help of gods. This was what created the *adbhuta* of which Bharata speaks.

CHAPTER – ELEVEN

An Enquiry into the *Rāga*-Time Association in the Light of History

Every Indian, at least every north Indian, whether he is a lover of classical music or not, believes that the hoary forms he is heir to, namely the *rāgas*, have important esoteric aspects besides the musical. I would like to discuss in this eassy one such aspect, viewing it in the perspective of history. I refer to what may be called the time aspect of a *rāga*. Each *rāga*, it is commonly held, in order to be truly efficacious has to be sung or played only at a particular hour of the day or night. A more informed listener will even assert that belonging to a specific part of the day or night is as essential a property of a *rāga*, as its tonal structure. He might then proceed to enumerate morning-*rāgas*, noon *rāgas*, evening *rāgas*, late-at-night *rāgas* and just-before-morning *rāgas*.

All of us, I am sure, have come across persons, obviously not very musical, not quite capable of distinguishing one *rāga* from another, who yet are deeply convinced that a *rāga* sung outside of its assigned hour creates a grating effect. Clearly, the notion that a *rāga* has inherent affinity with a certain part of the day is very deeply ingrained in our culture.

If you ask, 'how does one know which *rāga* belongs to what hour ?', the answer will be unanimous: the scheme has been fixed by a tradition reaching back to time immemorial. And, it would be added, it is not a meaningless conventional scheme but a living tradition which finds renewed sanction in the musical experience of every fresh generation.

But one might then put a further question: if the matter is one of direct musical experience, then the tonal or other more palpable features that are felt to be associated with the 'morning' or 'evening' quality of a *rāga* can surely be identified and distinguished. This seems an obvious question to ask and one would expect to find an answer to it in the older musical texts, but curiously enough, the first person to have asked it was a comparatively recent musician and scholar of music, Pandit Bhatkhande, whose works belong to the early years of our own century. He was also the first person who attempted to provide empirical tonal cognates for the 'morning', 'noon', 'evening' and similar time-realted properties of *rāgas*. The generalisations he arrived at, found common acceptance and still remain without any serious rival. His might almost be termed the 'official' theory in the matter, despite doubts and reservations felt in many circles — reservations which, however, do not go beyond matters of detail.

Whatever the merits of Bhatkhande's analysis, the very fact that he considered it an important enterprise in understanding and delineating Hindustani music is of great significance. He strongly felt that the notion of assigning a specific hour to every *rāga* was an essential element of Hindustani music, a major distinguishing mark. And this feeling, plainly, was the guiding motive behind his search for those patterns in *rāgas* which marked them as 'morning' or 'evening', and the like. In a, now historic, speech made at the first All India Music Conference in Baroda in 1916, he enumerated twenty significant features which, in his view, distinguished the Hindustani system, making it, in his words, as a 'system perfectly independent of the Southern or Karnatic'.[1] He set these features out in twenty separate and individually numbered clauses, of which as many as six, that is, numbers 5-10 are concerned with the time aspect of *rāgas*.

In clause number five he remarks:

"Stated times of the night and day are assigned to particular *rāgas*, according to a design which might suggest a psycho-physiological basis".

The next five clauses set-out certain specific features which 'enable a singer or listener to approximately determine the time

[1] The speech has been reproduced as 'A Short Historical Survey of the Music of Upper India', Bombay, 1934. See pages 41–42.

of the *rāga*'. He draws our attention to the crucial importance in this matter of the *tīvra ma*, the combinations *komala re-dha, ga-nī* and so forth — features which now form part of general musical knowledge and standard musical theory.

Pandit Bhatkhande, as he himself stresses, spoke of the notion of *rāgas* and their assigned hours with a specific purpose in mind: namely, to distinguish the Hindustani system from the Karnatic system of music. Thus in his days it was only the north Indian singers and listeners who felt that particular *rāgas* belong to particular hours of the night or day. South Indians, in contrast, did not share a similar feeling about their *rāgas*. Yet, though the southerner's music might be recognisably different from that of the northerner, there is an equally recognisable affinity and kinship between the two approaches to the art especially in their delineation of *rāgas*. *Rāga*-patterns, both in the south and the north, are based on formal principles that stem from an identical source and follow parallel streams of inspiration and development, interacting with each other to a no mean degree. Many *rāgas* of north India have such close counterparts in the South that even non-specialist listeners can recognise them as almost identical forms. This obvious feeling of consanguinity is, indeed, the inspiration behind a popular Vividha Bhāratī programme where north Indian *rāgas* are presented along with their south Indian siblings to reveal close kinship. But if many *rāga* patterns in the south and north are so conspicuously similar then they are bound to have formal features which are also essentially alike: features such as the dominant or exclusive presence of the *tīvra ma*, or the combination komala *re-dha, ga-nī* and the like, for these are tonal features as characteristic of Karnatic *rāgas* as of their Hindustani analogues. Yet Karnatic music knows of no 'morning', 'evening' or 'noon' *rāgas*.

The fact that there is in north India a definite design or scheme within which different *rāgas* have been assigned to different hours of the day suggests, according to Pandit Bhatkhande, a psycho-physiological basis for making such an assignment. He never, so far as I know, spelled out what he wished to indicate by speaking of such a basis. But if this basis is in any sense psychological or physiological then it must certainly be also a universal phenomenon common to both north Indians and south Indians, in fact, all mankind. Any sensitive listener, in other words, should be able to feel the 'morning' or 'evening' quality of a *rāga*. But no one except a north Indian, or a person duly initiated into the esoteric lore and conventions of Hindustani music, really responds to this quality in *rāgas*.

It is thus evidently a response which has to be learned. It is the product of a specific culture. If it seems natural and spontaneous to the Hindustani musician and listener, the reason lies in the fact that it has been so deeply ingrained through centuries of persuasive suggestion and habitual observance as to have become a reflex, almost a second nature. But the truth that it is a trained and not a natural response often shines forth in the untutored reaction of listeners from alien musical cultures, who though moved by a *rāga*, fail to detect its affinity with a particular time of the day or night. The perception of this affinity has to be taught to them, and, of course, many of them prove very dutiful students. But being a learned response it can also be unlearned. In truth, as a purely musical experience gains roots, and one begins to know and love a *rāga* for itself, one is quite able to detach it from such external associations as its relation with a particular hour of the day. This is especially true of practising musicians, who of all people are closest to the *rāgas*. Fox Strangways, writing almost contemporaneously with Bhatkhande — *The Music of Hindustan* by him was published in 1914 — speaks of 'advanced' musicians who found no meaning in ascribing hours of the day or seasons of the years to *rāgas*.[2] *Rāgas*, traditionally, belong not only to certain times of the day but also to particular seasons. The traditions behind the two ascriptions, seasonal and hourly, are equally old. The seasonal

---

2 A.H. Fox Strangways, *The Music of Hindustan*, p. 153. Interestingly, Fox Strangways had his own peculiar theory regarding structural properties that mark a *rāga* as 'morning' or 'evening'. He believed that morning *rāgas* had *aṁśas* ranging about G and the evening, about E. (Ibid).

ascription, indeed, as we shall see, is perhaps the more ancient one. The seasonal aspect of *rāgas* is no longer taken seriously even in the north except in the case of a few rain or spring *rāgas*, such as the various *malhāras, basanta and bahāra*, and these, too, are no longer kept tied down to their ascribed seasons, they are much too beloved for that. Yet, we still believe in keeping them confined to the boundaries of the hours within which they have been restricted by convention. There is plainly an inconsistency here: for if a *rāga* is just as sweet out of its assigned season, why should it not be equally sweet out of its ascribed hour ? The psycho-physiological basis, if any, is certainly the same in both cases. *Bhairavī* was allowed to break its bounds restricting it to the early morning, without any adverse effect being felt in its ethos. Who knows other *rāgas* may follow suit.

Musicians, in any case, cannot strictly observe the time rule, at least on the A.I.R., where they often sing 'morning', 'noon', 'evening', *rāgas* together in a single sitting. There are even signs of unrest concerning this limitation among concert goers. People have begun to miss morning *rāgas* in concerts, for most concerts are evening affairs. The south Indians too, once connected the *rāgas* to specific hours, as we know from the testimony of Rāmāmātya, who wrote his *Svaramelakalānidhi* in the 16th century, and is one of the oldest and most honoured authorities in the south.[3] They have given up the notion without any sense of loss.

It would be instructive to examine the history of the *rāga*-time tradition in the north, the weight of whose authority guides us in associating different *rāgas* with different hours of the day.

Most of us have a quite dim and shadowy notion of the antiquity and history of this tradition. If pressed we might say it is as old as the *rāgas* themselves which are very very old. Bhatkhande who was otherwise a very historically alert scholar, calls it a centuries old notion, without being interested in tracing its history in detail. He was of the opinion that though there have been changes in the time of the day assigned to different *rāgas*,

---

[3] *Svaramelakalānidhi*, See '*rāga prakaraṇa.*'

yet the concept that particular *rāga* belongs to particular hours has remained unchanged over the centuries. It was therefore to be honoured.[4]

Looking up the old texts we find that the *rāga*-time theory is certainly not as old as the *rāgas* themselves. The oldest *rāgas* that we know of are older than Bharata (2nd century BC to 2nd century AD), who has left behind instructions concerning the use of the *grāma-rāgas* in dramas. He makes no connection between them and the hours of the day. The first major available text written mainly about *rāgas* is the *Bṛihaddeśī* of Mataṅga. It belongs to the Gupta period or somewhat after, and is usually placed in the 7th or 8th century AD. The *rāgas* in Mataṅga's days, comprised a rich body of forms including *bhāṣā, vibhāṣā, antarabhāṣā*, besides *grāma-rāgas* and *rāgas* proper. This was already an old, well-entrenched corpus of music. Mataṅga speaks of various *gītis* or styles of *rāga* singing and of regional *rāgas* — *rāgas* born in or popular in specific regions[5] — but there are no traces in him of a time theory, as we know it today.

Abhinava Gupta writing towards the end of tenth and beginning of the eleventh century quotes an earlier authority called Kaśyapa, an ancient theorist whose date is unknown.

---

[4] B.N. Bhatkhande, *Ādhunika Hindustānī Rāga-paddhati evaṁ uske Adhyayana karne kī Saralatama Vidhī* — a speech published in *Bhatkhande Smṛti Grantha*. Khairagarh, 1966; see, p.439. Surprisingly, this does not seem to have led him to ask certain disturbing questions which such a realisation ought naturally to pose. One: Did the different *rāgas* assigned to the same hours of the day at different points in history, share certain tonal patterns in common? This seems unlikely, and I believe Bhatkhande would have agreed. Even if he were not to agree, another question arises: Were the tonal patterns which affiliated these *rāgas* to certain hours of the day, the same as those discovered by Bhatkhande? Again a difficult question to answer, but again the answer probably would be 'presumbably not'. What then are we to make of Bhatkhande's tonal affinities and their supposedly psycho-physical basis? This basis has certainly not changed over the last few hundred years, but tonal patterns corresponding to a particular time of the day appear to have done so. How is one to explain this change?

[5] cf. '*vangāldeśa sambhūtā vaṅgālī divyarūpiṇi/eṣā hyantarabhāṣā vai kāliṅge sā tu gīyate*: *Bṛhaddeśī*, p. 127 (Trivendrum edition). The second *rāga*, an *antarabhāṣā*, belonging to, or popular in, Orissa was named *Kālindī*.

Kaśyapa speaks of the seasonal aspect of *rāgas*:
"(*Rāga) preṅkholita* should be sung in spring, so should *mālavapañ-cama. Ṭakkarāga, gauḍakakubha, bhinnaṣaḍaja, kaiśika* and *bhin-napañcama* are favoured in summer and the subsequent seasons."[6]

Later *saṅgita* texts bracket Kaśyapa with Mataṅga and Yāsṭika and others as hoary teachers, Kaśyapa perhaps may be placed in the same period as Mataṅga, that is the 7th or the 8th century AD or perhaps, still earlier.

Nānyabhūpāla, a king of Mithilā, writing a century after Abhinava Gupta, is the first person, I have been able to discover, who speaks of a connection between musical forms and an assigned hour of rendering them. Beginning his chapter on *rāgas,* (chapter seven) in his *Bharata-bhāṣya,* he connects different *gītis* to different hours *(yāmas*) of the day. The two *gītis, śuddhā* and *bhinnā* are assigned to the first *yāma* or *prahara* (a three-hour period) of the day. The *gīti*, *gauḍī* is placed at mid-day, *vesarā* in the first part of the day and *sādharaṇā* is said to be '*sādhāraṇa*' or 'common to all hours of the day'.

These *gītis*, as is well-known, were not *rāgas* or similar forms, but various styles of rendering *rāgas*, akin to the *bānīs* of *dhrupada* and the different *gāyakīs* of present-day music. Immediately after speaking of *gītis* and their appropriate hours of singing, Nānya proceeds to proclaim:

"The *bhāṣās* of different *rāgas* fall within the same time bracket (*kāla*) as the *rāgas* to which they are attached".

He does not give details regarding the time of the day to which specific *rāgas* were to be rendered. He speaks only of the *gītis* and their time. However, different groups of *rāgas* were assigned to different *gītis*. The time of a *rāga* was presumably to be known through its *gīti.* What is more remarkable in this context is that Nānya assigns *gītis* or *rāgas* to specific hours

[6] Verses 74-75 of *Nāṭyaśāstra* with the *Abhinava Bhāratī*, G.O.S edition, Vol. IV, p. 78.

not because of aesthetic, but religious reasons. Unlike the listeners of today, he does not seem to have felt an affinity of 'mood' or 'ethos' between a specific hour and a specific *rāga*; what he said was that it is more 'auspicious' to sing a particular *rāga*, or a *rāga*-like form such as *bhāṣā*, at a particular hour. With this, too, he adds a rider: "All these (*bhāṣās*) are equally meritorious and result in eternal merit whenever they are sung; the rule concerning special hours of singing them is meant only for added religious merit (*śreyoviśeṣāya*)."[7]

For two or three centuries after Nānyadeva we have texts which, for our purposes, may be devided into two categories: those that speak of a connection between *rāgas* and their hour of singing and those that do not. Someśvara III, another king and a contemporary of Nānyadeva, who ruled in the Deccan in the beginning of the twelfth century, has a big section on music in his *Mānasollāsa*. He speaks of no connection between *rāgas* and hours of the day. The reason perhaps was that he was chiefly interested in music as a *vinoda*, a source of aesthetic pleasure: he is silent concerning the extramusical 'auspicious' qualities of *rāgas*.[8] This is not to imply that Someśvara was an irreligious man. Indeed, his section on song contains many hymns and ends with the exhortation that the *prabandhas* (musical compositions) he has spoken of, should be sung before the gods with due devotion.[9] But he evidently saw no merit, religious or other, in associating *rāgas* with particular hours. His son Jagadekamalla, too, wrote on music. Jagadekamalla's *Saṅgīta Cūḍāmaṇi* is also silent concerning *rāgas* and their specific hour of singing;

---

[7] *apāṁ śreyoviśeṣāya kālasya niyamaḥ smṛtaḥ/gīyate sarvakāle tu sarvā nityārtha-siddhaye*, Ch.VII verse 7. The First word in this verse, *apāṁ*, is clearly a scribal error; it makes no sense. Nānyadeva had written *āsāṁ*, referring to the *bhāṣās*. The edition of the *Bharatabhāṣya,* to which I refer is edited by Chaitanya P. Desai, pub. Indirā Kalā Saṅgīta Vishvavidyālaya, Khairāgarh.

[8] His section on music, Chap.16, *viṁśati* 4, of *Māmasollāsa,* is titled, '*Gīta-Vinoda*'.

[9] Ibid, verses 559-560, p. 81, Vol.III of the G.O.S edition of the *Mānasollāsa.*

though it does, at least on one occasion, speak of a seasonal connection, calling *deśīhiṇḍola* a spring-*rāga.*[10]

The two important texts after those of Nānya and Someśvara are the *Saṅgīta-samayasāra*, of Pārśvadeva and the *Saṅgīta-ratnākara* of Śārṅgadeva. Śarṅgadeva wrote early in the 13th century. Pārśvadeva's date is not certain. Many believe him to have been slightly earlier. Pārśvadeva does not speak of any connection between *rāgas* and a prescribed time of singing, though he speaks of *rāgas* in detail. Śārṅgadeva, however, diligently notes the hour of the day against every *rāga* that he describes, using phrases like *geyo'hnaḥ prathame yāme* (to be sung during the first *yāma* or *prahara* of the day), *madhyame'hno geyaḥ* (to be sung during mid-day) and the like.[11] Śārṅgadeva connects *rāgas* to seasons also.

Śārṅgadeva had avowedly based his description of *rāgas* on earlier authorities, which he copiously names. We do not know, however, his source for the ascription of hours to *rāgas*. Earlier works available to us, we have seen, do not make such ascriptions. Nānyadeva makes a connection between *gītis* and hours of the days, but his ruling is made very half-heartedly. The time factor in his view did not do more than to add a little more auspiciousness (*śreyo-viśeṣa*) to the rendering of a *rāga*. Perhaps the ascriptions noted by Śārṅgadeva were also made in the same spirit. Śārṅgadeva speaks of no aesthetic affinity, a kinship of ethos, between *rāgas* and hours of the day. And it would not be unreasonable to conjecture that he, too, like Nānyadeva, believed that to sing a *rāga* at a particular time made it more auspicious. He may have been guided in this by Nānya whose work he perhaps knew, for he was a very erudite scholar in *saṅgīta* texts.

In any case, neither he nor the tradition before him provides any basis for supposing that an intimate connection of 'ethos' or 'character' was felt by musicians or listeners between a *rāga* and

---

[10] See fn. on p. 75 of the G.O.S. edition of the *Saṅgīta-Cūḍāmaṇi.*

[11] See *Saṅgītaratnākara*, Chapter II, the '*rāgavivekādhyāya*', where such instructions are appended with every *rāga.*

its hour of singing or playing. That was to come later.

A rule which is believed to lead to greater auspiciousness, hence religious merit, tends to become a ritual and turns easily into established convention or customary practice; it thus becomes an ingrained habit; we keep following it even after religious connections are forgotten. This is what seems to have happened in the case of the *rāgas* and their connection with specific hours of the day.

Śārṅgadeva was greatly revered by authors who followed him. His work was accorded an almost canonic authority. The connection he made between individual *rāgas* and specific hours of the day became a convention with later authors, even though the *rāgas* themselves changed and the specific hours to which *rāgas* were connected also did not remain the same.

In the beginning, the *rāga*-time rule seems to have been only loosely observed and allowed flexibility. Pandit Bhatkhande quotes an old dictum to the effect that after ten *daṇḍas* of the night have passed any *rāga* can be sung.[12] Another dictum quoted in the *Saṅgīta Darpaṇa* is that if a king so orders any *rāga* can be sung at any time.[13]

Gradually, as the habit of singing particular *rāgas* at particular hours sunk in, it began to be thought that *rāgas* please only at their allotted hours — '*yathākāle samarābdhaṁ gītaṁ bhavati rañjakam*', as Dāmodara puts it. An aesthetic connection was thus made between a *rāga* and the time to which it had been allotted. Listeners and musicians began to feel that a *rāga* was deeply associated with an hour and so began to perceive an affinity of 'ethos' between the two. The category of the aesthetic was confused with that of the auspicious.

But it was only in modern times with Bhatkhande that an attempt was made to discover structural denominators common to *rāgas* placed in the same time-bracket. Bhatkhande succeeded in making a few generalizations which found great acceptance.

---

[12] *yathākāle samārabdhaṁ gītaṁ bhavati rañjakam/ daśadaṇḍāt paraṁ rātrau kāla-doṣo na vidyate//* quoted on p. 439. *Bhatkhande Smṛti Grantha.*

[13] *rājñādeśātsadā geyā na tu kālaṁ vichārayet-Saṅgīta Darpaṇa* 2, 26.

Modern Hindustani musical theory as well as practice have been greatly influenced by his views and teachings in other ways too.

Yet people have found faults with his generalisations, pointing out notable exceptions. And in any case, as I said earlier, no one has ever tried to display and work out in proper empirical detail the psycho-physiological basis which he believed was the ground for the *rāga*-time connection. It is one thing to find common features in *rāgas* that have been placed in a single time bracket but quite another to show that this points at a deeper psycho-physiological basis for the phenomenon. As will have been clear from the burden of my argument, I think that the association made between a *rāga* and its allotted time is an arbitrary association: it is not embedded in any universal human response, but is culturally conditioned. This I have tried to show through the brief survey of its history. This notion remains localised in the north — the reasons for which I would like to go into in another paper — and has been given up without any adverse consequences in the sister system of the south. Even a culturally-conditioned response may be valuable, but as I have pointed earlier, a deeper musical response tends to undermine rather than support the *rāga*-time association.

CHAPTER – TWELVE

Some Thoughts on the Early History of *Rāgamālā* Paintings

The history of *rāga* paintings shows two distinct phases. In the earlier phase *rāgas* and *rāginis* were conceived and painted as sculpturesque icons of deities. Very few paintings from this phase survive. In the middle of the sixteenth century we witness a transformation in *rāga*-portraiture: *rāga*-images acquire movement; they become dramatic, situational and poetic. *Rāga-mālās* from this later phase are plentiful. When thinking of *rāga-mālā*, it is these paintings that we generally have in mind. What I have to say here has mostly to do with the earlier phase of *rāga* paintings.

Since Sarabhai Nawab's publication of the *Masterpieces of Jain Kalpasūtra Painting* (1956), it has become generally known, that *rāga* miniatures had already come into vogue among Jain circles in the last quarter of the 15th century. Nawab has also pointed out the relation between the early *rāga* paintings and the descriptive *rāga-dhyānas* given by the Jain author Sudhākalaśa, in his 14th century text on music, the *Saṅgītopaniṣatsāroddhāra.*

Saṅgītopaniṣatsāroddhāra is believed to contain the earliest known *rāga-dhyānas*. These *rāga-dhyānas,* unlike the later, more commonly know *rāga*-portraits and descriptive verses, are conceived in the manner of iconic delineations of gods and goddesses.

Ebeling in his recent *Rāgamālā Paintings* has mentioned what he believes to be an earlier text on the subject, namely, the *Rāgasāgara.* This text passes under the hoary names of Dattila and Nārada. Perhaps for this reason Ebeling places the text in either the sceond or the eighth century AD[1] This conclusion does not seem to have been reached by Ebeling on his own, for on this point he quotes the authority of W. Kauffmann, who in his *Rāgas of North India* has dated the *Rāgasāgara* to the period noted above, and has

[1] 'Many believe that Nārada belonged to the second century AD, and Dattila to the eighth'.

also quoted *rāga-dhyānas* from it.

The *Rāgasāgara* is, however, not as early as Ebeling thinks. The reason why the text is sometimes attributed to Dattila or to Nārada is that it is written as a dialogue between Dattila and Nārada in the apocryphal manner of the *Purāṇas*. But apart from the names of the two '*munis*', partaking in the dialogue, there is nothing early about the *Rāgasāgara*. It is an eclectically put together text containing diverse and sometimes not quite well organised matter on various aspects of music. Verse 14 of its second *taraṅga* names the 13th century text *Saṅgītaratnakāra* and its author Śārṅgadeva. So the work was certainly written after him.[2] In classifying *svaras*, it speaks of *cyuta svaras*; and, moreover, it gives a detailed time-scheme for rendering various *rāgas*. Its *rāga-dhyānas* do not always depict the melody in the manner of the icon of a deity, but include dramatic or situational elements characteristic of later *rāga-mālās*. These are all factors which prove the work to be late. Its attribution to Dattila or Nārada is spurious.

In truth, it is unlikely that the notion of a *rāga*-picture, and the related idea of versified *rāga-dhyānas* (word-portraits of a *rāga*), goes back to a period earlier than the 13th century. The *Saṅgītaratnākara* written early in the 13th century has no *rāga-dhyānas* although it is a comprehensive work dealing in detail with all salient aspects of contemporary as well as ancient musical forms. *Saṅgītasamayasāra* by the Jain author Pārśvadeva may perhaps be of almost the same period as the *Saṅgītaratnākara*: this work, too, has no *rāga-dhyānas*. The earliest dated *rāga-dhyānas* are indeed to be found in the *Saṅgītopani-ṣatsāroddhāra* written in 1350. This work, as the name suggests, was an abridgement of the author's own, *Saṅgīopaniṣat*, written in 1324.[3] We can surely assume that

---

[2] *nanu ratnākare śārṅgadevena vikṛtāḥ svarāḥ dvādaśoktāḥ katham te tu saptaiva kathitāḥ svarāḥ. Rāgasāgara*-2, 14. (MS 15015 of the Madras Govt. MSS Library. Copy with the author).

[3] See Introduction to the G.O.S. edition of the *Saṅgītopaniṣatsāroddhāra.*

A seemingly earlier *rāga-dhyāna* also needs to be discussed here. Ram Krishna Kavi in his encyclopaedic, *Bharatakośa* quotes a single *rāga-dhyāna* from Jagadekamalla (1134-1150). The authenticity of this *dhyāna* is, in our view, extremely doubtful. Kavi says that for quotations from Jagadeka he had

this too recorded *rāga-dhyānas.*

There is another significant pointer towards the fact that *rāga-dhyānas* are a comparatively later phenomena. Rāṇā Kumbha of Mewar wrote a comprehensive treatise on music, the *Saṅgītarāja,* in the 15th century; like the *Saṅgītaratnākara* it is a detailed and thorough study of both ancient and contemporary music. Unlike the *Saṅgītaratnākara,* it does have *rāga-dhyānas.* Many of these *rāga-dhyānas,* with negligible modifications, are the same as those given by Sudhākalaśa.

---

consulted a MS of Jagadeka's *Saṅgitacūḍāmaṇi* which was incomplete and contained only the chapters on *tāla, rāga* and *nṛtya.* A *Saṅgītacūḍāmaṇi* has now been published by the Gaekwad Oriental Series (Baroda, 1958). The MS. which Kavi may have consulted was not available to the editor of this edition. The printed edition, too, has an incomplete text. Its section on *rāga* does not have many of the verses quoted by Kavi under the name of Jagadeka. Kavi quotes the descriptions of many *rāgas* from Jagadeka but, significantly enough, only one *rāga-dhyāna.* This is curious and unless the MS utilised by Kavi is examined, the authenticity of this single *rāga-dhyāna* is bound to remain questionable. Kavi has remarked: "There is a work in Malabar called *Sāra* which is only a recast of Jagadeka's work with later additions". He adds, "Pārśvadeva (author of *Saṅgītasamayasāra*) has incorporated Jagadeka's work seemingly as his own" (*Bharatakośa,* Introduction, p. iv). Pārśvadeva, we observe, gives no *rāga-dhyānas.* Further, Someśvara, the father of Jagadeka, and the author of *Mānasollāsa,* which contains a large section on music and describes many *rāgas,* also gives no *rāga-dhyānas.* All this casts great doubt upon the authenticity of the lone *rāga-dhyāna* quoted by Kavi from Jagadeka. We think that the quotation is really from the Malabar work cited by Kavi as *Sāra:* the work which Kavi calls a recast of Jagadeka's treatise and which also has much 'later additions'. It is not unlikely that Kavi has half-unthinkingly quoted a *dhyāna* from this work under the name of Jagedaka although the *dhyāna* was a later addition.

Another circumstance which points at the spuriousness of the alleged *dhyāna* from Jagadeka is the fact that Kavi also quotes *jāti-dhyānas* from him. *Jātis* were ancient melodies, pre-dating *rāgas.* In ancient works like the *Nāṭyaśāstra* and *Dattilam* which describe these melodies, no *dhyānas* are given. The idea of a *jāti-dhyāna* is indeed, entirely absent in subsequent works on music, too, where *jātis* are carefully described on the basis of ancient works. Authors like Abhinava (10th-11th centuries AD). Nānyadeva (11th century AD), Śārṅgadeva (13th century AD) and even Rāṇā Kumbha (15th century AD) describe *jātis* with a great wealth of detail, but they do not speak of *dhyāna* for these ancient forms. *Dhyānas* for *jātis* were, evidently, composed late in an age when the idea that every melody should have a *dhyāna* had become well-entrenched.

It is interesting to note that Kumbha does not give *rāga-dhyānas* for all the *rāgas* that he delineates. He gives *dhyānas* for only a group of comparatively later *rāgas*. Evidently, *rāga-dhyānas* had come into vogue only lately and it was not yet thought that every *rāga* should have a *dhyāna*.

The evidence leads us to infer that Sudhākalaśa, the Jain from Western India, is the earliest known author who gives us *rāga-dhyānas*. But certainly it would be hasty to assert that he was the first to compose *rāga-dhyānas*. This, however, would raise the question: Can we trace *rāga-dhyānas* which antedate him ? We shall attempt an answer to this question. Our answer has no claim to be conclusive, but we hope that it will throw an interesting light on the subject.

Introducing his section on *rāga-dhyānas*, Sudhākalaśa says that the number of *rāgas* is as great as sixteen thousand, for each of Kṛṣṇa's gopīs had created a *rāga*. It was, he adds, impossible to know so many *rāgas* and only some had retained a well-defined form.[4]

This seems to point at the fact that the notion of *rāga*-forms had Vaiṣṇava connections in Sudhākalaśa's mind. His remarks indeed, lead us to interesting thoughts. Many of us are familiar with the old story in the Vaiṣṇava tradition of how *rāgas* and *rāginīs*, personified as human beings, became deformed due to Nārada's faulty singing.[5] This story is revealing for our purpose in several ways. It occurs, what appears for the first time, in the *Bṛhaddharma Purāṇa*, a work of the *Upa-purāṇa* literature, which is perhaps earlier than the *Saṅgītopaniṣatsāroddhāra* of Sudhākalaśa.

It would be worthwhile here to recount the Nārada story as given in the *Bṛhaddharma Purāṇa* in some detail: Nārada had once called upon Nārāyaṇa in his heavenly abode, Vaikuṇṭha, where

---

[4] *Saṅgītopaniṣatsāroddhāra* 3. 72-73.

[5] Fox Strangways writing on Indian music in the early twentieth century, mentions this story. But he does not mention the source of the story. Fox Strangways, A.H., *The Music of Hindostan*, p. 75; (Oxford 1975, reprint from the first ediiton, 1914).

Nārāyaṇa was sitting with the goddesses Lakṣmī and Sarasvatī. Nārāyaṇa requested Nārada to sing. Nārada questioned him about the theory of music. Nārāyaṇa spoke to Nārada about *nāda* and *svara,* and also *rāgas* and *rāginīs*. He spoke of six *rāgas*, each of whom had six *rāginīs* as his wives. Every *rāga,* he said, had also a male attendent and each of the *rāginīs*, a serving maid.

After Nārāyāṇa's instructions, Nārada began to sing. His rendering of *rāgas* was not what it should have been, and Sarasvatī derisively laughed at him. Nārada became dejected. To cheer him up, Nārāyaṇa took him around Vaikuṇṭha. Nārada saw at one place a number of deformed beings and wanted to know who they were. Nārāyaṇa told him that they were the *rāgas* and *rāginīs* who had suffered mutilation due to Nārada's mishandling.

Nārāyaṇa then called upon Śiva to sing. Śiva sang a hymn to Kṛṣṇa in the *rāga gāndhāra*. The *rāga* himself appeared before those present. Another song was sung by one of Kṛṣṇa's female messengers. Śiva then sang again. His singing caused one of the wives of *gāndhāra rāga*, the *rāginī śrī* to present herself. *Gāndhārarāga* and *rāginī śrī* have been described as they appear. The descriptions bear definite and unmistakable characteristics of *rāga-dhyānas*; they are also similar in spirit to those of Sudhākalaśa. Gāndhāra is described in the following terms:

Resplendent in ornaments of gold,
Beautiful beyond compare
With a hue like that of a fresh rain-cloud
He wears a yellow dress
And holds in his hands a pair of lotus-flowers.[6]

Rāginī śrī has a description similar in spirit:

She has an unstained body like fired gold
In her two hands she holds a pair of lotuses.
Wearing ornaments of a great variety
and a bright dress

---

[6] *lasatsuhemābharaṇaṁ samujjvalannavāmbudabhāsamapūrvasundaraṁ gṛhītapītāmbarapaṅkajadvayam...*

Bṛhaddharmapurāṇa, madhyakhaṇḍa, 14, 86.

śrī rāginī shines with a similing face.[7]

R.C. Hazra has analysed the *Bṛhaddharma Purāṇa* in his *Studies in the Upapurāṇas*. He opines that the *Purāṇa* was composed towards the end of the 13h century. Unlike many other *Purāṇas*, the *Bṛhaddharma* forms a single unitary whole, and it seems that unlike many other *Purāṇas* all of it was composed at the same period.[8] If Hazra is right, then we have here *rāga-dhyānas* which antedate Sudhākalaśa.

Hazra's main arguments for dating the *Bṛhaddharma*, which, he says, was composed in Bengal, are therefore worth noting. The *Bṛhaddharma*, he argues, is post-Jayadeva, because Jayadeva's style is copied in the songs sung by Śiva and by Kṛṣṇa's *dūtī*.[9] The work, he further says, is pre-Caitanya, for its Vaiṣṇavism shows no Caitanya influence. Hazra further argues that the picture of Bengal reflected in the *Purāṇa* is of an age when Muslim rule in Bengal was yet quite recent and not yet total, since Hindu kings were evidently important and still held some power. There are, moreover, verses in the *Purāṇa* which, Hazra believes, exhort these Hindu rulers to muster arms in order to oppose the aliens.[10] This he says could have been meaningful only in the early period of Muslim conquest. These are the arguments which lead Hazra to place the *Purāṇa* late in the thirteenth century.

If the arguments are not clinching, they are surely suggestive. Swami Prajñānānanda, however, thinks that the *Purāṇa* was composed in the fourteenth or early fifteenth century.[11] He feels that the system of music reflected in the *Purāṇa* is a late system

---

[7] *jvalatsuvarṇāmalacārukāyikā karadvaye padmayugañca bibhratī vicitrabhūṣābharaṇojjvalāṁśukā śrīrāginī rājatasasmitānanā...*

Ibid, *madhyakhaṇḍa,* 14.93.

[8] Hazra, R.C., *Studies in the Upapurāṇas,* vol. II, p. 461 (Sanskrit College, Calcutta, 1963).

[9] The *dhruva* or refrain from the *dūtī's* song, in *rāginī śrī,* is as follows:
keśava kamalamukhīmukhakamalam
kamalanayanakalayātulamamalam
kuñjagehe vijanetivimalam.

[10] Hazra, R.C., *op. cit.*, p. 460.

[11] Prajñānānanda, *Rāga O Rūpa* (Bengali) p. 70, (Darjeeling, 1977).

belonging to these later centuries. Now, it is certianly true that the *rāga-rāginī* classification of musical forms recorded in the *Purāṇa* is of a comparatively later date, but there is no reason to believe that this system was unknown in the late thirteenth century. *Saṅgītamakaranda*, attributed to Nārada, contains such a classification and it is perhaps a text of this period. *Aparājitapṛcchā,* a text which can be dated much more securely to the middle of the 12th century,[12] already contains a *rāga-rāginī* classification. This text speaks of six *rāgas* and thirty-six *rāginīs:* each *rāga* being associated with six *rāginīs,* as in much of later classifications. The *rāginīs* are spoken of as having emerged from the *rāga* with which they are associated.[13] Yet a man-wife relation is also implied between a *rāga* and its associated *rāginīs*: a *rāginī,* it is said, should be sung only with the *rāga* from which it has emerged, for making any other association would be like committing adultery.[14]

Though the *Bṛhaddharma* cannot be placed in a period antedating the *Saṅgītopaniṣatsāroddhāra* with absolute certainty, there is a strong likelihood that the *Purāṇa* is an earlier work. And, what is more significant, like other *Purāṇas*, it certainly contains myths and legends which were formulated before the period when the *Purāṇa* was actually written down.

To my mind, one myth which shows a tell-tale sign of belonging to a period prior to the *Saṅgītopaniṣatosāroddhāra* is

---

[12] M.P. Vohra and M.A. Dhaky: 'The date of the *Aparājitapṛcchā*', *Journal of the Orietnal Institute*, Baroda, vol. IX., 1960.

[13] The six *rāgas* listed are: *Śrī-rāga, Vasanta, Pañcama, Bhairava, Megharāga* and *Naṭṭanārāyaṇa.* Each has the following *rāginīs:*
śrī-rāga: gaurī, kolā, gāndhārī, drāviḍī, mālakośikā, devagāndhārī.
vasanta: hiṇḍolā, kośikā, rāmagirī, padmamañjarī, guḍagrīvā, deśākhyā.
bhairava: bhairavī, gurjarī, bhāṣā, velāvalī, karṇāṭī, kalahaṁsā.
pañcama: triguṇā, khambhāvatī, ābherī, kakubhā, virāṭī, sāverī.
megharāga: baṅgālī, mādhurī, kāmodā, sādhakā, devaśrī, devamālā.
naṭṭanārāyaṇa: troṭakī, moṭakī, dumbinaṭṭā, varāṭakā, gāndhārī, sindhumalhārī.

Aparājitapṛcchā, sūtra 238, 15-21.

[14] *yadrāgadyāḥ samutpannāḥ gīyate tena tāḥ saha/ yadanyathāmiśritaṁ taddușyate paradāravat//*

Ibid. *sūtra* 238, 22.

the Nārada myth we have just related. The reason why I think it to be older is that here in this story we seem to see the idea of *rāga-dhyānas* taking shape in a seminal form as it were. The story, I think, presents us with the mythopoeic process by which *rāga-dhyānas* came into being.

Musical experience convinces us that every *rāga* has a *rūpa* of its own and that this is a living, dynamic *rūpa* both in form and spirit. Every *rāga*, in other words, has a distinct personality. The metaphor of a living and individual human being naturally comes to the mind. It was certainly this metaphor which gave rise to the idea of personified *rāgas* with *rāginīs* as their spouses. Nārāyaṇa's music lesson to Nārada in the *Bṛhad-dharma* assumes the existence of such personified *rāgas*: a notion already present in the *Aparājitapṛcchā*. But this metaphor of *rāgas* in human form is then carried a step forward by the Purāṇic poet and used to construct the allegory of *rāgas* becoming deformed in limb and body through Nārada's mishandling. Later in the story, the *Purāṇa* illustrates how a proper rendering could manifest a *rāga* in its undeformed, resplendent form. On this occasion the two *rāgas* (a *rāga* and a *rāginī*) sung by Śiva, appear bodily on the scene as individuals. It was felt as appropriate by the Purāṇic poet to describe these two *rāgas* as they appear as persons. The *rāgas*, however, could not be described as if they were ordinary men and women: they were thought to be transcendent entities. The Purāṇic poet found it fit to describe them in terms of iconic features associated with deities.

The *rāga-dhyānas* occuring in the *Bṛhaddharma* seem clearly to show a Tantra-like iconography. The Tāntric pantheon had innumerable deties both male and female. Each was characterised distinctively, often for the purpose of making plastic images or pictures. This resulted in a large gallery of iconic portraits, to which new additions were ever being made. It was easy, and, indeed, fitting, to multiply deities in the Tāntric manner; a number of set iconic elements had become established for the purpose which could be readily handled, permuted and combined to form new iconic forms. The *Bṛhaddarma* uses a well-travelled Tāntric *mārga* to create new icons for *rāgas* and *rāginīs*, which it saw as deities.

The *Bṛhaddharma Purāṇa* has definite Vaiṣṇava leanings, but it also evinces a great influence of Tāntrism, which, in medieval times, exercised sway over every *sampradāya*. This influence was felt all the more in Bengal where the *Bṛhaddharma* was written. Its poet when called upon to portray a *rāga* and a *rāginī* must have found it the most natural of things to employ the ready-to-hand and readily malleable repertoire of iconic forms in which Tantra was so rich. Elsewhere, too, the *Bṛhaddharma* employs the same method in calling up new iconic portraits, as for instance, in picturing the plant *tulasī*[15] or the twelfth day of the lunar month, *dvādaśī tithi* as deities.[16]

The idea of a *rāga-dhyāna* can, I think, be traced thus to the Nārada-story in the *Bṛhaddharma*. The idea was not an entirely novel conception: since early times it was believed that each musical note had a colour, a *varṇa* (in the sense of social class) and also a specific deity, though the note was not itself deified. What was new in a *rāga-dhyāna* was that *rāgas* themselves were turned into some kind of minor deities, and portrayd in iconic forms.

Once the idea of *rāga-dhyāna* was fomulated, it quickly disseminated and acquired various forms. The painterly forms given to *rāgas* have never been uniform. Throughout the history of *rāga* painting, *rāga*-portraiture has had many different, and distinct schools. The very classification of *rāgas*, and, indeed, even the names of *rāgas* that are included in different lists of major forms have followed different traditions. The *rāga*-list given in the *Saṅgītopaniṣatsāroddhāra* is quite distinct from that of the *Bṛhaddharama*. The *rāga-dhyānas*, too, are different, though they follow the same Tantra-like iconic pattern. The *Saṅgītopaniṣatsāroddhāra* has, in addition, *dhyāna*-verses not only for *rāgas* but also for such smaller units of musical structures as

---

[15] *Bṛhaddharma Purāṇa, pūrvakhaṇḍa,* 8, 5-6. Tulasī is described as:
śyāmāṅgi cāruvadanā divbhujā smitabhaṣiṇi
śaṅkhapadmakarā śvetavasanā yuvatī satī
nānālaṅkārabūṣāḍhyā sindūrāruṇamālikā.

[16] She is described as *gaurāṅgi, pītavasanā, dvibhujā* and *śyāmapṛṣṭhikā*. Ibid., *pūrvakhaṇḍa*, 23, 51.

tāna, mūrchanā, śruti and *svara*. In some early *Kalpasūtra*-miniatures, these, too, have been painted as if they were icons.[17]

Rāga-dhyānas and *rāga-mālā* paintings, generally known today are quite different in form and spirit from the descriptions in the *Saṅgītopaniṣatsāroddhāra* and from the *rāga* paintings found in late fifteenth century illustrated *Kalpasūtras*. Later *rāga-mālā* paintings and their associated *dhyānas* do not portray *rāgas* as icons, but picture them as characters within some kind of an episodic situation. A personified *rāga*-form is presented within what may be likened to a dramatic tableau. As a result, unlike earlier *rāga*-paintings, the later *rāga-mālā* is marked by action. A *rāga* is usually pictured as a man or a woman performing some action, or as the centre of some action, within a landscape or an architectural setting or an interior, or as is often the case, a combination of these.

In a *rāga-mālā* picture the character representing the *rāga* is usually easy to recognise. But the important thing is that it does not alone represent the *rāga*: the *rāga* is represented by the whole situation within which the *rāga*-character forms only a part. This is quite distinct from earlier iconic representations of *rāgas* where the icon of a personified deity was all important. In later *rāga-mālās*, the situational or 'dramatic element' is so important that in some cases where the painting of a *rāga* shows more than one person, it is difficult to say which of them represents the *rāga*. In a representation of the *rāginī śyāma-kalyāṇa*, from an eighteenth century Deccan set (in the collection of the Archaeological museum, Hyderabad, reproduced in Ebeling, *Rāgamālā Painting* p. 203 fig. 99), two ladies are shown sitting in a pensive mood. One has a female attendant wielding a *camara*. It is difficult here, as Ebeling has also remarked, to say which lady represents the *rāginī*. Evidently, the whole picture represents the *rāginī*. In another miniature showing the rāginī *vasantī* (reproduced in Ebeling, *Rāgamālā*

[17] Nawab, Vidya Sarabhai, 419 *Illustration of Indian Music and Dance in Western Indian Style,* figures: 1-107. (Ahemedabad, 1964).

Painting, p. 288), two girls are shown picking flowers. Again it is not possible to say which of them is the *rāginī*: apparently, both together are.[18]

Though a *rāga* is shown within an episode, its picture is limited to that one single episode. It is not made to move from one episode to another like Kṛṣṇa in a *Bhāgavata* or a *Gīta-Govinda* set or like Ḍholā in a *Ḍholā-Mārū* set. In this, the *rāga*-image is more like paintings illustrating *nāyikā-bheda* poems where every painting represents a single specific situation. Indeed, if one sees the same *rāga* in another situation, one can be sure that the image belongs to another school of *rāga-mālā* painting.

Limiting a *rāga* to a single situation or image seems surprising, for a *rāga* as rendered musically, shows changing moods unfolding over a period of time. Its visual representation seems to demand a similar unfoldment through multiple images woven together. The only ambitious attempt that I know of at visualising musical movement through a series of suitably changing images has been made by Walt Disney in his film Eroica based on Beethoven's well-known symphony of the same name. The dynamic movement possible in a film is not possible in painting, yet the miniaturist could have represented a *rāga* through a set of paintings rather than one single miniature.

The images in later *rāga-mālās* are conceived as images diffused with a poetic rather than an iconic spirit. The influence of the *rīti* poetry of the age, dominated by themes of love, is palpable in many of the images. A great number of images found in later *rāga-mālās* are obviously drawn from the *nāyaka-nāyikā* poems of the age. Their painterly-style or *kalam* is also modelled on the representations of the *nāyaka-nāyikā* theme which had begun to be popular among patrons of the miniature during the fifteenth century and after. The earliest of the new style *rāga-mālās* (middle and late 16th century) already echo the

[18] The same difficulty of identification can be noted in the representation of *gajadharā*, a *putra* of *megha*; *surmanad*, a *putra* of *hiṇḍola* and *mālava*, a *putra* of *śrī*, reproduced in Ebeling, *Rāgamālā Painting* p. 296. These representations show two people engaged in a fight: either could be the *rāga* in question.

style of early miniatures based on *Vasanta-Vilāsa* (1451), *Caurapañcāśikā* (1550) and *Laura Candā* (1550).

The changes in form that took place in the later *rāga-mālā* are indicative of a change in spirit. What was an icon with trans-human meanings was now brought down to a human plane, albeit with few exceptions as in the case of some *rāgas* like *Bhairava*. The process of transformation is not very clear. Few texts and paintings survive from the period of transition and these provide no clue in this matter. The newer taste was for greater movement and a more episodic and dramatic manner of painting. *Rāgamālā*, as a genre, could have appealed to the newer taste only if it could mould itself to the new manner of painting. And this is, indeed, what happened. *Rāgas* as deities were in this process, desecrated. But this aroused no feelings of compunction, for though imagined as deities, *rāgas* were never part of any cult or divine pantheon. Their portrayal could be suitably transformed to occupy a place in the repertoire of themes that had begun to capture the imagination of painters and patrons of a newer age. This done, the *rāga-mālā* entered the mainstream of the new schools of miniaturists.

An interesting question may be asked here: Did the transformation in *rāga-mālā* reflect in any way a similar transformation in music? This is difficult to answer, though a transformation in music contemporaneous with the transformation in *rāga-mālā* painting does not seem to have occurred. What did occur was a major transformation in the art of painting of which *rāga-mālā* was only a genre. It was, I think, this change in the painter's approach to his art that entailed a change in the conception of *rāga*-portraiture. A similar thing can be witnessed today. Over the last hundred years, no radical transformation has occurred in music, but *rāga*-images painted today by such modern painters as M.F. Hussain and Laxman Pai are certainly very different in spirit and form from those of the preceding period. What has happened is a transformation in the painter's attitude to his art.

CHAPTER – THIRTEEN

Some Reflections on the *Vīṇā* in Gupta Coinage

Samudragupta's *praśasti* calls him a great musician. He is described as surpassing Nārada and Tumburu in musical skill.[1] The *vīṇā* type coins minted by Samudragupta show him as playing the *vīṇā* (Pl.VIII. 8). They are proof that the *praśasti* — allowing for the usual poetic exaggeration — was not voicing an empty praise. The coins also reveal that Samudragupta took great pride in his musicianship, for no king before him had minted coins of this kind.

Samudragupta was not the only Gupta king who minted *vīṇā* type coins. Similar coins minted by his grandson, Kumāragupta-I, have also come to light (in the Bayana Hoard). Presumably, Kumāragupta-I, too, was a *vīṇā*-playing musician. But no *praśasti* extolling Kumāragupta's musicianship has been uncovered. It might be argued that Kumāragupta-I, was merely emulating his illustrious grandfather in minting a coin-type initiated by him, without having any active personal interest in *vīṇā*-playing. There are, however, strong grounds which suggest that Kumāragupta-I, too, was, in all likelihood, a musician. Skill in music was not a rare thing among ancient Indian kings.

Kṛṣṇa and Arjuna, the royally-born heroes of the *Mahābhārata*, were renowned for their skill in music. The *Harivaṁśa* ascribes to Kṛṣṇa the authorship of a new kind of music, the *chālikya-gāndharva*.[2] Coming to a "historical" period, we hear of Udayana's excellence on the *vīṇā*. So famous was this 6th century BC king of Kauśāmbī for his *vīṇā* that legends have preserved the name of his instrument also. His *vīṇā*, called the *ghoṣavatī*, evidently played a central role in Udayana's chief exploit, the wooing and winning of

---

[1] *niśitavidagdhamatigāndharvalalitairvrīḍitātridaśapatigurutumburunār-adādeḥ*... Fleet, *Gupta Inscriptions* No.1, p.8.

[2] *Harivaṁsa*, 89, 66-83 (Citraśālā press edition).

Vāsavadattā, daughter of Pradyota, king of Mālavā. Many stories of the magical powers of this *vīṇā* were current during ancient times. The *ghoṣavatī*, it was said, could subdue the wildest and the most violent of raging elephants with ease.

King Khāravela who ruled over Kaliṅga in the second century BC was another king who prided in his proficiency in music. The Hathi-gumpha inscription speaks of his skill in the art.[3] Another ruler, Mahākṣatrapa Rudradāman in the Junagadha inscription of 2nd Century AD speaks of his mastery over music.[4] Early Buddhist literature speaks of many kings and princes who were experts in music.[5] Kālidasa in his *Raghuvaṁśa* says that the royal laps of Agnivarṇa were graced equally by his sweet-spoken queen and his sweet-voiced *vīṇā*.[6]

Evidently it was not uncommon for kings to be musicians. Many ancient authorities speaking of the education of kings had, indeed, prescribed music as part of a princes'curriculum. Bhīṣma, lecturing Yudhiṣṭhira on polity (*rājadharma*) in the *Anuśāsanaparva* of the *Mahābhārata* advises him that he should, as a king, acquire a knowledge of music along with other skills and arts necessary for a good ruler.[7] *Rāmāyaṇa* also includes music among the branches of learning that a prince was required to be versed in.[8] The Hathigumpha inscription of Khāravela informs us that the king had learnt music along with military arts

---

[3] *'tatiya puna vase gamdhavvavedabudho dapanatagītavāditasandaṁsanāhi usava-samājakarāpanāhi kiḍāpayati nagarī': Epigraphica Indica*, Vol. 20, p. 79.

[4] *'gāndharvanyāyādyānāṁ vidyānāṁ mahatīnāṁ pāraṇadhāraṇavijñāna-prayogāvāptavipulakīrtinā... mahākṣatrapeṇa rudradāmnā:* Ibid., Vol. 8, p. 44.

[5] *Mahāvagga* 10, 2 (p. 376 of the Pali Publication Board edition brought out by the Bihar Government). See the story of Prince Dīghāyu. Also Kusa Jātaka (No. 531). Mahāumagga Jātaka (No. 546) etc. Buddha himself was taught music (*Lalitavistara*, Ch. 12, p. 108 of the Mithila Vidyapitha edition). The story of Kuṇāla who sang under the balcony of king Aśoka is also noteworthy.

[6] *aṅkamaṅkaparivartanocite tasya ninyaturaśūnyatāmubhe vallakī ca hṛdayaṅgamasvanā valguvāgapi ca vāmalocanā. Raghuvaṁśa* 19, 13.

[7] *Mahābhārata, Anuśāsanaparvan* 104, 46-50.

[8] *History of Dharmaśāstra,* P.V.Kane, Vol. III, p. 49. Rāma and his brothers, says Kane, are described as proficient in *Vedas, vedāṅgas, rājavidyā, dhanurveda* and also *gāndharvaveda.* (*Rāmāyaṇa* 1, 18, 24, 26; 2, 1, 20; 2, 21, 34-35; 5, 35, 13-14).

as a prince.[9] The practice of teaching music to princes doubtless continued during Gupta times and after. It certainly was in vogue during Harṣa's period. Bāṇa in his *Kādambarī* speaks of princes being trained in music.[10]

The vast Jain literature of popular tales records many stories of princesses who held *svayaṁvaras* in which the condition for winning the hand of the princess was to excel her in playing the *vīṇā*. An early example of such a story is to be found in the, significantly named, *Vīṇālambhaka* of *Vasudeva Hiṇḍī,* a work noticed before the seventh century AD, and perhaps composed during the Gupta age or immediately after. In later Jain tales the *vīṇā-svayaṁvara* became an established and oft-repeated motif; it occurs in the works of Hariṣeṇa (9th century AD), Vādībha (11th century AD), Haricandra (13th century AD), and others. Stories of princesses being won in *vīṇā-svayaṁvaras* belong to the realm of imagination, but they are nonetheless symptomatic of the fact that *vīṇā*-playing was a well-respected art, cultivated even by royalty.

It would not, then, have been out for the ordinary Kumāragupta-I to have been a musician like his grandfather Samudragupta.

The Udayana legend records another intriguing fact. It was believed that the *vīṇā ghoṣavatī* as well as the skill in playing on it was handed down from father to son in the Kasusāmbī royal family to which Udayana belonged. In Bhāsa's *Pratijñāyaugandha-rāyaṇam* a play, the script of which, in the main, may perhaps go back to the third century BC, Pradyota, king of Avantī, speaks of Udayana's supreme haughtiness of character. One of the principal reasons he gives is "*darpayati cainaṁ dāyādyakramāgataḥ gāndharvo vedaḥ*" (his skill in music which he has received as part

---

[9] Ibid. *loc.cit.* Khāravela states that he learnt *gāndharvaveda* along with *lekha, rūpa* (currency) *gaṇanā* (accountancy) and administration of justice when he was a crown prince. *(Epigraphica Indica* vol. 20, p. 79).

[10] Candrāpīḍa was trained, among other things, in '*vīṇāveṇumurajakāṁsyatāla darduraputaprabhṛtiṣu vādyeṣu*' and '*nāradīyaprabhṛtiṣu gāndharvavedaviśeṣeṣu*': *Kādambarī*, p. 168 (Nirṇayasāgara edition).

of his inheritance makes him insolent).[11]

Another important play on the Udayana-Vāsavadattā theme is the *Vīṇāvāsavadttam.* It has been ascribed by some scholars to Śūdraka. This may well be doubted; but though the problem of its authorship cannot be satisfactorily resolved, the tone, structure and ethos of the play are reminiscent of the Bhāsa dramas (it too, was, moreover, recovered in Kerala), and it bears the mark of being a fairly old production.[12] Udayana's *vīṇā* figures prominently in the play — as the name *Vīṇā-vāsavadattam* implies. The *vīṇā* has been described as '*vatsarājakula-sarvasvaṁ vīṇāratnam*' (Jewel of a *vīṇā*, the ultimate treasure of the Vatsa kings').[13] This allusion lends weight to the story as recorded in Bhāsa's play.

In the Udayana story we have an example of a royal family which treasured musical skill as a family heritage. May this not have been true of the Gupta royal family too? It would be too much to expect that music was literally handed down from father to son, but there is certainly nothing fantastic in thinking that the father was an example to the son, and had him learn music, and the son eventually came to cherish it. No positive proofs can, of course, be adduced. But we do have the fact that grandfather and grandson both played the *vīṇā* and cared enough about music to mint coins showing them as *vīṇā* players. Moreover, given the fact that skill in music was cherished in many royal households throughout the ancient period — and the telling evidence of the Vatsa kings of Kausāmbī — it becomes certainly within the realm of reasonable plausibility that the Gupta household, too, treasured music as a family skill.

There is however one obvious lacuna in our suggestion: there is no evidence that Chandragupta-II was also a musician. Though

---

[11] *Pratijñāvaugandharāyaṇam*, Act. II.

[12] *Vīṇāvāsavadattam.* See Introduction by K.V. Sarma and Preface by V. Raghavan to the Kuppuswami Sastri Research Institute.

[13] *op.cit.*, Act IV (p. 69). (*praviśya vīṇāhastaḥ kañcukīyaḥ*): *"jayatu mahārājaḥ idaṁ khalu śāḷaṅkāyanena preṣṭaṁ vatsarājakulasarvasvaṁ vīṇāratnam".*

Chandragupta-II issued more coin-types than his father Samudragupta, no coin of his showing him as playning the *vīṇā* has yet come to light. But before giving up our theory, let us pause and reflect a little more on the available evidence, and the absence of it. Firstly, we must not lose sight of the truth that recovery of material evidence - such as coins - from the ancient period has a great element of chance or accidentality. The fact that non-*vīṇā*-type coins of Chandragupa-II have been recovered, does not necessarily mean that no such coins were minted. Prior to the finding of the Bayana Hoard, *vīṇā*-type coins of Kumāragupta-I were also unknown.

Again, the *vīṇā* coin-type was not issued as a major gold coin by any of the emperors. And the ratio of available *vīṇā*-type coins is noticeably small in comparison with the total body of discovered coinage; suggesting that the actual issue, too, was numerically small. Coins of the *vīṇā*-type show Samudragupta at leisure and were perhaps issued as a graceful gesture accompanying the achievement of empire, prosperity and well-being. Significantly, the ratio of coins showing Chandragupta-II as indulging in gracious living is also very small. Of some types, only three or four specimens are known. And one coin type, the so-called king-and-queen-on-couch type, where the king is shown drinking wine — a coin which has formed the basis of much speculation regarding the character and personal traits of Chandragupta-II — is known through only a single specimen. This being so, the fact that no *vīṇā*-type coin of Chandragupta-II is known, can be reasonably said to be due to the vagaries of discovery.[14]

---

[14] However, a gold coin *has* been found which, as described in the *Progress Report of the Archaeological Survey of India*, Western Circle, 1916-17, may be an example of a *vīṇā*-type coin issued by Chandragupta-II. But the identification remains uncertain as no photograph of the coin has been published. The legend on it, as well as its reported description — which itself leaves rooms for doubt — cannot be verified. Its description is as follows:

Obverse: King seated on a high-backed couch, with one foot hanging; wearing waist cloth; hand to the left touching lyre or feeding some animal; legend — *paramabhāgavata maha.*

Reverse: Figure of Lakṣmī seated on a footstool with a seat over it; holds uncertain object in hand; to left crescent; legend — *vikramāditya* (*ḥ*).

Secondly, it has been suggested by Altekar that the letters construed as *rūpākṛti* on one of the couch type coins of Chandragupta-II, actually form the word *rūpakṛtī* and mean, a creator of dramas. Thus Chandragupta-II was perhaps a playwright.[15] If this be true, it would not be surprising if Chandragupta-II also took on active interest in music; for drama, as Kālidāsa says, is a performance-oriented art[16] and music in ancient times was an integral part of drama.[17] Besides, the image of Chandragupta-II, as suggested by some of his coins, is that of a person with epicurean tastes. This, coupled with his interest in literature — of which he is also believed to have been a great-patron — recalls the portrait of a well-cultivated, sophisticated *nāgaraka* as painted by Vātsyāyana in his *Kāmasūtra.* The *vīṇā* always adorned the room of such *nāgarakas.*[18]

There is thus a distinct possibility that Chandragupta-II, too, like his illustrious predecessor issued a *vīṇā* type coin, and it would be premature to conclude that no such coin was ever minted on the strength of the fact that no such coin has been so far recovered. After Kumāragupta-I, Skandagupta was too busy in saving an endangered empire. We expect that he was also taught music as a family tradition or *vidyā-saṁskāra*, but he could not, or did not, keep up the flourishes of his predecessors in minting coins about this or other leisurely occupations. Only three coin types of his have come to light.

As evinced from this description the coin certainly bears resemblances to the *vīṇā* type, especially, with that issued by Kumāragupta-I, where the figure of Lakṣmī(?) is shown as seated on a footstool.

See also, in this connection, fn.2, p. 35'A Lyrist Type Copper Coin' by Bratindranath Mukherjee in the *Journal of the Asiatic Society*, Vol. I, No. I, 1959.

[15] *The Coinage of the Gupta Empire*, pp. 133 -34.

[16] *Parivrājikā*: *deva prayogaprādhānaṁ hi nāṭyaśāstram. kimatra vāgvyavahāreṇa. Mālavikāgnimitram,* Act I.

[17] *Nāṭyaśāstra* (Gaekwad edition) Vol. IV, 28, 7 and *ṭikā*; also 32, 425 and 436.

[18] *Kāmasūtra,* 1, 4, 4. The *sūtra* describing the room of a *nāgaraka* contians the item: *nāgadantāvasaktā vīṇā.* See also *sūtra* 1, 3, 15 where *vīṇā* playing is included among the fine arts to be learnt by the cultivated person.

II

The kings on Gupta coinage are shown as playing a harp *vīṇā*.[19] *Vīṇās* of this type are quite common in early sculptures at Bharhut, Besnagar, Amaravati and the Buddhist caves of Pitalkhora,[20] besides other sites. This *vīṇā* was shaped like a bow that faced down with a tilt or an angle with one end portruding upward, and the other, lower end, forming a hollow belly which served as the sounding board of the instrument. The *vīṇā* strings were stretched across the structure like bow-strings. In playing, the sounding belly was usually placed on the laps. Strings were so arrayed, that in the playing position, the lower a string, the shorter its length. The still surviving south Indian instrument *yāzh* resembles this old *vīṇā*; most similar in structure to the ancient one, however, is the Burmese harp which seems to have been handed down in an almost unchanged form since ancient times.[21]

In the *vīṇā*-type coins, the king is shown sitting on a couch with both legs resting on a foot-board and holding the *vīṇā* on his laps. He is portrayed in profile. The right hand is stretched slightly away from the torso, and is shown striking the strings, while the left hand lies stretched across the lap above the hollow belly of the *vīṇā*. The left hand lies at ease and the palm forms a *mudrā*-like gesture — to which we will have occasion to return. The thumb and fore-fingers are, in some coins, projecting slightly outwards while in others they are bent towards each other in more than a semi-circle. The open palm faces upward with a slight tilt towards the torso. The remaining

---

[19] "The lute of Samudragupta's coins has a long hollow belly covered with a board of seven strings". *The Gupta Gold Coins in the Bayana Hoard,* Altekar, Introduction p. 1 xviii. The instrument is actually of the harp type, one of the most ancient musical instruments, common to all old cultures. The strings are tied across a triangular frame; each string producing a single musical note. The use of the word 'lute' by Altekar here is unhappy.

[20] *The Coinage of the Gupta Empire*, p. 74.
'Saptatantri Veena in the sculptures of Buddhist caves of Pitalkhora': Swami Prajnananand in *Roopa-Lekha,* Vol. XXXII No. 1, July 1961.

[21] For an illustration and description of the Burmese harp *see 'Die Musikinstrumentre Indiens Und Indonesiens',* Curt Sachs, pp. 140-41.

three fingers are bent palm-wards.[22]

Scholars have talked of the Gupta kings as *vīṇā* players only. But some important considerations have led us to think that the kings are shown as singing, and that *vīṇā*-playing is, in the coin-portrayal, an auxiliary activity. This might appear a little startling, for the *vīṇā* is evident in the picture while singing is not; the kings are shown as actually playing it, while there are no signs to indicate that they were singing. However, we should like to place our considerations and reasoning before you, and perhaps, then, our suggestion will not appear as something bizarre or merely eccentric. Let us, to begin with, consider some common portrayals of modern Indian classical singers. Numerous sketches, paintings or photographs of singers show them sitting with a big *tānpūrā*, their right hand on the strings of the instrument, and the left lying idle on the hollowed-out gourd which acts as the sounding belly. In such portraits, the *tānpūrā* looms literally large; even appearing sometimes to overshadow the singer in size and prominence. Yet, we know that the musician portrayed is a singer, not an instrumental player and that the purpose of the instrument is to act as an accompaniment to the vocal melody.

The *vīṇā* of Samudragupta and Kumāragupta-I, we believe, was also acting as a singer's accompaniment. We will outline our reasons.

Musical instruments of the string group, especially of the harp type, were commonly used in ancient times to accompany song, which was the dominant musical form.[23] It was common in

[22] The kings' posture is almost identical on all *vīṇā*-type coins, though the impression is not always clear. For a fairly clear impression, see the reproduction given by Altekar in *The Coinage of the Gupta Empire*, plate III, No. 16. In this coin thumb and fore-finger are projecting slightly outward. In a coin of Kumāragupta-I, thumb and fore-finger are clearly seen to be inclined towards each other so as to make a circle-like form; see Altekar, *The Gupta Gold Coins in the Bayana Hoard,* plate XXXI, No. 5.

[23] (A famous remark of Śārṅgadeva runs: '*nṛttaṁ vādyānugaṁ proktaṁ vādyaṁ gītānuvarti ca,* (*Saṅgīta Ratnākara* I, 24). Vocal music has traditionally been the major form in India. Ancient musical genres or types were distinguished on the basis of song. *Sāma,* a basically sung form, gave rise to the *jāti*, predominantly a vocal genre. In fact *gāndharva* — the ancient word for

ancient India for singers to accompany themselves on the *viṇā*. Many references can be evinced from literature.

Udayana's legendary *viṇā* is well known to scholars and students of hisotry; what is less known is that legends also speak of Udayana's singing. In the play *Viṇāvāsavadattam,* the *viṇā ghoṣvatī,* whenever played, is used as accompaniment to song. The first instance of its use is in the episode where Udayana sets out to catch a wild elephant. The dramatist portays Udayana as approaching the raging beast with his *viṇā* — which had powers to cast a spell on the wildest of animals.[24] When he comes near the beast, he sings a spell, accompanying himself on the *ghoṣavatī.*[25] Later in the play — in act VIII — Udayana goes to Vāsavadattā's apartments to give her lessons on the *viṇā.* During the first lesson, Vasavadatta feels too shy to make music. Sāṅkṛtyāyanī, the elderly female monk who is Vasavadatta's companion, then requests the king: '*prakṛtyaiva sāpatrapā khalviyam, sandarśanaṁ ca prathamam, tasmādaśaktā devī gātuṁ tantrisparśanādeva vidyārambhaḥ kṛto bhaviṣyati*' ('the lady is bashful by nature. And, as she is meeting you for the first time, she cannot bring herself to sing. Let her be initiated into the art by merely touching the strings'). It is clear from this little speech that learning the *viṇā* implied learning to sing. Indeed, following Vāsavadattā's inability to sing, Sāṅkṛtyayānī asks the king to sing to them an auspicious song, as an appropriate beginning to the lesson. The king complies with a hymn to Viṣṇu accompanying himself on the *viṇā.*[26] His hearers are enthralled, and he sings

---

music — has been defined in the *Nāṭyaśāstra* and *Dattilam* as containing three elements: *svara (*tones) *tāla* (rhythm) and *pada* (words). Clearly the ancients, in thinkiņg of music, thought primarily of songs. In Greece lyric singers used to accompany their songs on the lyre — the songs were, for this reason called lyrics.

[24] Incidentally, in the *Vidhura Paṇḍita Jātaka* (No. 546), we hear of a *hatthi-kānta-viṇā* (*hasti-kānta-viṇā*). This *viṇā* had powers to tame elephants. It may have been used by elephant catchers in ancient times, and, perhaps, the stories of *ghoṣavatī's* power over elephants may have originated out of tales told among elephant-catching circles relating to the power of the *hatthi-kānta-viṇā.*

[25] *Viṇāvāsavadattam*, Act II, *op.cit.*, p. 27.

[26] *Viṇāvāsavadattam*, Act VII, pp. 114-15.

two more songs, one a *praśasti,* the other a love-song. Vāsavadattā's lessons continue, and her love for Udayana grows with her knowledge of the *vīṇā*. In Act VIII, we find that she has become an expert musician. She is requested by her companions to set to music two love-poems which Udayana had sent her. She sings the poems, accompanying herself on the *vīṇā*. Sāṅkṛtyāyanī praises her music, exclaiming that the *vīṇā* playing was wonderfully synchronised with the song.[27]

The practice among singers to accompany themselves on the *vīṇā*, goes back to a still remote antiquity. The *Sūtra* works speak of *vīṇāgāthins* — a class of *brāhmaṇa* or *kṣatriya* singers[28] who, as the name, suggests, accompanied themselves on the *vīṇā*. These singers were employed to sing *gāthās* during sacrificial ceremonies.

---

[27] *tantrīsvarāṇi akṣarāṇi ca anyonyam anupraviṣṭaniva,* ibid., Act VIII (p. 137).

Udayana's *vīṇā*-playing was associated with singing even in some later versions of the Udyayana-Vāsavadattā romance. In Somadeva's *Kathāsaritsāgara,* Udayana has been portrayed as singing while playing the *vīṇā* when approaching the false elephant. He has been described as:
ekākī vādayan vīṇāṁ cintayan bandhanāni saḥ madhuradhvani gāyaṁśca śanairupajagāma tam: Kathāsaritsāgara, 2, 4, 17.
Later in the story, as Vāsavadattā's tutor, he is pictured in a charming verse as:
aṅke ghoṣavatī tasya kaṇthe gītaśrutistathā
puro Vāsavadattā ca tasthau cetovinodinī. Ibid. 2, 4, 32.
It is quite likely that the description of Udayana as both singing and playing the *vīṇā* was part of the original tale as told by Guṇāḍhya; for, significantly enough, we find that Kṣemendra in his *Bṛhatkathāmañjarī* also pictures the king with words like:
kūṭakuñjaramālokya vīṇāmadhuragītibhiḥ... Bṛhatkathāmañjarī 2, 2, 39.
and again:
vīṇāgeyakalājñāne śiṣyeyaṁ bhavatāmiti: Ibid., 2, 2, 47.

[28] The *Hiraṇya Śrauta Sūtra* speaks of *'brāhmaṇau vīṇāgāthinau gāyataḥ'* (14, 2, 6) and again *'rājanyau vīṇāgāthinau gāyataḥ'* (14-2, 17-18). Also *Āpastamba Gṛhya Sūtra*: *gāyatāmiti vīṇāgāthinau śaṁsasti*' (14, 6, 4)..
Sahani in his paper entitled '*Vīṇā* coin-type of Samudragupta and Kumaragupta-I' — *Journal of the Numismatic Society of India,* Vol. XIX — puts forward the suggestion that Samudragupta issued the *vīṇā*-type coins after performing the *aśvamedha* sacrifice — which, too, was celebrated through the issue of appropriate coins — and that he might have played the *vīṇā* in this sacifice as the ritual demands. Perhaps he did, and perhaps he acted as a *vīṇāgāthin,* in which case he would also have rendered songs.

Singing of epic-ballads was another ancient art. The *Rāmāyaṇa*, traditionally considered the *ādikāvya* — the first 'composed' poem as opposed to the 'revealed' body of Vedic *mantras* — was associated with singing right from the inception of its first *śloka* by Vālmīki. The sage, as soon as he had uttered the celebrated *śloka* cursing the *niṣāda*, put it to music and sang it in accompaniment to a string instrument.[29] Later Lava and Kuśa sang the *Rāmāyaṇa* in the court of Rāma in the presence of a distinguished gathering, which included experts in music. Again there was string accompaniment to their singing.[30]

In the *Dīghanikāya* there occurs the story of Pañcaśikha who sings some *gāthās* to the Buddha. He plays the *vīṇā* to his own singing, and so excellent is the total effect that Buddha commends him, saying that his song and his *vīṇā* were in beautiful harmony with each other.[31] The *Mahāvagga* contains the story of prince Dīghāvu, son of Dīghiti, king of Kosala, fallen on bad days, who sang a sorrowful song to his own *vīṇā*-accompaniment, in the elephant-stables of Brahmadatta, king of Kāśī.[32]

In the *Jātakas* there are quite a few instances of singers accompanying their song on the *vīṇā*. The love-lorn king Kusa, whose story is told in the *Kusa Jātaka* (No. 531), plays the *vīṇā* and sings songs of love to attract his estranged queen. The *Cullapralobhana Jātaka* (No. 263) speaks of a dancer who sang with a *vīṇā* in order to arouse passion in the heart of the prince of

---

[29] *padabaddho 'kṣarasamaḥ tantrīlayasamanvitaḥ śokārtasya pravṛtto me śloko bhavatu nānyathā. Rāmāyaṇa,* 1, 2, 18 (Gita Press edition).

[30] Ibid. 7, 94, 2-7.

[31] *'bhagavā pañcaśikhaṁ gandhabhadevaputtaṁ etadavoca - 'samvandanti kho te, pañcaśikha, tantīsaro gītassareṇa gītassaro ca tantīssareṇa; na ca pana pañcaśikha, tantīssaro gītassaraṁ ativattati, gītassaro ca tantīssaram'. Dīghanikāya, Mahāvagga, Sakkapaṇhasuttam.* (pp. 199-200, Pt. II of the Pali Publication Board edition brought out by the Bihar Government).

[32] *'atha kho bhikkhave, dīghāvu kumāra rāttiyā paccūsasamayaṁ paccutthāya hatthisālāyāṁ mañjunā sareṇa gāyi, vīṇāṁ ca vādesi'. Mahāvagga* 10, 2 (p. 376 of the Pali Publication Board edition).

Vārāṇasī. So skillfully balanced was her music-making that the *vīṇā* playing and the singing appeared as one single melody.[33] The *Kākatī Jātaka* (No. 327) has a musician (*gandharva*) who sang *gāthās* to his own *vīṇā* accompaniment.

The *Laṅkāvatara sūtra* (composed sometime during the first two or three centuries of the Christian era) gives a very graphic description of Rāvaṇa, the *rākṣasa* king, who with his retinue attended upon Buddha and sang panegyrics to his glory. He accompanied his song on the *vīṇā*, tuning the strings to the appropriate notes. His song merged effortlessly with the melody produced on the *vīṇā*.[34]

Kalidāsa in the *Uttaramegha* of his *Meghadūta*, portrays the folorn *yakṣiṇī* in a series of poignant word-pictures. One moving *mandākrāntā* verse delineates the *yakṣiṇi* with *vīṇā* on her laps, desiring to while away her sorrow in singing songs marked with the name of her lover; but her falling tears wet the strings of her instrument, making it difficult for her to tune it.[35] Cārudatta, the hero of Śūdraka's *Mṛcchakaṭika,* praising the singing of his friend Rebhila, says that the singing was closely synchronised with string-playing[36] referring evidently, to *vīṇā* accompaniment. In another play by Śūdraka, a *bhāṇa* called *Padmaprābhṛtaka*[37] *vīṇā*-playing with song is clearly alluded to: the haetara Śoṇadāsi

---

[33] '*-tantīssareṇa gītassaraṁ gītassareṇa tantīssaraṁ ca*', quoted in *Prācīna Bhārata men Saṅgīta,* p. 26, fn. 2. The words are reminiscent of Buddhas commendation of Pañcaśikha's playing quoted above.

[34] '*atha rāvaṇo rākṣasādhipatiḥ saparivāraḥ pauṣpakaṁ vimānamadhiruhya yena bhagavānstenopajagāma, upetya vimānādavatīrya saparivāro bhagavantaṁstrikṛtvāḥ pradakṣaṇīkṛtya tūryatalāvacaraiḥ pravadayadbhirin-dranīlamayena daṇḍena vaidūryamursara pratyuptāṁ vīṇāṁ priyaṁgupāṇ-ḍunārdhyena vastreṇa pārśvālambitāṁ kṛtvā, saharṣya, ṛṣabha, gāndhāra, dhaivata, niṣāda, madhyama, kaiśika, gītasvaragrāma-mūrchanādiyukte-nānusāryāṁ salīlaṁ vīṇāmanupraviśya gāthābhirgītairanugāyati sma*'. *Laṅkāvatara Sūtra.*

[35] *Meghadūta, Uttaramegha*, 23(Nirnaya Sagara edition).

[36] '*taṁ tasya svarasaṅkramaṁ mṛdugiraḥ śliṣṭam ca tantrīsvanam*'. *Mṛchchakaṭika,* Act III, verse. 5.

[37] The attribution is, in this case, less certain.

is pictured in a sad mood singing softly and playing the *vīṇā* which rests on her lap.[38]

Another old *bhāṇa, Pādatāḍitakam*, by Śyāmilaka — who is believed, by some scholars, to have composed it during the reign of Chandragupta-II[39] — also has a similar picture: a restless (*utkaṇṭhitā*) haetara, awaiting her lover, expresses her feelings in a sweet song, accompanying herself on the *sapta-tantrī vīṇā*.[40] Another *bhāṇa*, attributed to Vararuci, called *Ubhayābhisārikā*, pictures a man tormented by love singing songs in the *vaktra* and *aparavaktra* metres while playing the *vīṇā*, tuned appropriately to his song.[41] Dr. Motichandra, on internal evidence, assigns this play to the reign of Kumāragupta.[42]

There is the well-known scene in Bāṇa's *Kādambarī* where Candrāpīḍa first meets Mahāśveta. He is attracted to her by her out-of-the-world music: she had been singing to her own *vīṇā* playing in a lonely Śiva-temple.[43] In Jain stories of *vīṇā-svayaṁvara*, though ostensibly the competition seems to involve *vīṇā*-playing alone, yet singing is taken for granted as associated with the *vīṇā*. In *Vasudeva Hiṇḍī,* Vasudeva sings the *viṣṇu-gītaka* with the *vīṇā* in the competition which won him a bride. Later works make a similar association of *vīṇā*

---

[38] '...*aṅkādhirūḍhāṁ vallakīmiṣatkararuhairavaghaṭṭayantī kākalimandamadhureṇa svareṇa kūjayantī tiṣṭhati' Padmaprābhṛtaka;* see p. 44 of *Caturbhāṇī,* translated into Hindi and edited by Motichandra, Pub.: Hindi Grantha Ratnakara Karyalaya, Bombay, 1959.

[39] See Introduction to the *Caturbhāṇī, op. cit.*, p. 7.

[40] '...*asau saptatantrīrnakhairghattayantī kalaṁ kākalipañcamaprāyamutkaṇṭhitā valgugītāpadeśena vikrośati': Pādataḍitakam, Caturbhāṇī, op. cit.*, p. 177.

[41] '*aśokavanikābhyāse kopi khalu puruṣaḥ sandaṣṭa iva madanenāvyaktakākalīṁ racanāmūrchanāṁ vīṇāṁ kṛtvā ime vaktrāpavaktre gāyannātikrāntaḥ*' (the two poems follow). *Udhayābhisārikā, Caturbhāṇī*, op. cit., p. 144.

[42] Introduction, p. 8, *Caturbhāṇī op. cit.*

[43] '*anavaratagītaparisphuritādharapuṭavaśādatiśucibhiḥ... snapayantīṁ gaurīnātham... dakṣiṇakareṇa vīṇāmāsphālyantīṁ, pratyakṣamiva gāndharvavidyām...' Kadambari, pūrvabhāga,* pp. 281-83 (Nirnaya Sagara Press ed.).

with song in the bridal competition.[44]

Many more instances can be quoted, but these, we hope, will suffice to indicate a close association between song and *vīṇā*. We do not mean to suggest that the *vīṇā* was always associated with song. Our intention is to bring out the fact that such an association was common. In the instance of the Gupta kings, such an association is strongly indicated by another circumstance. The *vīṇā* type coins, as the experts have remarked, picture an instrument with seven strings. The *saptatantrī-vīṇā* or the seven-stringed harp was, indeed, a popular ancient instrument. It is mentioned in the *Jātakas*. One entire *Jātaka* story centres round the *saptatantrī (Guttila Jātaka*, No. 243). The *Vimānavatthu* speaks of the sweet-sounding *saptatantrī* (*satatantīṁ sumadhurāṁ*).[45] Śyāmilaka in his *Pādatāḍitakam*, describing a haetara singing (see above), speaks of her as playing the *saptatantrī*.[46] Altekar, in calling Samudragupta's *vīṇā* a *saptatantrī*, has pointed out that representation of this instrument abounds in the sculpture of Bharhut, Besnagar and Amaravati.[47] Swami Prajñānānanda in his *A Historical Study of Indian Music* cites illustration of the *saptatantrī vīṇā* at the Pitalkhora caves.[48]

Another point suggests the *saptatantrī*. Harp-*vīṇā* in ancient times was played both with a plectrum (*koṇa*) and the fingers. The Gupta kings on their *vīṇā* coins are shown as playing the instrument with their fingers, for the gesture of the right palm does not appear to

---

[44] e.g. *Bṛhatkathākośa* of Hariṣeṇa (c.10th century AD), see the story of Gandharvadattā (114, 6). Also *Gadyacintāmaṇi* of Vādībha Siṁha Sūri, *Lambha* 3. The work is assigned to the 9th century by Panna Lal Jain; see introduction pp. 15-16, to the Bhāratīya Jñānapīṭha edition; K.K.Handiqui assigns it to the 11th century, see his foreword to the *Jīvandhara campū*, Bhāratīya Jñanapīṭha edition). Both Jīvandhara, and the princess he competes with, sang hymns of the Jina on the *vīṇā,* pp. 175-79, Bhāratīya Jñānapīṭha edition. See also the same episode in *Jīvandhara Campū* (Ca. 13th century) *Lambha*, 3, verses 31-32, p. 64 of the Bhāratīya Jñanapīṭha editon.

[45] *Vimānavatthu*, 32, 2, 5, 1.

[46] See fn. 2 on p. 16 above.

[47] *op.cit.*, *loc.cit.*

[48] The book is published by Anandadhara Prakashan, Calcutta. See Chapter 6 of the work and illustrations.

indicate that the king was holding a plectrum. This, along with other circumstances, also points to a seven-stringed instrument; for Bharata in distinguishing between different *vīṇā*s and their number of strings, remarks that *citrā*, the *vīṇā* with seven strings was played with the fingers[49] Śyāmilka's haetara, who plays a *saptatantrī*, does so with her nails (*nakhairghaṭṭayantī*).

Now, if it be true that the Gupta kings are shown playing a seven-stringed harp, then certain implications follow which are meaningful in the present context. A seven-stringed harp can logically be tuned to only seven notes. It can produce only one octave with the seven regular notes of the ancient scale, unless one or more note be dropped; in which case, too, the range will not significantly increase. Dropping of too many notes in order to achieve a greater range of pitch would produce so much tonal gap between notes as to make the resulting melody musically poor or threadbare. In truth, only a single octave can be effectively achieved with seven strings on a harp. But effective music cannot be made if one only has the range of a single octave at one's command. Ancient music recognised a range of three octaves, known as the *mandra, madhya* and *tāra.* This was the range theoretically envisaged on the basis of the fact that the gifted voice when rightly trained can attain a range of three octaves.[50] Of the harp *vīṇās*, the *mattakokilā*, which

---

[49] *saptatantrī bhaveccitrā vipañcī tu bhavennave/ koṇavādyā vipañcī syāccitrā cāṅgulivādanā. Nāṭyaśāstra* (Gaekwad Oriental Series Edition), Vol. IV, 29, 118.

[50] This is normal; some rare voices can attain more, and *ati-tāra* and *ati-mandra* were not unknown to ancient theoreticians, too. Only the range of folk-melodies is often restricted to less than an octave, but the Gupta king, in age when art-music had reached great sophisticated heights, was certainly not rendering folk-music. Moreover, in folk forms, song is supreme; instrumental playing of folk-melodies makes little musical sense. The intimate connection between the human voice and the range in octaves of melodies in ancient times is apparent in the ancient notion of '*sthāna*'. *Sthāna* was the generic term for the octaves. At the same time, the term also denoted the anatomic seat within the human body from which, in singing, the octaves were believed to be produced. Thus the *sthāna* for the *mandra* octave was the chest, for the *madhya* octave the neck region and for the *tāra* octave the head. A note in the *mandra* octave was often referred to as a chest note; a note in the *madhya* octave could be called a *kaṇṭha* -note or a note of the neck; *tāra* notes were head-notes.

had twenty-one strings was the most appropriate *vīṇā* for giving an instrumental rendering of melodies in their optimum form.[51] It could do justice to the most ambitiously wide-ranging melody then current. But the *mattakokilā* was evidently a later innovation. it is conspicuously absent in the *Nāṭyaśāstra*. It is also noticeably missing from the works of the early poets who name other *vīṇās*. Obviously, even though it may have been known in the Gupta age or perhaps earlier, it was not a dominant instrument. Abhinava is the first writer on music who speaks of the *mattakokilā* with twenty-one strings as the chief of the *vīṇās*. He cites in this connection a passage from an unnamed earlier authority. In this passage, the *mattakokilā* is listed along with a number of other *vīṇās*, but its dominance is neither stated nor implied. The number of its strings is also not mentioned.[52] The *Amarakośa* names three *vīṇās*: *vallakī, vipañcī* and *parivādinī* - these are names quite familiar from ancient *kāvya* literature. The *vipañcī,* according to Bharata, had nine strings, the *parivādinī*, says Amara, had seven,[53] the *vallakī,* too, was certainly not a many-stringed *vīṇā*. The fact that Amara does not mention the *mattakokilā* is certainly an added evidence for its lateness. There is another significant testimony: *Rājapraśnīyam*, the Jain canonical text, which perhaps belongs to the Gupta age. It lists a large variety of *vīṇās*, but the *mattakokilā* is not named.[54]

Significant music can be made even with a range of two octaves, which is all that many of our best singers command, and doubtless this was true of ancient musicians also. But this is a

---

[51] *tatra mattakokilā pradhānabhutā. ekaviṁśatitantrīkatvenānyūnādhikāṁ tristhānagatasvarasāraṇājātigītivīṇāśarīramucyate. tadgataśca dhātuprayogā uktāḥ. tadupajīvakatvenāparā bhavantīti.* Abhinava on *Nāṭyaśāstra* 29, 112. (See Gaekwad edition, vol. IV).

[52] Ibid; see verses quoted in commentary on *Nāṭyaśāstra* 29, 112.

[53] *vīṇā tu vallakī sā tu tantrībhiḥ saptabhiḥ parivādinī: Amarakośa* 1, 7, 3.

[54] The work contains a detailed description of a very elaborate ballet-like dramatic pageant which the *gandharva* Sūryābha presented before Lord Mahāvīra. The following passage lists the *vīṇās* that were played during the performance: *muccijjantāṇāṁ vīṇāṇāṁ vipañcīṇāṁ vallakīṇāṁ kuṭṭijjantāṇāṁ mahantīṇāṁ kacchapīṇāṁ cittavīṇāṇāṁ sarijjantīṇāṁ vaddhisāṇāṁ sughoṣāṇāṁ nandīghoṣāṇāṁ phuṭṭijantīṇāṁ bhamarīṇāṁ chabbhamarīṇāṁ parivāinīṇāṁ chippantīṇāṁ tūṇāṇāṁ tumbavīṇāṇāṁ."* *Rājapraśnīyam, Sūtra* 41.

limitation that the voice has perforce to submit to. An instrumentalist, with a mechanism that can readily be made to cover a wide range, need not be so limited. To deliberately restrict oneself to just one octave can have no justification — unless the instrument being played was not the chief tool for rendering the melody. This, we suggest, is what obtained in the case of Samudragupta and Kumāragupta-I. They were making vocal music. Musical range and melodic finesse was attained through the voice; the *saptatantrī vīṇā* served mainly as instrumental support; for though the *spatatantrī* could not provide range, it could yet give all the necessary notes in the octave of any desired scale for the sake of accompaniment.

It can here be argued that even on the open string of a *vīṇā* of the harp variety, great musical range can be achieved by playing the string in the manner of the Hawaiian guitar, or the modern *vicitra-vīṇā* or the south Indian *goṭṭuvādyam*. A single string can produce more than one octave if properly manipulated by an object which can press it and glide over it. However, such playing needs both hands, one to strike and another to play the string. The Gupta kings are playing the instrument with only one hand, the other lies idle on the sounding belly of the *vīṇā*.

The gesture and position of this idle hand is suggestive. Altekar, in his famous work, *The Gupta Gold Coins in the Bayana Hoard* wonders why the left hand is above the sounding board and not below it, where it could have lent proper support to the instrument.[55] One could have expected the musician to be holding tight to the *vīṇā* had the attention of the musician been primarily directed towards the instrument, had he, in other words, been making instrumental music. But if vocal music was the king's chief concern, he would be merely strumming the *vīṇā*, merely sounding the principal note or notes around which he happened to be weaving his vocal melody.[56] A hand loosely

---

[55] 'One expects the left hand to be placed under the lute in order to support it'. *The Gupta Gold Coins in the Bayana Hoard,* Altekar, Introduction, p. 1xix.

[56] This may have been done in ways similar to those employed by modern Hindustani vocalists who use the *svaramaṇḍala.* The *svaramaṇḍala* is an old

placed above the sounding board can make the instrument secure enough for his purpose. In fact, many modern singers too, while strumming the *tānpūrā* with their right hand, place the other loosely on its round belly.

The gesture of the left palm is also noteworthy. It has been suggested that this is the natural gesture of a musician deep in his music. This may be so; and if so, such a gesture is more common with singers than players; for players usually have both their hands full. We suggest another possibility. The gesture, forms what was known as the *vyākhyāna mudrā* — though it has not been looked at this way;[57] except that the arm is not raised towards the chest as is usual in this *mudrā.* But this is easily explained; a person engaged in *vīṇā*-playing could not have raised his free arm as it did act as a support to the *vīṇā.*

In ancient iconography, the *vyākhyāna mudrā* suggests speech, exposition, teaching — in short, uttering of words. The lips are not shown as parted as this would hamper the expression of serenity and composure associated with *vyākhyāna.* The *mudrā* itself is symbolic of utterance. The *vyākhyāna mudrā* found in association with the *vīṇā* surely symbolized the act of singing, which too involves a kind of utterance.

---

instrument in India, though in its current form it has obviously been influenced by the East European Zither. The *svaramaṇḍala* has a direct kinship with the older harp-*vīṇā,* especially the *mattakokilā.* Kallinātha commenting on *Saṅgīta Ratnākara* 6, 109-113 says: *mattakokilaiva loke svaramaṇḍalamityucyate.* The *svaramaṇḍala* never lost its popularity. Abul Fazl lists it among the instruments used during Akbar's reign. Maharaja Sawai Pratap Singh Deva of Jaipur, testifies to the use of the instrument during the end of the eighteenth century in his *Sangīta-Sāra (Hindi):* See Part II, pp. 7-8 of the Poona Gyan Samaj edition, Poona, 1910.

It is, indeed, a curious fact that the modern parallels of the ancient kings' *vīṇā*-playing portraits are the familiar photographs or paintings of such singers as Bade Ghulam Ali Khan singing with their *svaramaṇḍalas* on their laps.

[57] There was no single fixed gesture for the palm in the *vyākhyāna mudrā.* But there are a number of loosely related variations. On some *vīṇā* type coins the left thumb and fore-finger are shown as projecting slightly outwards, while in others they bend towards each other in more than a semi-circle. In his *The Development of Hindu Iconography,* J.N. Banerjea notes that both these positions are found depicted in ancient sculpture, pp. 254-55.

The use of this *mudrā* was a happy stroke on the part of the mint designer. He had so composed the figure as to show the king in profile, thus pushing the *vīṇā* towards the side and making the figure of the king more prominent. To have shown His Majesty in this posture with his lips parted in song would have resulted in a very uncouth beak-like effect.

III

Finally, a few words about music, kingship and a historical generalisation commonly made. Historians often speak of music as the tempting devil who lures a king away from his stern regal duties, into the soft arms of decadence, the result being inevitable decay and loss of power. The example of the Gupta kings, especially that of Samudragupta, should make up stop and think before becoming a party to such a generalization. Here were kings, who at the height of power and glory, took active interest in music, without wallowing in decadence. The truth is that music, like any other pursuit, can be the expression of inner strength, power and glory as well as moral weakness and decadence, for music is as complex and multifaceted as the human mind which uses it as a medium of expression.

CHAPTER – FOURTEEN

The Music of *Gītagovinda* and its Antecedents: Some Historical Observations

I

Since the earliest histories of Sanskrit literature began to be written, scholars have assigned to the *Gītagovinda* of Jayadeva a unique place in Indian literary writings. One reason for the uniqueness of the *Gītagovinda* is its form. It is quite unlike any preceding lyric in Sanskrit. The cause lies in the fact that no lyric before it was so palpably connected with music.

One of the most well-known verses from the *Gītagovinda* is that in which the poet proudly proclaims his excellence in having composed the most sweet and mellifluous verse.[1] In another verse which is not so well-known, Jayadeva has claimed an equal excellence for his music: In verse 10 of the last *sarga* (one of the verses attached as an epilogue to his work) Jayadeva exclaims —

> *yadgāndharvakalāsu kauśalamanudhyānaṁ ca yadvaiṣ-ṇavaṁ*
> *yacchṛṅgāravivekatattvaracanā kāvyeṣu līlāyitam/*
> *tatsarvaṁ jayadevapaṇḍitakaveḥ kṛṣṇaikatānātmanaḥ*
> *sānandaḥ pariśodhayantu sudhiyaḥ śrīgītagovindataḥ//*

(Excellence in the skill and subtleties of music; the path of meditation on God according to the *Vaiṣṇava* tradition; the proper assimilation and play of the deepest and truest *sṛṅgāra* in poetry: may the learned gather (or expect) these things from *Gīagovinda* of the pandit-poet Jayadeva).[2]

---

[1] *Yadi harismaraṇe sarasaṁ mano yadi vilāsakālasu kutūhalam/ madhurakomala-kāntapadāvalīṁ śṛṇu tadā jayadevasarasvatīm. Gītagovinda, sarga* 1, verse 4.

[2] Kumbha explains the last line in such a way that it expresses an uncharacteristically modest rather than a boastful thought: "*he sudhiyaḥ jayadevapaṇḍitakavestatsarvaṁ gītagovindataḥ. atra tasil sārvavibhaktikatvā-tsaptamyarthe upapattiḥ. gītagovinde pariśodhayantu, śuddhaṁ kurvantu*". But Kumbha adds: *gītagovinde vā śuddhaṁ jānantu*".

This is a verse which occurs in most manuscripts of the *Gitagovinda*. The claim made here by Jayadeva reveals that in presenting the *Gitagovinda* to the connoisseurs of his day, the poet wanted them to admire his musical as much as his poetic skill.

The larger part of *Gītagovinda* comprises, what have been called *aṣṭapadīs* in almost all manuscripts of the work. The *aṣṭapadīs* number twentyfour and contain eight stanzas each (the first *aṣṭapadī,* a hymn to the ten incarnations of Kṛṣṇa, however, has eleven). The *aṣṭapadīs* have been thematically linked with each other into a drama-like episodic scheme with the help of small groups of intermediate poetic verses. These are composed in the familiar manner and metre of classical Sanskrit poetry. But the *aṣṭapadīs* are revealed to be quite different even at a cursory glance: not only is the flow of words and diciton in them composed with an eye to music, their metre, too, forms a class apart from customary Sanskrit poetic metres.

There are, indeed, many indicative factors which disclose the song aspect of the *aṣṭapadīs* and reveal their kinship with forms conceived in the musical as distinguished from the purely poetic tradition:

1. Each *aṣṭapadī* contains a refrain, a *dhruvapada*, which was a characteristically musical feature.[3]
2. Almost all manuscripts caption each *aṣṭapadī* with the name of the *rāga* and *tāla* to which it was to be sung.
3. And lastly, the end verse of each *aṣṭapadī* includes the name of the poet.[4]

---

[3] In the *prabandha* genre of medieval songs — to which, as we shall argue, the *Gītagovinda* belonged — the *dhruva* was that musical part or movement which was essential to all *prabandhas*. Some other features being optional. The *dhruva,* like the theme in western music and the '*sthāyi*' in current Hindustani music, was to be often repeated. Someśvara in his *Mānasollāsa* defines *dhruva* as: '*paunaḥpunyād dhruvattvācca dhruvakaḥ parikīrtitaḥ*'; *Mānasollāsa* 4, 16, 442. See also *Saṅgīta-ratnākāra* (henceforth shortened as S.R.) 4, 9 and the commentary of Kallinātha.

[4] This feature is indeed decreed for *prabandha* songs: In the last movement, of the *prabandha*, termed the *ābhoga,* the poet-composer, says Śārṅgadeva, should include his name:*syādābhogastadanantaraṁ geyo vāggeyakāreṇa svābhidhānavibhūṣitaḥ.* S. R. 4, 38.

These are features found associated with song-forms and are quite alien to Sanskrit poetic practice. They have been part of our musical tradition and are still to be found in the practice of song writers who compose in classical forms such as *dhrupad, khyāl, ṭhumrī* etc. The *padas* of the medieval poet-saints which were composed as songs are also seen to incorporate these features. They have a long past and can be traced back at least to the songs of the early medieval '*siddha*' poets such as Sarahapāda, Kanhupāda and others, the earliest of whom goes back to the eighth century AD. The compositions of these '*siddha*' poets were *geya-padas* (or songs). These early *padas* are found to contain all the features stamped also upon the *aṣṭapadī:* they include a *dhruva-pada* or refrain; they record the name of the poet (the '*bhaṇitā*' as it is called) and, moreover, manuscripts of the text of these songs, dating back, according to their discoverer Hara Prasad Sastri, to a very early period — also mention the name of the *rāga* to which each song was to be sung.

Thus the *aṣṭapadī* is seen to have a strong kinship with forms belonging to the musical tradition. In fact, the name *aṣṭapadī* itself indicates the musical affinities of the form. The *Bṛhaddeśī* of Mataṅga, a well-known and influential text on music, placed usually in the seventh-eighth centuries AD, lists the *tripadī, castuṣpadī* and *ṣaṭpadī* as long-standing song-forms belonging to the large genre called *prabandha* (*Bṛhaddeśī*, verses 380 and 386). These forms are classified under *prabandha* in subsequent *saṅgīta*-texts, too. Śārṅgadeva, the famed authority on music, who may have been a younger contemporary of Jayadeva (he composed his *Saṅgīta-ratnākara* in the reign of the Yādava King Siṅghaṇa ruling at Deogiri, modern Daulatabad, between AD1210 and 1247*)*,[5] lists these forms and delineates their characteristic features.[6] Another work, the encyclopaedic *Mānasollāsa* (also known as the *Abhilaṣitārthacintāmaṇi)* is most interesting in this context. It covers a large range of diverse

---

[5] S.R. (Adyar Library edition), Vol. I, Introduction, p. x.

[6] S.R. 4, 29-30 and 4, 268-274.

subjects including music. The work was, purportedly, written by king Someśvara of the Western Cālukya dynasty; though it has been argued that the actual author was a learned pandit in the employ of the king.[7] Someśvara ascended the thorne at Kalyāṇī in the third decade of the 12th century AD, and the *Mānasollāsa* was composed perhaps in the next decade.[8]

The *Mānasollāsa* provides many valuable cues to the understanding of the song-tradition in which the *Gītagovinda* was composed. It gives the texts of many a song actually sung during the period. Other technical works on music rarely do so. The material in this work is especially valuable as it was composed some decades before the *Gītagovinda,* which is generally placed towards the end of the 12th century AD. The *Mānasollāsa* has a long section (in the 16th chapter of the 4th *viṁśati*) on *prabandha* songs. Numerous samples of song-texts are given and these provide us with interesting antecedents of the form adopted by Jayadeva in his *aṣṭapadīs.* The *prabandha* genre included a rich variety of forms and though Someśvara quotes dozens of examples he says that he is illustrating only those *prabandhas* where he could not find a well-known prevalent song.[9] The songs given are not always complete, for only a few lines are thought as sufficiently illustrative; still, many of the songs contain the name of the professed composer Someśvara at the end[10] much in the same manner as *lakṣaṇa-gītas*, illustrative of particular *rāgas*, contain the name of the composer in the classical songs of today.[11] We find in the *Mānasollāsa* many a song which

[7] *Mānasollāsa*, G.O.S. edition, Vol. I, Introduction, p. vi.

[8] Ibid., pp. vi-vii.

[9] *lakṣaṇena prabandhānāṁ yatra lakṣyaṁ pratīyate na tatrodāḥṛtiḥ proktā, sāpekṣyeṣu nigadyate; Mānasollāsa* 4, 16, 199.

[10] Ibid., 4, 16, 476; 412; 495 and etc.

[11] Let us take an example: Pandit Bhatkhande who composed under the name of Catura, gives the following '*sthāyī*' for the *lakṣaṇa-gīta* of *rāga śyāmakalyāṇa: 'śyāmakalyāṇa gāvat nisadina catura guṇī, (Hindustānī Saṅgīta Paddhati,* Pt. V, p. 76). Compare this with the following in Someśvara: After saying that he is going to illustrate the *prabandha* called *haṁsavatī* belonging to the '*elā*' class (*Mānasollāsa* 4, 16, 456), Someśvara gives the song, ending with '*ā someśvaradeva viracita elā haṁsavatī.* At the place of the *ā* syllables a free musical passage was, perhaps, to be sung.

foreshadow the manner, diction, style and even to some extent the theme of the *aṣṭapadīs* — though the poetic skill and the well-measured flow of the *Gītagovinda* are absent here. It would be worthwhile to take a few examples:

1. One of the *prabandhas*, called *jayamālikā* (perhaps because every new line began with the word '*jaya*') composed as a hymn, bears similarities with Jayadeva's famous *aṣṭapadī* on the *daśāvatāra* theme. The metre in Someśvara's song is irregular as is often the case with the texts of songs even today. The first three lines are—

jaya bhujaparighadhṛtagovardhanadharādhara
jaya kalpāntakakālakesarikarālākārakāliyapralayakārin
jaya madhuvadhūvidhuntuda[12] etc.

2. Another *prabandha*-hymn contains a rhyme scheme and has fluid-flowing *samāsas* like Jayadeva:

nijavibhavaracitadaśāvatāram
niśitaśaraśatakṣatadanujabhāram[13] etc.

Yet another in the same strain, reads:

sudarśanadalitabāṇabāho
śiromātrāvaśeṣīkṛtarāho
niravadhiśāstropadeśadakṣa
saṅgararaṅgadalitahiraṇyākṣa[14] etc.

3. There are expressions also of the *Kṛṣṇa-gopī* love theme in the liquid style made famous by Jayadeva:

Yauvanabhūṣitagopavadhūmukhapadmamadhukara
śyāmalavigrahakāntivinirjitanavyajaladhara
śṛṅgārasadanasmerasaroruhasañcayapiñjara[15] etc.

Even Rādhā is mentioned in a hymn where Kṛṣṇa is addressed as:

samarabharavivaśarādhāhṛdayavallabha[16]

The *Gītagovinda* reflects a much deeper awareness of poetic

---

[12] *Mānasollāsa*, 4, 16, 309.
[13] Ibid., 4, 16, 501.
[14] *Mānasollāsa*, 4, 16, 356.
[15] Ibid., 4, 16, 451.
[16] Ibid., 4, 16, 370.

values than do Someśvara's songs, but then, Jayadeva had poetic as well as musical ambitions. Yet the songs quoted here suffice to show that the *Gītagovinda aṣṭapadīs* were composed within the well-established tradition, scheme and strand of *prabandha* songs.

One stray song of the species illustrated in the *Mānasollāsa* occurs even in a non-musical Jain Prakrit literary work, the *Kathā-kośaprakaraṇa* of Jineśvara Sūri, who composed his collection of stories in AD 1051,[17] many years before the *Mānasollāsa.* In the story of prince Sīhakumāra (*sīhakumāra kathānakam*), the main character Sīha is described as an expert in the art and technique of music. Sīha, when asked to show his skill in the court of his father, sings a song, which Jineśvara has called a *cauppadikā bandha*, evidently meaning a composition in the *catuṣpadika* i.e. a *prabanda* song of the *catuṣpadī* variety. Jineśvara gives us the text of the song, which is a hymn in Prakrit to Mahavira. The song has many points of interest. It contains four stanzas in a more or less regular rhyming metre, as in Jayadeva. It has a refrain in the form of a line which is repeated after every stanza — this is evidently the '*dhruva*' though not actually called so. The name of the composer Sīhakumāra occurs in the line which acts as the *dhruva*. We quote two stanzas:

Saṁsārasamuddagatabhavika uddharaṇā
Kāmakohamayamohamicchatta avaharaṇā
eṣiṁ kari gāyai rāyasīhakumārā
vīra tuha pāyavirahi sayalu andhārā

(This stanza is repeated as *dhruva*)

Devasuramanuyasivasampayatarukaṁdā
narayaduhatiriyabhavasantativicchedā
esiṁ kari gāyai.............etc.[18]

One here observes many notable formal similarities with the *Gītagovinda aṣṭapadī:* the rhyme scheme is of the same nature; the poet's name is included in the song, and there occurs a refrain; and indeed, the very name of the form, *catuṣpadī,* cannot

[17] See the Introduction to Jineśvara Sūri's *Kathākośaprakaraṇa,* Singhī Jaina Granthamālā No. 11, Published by Bhāratīya Vidyā Bhavana, 1949.

[18] Ibid., text, p. 42.

but remind us of the *aṣṭapadī*. This song was recorded more than a century before the composition of the *Gītagovinda*.

II

There is, then, a strong case for believing that the *aṣṭapadī* belonged to genre of the songs called the *prabandha*. Jayadeva, too, has himself called his poem a *prabandha* in a celebrated verse:

vāgdevatācaritacitritacittasadmā
padmāvatīcaraṇacāraṇacakravartī/
śrīvāsudevaratikelikathāsametaṁ
karoti jayadevakaviḥ prabandham//[19]

The word *prabandha* was used also for any literary composition and this is the sense in which it is generally understood in this verse. But in the view of the extermely suggestive evidence that has been presented above, one can reasonably maintain that the word in this context denotes the *prabandha* genre of songs, too, if not song alone.

There is another suggestive point that emerges from the verse in this connection. Jayadeva here names a woman, Padmāvatī, in tones of obvious tenderness and love. Padmāvatī was, according to well-known legends, Jayadeva's wife. Jayadeva remembers her again with affection and pleasure at the end of an *aṣṭapadī* in the 11th *sarga*:

vihitapadmāvātīsukhasamāje
kuru murāre maṅgalaśatāni
bhaṇati jayadevakavirājarāje[20]

(O Murari, bestow a hundred blessings on Jayadeva the king of poets who sings to you — Jayadeva who has often been a source of great happiness to Padmāvatī).

---

[19] *Gītagovinda*, *sarga* 1, verse 2.

[20] According to one reading, the *aṣṭapadī* no. 19, *sarga*, 10, also mentions Padmāvatī in the last verse, where Jayadeva refers to himself as the 'beloved or husband of Pādmāvatī': *jayati padmāvatīramaṇajayadevakavibhāratī-bhaṇitamatisāram.* This is a *pāṭhabheda* quoted in both the Nirṇayasāgara edition of the *Gītagovinda* (see p. 133) and the Lālbhāi Dalpatbhāi edition with Mānāṅka's *ṭika*; see p. 87.

Mentioning one's beloved in a poem (even if she was a wife) was considered as a highly unorthodox — not to say unseemly-poetic practice, and some commentators have tried to explain Padmāvatī as denoting the Goddess Lakṣmī — though such a name for Lakṣmī hardly occurs anywhere. But while we find no precedents where a Sanskrit poet has openly inserted the name of his own wife or beloved within his poem, such a practice seems to have been quite in order among singers and composers of songs. Witness Kālidāsa's *yakṣiṇī*, who tried to while away her sorrow by singing songs with her beloved's name in them.[21] In the case of *prabandha* singers we even find a near-authorization for such a practice in the *Mānasollāsa* where Someśvara states: "A musician should sing to (or of) the king or chief prince who are endowed with the qualities of the great and possess great power; or he should sing to (or of) the chief queen or the great queen or to a woman of distinction whom he loves; to (or of) these he should sing, whomsoever he feels inclined towards; but a *prabandha* should never be composed with a view to please anyone else even for the sake of money."[22] In the light of this statement, we can see that Jayadeva was not violating any code of propriety in having fondly put in the name of his beloved in the body of his composition.

Although the form, the manner of composition, and other peculiarities of the *aṣṭapadī* reveal it as a *prabandha*-song, yet the name *aṣṭapadī* as such does not occur among lists of *prabandhas* in *saṅgīta* texts. But this is not surprising. The *prabandha* was a very large genre comprising a vast number of varieties. These were distributed into classes and sub-classes by theorists with their love for categorization. Not all forms could

---

[21] *madgotrāṅkaṁ viracitapadaṁ geyāmudgatukāmā: Meghadūta, Uttaramegha,* 23. I am indebted to Professor G.C. Pande for this suggestion.

[22] *nṛpaṁ vā yuvarājaṁ vā mahāśaktiguṇorjitam/mahādevīṁ bṛhaddevīṁ priyāṁ vā yoṣiduttamām/gāyennijecchayā gātā yatra cittaṁ pravartate/ arthalobhāttathānyeṣāṁ prabandho naiva gīyate/ Mānasollāsa,* 4, 16, 562-563. '*Priyāṁ vā yoṣiduttamām*' may, of course, refer to a king's favourite and not the composer's beloved.

be listed and described, for that would have over-burdened even the most ambitious *śāstric* work. Śārṅgadeva divides *prabandhas* into three classes: *sūḍa, āli* and *viprakīrṇa* (lit. 'scattered', i.e. miscellaneous).[23] The third class included *tripadī, catuṣpadī* and *ṣaṭpadī,* and comprised a large corpus of forms. Of these Śārṅgadeva proposes to describe only a few well-known ones.[24] It is quite likely that the *aṣṭapadī* was one of the obscure and lesser-known forms of this class and came into prominence later, due, may be, to the attention bestowed upon it by the genius of Jayadeva.

Song-composers in early medieval times were called *vāggeyakāras*[25] i.e. creators of words and (accompanying) music. *Vāggeyakāras* were classified according to their talents and capabilities. The best of them was a master poet-cum-musician in whose compositions both the poem and its music were new and original and embodied the great creative genius (*prabhūtapratibhā*)[26] of the composer. Jayadeva evidently, was a truly *pratibhāvān vāggeyakāra.*

There was no false modesty in Jayadeva. A *vāggeyakāra*, says *Śārṅgadeva,* should put his name in the last movement of a *prabandha* song;[27] this Jayadeva has proudly done in all his *aṣṭapadīs.* He often also adds an invitation to the *rasikas* and *paṇḍitas* to admire his sweet artistry.[28] The foremost *vāggeyakāras*, says Śārṅgadeva, are '*vastukavis*' (S.R. 3, 11) — this Kallināttha explains as meaning a *kathākavi*: a poet whose poem weaves a story. Jayadeva, indeed, claims that the subject

---

[23] S.R. 4, 22-23.

[24] *tato 'nye viprakīrṇāstān prasiddhān katicid bruve.* S.R. 4, 28.

[25] *vāṅ māturucyate, geyaṁ dhāturabhidhīyate/vācaṁ geyaṁ ca kurute yaḥ sa vāggeyakārakaḥ, S.R.* 3, 2,.

[26] S.R. 3, 6 Kallinātha quoting from another text explains *pratibhā as: 'prajñāṁ navanavonmeṣaśālinīṁ pratibhāṁ viduḥ'.*

[27] S.R. 4, 38; quoted ante. See footnote 4.

[28] *śrījayadevabhaṇitarativañcitakhaṇḍitayuativilāpam/śṛṇutasudhāmadhuraṁ vibudhā vibudhālayato' pi durāpam: Gītagovinda sarga 8,* last verse of *aṣṭapadī.* Also; *śrījayadevabhaṇitamatilalitam/ sukhayatu rasikajanaṁ haricaritam. Gītagovinda sarga 9,* last verse of *aṣṭapadī*

of his *prabandha* is a *kathā* - the tale of Kṛṣṇa's loves — (*vāsudevaratikelikathāsametam/karoti jayadevakaviḥ prabandham*).

Legends recorded about Jayadeva by Nābhādāsa in his *Bhaktamāla*, and following him by Jayacanda, portray Jayadeva as a singing poet and a dancer dedicated to the service of Lord Kṛṣṇa. He was, it is related, a simple, unlearned *brāhmaṇa* who sang and danced before Lord Kṛṣṇa out of spontaneous devotional fervour. Such a picture of Jayadeva's personality is however, belied by the *Gītagovinda*, which is the creation of a deeply sophisticated man, a *nāgaraka*, a *vidagdha* (in the language of Jayadeva's days), who was one of the best products of the urbane culture and refinement attained in the cultivated circles of the age. Jayadeva's Mīrā-like image of a simple spontaneous *bhakta*, which was the ideal of this devotional movement, was transposed upon the memory of Jayadeva, transforming his character completely. But the picture of Jayadeva as a poet-musician is certainly rooted in fact. The *Sekaśubhodaya*, a 16th century collection of legends centring around the court of King Lakṣamaṇasena, portrays Jayadeva in a manner quite different from the image of him as a simple devoted *bhakta*. Jayadeva is presented here as the court musician of Lakṣamaṇasena; Padmāvatī is his wife; both are reported to have supernatural powers in their music, powers such as those told of Tānsen, Baijū Bāvarā and other renowned musicians (*Sekaśubhodaya*, Ch. 13).[29]

III

The *prabandha* form of music which Jayadeva, from all signs, appears to have adopted for his song, had, we have seen, a tradition antedating him. We have given examples from antecedents composed in the 12th century AD, but the form itself was much older. It was an already well-established, well-regulated form when Mataṅga wrote his *Bṛhaddeśī*, in the

---

[29] The text has been published by the Asiatic Society of Bengal, Calcutta 1963, with an Introduction and translation in English by Sukumar Sen.

seventh or eight century.[30] The form was, in other words, a well-cultivated classical form by the time Jayadeva sang in it.

However, the links that the *Gītagovinda* bears with its *prabandha* antecedents appear to have been overlooked by modern historians of Sanskrit literature. They have put forward the hypothesis that Jayadeva was inspired by folk and rustic forms. Schroeder called the work a 'refined *yātrā*'. Winternitz opined that 'rustic dance games with music served him (i.e. Jayadeva) as models for the songs which form the nucleus of the work'. This view is still the generally current view, and needs to be revised in the light of *saṅgīta*-works.

The *prabandha* is now an extinct form, but technical descriptions of its musical structure are to be found in *saṅgīta*-texts. It, plainly, stands out as a refined form of high art-music.

The musical movement of the *prabandha* has a four-part structure: it began with the *udgrāha*, after which came *melāpaka, dhruva* and *ābhoga*. The structure has a distant parallel in the four-part *dhrupad* form which was born out of the *prabandha*.[31] Of the four basic movement of the *prabandha* structure, two, namely, *melāpaka* and *ābhoga*, did not occur in certain *prabandhas*;[32] the other two, *udgrāha* and *dhruva*, were essential.

---

[30] Mataṅga describes a host of forms in terms echoed and often quoted by later authorities. He begins a survey of *prabandhas* with the statement that they are innumerable and that he has chosen to describe only a prominent few: *deśīkāraprabandho'yaṁ haravaktrābhinirgataḥ/kaścitkhyātāstu kathitā na jñāyate'l- pabuddibhiḥ/teṣāṁ madhyāt samuddhṛtya yuktalakṣaṇalakṣitān/ śrīmataṅgamuniḥ prāha munīnuddiśya tadyathā. Bṛhaddeśī* 376-77.

[31] Nāyaka Gopāla, one of the earliest known *dhrupad* composers whose compositions, however transformed, have come down to us, has been referred to by Kallinātha (15th century AD). as a composer of *prabandhas* (see his *ṭīkā* on S.R. 4, 253-256). Nāyaka Gopāla is believed to have lived in the period of Alauddin Khilji (AD 1296—1316). The fact that Nāyaka Gopāla is associated both with the *prabandha* and the *dhrupad* is indicative of the link between the two forms of musical composition. Sadāraṅga, to whom we owe the present *Khyāl* style, had similar links with the older *dhrupad* form.

[32] S.R. 4, 11; See also Parśvadeva as quoted by Siṁhabhūpāla on S.R.: 4, 1-19. Also *Mānasollāsa*, 4, 440-43.

The general *prabandha* structure was further analysed into six elements, metaphorically referred to as the six limbs of the *prabandha-puruṣa.*[33] These elements were: *svara, biruda, pāṭa, tenaka* (also called *tennaka*, *tenna* or *tena* in some works), *pada* and *tāla.*[34]

Svara, in this context, denoted the singing of sol-fa notations.[35] Siṁhabhūpāla[36] here explains: *svara* stands for the singing of the syllables, *sa ri ga ma pa dha ni* at their appropriate pitches".[37] This is what is known as singing of '*sargams* in modern musical parlance. *Pada* stood for the words of the sung text (S.R. 4, 16). *Tenaka,* signified the singing of the two syllables '*te na*' repeatedly, and seems to have been the forebearer of our own '*nom tom*' vocables in singing. The syllables '*tena*' were believed to represent the *mahāvākyas* like *'om tat sat'* and '*tattvamasi';* consequently, their employ during singing was considered auspicious.[38] *Pāṭa* was the technical term for the different syllables conventionally employed to represent the different sounds produced on the drums — what we today call tablā or *mṛdaṅga 'bols'.*[39] The term *tāla* had the same meaning as it has today: i.e. a rhythmic cycle of numbered beats distributed in a particular pattern. *Biruda* meant a laudatory epithet. Its position and significance in the context of the *prabandha* is not clear.

---

33 S.R. 4, 12-13.

34 Ibid.

35 *svarāḥṣaḍjādayasteṣāṁ vācakāḥ sarigādayaḥ/svarābhviyakti saṁyuktāḥ svaraśabdena kīrtitāḥ.* S.R. 4, 15-16.

36 He wrote his *ṭīkā*, entitled *Saṅgītasudhākara,* on the S.R., towards the close of the 14th century AD.

37 *"svarā iti. ṣaḍjādayaḥ svarāḥ pūrvamuktāḥ teṣām vācakāḥ sarigamapadhanīti varṇāḥ tattatsvārabhivyaktisahitāḥ svaraśabdenocyante: Saṅgītasudhākara* on S.R. 4, 1.9. Kallinātha's commentts are also revealing: *"svarasya ca sakalaprabandhagatatve'pi ṣaḍjādivācakānāṁ sarigādīnāmeva svarābhivyaktihetutvādasādhāraṇyenāṅga-tvavyapadeśaḥ."*

38 *teneti śabdastenaḥ syānmaṅgalārthaprakāśakaḥ/oṁ tatsaditi nirdeśāttatvamasyā-divākyataḥ/tadittu brahma tenāyaṁ brahmaṇā maṅgalātmanā/lakṣitastena teneti......* S.R., 4, 17-18.

39 *pāṭo vādyākṣarotkaraḥ.* S.R. 4, 18.
Siṁhabhūpala explains: *"vādyākṣarāṇāṁ dhigdhigādīnāmutkaraḥ samūho, vādyād-hyāye vakṣyamāṇaḥ, pāṭa ityucyate".*

This brief technical account of the *prabandha* form should, we hope, suffice to sketch before us the picture of its complexities. It was, obviously, a highly developed art-form and bears many suggestive parallels with present classical forms.

A confusion can perhaps arise here: The *prabandha* has been included by theorists in the category of *deśī* music, and *deśī* has been defined as popular, regional music unbound by rules. But one should not on this score be led to think that all so-called *deśī* music was of a folk or rustic character. After all, our own complex and subtle art music is but *deśī* music; for *deśī* is, in *śāstric* works, a category opposed to *mārga*, a term which denoted the most ancient forms of music predating the medieval period, and all *mārga* forms were already extinct by the 16th century AD. Our art-music also is thus *deśī*. The term, then, need not necessarily signify a crude folk form.

There, certainly, must have been folk elements in the *prabandha* as there are in all cultivated art-forms. Both Indian and western art-music contains demonstrable elements traceable to 'folk' sources. Indeed living art-music keeps continuously being renewed through assimilation of influences that have a 'folk' derivation.[40] *Prabandha*, too, seems to have emerged out of *mārga* forms due to a gradual absorption of new folk forms, and it is in this sense that it was *deśī* music. But it certainly could not have been rustic music. As early as in the period of Mataṅga, the *prabandha* forms had acquired a standardised structure. And after Mataṅga too, we come across *saṅgīta*-texts, separated from each other both in time and in space, which describe the *prabandha* in an almost like language and manner. Authorities belonging to different times and regions such as Pārśvadeva (ca. 12th century AD, hailing from western India), Nānyadeva (king of Mithila, early 12th century AD), Someśvara, (Cālukya king of Kalyāṇī, reigning during the 1130s), and Śārṅgadeva (who wrote his *Saṅgītaratnākara* in early 13th century AD at Devagiri, modern Daulatabad) have all described the *prabandha* in similar

[40] Both the *ṭhumrī* and the *ṭappā*, for example, have developed in this way.

terms. It was no regional style. It was a form cultivated country-wide over the centuries. Formal rules had to be carefully observed in singing a *prabandha*.[41] *Prabandhas* were sung in Prakrit or the vernacular, but also in Sanskrit, the 'cultivated' tongue. The *vāggeyakāras* who composed and sang *prabandhas* were honoured in the court of cultured kings.[42] The *prabandha* singer's art was an exacting art demanding control over many intricacies and a high degree of finesse and perfection. Critical appreciation was well-developed among discriminating listeners and *saṅgīta* texts describe in detail the *doṣas* to be avoided, and extol the *guṇas* to be cultivated.[43] Most of the observations made in these texts are still valid for classical music today.

IV

Jayadeva, we have seen, wanted his audience to admire both his musical and poetic achievement in the *Gītagovinda*. He must have belonged to that charmed group of *vāggeyakāras* who could compose both the poem and the music of a song with genius. His art received a ready response from his public and his fame spread far even in those troubled times. A verse of his has been quoted in a rock edict from Patan, dating AD 1292.[44]

A living tradition treasures and preserves the creations that it deems as works of genius. Yet, though we have the *Gītagovinda* poem, its original music has been lost. There exist many current styles of *Gītagovinda* singing, especially in the east and the south, but none can be traced back with any certainty to the medieval

---

[41] Someśvara, who was directly acquainted with *prabandhas*, observes: *vidhiryeṣāṁ prabandhānaṁ yādṛśaḥ parikīrtitaḥ/ tālena bhāṣayā rāgaiḥ svaraiḥ pāṭaiśca tenakaiḥ/vidhinā tena te geyā na vidhiḥ pratilaṅghyate/ vidhilope bhaveddoṣo na samyaglakṣaṇaṁ bhavet: Mānasollāsa* 4, 16, 556-557.

[42] Music and dance performances were presided over by the king, and he was expected to be a connoisseur versed in the mysteries of the art (*Mānasollāsa* 4, 16, 2-5). The best *vāggeyakāras* were given seats of honour with the nobility in a *saṅgīta-sabhā*. Ibid., 4, 8, 12-13).

[43] S.R., 3, 13-86; *Mānasollāsa* 4, 16 15-87 and other texts.

[44] *History of Indian Literature,* Winternitz Vol. III, pt. 1, p. 136, and other standard works.

period. The earliest tradition may perhaps, in some form, have its source in the *bhakti* period, but even this cannot be really authenticated. Some manuscripts, however, may go back to an earlier period, and these give us the names of *rāga* and *tāla* for each *aṣṭapadī*. But there is no unanimity even in this very meagre musical information. Different manuscripts are seen to give different sets of *rāga-tāla* for many of the *aṣṭapadīs*,[45] and none of the manuscripts can be directly linked with Jayadeva, or his immediate tradition.

Jayadeva's own music does not appear to have survived the poet himself for long. Indian music is almost entirely unnotated, and was much more so before the modern period. Music is handed down in a *guru-śiṣya-paramparā*, and hence its forms need a much greater social stability for preservation than do manuscripts of the written word. The turbulent period which followed Jayadeva — who most probably was patronised by Lakṣmaṇa Sena of Bengal towards the end of the 12th century AD — destroyed many forms and traditions; there is nothing to wonder if Jayadeva's music, too, was lost.

Certainly no authentic and generally accepted music attributed to Jayadeva himself was surviving when Rāṇā Kumbha wrote his *Rasikapriyā ṭikā* on the *Gītagovinda* in the middle of the 15th century AD.[46] Kumbha in his prologue

---

[45] We have no direct access to manuscript material, but we give a few striking examples from two printed texts of the *Gītagovinda*, and the *pāṭhabhedas* they record. The texts are (1) the Nirṇaya Sāgaṛa edition with the *ṭikās* of Kumbha and Śaṁkara Miśra, (2) and the Lalbhai Dalpatbhai, Bharatiya Sanskriti Vidyamandir, Ahmedabad, edition with the *ṭikā* of Mānāṅka. The different *rāgas* and *tālas* recorded for the 10th *aṣṭapadī* are: (a) *rāga deśavarāḍī, paḍimaṭha tāla*, (b) *rāga deśākha, virādī* (?) *tāla*, (c) *rāga gauḍī, parimaṭha tāla* (d) *rāga deśavarāḍi, rūpaka tāla*. The 16th *aṣṭapadi* has: (a) *rāga desākha, gauḍivamaṭha* (?) *tāla*, (b) *rāga mālava gauḍa*, (c) *rāga deśākha, ekatālī tāla*, (d) *rāga deśavarāḍī, rūpaka tāla*. The 17th has: (a) *rāga bhairavī, yati tāla*, (b) *rāga bhairava, yati tāla*, (c) *rāga megha*. The differences recorded here are apart from those given by Kumbha; he had used an entirely different set of *rāgas* and *tālas* for the *aṣṭapadīs*.

[46] Kumbha reigned from AD 1433 to 1468. He seems to have composed the *Rasikapriyā* towards the end of his reign after having fought and won many battles. Verse 14 in the prologue to his *ṭikā* reads:

laments the fact that no *ṭīkā* on the *prabandha* composed by Jayadeva exists which deals with all the aspects of the song. By this he meant that commentators had confined themselves to explaining the text alone. He proposes to fill in the existing gap by indicating the *svara* and other six limbs of a *prabandha* (such as *pāṭa, tena* etc.) as they should be musically arranged in the sung form of the poem.[47]

But the music to which Kumbha here alludes, was not a traditionally current form, but one which he had himself composed to the *Gītagovinda*. Repeatedly he informs us that he himself was putting the text composed by Jayadeva to music. Beginning his *ṭīkā* on *sarga* two, he says — using the musical parlance of his day — that he was adding his own *dhātu* to Jayadeva's *mātu: dhātu* and *mātu* meant in medieval times, what the words '*svara*' (music) and '*bol*' (words) mean today.[48] Kumbha makes the same assertion at the commencement of his comments on the third, fourth, fifth, eighth and other *sargas*.

Kumbha in his *Rasikapriyā* often refers to and quotes from his great tome on music, the *Saṅgītarāja.* It appears that Kumba had set the *Gītagovinda* to his own music in the *prabandha* idiom, even before he wrote the *Saṅgītarāja*, for in this text he says that he has composed 28 *prabandha* songs to the text of the *Gītagovinda*. He classifies these *prabandhas* as belonging to the *miśrasūḍa* class, and lists them with the words:

aṣṭāviṁśatirete' tra prabandhāḥ kṛṣṇabhūbhujā

---

jitvā tu pṛthviṁ kṛtvā tatpatīnkaradāyinaḥ/rādhāmādhavasārasya rasiko ramate'dhunā.

[47] *pratyajñāyi prabandho yo jayadevena dhīmatā na tasya vidyate lakṣma* sarvāṅgairupalakṣitaḥ *ataḥ svarādibhih ṣaḍbhiraṅgaiḥ saṁyojya tathyatāṁ/ nītvā, gītvā tadā hitvā kutukāttu pravartyate. Rasikapriyā,* prologue verses 14-15. In the same passage Kumbha again says:

atha kumbhakarṇanṛpatiḥ stutvā natvā sarasvatīṁ devīm/svarapāṭatenakānāṁ karoti gumphaṁ sumānārtham. Ibid., verse 21. The printed text reads '*pāṭha*', in the second line; but the association with *tena* and *svara* clearly indicates that the reading should be *pāṭa.* Elsewhere Kumbha calls his *ṭīkā* a 'total *ṭīkā*' *kḷptavivṛti* and a *ṭīkā* which illumines the music of the *Gītagovinda* (See verse 7 in the *Rasikapriyā* on *sarga* 3).

[48] S.R. 3, 2; quoted earlier; see footnote 25.

svopajñagītagovindamiśrasūḍe prapañcitāḥ
(*Saṅgītarāja* 2, 4, 2, 29)

(These 28 *prabandhas* are arranged by Kumbha in the *Gītagovinda miśrasūḍa* — a class of *prabandhas* — which he has himself composed) Kumbha had given to these *prabandhas* names inspired by Jayadeva such as: *sāmodadāmodarabhramarapada, akleśakeśavakuñjaratilaka, amandamukundamakarandaḥ*, and such like.

Kumbha's comments can give us no idea as to how Jayadeva had composed the *prabandhas* almost three hundred years earlier, but they can certainly give us some notion as to how the text of a song was moulded to the *prabandha* form. This notion, too, can be but a faint shadow of what Kumbha had musically achieved, for he does not give us any notations. And even if he had, they would have been like an undecoded language to us, because the tonal values of notations found in old *saṅgīta*-texts are far from being satisfactorily known.

Still, with these reservations in mind, let us take a few examples of how Kumbha had applied the formal musical elements of the *prabandha* genre to the *Gītagovinda*. This will at least give us an inkling of the nature of the *prabandha* idiom:

1. The second *aṣṭapadī* is the hymn beginning with:

śritakamalākucamaṇḍala dhṛtakuṇḍala e
kalitalalitavanamāla jaya jaya deva hare

In this song an *ālāpa* — a free improvised musical passage, devoid of words[49] — was to be effected with the last syllable 'e' of the first line *(atra ekārādirālapo jñeyaḥ)*. The first line of every stanza in this *aṣṭapadī* ends with an *ekāra:* all were to be followed by an *ālāpa*; the purpose being to give a proper musical form and expression to the *rāga* being sung.[50] The *ālāpa* was to be rich in the use of *gamakas*.[51]

---

[49] *rāgālāpanamālaptirbhūribhaṅgimanoharā / prayogādvā tathālāpasaṁjñā sākṣaratārjitā: Saṅgītarāja*, 2, 2, 3, 52.

[50] *'e' iti etadante rāgapūrtyai gānavelāyāṁ pratipadaṁ etāvadpadam. Rasikapriyā, sarga* 1, *aṣṭapadī* 2.

[51] *ālāpaṁ ca pratipadaṁ nānāgamakapeśalaḥ. Ibid.*

In current classical music, too, the singing of a poetic text is interspered with purely musical passages so as to give shape to the *rāga.*

2. The celebrated *aṣṭapadī* beginning with *'lalitalavaṅgalat-āpariśīlanakomalamalayasamīre'* was also to be interspersed with *ālāpas* rich in *gamakas*. At the end of the poem were sung the auspicious *'tena'* syllables followed by *pāṭa-akṣaras* or *mṛdaṅga* bols, after which '*saragam's* were sung.[52]

3. The fourth *aṣṭapadī (candanacarcitanīlakalevara-pītavasana-vanamālī..)* was set to *rāga gurjarī* and *jhampa tāla.* At the end of its last musical movement, called *ābhoga, sargams* were sung, followed by *mṛdaṅga* bols (i.e. *pāṭa*), after which a few stanzas of the song were repeated.[53]

Similar formal elements are found in the composition of other *aṣṭapadīs*. These features of the *prabandha* idiom, remind us of our own approach in musically interpreting poetic texts in the classical style of singing, and can help us imagine the expressive richness of the *aṣṭapadī* form.

---

[52] "*teneti maṅgalavācakam. tata pāṭavādyākṣarotkaraḥ. tataḥ svaraḥ ṣaḍjādiḥ*" Ibid., *sarga* 1, *aṣṭapadī* 3, also in the same context:

gamakālaptibhūyiṣṭhaḥ pūrṇakalpaḥ prakīrtitaḥ pūrtau punastena-pāṭasvarāṇi...

[53] Ibid., *sarga* 2. *aṣṭapadī* 1.

CHAPTER – FIFTEEN

Music in the *Ṭhāṇaṁga Sūtra*

Aṅga is the primary canon of the Jains. Śvetāmbara Jains have preserved eleven of the originally twelve *aṅgas* in a redaction made by Devarddhigaṇi in the Fifth century AD. *Ṭhāṇaṁga* is the third *aṅga*. This *aṅga* is a store-house of varied lore. Together with matter relating to Jain doctrine and conduct, it also contains much information on many secular arts, skills and sciences.

The arrangement of contents in the *Ṭhāṇaṁga* follows a plan based on numbers. The work is divided into ten *sthānas* (*thāṇas*), and music is placed in the seventh *sthāna* because the basis of music is the seven-note octave.

The *Ṭhāṇaṁga* account of music is short and cursory. It is unsatisfactory as a systematic and comprehensive delineation of ancient Indian music, and is similar in this respect to the description of the subject as found in *Purāṇas* such as the *Mārkaṇḍeya* and the *Viṣṇudharmottara*. It has, nevertheless, many points of interest. Early texts on music are rare and the *Ṭhāṇaṁga* description is valuable on this count also, for it belongs to a period from which few texts survive.[1]

The text on music as found in the *Ṭhāṇaṁga* also occurs almost verbatim in the *Aṇuŏgadāra*, another canonical work of the Jains. *Aṇuŏgadāra* is part of the secondary Jain canon.[2] The

---

[1] The *aṅgas* contain material much antedating Devarddhigaṇi who was primarily a compiler. However, certain minor changes, deletions and additions in the *aṅgas* did occur as the discrepancies between the contents of the texts as available and as noted in the later portions of the canon or reported by early *ṭikākāras* show. Muni Nathamal in his editor's preface, pp. 5-6 to the Jain Śvetāmbara Terāpanthī Mahāsabhā, Calcutta, edition of the *Āyāra* text gives some examples of such changes in the case of *Ayāra*. See also *A History of Indian Literature*, Winternitz Vol. II, foot note 3 on p. 47.

[2] *Aṇuogaddāra* is classed by some as a *mūla sutta* and as *cūlikā* by others (see Introduction to *Dasaveyāliya*, edited by Amolak Chandra Surpuria,

material on music in this text seems to have been borrowed from the *Ṭhāṇaṁga*, which being an *aṅga,* contains earlier material.

The purpose of including music as a topic in the *aṅga* was, evidently, to give the Jain monks a modicum of acquaintance with the art. The *Ṭhāṇaṁga* account has no further ambitions and for a fuller and more detailed understanding of the subject one has to turn to texts like the *Nāradīya Śikṣā, Nāṭyaśāstra* and *Dattilam*.

II

As the *Ṭhāṇaṁga* dissertation on music is short and also little known, we give here a full translation of it. We will then attempt at a study and analysis of the text in the light of other ancient accounts.

THE TEXT[3]

Names of notes

Musical notes (*svaras*) are said to be seven in number. They are: *ṣaḍja, ṛṣabha, gāndhāra, madhyama, pañcama, dhaivata* and *niṣāda;*[4] thus are the seven notes termed.

Svarasthānas

There are said to be seven *sthānas* for these seven notes: *ṣaḍja* is produced from the tip of the tongue (*aggajibbhaeṁ*), *ṛṣabha* from the chest (*ureṇa*), *gāndhāra* from the throat, *madhyama* from the middle of the tongue, *pañcama* from the nasal region, *dhaivata* from the area of the lips and the teeth, and *niṣāda* from the roof of the palate. Such are the *svara-sthānas.*

---

published by Raibahadur Motilal Mutha, Bhavani Peth, Satara). Winternitz classifies *Aṇūoga* with *Nandi* as an independent canonical text and mentions that some classify them as *prakīrṇas* (op. cit., pp. 429-30).

[3] We have used the text as given in the edition published by the Akhila Bhāratīya Jaina Śāstroddhāra Samiti, Rajkot, 1965. The text includes a *ṭikā* in Sanskrit and explanations in Hindi and Gujarati by Muni Ghāsīlāljī. See Appendix II for the original Prakrit.

[4] We will give Sanskrit terms as they are more familiar than Prakrit.

Svaras produced by living beings

Seven *svaras* are said to be produced by living beings (*jīvanissiyā*), in this manner: *ṣaḍja* is sounded by the peacock, *ṛṣabha* by the cock, *gāndhāra* is the call of the swan, and *madhyama* that of sheep. In the (spring) season when flowers bloom, the *kokila* sings the *pañcama*. The sixth note is (in the call) of the *sārasa*, and the *krauñca* bird sounds the *niṣāda*.

Svaras produced by non-living objects

Seven svaras are said to be produced by non-living objects (*ajīvanissiyā*), as follows: *ṣaḍja* is the sound of the *mṛdaṅga*, *ṛṣabha* of the (instrument called) *gomukha*;[5] the conch sounds the *gāndhāra*, and *madhyama* is sounded by the *jhallarī*;[6] the *godhikā* with a four-legged stand[7] sounds the *pañcama*; the *āḍambara*[8] sounds *dhaivata* and the seventh (note) is (sounded by) the *mahābherī*.[9]

Svara lakṣaṇas:

There are said to be seven *svara-lakṣaṇas* related to these seven *svaras*. These are (as follows):

With *ṣaḍja* a person acquires livelihood (*vittiṁ*) and (his) actions do not remain fruitless;[10] he comes to possess many cows, friends and sons and is loved by many women.

With *ṛṣabha* (a person) acquires power (*esajjaṁ*); (he) becomes a commander of armies and accumulates great wealth. He comes to possess (rich) clothes, perfumes, jewellery, many couches and many women. With *gāndhāra* (a person) acquires proficiency in the science of music; (he) acquires an excellent

[5] A musical instrument perhaps of the horn variety.

[6] A kind of drum or may be a cymbal.

[7] The *sūtra* has *caucalana paiṭṭhāna gohiyā*'. '*Gohiyā* is explained as a kind of drum also called *dardarikā* by Ghāsīlālji. The descriptive epithet '*caucalana paiṭṭhāna* was evidently the distinctive trait of a special type of *godhikā*.

[8] Another kind of drum; also mentioned in *Śatapatha Brāhmaṇā*, 14.

[9] Another horn.

[10] The text reads '*kayaṁ ca na viṇassaī*'.

livelihood (*vajjavitti*) and becomes a master of many arts and skills. Poets, wise men and those learned in the *śāstras* (are persons who are characterised by *gāndhāra*).

Persons who are characterised by the note *madhyama* (*majjhimasarsampannā*) are people with a happy disposition (*suhajīviṇo*). They are generous, they eat, drink (and make merry): Such is the (disposition) depending upon the note *madhyama.*

Persons characterised by the note *pañcama* become kings; they are brave, they gather together a great number of men[11] and become leaders of vast multitudes (*aṇekagaṇanāyagā*).

Persons characterised by the note *dhaivata* are of a quarrelsome nature. They become bird catchers (*sāüṇiyā*), hunters (*vagguriyā*), boar-catchers and fishermen.

People whose disposition depends upon *niṣāda* are *caṇḍālas*, professional boxers (*muṭṭhiya*), lowly people, sinners of various kinds, thieves, and killers of cows.

The three grāmas:

There are three *grāmas* relating to these seven *svaras*. The *grāmas* are: *ṣaḍja-grāma*, *madhyama-grāma* and *gāndhāra-grāma.*

Mūrchanās:

Ṣaḍja-grāma is said to have seven *mūrchanās*: *mārgi, kauravīyā, hari, rajanī, sārākrāntā, sārasī* and *śuddhaṣaḍjā.*

Madhyama-grāma is also said to have seven *mūrchanās*: *uttaramandrā, rajanī, uttarā, uttarasamā, samavakrāntā, sauvīrā* and *ābhīrī*, the seventh. *Gāndhāra-grāma*, too, is said to have seven *mūrchanās: nandī, kṣudrikā, pūrimā, śuddhagāndhārā* the fourth, *uttara-gāndhārā* the fifth, and *suṣṭhuttarāyāmā*, the sixth as per rules, and finally *uttarāyatā*, the seventh and last of the *mūrchanās.*

Questions relating to song techniques

Wherefrom are the seven notes produced ? What is the

---

[11] The expression is '*saṅgahakattāro*' which may also mean 'accumlators (of wealth).'

fountainhead (*yoni*) of song ? of what duration is the breath (in singing) ? How many are the processes *(āgārā)*[12] in a song ?

The answers

The seven *svaras* are produced from the region of the navel.

Lament is the fountainhead of song (*ruīyajoṇiyaṁ*).[13] The duration of the breath should be equal to one metric foot (*pāda*).

There are three processes (*āgārā*) in a song: (a song is) soft in the beginning, sustained in the middle and ends with a fury (*avasāne tajjavinto*).[14]

Criteria for a good singer

One who is properly trained and knows the six faults, the eight merits and the three *vṛttas* of song becomes proficient enough to sing in theatre-halls (*raṁgamajjhammi*).

The six faults

One should not sing timidly, or in too fast a tempo, or in a manner that cuts short the melodic movement; one should not stray away from the rhythm (*tāla*); (moreover, to sing in) a croaking crow-like voice and a nasal tone; these are the six faults in a song.

The eight merits

The eight merits in a good song are: fullness, affectiveness, melodic grace, clarity, avoidance of mere loudness, sweetness, evenness and charm.

---

[12] *Āgārā* literally means, 'forms', but what is signified seems more akin to processes or rather 'phases,' as the answer to this question implies.

[13] The question 'what is the *yoni* of a song' could mean 'what is nature or characteristic of a song, or 'to what class of things does a song belong'; the answer consequently would mean 'a song is of the nature of a lament or belongs to the same class as a lament.' See also Appendix I, at the end.

[14] Ghāsīlālji translates '*tajjavinto*' as '*kṣapayantaḥ*' which seems to be off the track. The *Pāia-sadda-Mahaṇṇavo* equates '*tajja*' with '*tajjay*' and gives the meaning as, 'to threaten,' 'to deride'. There is, however, a variant reading suggesting, *kṣapayantaḥ;* See Prakit text, Appendix II.

Aesthetic elements of a good song

A good song is fluent (*pasattha*) in all three octaves: *mandra, madhya* and *tāra*;[15] it is sung with an enticing flow of words; it is synchronised with the resounding *tāla*-beats *(samatālapaḍukkhevaṁ)* and is intoned with an even application of all seven *svaras*: It has depth *(sāramanta)* and grace; it is devoid of faults, rightly applied, sweet, and is sung with due deliberation over its various elements *(uvaṇītaṁ sovacāraṁ)* and with an eye to measured form *(mita)*.

Vṛtta

Vṛttas are of three kinds: *sama, ardhasama,* and *viṣama* in all respects — there is no fourth.

Languages of songs

Utterances are said to be of two kinds: Sanskrit and Prakrit, (both) are sung to the whole gamut of notes *(saramaṇḍalammi)*. The *Ṛṣibhāṣ-itas*[16] are the best songs (*pasattha*).

Different women and their inherent qualities as singers

Which women sing sweetly ? and which sing with a rough harshness ? which sing skilfully ? which sing at an (unduly) slow

[15] The text has '*urakaṇṭhasirapasatthaṁ*' '*ura*', '*kaṇṭha*' & '*sira*' were considered to be the three seats or abodes of the three octaves, *mandra, madhya* and *tāra*, respectively. The use of the terms '*ura*' etc. is, in this context, obviously indicative of the octaves which were said to reside in them. We come across similar figurative usage in other text too. See for example *Nāṭyaśāstra* 29, 43 (Gaekwad edition; this is the edition we will refer to throughout this paper); here the same *alaṅkāra* has different names when produced in the *kaṇṭha* (i.e. the *madhya* octave) and in the *śira* (the *tāra* octave).

[16] Ghāsīlālji interprets the phrase as a clause qualifyng the precedent statement. The meaning he gives is: 'they (Sanskrit and Prakrit) are commendable since they have been uttered by Ṛṣis.' But, Prakrit and not Sanskrit was the Jain *ārṣa* language. The reference is here perhaps to the Canon called *Ṛṣibhāṣita* or *Isibhāsiyāiṁ*. H.R. Kapadia also interprets the reference here as pointing to *Isibhāsiyāiṁ*, the canonic text. *(The Canonical Literature of the Jainas,* footnote on p. 125.) The *Isibhāsiyāiṁ* has 45 chapters, each a biography of one 45 of the '*pratyekabuddhas*' like Nārada, Aṅgarisi, Valkalacīrī and others. Many chapters are in verse and may have been set to music.

tempo ? which at a (misplaced) fast one and which stray out of a tune ?

Young and pretty women *(śyāmā)*[17] sing sweetly; dark ones sing with a rough harshness, fair women are skilfull in song; one-eyed women sing with an undue slowness and blind women with undue speed. Brown-eyed women[18] sing out of tune.

Well-synchronised song

(Songs sung with) the seven *svaras* (ought to be) well-synchronised with the accompanying instruments, the *tāla*, the prosodic measure (*pāda*), the tempo (*laya*), the *graha*,[19] and the melodic movement; (it should be) well regulated in breathing in and out.

The svaramaṇḍala

The seven notes, the three *grāmas*, the twenty-one *mūrchanās*, the forty-nine *tānas*: these constitute the *svara-maṇḍala*.

III

We observe that the delineation is fragmentary, eclectic and disjointed. Only a few stray topics of the ancient musical system are treated, and these, too, are merely noticed. The account tells us little of the forms and techniques of ancient music, but seems rather to be a randomly collected popular digest of musical lore. Purāṇic accounts of music are similar in character, and were, evidently, collected with a similar populistic aim.[20]

The theoretical framework within which ancient musical forms and structures were interpreted and morphologically analysed had developed quite early into an organised discipline.

---

[17] Literally, '*śyāmā*' means 'a girl with a darkish complexion': it also denotes a 'young and pretty girl'. Kālidāsa uses the word in this sense in the *Meghadūta,* when describing the *yakṣiṇī* as '*tanvī śyāmā...*'

[18] The term is '*piṁgalā.* It perhaps also signified women with hazel-brown eyes, or pigmented brownish skins. A *piṁgalā* was, obviously, not admired.

[19] *Graha* was the initial *svara* in a melodic pattern.

[20] For a collection of Purāṇic records on music see '*Textes des Purāṇas Sur La Theorie Musicale'*, Alain Danielou and N.R. Bhatt, Pondicherry 1959. The records in different *Purāṇas* are not all of the same length and scope, but they all share a populistic tendency. The *Purāṇas* were, after all, 'popular' works.

Already in the *Nāṭyaśāstra* — which had acquired its present form by the second or third century AD — we find a fully developed scheme hierarchically arranged into basic and secondary categories and concepts. *Nāṭyaśāstra* does not name earlier musical authorities but it alludes to an authoritative tradition[21] and certainly had many precursors.

The *Ṭhāṇaṁga* barely lists four concepts of the ancient musical scheme, namely *grāma, mūrchanā, sthāna* and *tāna.*

The text does no more than record the names of the three ancient *grāmas*. Of these, the *gāndhāra-grāma* was an obsolete *grāma* and survived only in memory. The *Nāradīyā Śikṣā* speaks of it as existing with the gods alone.[22]

Ṭhāṇaṁga also names the *mūrchanās* of the three *grāmas.* The names recorded are quite at variance with other ancient lists.[23]

---

[21] *Nāṭyaśāstra* refers to *āptopadeśa'* — 'ancient authoritative decree' — in speaking of the two *niṣādas* (28, 34); in describing the *jātis* — ancient *rāga*-like formations — it often refers to rules or formulations as being '*smṛtāḥ*' or '*prakītritāḥ*' etc. i.e. 'traditionally current' (28, 64; 83; 85; 88; 90; 92; etc.). Similar expressions occur in the description of *tāla* structures (31, 106; 109; 125; 144, etc.).

[22] *Nāradīyā Śikṣā,* 1, 2, 7.

[23] The *Nāradīyā Śikṣā* enumerates two sets of *mūrchanās*, without clearly assigning them to any specific *grāma.* The first set has: *nandī, viśālā sumukhī, citrā, citravatī, sukhā* and *valayā* (the text reads *valaya*). These are called the *mūrchanās* of the gods. The enumeration of the second set is couched in a language which suggests that the *mūrchanās* belong to the *ṣaḍja-grāma:*

ṣaḍje tūttaramandrā syādṛṣabhe cābhirudgatā
aśvakrāntā tu gāndhāre tṛtīyā mūrchanā smṛtā
madhyame khalu sauvīrā hṛṣyakā pañcame svare
dhaivate cāpi vijñeyā mūrchanā tūttarāyatā
niṣādādrajanīṁ vidyādṛṣiṇāṁ sapta mūrchanā

(*Nāradīyā Śikṣā,* 1, 2, 9-12)

The *Nāṭyaśāstra* gives almost the same set of names for the *ṣaḍja-grāma mūrchanās* as the *Nāradīyā Śikṣā* with a little difference in the sequence of names (*Nāṭyaśāstra* 28, 27-28). This text lists another set of *ṣaḍja-grama mūrchanās* which is again the same as that of Nārada *and* is given in the very same language (ibid. 28, 29-30). The *madhyama-grāma mūrchanās* in the *Nāṭyaśāstra* are *sauvīrī, hariṇāsvā, kalopanatā, śuddhamadhyā, mārgī, pauravī* and *hṛṣyakā* (ibid. 28, 31).

The *Vāyupurāṇa* gives the same *mūrchanās* for the *ṣaḍja-grāma,* and enumerates them in the same sequence as in the first set listed in the *Nāṭyaśāstra*

Nowhere does the *Ṭhāṇaṁga* account suggests that only two *grāmas* were employed in actual musical practice. Yet the tenor of the text in its present form does not bespeak of an antiquity so high as might lead us to infer that it was composed when the three-*grāma* system was prevalent. The *Ṭhāṇaṁga* account, on the whole, assumes the same framework of ideas and notions as are embodied in the *Nāradīyā Śikṣā* which belongs to a period when *gāndhāra-grāma* was quite obsolete.

We do not know when the *gāndhāra-grāma* became obsolete. The earliest known texts were all written within a two-*grāma* system which had already become firmly established by the period of the *Nāṭyaśāstra* and must have been the ruling musical system for some centuries before.

Still we must not forget that there certainly was a *gāndhāra grāma* once. Musical tradition has never let the memory of it die. Some latter-day theorists — like Nānyadeva in his *Bharatabhāṣya* — even constructed a tonal structure for it in order to give it a greater semblance of reality.

The *Ṭhāṇaṁga* account of music is a heterogeneous juxtaposition of diverse material; perhaps in its diversity it also preserves several layers of material representing diverse periods of musical history. The nucleus of the *Ṭhāṇaṁga*, in all probability, goes back to Mahāvira's immediate disciples. It is likely that the record hearkens back to an age when the *gāndhāra-grāma* was an actuality, or at least still fresh in people's memory.

Much of the *Ṭhāṇaṁga,* however, bears the stamp of a relatively later date. It reflects the same milieu of musical culture as is pictured in the *Nāradīyā Śikṣā,* and the *Nāṭyaśāstra.* The *Śikṣā* is believed to have been composed in the beginning of the Christian era; the *Nāṭyaśāstra* may be a century or two later. Both texts utilised earlier material.

(see *Texts des Purāṇa Sur La Theoris Musicale,* p. 32). This *Purāṇa* also gives a list of *gāndhāra-grāma mūrchanās: ālāpā, kṛtrimā nandinī, viśuddhagāndhārī. gandhārī, uttarā, ṣaḍjā* and *pañcāyatā* (ibid. p. 36). Barely a few names here bear a resemblance with the *Ṭhāṇaṁga* list of *gāndhāra-grāma mūrchanās.*

The present *Ṭhāṇaṁga Sūtra* mentions an event which occurred six hundred years after the *Nirvāṇa* of Mahāvīra. This *aṅga,* then, was certainly retouched in the 1st-2nd Centuries AD. Perhaps at this period new matter was also added to the work in order to enlarge its encyclopaedic scope; the section on music, too, evidently received its share of accretions. The older nucleus — containing the enumeration of three *grāmas* and their *mūrchanas* must have been preserved — albeit with certain changes or alterations — as part of a hallowed memory. Nor was it thought necessary to point out that the three-*grāma* system no longer prevailed; for the purpose of the text was not to serve as a practical guide to music but only as a record of popular lore. Often in popular descriptions of this sort entities which no longer hold sway in practice continue to figure as important, echoing the fact that these entities, too, had their day. Thus we see even today that in many popular enumerations of major *rāga*-forms, the name of *rāga dīpaka* looms large. Although *dīpaka* has been a lost *rāga* for long.

The Purāṇic texts on music, which, too, are popular accounts, also presume a three-*grāma* system like the *Ṭhāṇaṁga*, despite the fact that in their present form the *Purāṇas* are probably later than the *Ṭhāṇaṁga*; for they were, in their extant form, composed in the Gupta age or after.

Another fact is worth noting: the *Nāradīyā Śikṣā* suggests that *ṣaḍja, ṛśabha* etc. were comparatively later names for the *svaras*; in the older *sāma* music the *svaras* had another set of names.[24] *Ṭhāṇaṁga*, gives the later *svara*-names and shows no awareness of any older nomenclature. This, however, does not detract from the value of *Ṭhāṇaṁga* as recording old traditions, for the *ṣaḍja-ṛṣabha* nomenclature is not necessarily of a later date than the period of the three *grāmas*.

Besides *grāma* and *mūrchanā*, the *Ṭhāṇaṁga* also speaks of *sthāna*.

The notion of *sthāna* or 'abode' was in ancient musical

---

[24] *Nāradīyā Śikṣā,* 1, 1, 12.

theory based on a principle which related the octaves in singing to various regions of the human anatomy. Ancient music was usually conceived of as having a range of three octaves: *mandra* (Lower), *madhya* (middle) and *tāra* (upper). Chest was the abode of the *mandra*; it was from the chest that this octave was thought to be produced. The throat and head regions were similarly the abodes of *madhya* and *tāra*, respectively.

The *Nāradīyā Śikṣā* has named these three *sthānas.*[25] The *Śikṣā* also gives another, quite different category of *sthānas* for each of the seven *svaras,* severally: *ṣaḍja* is said to be born from the throat, *ṛṣabha* from the head, *gāndhāra* from the nasal region, *madhyama* from the chest, *pañcama* from the three regions of the chest, head and throat, *dhaivata* from the forehead and *niṣāda* from all the above regions.[26]

The *Ṭhāṇaṁga* account of *sthāna* is akin to the second category of *sthānas* given in the *Nāradīyā Śikṣā*. But the details are quite at variance; the *Ṭhāṇaṁga* relates the *svaras* to different regions situated almost exclusively in the buccal cavity much in the manner of ancient Sanskrit grammarians recounting the '*sthānas*' of different Sanskrit phonemes.[27] There seems to be an attempt here, both by the *Śikṣā* and the *Ṭhāṇaṁga* to extend the concept of *sthāna,* as a concept which pictures the

---

[25] *Nāradīyā Śikṣā,* 1, 1, 7-8; also *Dattilam,* 8 and 42.

[26] *Nāradīyā Śikṣā,* 1, 5, 5-6. This passage in the *Śikṣā* is followed by a set of details of the same category but at variance with it. The relation between the two different sets of details concerning the same aspect of *sthāna* is not made clear. The second set of details is as follows: *ṣaḍja* is produced when the breath strikes these six *sthānas*: nose, throat, chest, roof of the palate, tongue and teeth; *ṛṣabha* is produced when the breath strikes the throat and the head; *gāndhāra* is produced on the breath striking the throat, the head, and also the nose, and *pañcama* is prodused when the breath strikes the chest, the heart, the throat and the head: *Nāradīyā Śikṣā,* 1, 5, 7-10.

[27] The *Ṭhāṇaṁga*, however, shows awareness of the idea that chest, throat and head were the 'abodes' of the three ancient octaves, for it uses the terms *ura, kaṇṭha* and *śira* to denote the three octaves that were produced from these *sthānas.* It·also mentions the related process of the way that *nāda* (voice) was produced in the human body when it says that 'the seven *svaras* are produced from the navel' (cf. *Nāradīya Śikṣā,* 1, 5, 7-10).

physiology of sound-production through the human-frame, from the field of grammar to that of music. But the concept remains a mere copy; it is not given any empirical basis that could be really said to *describe* the actual processes of producing different *svaras* in terms of different physiological *places* related to them. Empirically, indeed, quite unlike grammar, the processes described have nothing to do with the actual physiology of *svara* production. In fact, there seems to be no process of *svara*-production which can be said to bear any semblance with the grammatical notion of *sthāna,* and the production of different phonemes through the voice.[28]

The *Ṭhāṇaṁga* text closes with a definition of the ancient notion of '*svaramaṇḍala*'. The verse here is almost an exact Prakrit parallel of the verse in the *Nāradīyā Śikṣā* containing the same idea.[29] The *Ṭhāṇaṁga* mentions the concept of *tāna* in this passage but does not explain it, nor does it name the *tānas.*

IV

Though unsatisfactory as a guide to the schema and forms of ancient music, the *Ṭhāṇaṁga* text outlines certain ideas and notions that formed the metaphysical and aesthetic perspective in which music was generally envisioned and evaluated.

One deep-rooted ancient idea was that musical tones had a series of extra-musical dimensions. The seven *svaras* were perceived to have attributes correlating them with phenomena which, apparently, have nothing to do with tones: a *svara* was not only a pleasing sound, it had a colour, a social caste and also a deity.

The *Nāradīya Śikṣā* lists the following series of these attributes:

The colours of *svaras: ṣaḍja* is said to possess a lotus hue, *ṛṣabha* has a tawny parrot-green colour, *gāndhāra* is golden,

[28] For further discussion, the reader might like to see another essay in this collection, 'The Body As An Instrument'.

[29] *saptasvarāstrayo grāmā mūrchanāstvekaviṁśatiḥ/ tānā ekonapañcāśadityetatsvara-maṇḍalam. Nāradiya Śikṣā,* 1, 2, 4. The notion of *svaramaṇḍala* is differently conceived in the *Nāṭyaśāstra* and the *Dattilam.* These two texts relate the notion to the *śruti*-intervals between *svaras* (See *Dattilam* 15; *Nāṭyaśāstra* 24).

madhyama is the colour of reddish-white oriander *(kunda)*, *pañcama* is black (or dark blue: *kṛṣna*). *dhaivata* is yellow and *niṣāda* possess all the colours.

These are the '*varṇas*' of *svaras* but each has a *varṇa* also in the sense of social caste: *pañcama, madhyama* and *ṣaḍja* are *brāhmaṇas; dhaivata* and *ṛṣabha* are *kṣatriyas*, while *gāndhāra* and *niṣāda* are half-*vaiśya*, half-*śūdra*.[30]

Svaras also have transcendental attributes. Every *svara* has a specific deity (*adhiṣṭātṛ devatā*): *ṣaḍja* has Brahmā for its deity; *ṛṣabha* has Agni — 'because this *svara* radiates a fiery brilliance;' *gāndhāra* has the cow — 'because it is pleasing to the cattle, and the *saurabheyas* (i.e. 'cattle', but also 'Rudra') come running on hearing it; *pañcama* has as its deity, Soma — 'for in the different musical *grāmas* this *svara* like the Moon, waxes and wanes in measure; *dhaivata*, too, for the same reason, also has Soma for its deity and *niṣāda* has Āditya — 'since this *svara* overpowers all others.'[31]

Later texts also record attributes of this kind. Mataṅga (ca. 7th century AD) and Śārṅgadeva (13th century AD), for example, give similar lists. Their list of deities is however, quite at variance with that of the *Nāradīyā Śikṣā*.[32] There were, clearly,

---

[30] *Nāradiyā Śikṣā*, 1, 4, 1-4.

[31] *ādyasya daivataṁ brahmā ṣaḍjasyāpyucyate budhaiḥ*
tīkṣṇadīptiprakāśatvādṛṣabhasya hutāśanaḥ
gāvāḥ pragīte tuṣyanti gāndhārastena hetunā
śrutvā caivopatiṣṭhanti saurabheyā na saṁśayaḥ
somastu pañcamasyāpi daivataṁ brahmarāṭ smṛtam
nirhrāso yaśca vṛddhiśca grāmamāsādya somavat
tasmādasya svarasyāpi dhaivatatvaṁ vidhīyate
niṣīdanti svarā yasmānniṣādastena hetunā
sarvāṁścābhibhavatyeṣa yadādityo'sya daivatamiti.

Nāradīyā Śikṣā, 1, 5, 12-18.

The deity for *madhyama* is missing from the text. Bhaṭṭa Śobhokara in his *ṭīkā* interprets the passage as recounting Āditya for both *dhaivata* and *niṣāda*. This, we think, is misconstrued. *Dhaivata* has been bracketed with *pañcama*, not *niṣāda*. Like *pañcama*, *dhaivata* was the only other note which underwent an increase and decrease in measure in the two ancient *grāmas*. Nānyadeva in this context clearly says: '*somavad vṛddhimāpanno dhaivataḥ somadaivataḥ*': *Bharatabhāṣya*, 3, 17.

[32] *ṣaḍjasya daivataṁ brahmā ṛṣabho vahnidaivataḥ*
gāndhāro bhāratīdevo madhyamo haradaivataḥ

different traditions in this matter. The *varṇas* given in all texts are, however, identical.[33]

Envisioning such attributes was part of the ethos of the period when early theorisings on music and speech-sounds developed. The *Yājñavalkya Śikṣā* gives a similar scheme of attributes for the phonemes and syllables of Sanskirt speech.[34] The concept of such attributes had, evidently, arisen out of a perception of affinity or identity felt at an intuitive, psychic plane.

In later ages enumerating these extra-musical attributes of *svaras* became a part of the mythical lore that grew around music. But this lore appears to have survived as a pious convention alone and not in spirit. Yet we can, to some degree, still sense the genuine core of psychic intuition that lay at the root of this convention, because we still have a 'feel' for qualities in music which are somewhat analogous in nature. We still feel that different *rāgas* have an inner affinity with different hours of the day and with different seasons of the year (at least we do so in the Hindustāni tradition). A morning *rāga* sung in the evening offends our sensibilities; the *rāga malhār* invariably reminds us of rains.[35]

The later medieval phenomenon of picturing *rāgas* as elaborate deities — of which we find the first evidence in the 14th century,[36]

---

pañcamaḥ śatayajñastu dhaivato gaṇanāyakaḥ
niṣādo bhānudevastu ityete svaradevatāḥ. *Bṛhaddeśī* 79-81.

Śārṅgadeva's list has many deities in common with this but not all: *Saṅgītaratnākara* 1, 3, 57-58.

[33] Nānyadeva (12th century AD) has '*karbura*' for *niṣāda: Bharatabhāṣya* 3, 4. Śārṅgadeva has the same: *Saṅgītaratnākara* 1, 3, 55. But this is not essentially different from the colour given by Nārada, since '*karbura*' also means 'of a variegated colour,

[34] *Yājñavalkya Śikṣā* 86-92. We refer to the edition published in the Banaras Sanskrit Series, by Griffith and Thibaut, Banaras 1891.

[35] For a very different view of the concept of the affinity between seasons and times of the day and *rāgas,* see the essay, 'An Enquiry Into The *Rāga* — Time, Association In the Light of History,' recorded earlier in this collection.

[36] The earliest *rāga-dhyānas* are found in the *Sangītopaniṣatsāroddhāra* of Sudhākalaśa (AD 1350) — see ch. 3 verses 72 to 111. The trend may have begun a century earlier. See also the essay, 'Some Thoughts On The Early History of Rāgamālā Paintings' in this collection.

— and as painterly images in the later *rāga-mālā* paintings, too, can certainly be traced to the early concept of assigning a deity and a colour to every *svara.*

The *Ṭhāṇaṁga* does not list the kind of extramusical *svara*-attributes that other ancient texts do. It, however, speaks of another: it identifies each *svara* with the call of a specific bird or animal. This, too, was a generally held notion, and the *Ṭhāṇaṁga* enumeration has its counterpart in the *Nāradīyā Śikṣā* and other texts, both early and relatively modern. The language in which the descriptions are couched suggest that the relation in this case was considered to be an actual physical one: the peacock is said to intone the note *ṣaḍja*,[37] the sheep bleat out the *madhyama*, the *kokila* actually sings in the *pañcama* and so forth.

The implications are intriguing. Did the ancients really recognise the *svaras* of their octave in the cries of certain birds and animals ? The expressions in the texts do seem to suggest so, yet there are certain difficulties in accepting this as a fact. Let us consider them.

To picture an actual correspondence one may postulate that the ancients had standardised the pitches for different notes just as one finds in modern western music.[38] Tuning forks are used in the west to provide conventionally fixed pitches. Cries of birds and animals, we may imagine, similarly acted as live tuning forks for the ancients; so that if one wanted to arrive at the standard pitch of the *ṣaḍja,* one only had to listen to the wail-like cry of the peacock. Other notes could similarly be arrived at. But this picture, though appealing, cannot hold ground for a number of reasons.

---

[37] Note Kallinātha's comments on *Saṅgītaratnākara* 1, 3, 46-47: *'lokato' pi ṣaḍjā-disvarūparijñānāya mayūrādiprāṇiviśeṣadhvaniṁ nidarśanābhiprā-yeṇāha "mayūreti".*

[38] We must not forget that the evidence from *Dattilam* seems to battle against this assumption. Dattila says that any sound whatever could be taken as the *ṣaḍja,* and other notes followed through a fixed ratio of tonal relations; *Dattilam* 12. It might, however, be argued that by the time of *Dattilam* the older tradition was already lost.

Firstly, there is the difficulty of variant traditions. Different accounts equate the *svaras* with the cries of quite different birds or animals. The enumeration in the *Nāradīyā Śikṣā* sharply diverges from the one in *Ṭhāṇaṁga*. *Ṛṣabha* in the *Ṭhāṇaṁga* account is the cry of the cock but the *Nāradīyā Śikṣā* names the cow; *gāndhāra* according to the *Śikṣā* corresponds to the bleating of sheep or goats (*ājāvika*) but *Ṭhāṇaṁga* equates it with the call of the swan, and according to this text the sheep (*meṣa*) bleat in the note *madhyama*, not *gāndhāra*. The *Śikṣā* equates *dhaivata* and *niṣāda* with the calls of horses and elephants respectively[39] but *Ṭhāṇaṁga* in these cases names the *sārasa* and the *krauñca*. One contradiction especially stands out: the *krauñca* bird according to the *Śikṣā* calls in the *madhyama* but according to the *Ṭhāṇaṁga* the *krauñca* calls in the *niṣāda*, a note half an octave away from *madhyama*. Later texts report other traditions. Mataṅga, quoting Kohala,[40] equates *ṛṣabha* with the call of the *cātaka* bird and *dhaivata* with the croaking of the monsoon frogs.[41] The rest of his list is as in the *Nāradīyā Śikṣā*.

Still, we find two constants: all known traditions equate *ṣaḍja* with the peacock's call and *pañcama* with the cooing of the *kokila*. These two equations had become almost axiomatic. Kālidāsa, thus, speaks of the '*ṣaḍjasaṁvādinīḥ kekāḥ*' ('the peacock's call, harmonious with the *ṣaḍja*') while the *pañcama* of the *kokila* was almost a by-word, as it still is. With these notes as our axis-sounds, notes which had an acoustically harmonic relation with each other in the ancient *ṣaḍja-grāma*, we can, in

---

39 *ṣaḍjaṁ vadati mayūro gāvo rambhanti cārṣabham*
ājāvike tu gāndhāraḥ krauñco vadati madhyamam
puṣpasādhāraṇe kāle kokilā vakti pañcamam
aśvastu dhaivataṁ vakti niṣādo vakti kuñjaraḥ

Nāradīyā Śikṣā, 1, 5, 3-4.

40 There is a confusion in the text on this point. The text quotes the passage with the words: '*tathā cāha kohalaḥ maheśvaraḥ*'. Kohala was a well-known ancient authority; the word *maheśvara* is out of place and seems to have been inserted by an inadvertent scribe.

41 *Bṛhaddeśī, vṛtti* on verse 62. The same tradition is given by Śārṅgadeva: *Saṅgītaratnākara*. 1, 3, 46-47.

principle, arrive at the other notes. But again there is a difficulty. None of these two birds produce sounds that are themselves constant, meaning that the birds do not produce single sounds. The peacocks call is distributed over a range of at least two tones and the *kokila* makes a whole melodic movement consisting of a large cluster of notes. How is one to pick out *ṣaḍja* and *pañcama* from this range of pitches ?[42]

The *Ṭhāṇaṁga* account makes another classification on this point which is relevant to our discussion. It equates the *svaras* not only with the calls of birds and animals but also with sounds produced by what it terms as 'non-living objects;' these being, in this instastce, musical instruments. An equation of this kind is not found in any non-Jain text.[43]

Ṣaḍja, the *Ṭhāṇaṁga* says, is produced by the *mṛdaṅga, ṛṣabha* by the *gomukha*, and so forth. The instruments named are of the percussion or the horn group — instruments that have a relatively limited range of tones — and yet none of them are instruments that sound at a constant pitch.[44] They could not have acted as tuning forks. They must, moreover, have come in different shapes and sizes and consequently they must have had different ranges of pitch. It is difficult to imagine of any specific instrument inherently producing only one definite *svara.*

We can only conclude that in all probability the relation between *svaras* and the sounds of birds, animals as well as musical instruments was also conceived on a psychic rather than a physical plane. This may also account for the difference we

---

[42] It must be added here in good faith that an acoustic study of the ratios between the sounds made by the various animals listed in ancient texts might, perhaps, provide a clue as to the pitch-positions, and tonal relations of ancient *svaras.*

[43] Sudhākalaśa, a Jain author of the 14th century, makes a similar classification of notes into *jīva,* and *ajīva* categories: '*sacetenakṛtāḥ ke' pi kecinniścetanodbhavāḥ; Saṅgītopaniṣadsāroddhāra* 1, 10. This classification was, evidently, borrowed from the *Ṭhāṇaṁga.*

[44] Bharata indeed speaks of tuning them: see *Nāṭyaśāstra* 34, 217; notice especially the expression '*śithilāñcitavadhrastaniteṣu yathāgrāmarāgamārjanalipteṣu mṛdaṅgeṣu...'*

find in the traditional lists of birds and animals, since flexibility is quite conceivable in matters perceived on a supra-sensory plane, without detracting from the value of the perception itself. We can, for instance, validly question if a particular *rāga* should indeed be called a 'morning' *rāga* rather than an 'evening' *rāga,* without questioning the principle of assigning such affinities.[45]

V

Music had developed into a consciously cultivated art at an early period. As a corollary it had also acquired a significant body of critical terminology. The very early history of music-criticism, as of the theoretical scheme of musical forms and structures, is obscure. Already in the *Nāradīyā Śikṣā*, critical criteria for evaluating music acquire an organised plan and vocabulary. The *Śikṣā* classifies and lists the *guṇas* (merits) and *doṣas* (faults) of performances much in the same way as the early *ālaṅkārikas* classified the *guṇas* and *doṣas* of poetry.

The *Ṭhāṇaṁga* enumerates eight merits and six faults. It gives us just a string of critical terms without explaining them. However, in many cases the terms are almost self-explanatory; though, of course, we cannot recapture the nuances they must have possessed in a living musical milieu.

The *Nāradīyā Śikṣā* lists ten *guṇas* and fourteen *doṣas*. It also has short prose passages defining and explaining the *guṇas*.[46] Most terms in the *guṇa*-enumeration are common with the *Ṭhāṇaṁga* list — six to be exact — though there is a difference in the number of terms.[47] But the *doṣa*-lists in the two

---

[45] Lively controversies occur among musicians regarding the 'morning' or 'evening' properties of many *rāgas*, especially newly composed ones.

[46] The *doṣas* are only listed, not expounded. The *Śikṣā* as we have it has some textual lacunae and irregularities. The original text might have contained expositions of the *doṣas*, too. *Nāradīyā Śikṣā,* 1, 3, 1-13.

[47] The *Śikṣā* list is: *gānasya tu daśavidhaguṇavṛttistadyathā: 'raktaṁ pūrṇamalaṅkṛtaṁ prasannaṁ vyaktaṁ, vikruṣṭaṁ ślakṣṇaṁ samaṁ sukumāraṁ madhuramiti guṇāḥ.' Nāradīyā Śikṣā,* 1, 3, 1. *Ṭhāṇaṁga* does not have *prasanna, vikruṣṭa, ślakṣṇa* and *sukumāra*. Instead it has *avighuṭṭha* and *sulaliya.*

texts have a great divergence.[48]

The *Nāṭyaśāstra* devotes a large section to the examination of *guṇas* and *doṣas* in music (ch-33). Merits and demerits of singing and instrumental playing are presented in the perspective of ancient theatre where music had a major role to play. The material is presented in a much more organised form than in the *Ṭhāṇaṁga* or the *Nāradīyā Śikṣā*. The delineation is, moreover, wider in scope; the merits of singers, players on different instruments and also instructors of music have been distinguished and separately treated. The treatment has many critical notions in common with the *Ṭhāṇaṁga* and the *Nāradīyā Śikṣā*. These must have part of the general milieu. But textual resemblances are superficial. The tenor of Bharata's text is quite different in mode and exposition.

Apart from a list of *guṇas* and *doṣas*, the *Ṭhāṇaṁga* also contains certain observations regarding the principles governing the forms and the aesthetics of ancient music, especially song. These observations are not found elsewhere — at least not in the same form — and are worthy of consideration.

The *Ṭhāṇaṁga* speaks of three '*āgāras*' of songs — a notion unique to *Ṭhāṇaṁga*. Songs it says, begin softly, they are sustained in the middle and end with a fury. The description, inspite of being laconic, is quite suggestive. It, apparently, outlines the general phases of melodic movements made in ancient renderings of song. The suggested formal contours remind us of our own classical singing which usually begins at a slow-soft pace, and gathering momentum as well as melodic wealth, ends with a fast turbulent movement.

After listing *guṇas* and *doṣas*, the *Ṭhāṇaṁga* sums up the

[48] The *Śikṣā* lists: *śaṅkitaṁ bhīta(ma)mudghuṣṭamavyaktamanunāsikaṁ*
kākasvaraṁ śirasi gataṁ tathā sthānavivarjitam
visvaraṁ virasaṁ caiva viśliṣṭaṁ viṣamāhatam
vyākulaṁ tālahīnaṁ ca gītidoṣāścaturdaśāḥ

Nāradīyā Śikṣā 1, 3, 11-12. Only three terms are in common with *Ṭhāṇaṁga* (if we read '*bhītam*' and not '*bhīmam*)'. The *Ṭhāṇaṁga* has '*duyaṁ*' '*rahasaṁ*' and '*uttālaṁ*' which are absent from the *Śikṣā* list.

qualities expected of a good song in a few pithy phrases. Such aphoristic passages were, no doubt, intended to serve as memorisable guide-lines for aspiring musicians as well as discerning listeners.

Another such aphoristic passage occurs at the end of the *Ṭhāṇaṁga* account and states a maxim in a nutshell, namely, that synchronisation or harmony (*samatva)* must pervade a song in all its parts. Especially interesting here is the notion of synchronised breathing. The advice — stated earlier in the text — that the breath should be equal in measure to a single metric foot is, evindently, a related idea. A metric foot usually marks a break or pause in the syntax of a poem; singers are, therefore, asked to regulate their breathing in such a manner that a pause in their singing should coincide with that in the sung text.

Such a notion of pause recalls the concept of *vidārī* (musical pause) as defined by Bharata in relation to theatric songs *(dhruvā)*. Bharata lays down the rule that in singing songs during dramatic performances a *vidārī* should be made to coincide with the consummation of a sentence or a clause.[49]

There is a tantalising, though cryptic, remark in the *Ṭhāṇaṁga* about the essential nature of song or the source of the impulse to sing. The remark is evocative of certain well-known and penetrating reflections on the origin of the poetic impulse. Songs, the text says, are '*ruditayoni*': they are of the nature of a lament or have their source in a lament. We are reminded of Shelley's famous line: 'Our sweetest songs are those that tell of saddest thought'. The remark also brings to mind Bhavabhūti's celebrated statement that all poetry expresses but one sentiment, the *karuṇa* — pathetic — others are nothing but *karuṇa* in different garbs.[50] Similar in spirit is the poignant story of how

[49] '*padavarṇasamāptistu vidarītyabhisaṁjñitā.*' *Nāṭyaśāstra* 32, 17. Abhinava clarifies: '*avāntaravākyasamāptau sthāyyādivarṇasyāpanyāsena nyāsena vā samāptirvidārī.*' It should be remembered that *vidārī* was intimately related to the meaning of a poem only in certain types of songs; it could also relate to melodic content alone.

[50] '*eko rasaḥ karuṇa eva nimittabhedādbhinnaḥ pṛthag pṛthagivāśrayate vivartān*'

Vālmīki, the *ādikavi,* (the primeval poet) composed the world's very first stanza of poetic verse at being deeply moved by the sorrow of a *krauñca* bird wailing for its dying mate.[51]

It is remarkable that most of the critical notions we find recorded in the *Ṭhāṇaṁga* (and other ancient texts) are still pertinent to our music-making today. Indeed, many ancient expressions can be discovered in current vernacular musical vocabulary; they are a living testimony to certain essential continuities of our art. No doubt, many of the notions are truisms and apply to all music, but a significant number of them are specific to the musical culture as developed in India.

VI

The *Ṭhāṇaṁga* text on music contains quite a motley collection of material within its small radius. It also records some interesting oddities of musical lore.

A longish passage expounds what the text terms *svara-lakṣaṇas*. The contention of the passage may be explained as an extended application of the principles of palmistry. The passage correlates the fortunes and the disposition of a person with his specific '*svara*'.

Similar divinations were part of the ancient science of *aṅgavidyā,* according to which any characteristic physical trait of a person could be a 'sign' (*lakṣaṇa*) or indication of his fortunes. Every man has a vocal chord which is as distinctive as the lines of his palm. Voice can thus form the basis of prognostication, and it was part of the business of *aṅgavidyā* to 'read' voices.

Not much literature on *aṅgavidyā* survives, though it must have been a very popular *vidyā.* We have fortunately one major ancient text in Jain Prakrit on the subject, entitled *Aṅgavijjā.* The work is classed by Jains as a canonical text of the *paiṇṇa* (*prakīrṇaka*) group and is assigned to the 4th century AD.[52] The

---

[51] See also Appendix I, at the end, for a discussion of a very different interpretation of passage in view here.

[52] See Dr. Motichandra's introduction to *Aṅgavijjā,* p. 35; text published by the Prakrit Text Society, Banaras 1957.

37th chapter of this work speaks of *lakṣaṇas* (the chapter is called *Lakṣanādhyāya*). A *lakṣaṇa* in this context meant the physical trait of a person: such as complexion *(vaṇṇa)* gait *(gati)* and the like. *Svara* is recounted as one of the *lakṣaṇas*. The word '*svara*' here is used in the sense of 'a sweet pleasant voice' and not to signify musical tones. Persons who possess *svara* — or in other words people with pleasant voices — are according to *Aṅgavijjā*, the lucky ones; they attain to great power *(issariya)*, or a like stature *(issariyasamāṇa)*, they acquire proficiency in speech *(gahiyavakkaṁ)*, and in the sciences, and become well-known and far-famed. Those devoid of *svara* are misfortunate in these respects.[53]

The *svara-lakṣaṇas* recorded in the *Ṭhāṇaṁga* are much more specific. Here the word '*svara*' denotes a particular musical tone. People with different *svaras* have different fortunes. And unlike the *Aṅgavijjā* account, possessing '*svara*' is not by itself considered beneficial; much depends on which *svara* one has: *dhaivata* and *niṣāda* are certainly not the right notes to have. But how is one to know the *svara* of a person ? No criteria are given. Perhaps, this, too, was a matter of psychic vision. Some occultists believe that every person emanates an aura of a specific colour. The *svara* of a person was, perhaps, similarly envisaged.

Another curious passage occurs among the remarks on musical aesthetics. The musical propensities of women are related to their looks and physical make-up. The basic criterion is simple: beautiful women sing beautifully, ugly ones make poor singers. The attitude reflects the ancient adage — '*yatrākṛtirtatra guṇāḥ*' ('excellence is where beauty is').

Women who are classed as *śyāmā* — a type universally lauded in ancient times — are described as the most excellent singers. Bharata, too in a similar context, has a good word to say

---

[53] *sarasampanne issariyaṁ issariyasamāṇaṁ kittijasasampannaṁ ca gahiyavakkaṁ vijjābhāgī ya sarasampanne bhavati sarahine etesiṁ vivatti. Aṅgavijjā*, ch. 37 (p. 174).

about women of the *śyāmā* type.[54] Abhinava, by way of explanation, comments that only a *śyāmā* could stand up to the rigours of musical training.[55] Bharata, however, refrains from going into details about types of women and their capabilities as musicians. He makes a general statement that in dramatic performances songs are often sweeter if sung by women, since women have a naturally melodious voice; recitative prose passages, he says, are more effectively spoken by men because of their vigorous voices.[56]

VII

We have said that the *Ṭhāṇaṁga* account of music is a kind of digest. It contains material compiled from various sources. As in Purāṇic compilations of this nature, sources are not mentioned.

Tracing such material to its source can become mostly an exercise in futility because little from ancient times survives.

But we have noted one remarkable parallel with the *Nāradīyā Śikṣā* where there is an almost word to word correspondence. This is no doubt a significant clue, but to presume a direct borrowing either way could be misleading. Musical lore like other ancient lore seems to have had a body of material traditionally handed down. It formed a kind of common pool from which all writers on the subject could draw. The passage which occurs both in the *Nāradīyā Śikṣā* and *Ṭhāṇaṁga* may have been part of this common heritage. Many early *Śikṣā* works likewise share certain passages in common and the question who borrowed from whom is quite misplaced in such cases.

A fruitful conjecture might yet have been possible if one could be sure of the relative chronology of the *Ṭhāṇaṁga* and the

---

[54] *suvihitagamakavidhāyinyo'kṣobhyā tālalayakuśalāḥ / ātodyārpitakarṇā vijñeyā gāyikāḥ śyāmāḥ. Nāṭyaśāstra* 33, 34.

[55] '*śyāmā iti taruṇyaḥ tadvarṇā eva kleśasahatvāt.*' Abhinava on above.

[56] *prāyeṇa tu svabhāvāt strīṇāṁ gānaṁ ruciraṁ ca pāṭhyavidhiḥ, strīṇāṁ svabhāvamadhuraḥ kaṇṭho nṛṇāṁ balitvaṁ ca. Nāṭyaśāstra* 33, 5.

Nāradīyā Śikṣā. But this, too, is uncertain ground and we are left with no threads to follow.

In truth, analysis shows that there are more textual divergences than similarities between the *Ṭhānaṁga* and the *Nāradīyā Śikṣā.* We can even go further and say that there are certain elements in the *Ṭhāṇaṁga* account which are either absent from or at significant variance with the material available not only in the *Nāradīyā Śikṣā* but also the *Purāṇas,* and later musical texts which rely, in many matters, on earlier works. It seems that the compiler of the *Ṭhāṇaṁga* section on music had borrowed much material from a school of musical theorists with a distinct stance and vocabulary on certain moot points.

Chapter – Sixteen

The Body as an Instrument
A Theoretical Choice Made by Śārṅgadeva

I wish to discuss an interesting section which occurs right at the beginning of Śārṅgadeva's *Saṅgītaratnākara.* It concerns the question of what the text calls, *nādotpatti*, the process by which sound is produced in the human body. Clearly, however, what Śārṅgadeva wanted to do was not only to explain *nādotpatti*, the production of sound in general through the human frame, but to picturise *svarotpatti,* the more specific process by which musical tones arise in the body.

Śārṅgadeva's handling of his material is worthy of attention. He had, we find, three different theoretical pictures of the process before him, which were available to him from widely different disciplines and approaches to the human body. He outlines all three of them and then quite perceptibly makes a choice from among them, picking the one most appropriate for his purpose as a *saṅgīta-śāstrī*. His understanding of the human body as it emerges from the stand-point he opts for, is to treat the human body as an instrument which the soul, or rather the embodied soul, the *jīvātman,* uses for its own creative purpose of making music.

Interesting as the view which Śārṅgadeva accepts as an answer to the question of how sound is produced through the human body is in itself, what I find even more interesting is to observe him making a choice between available alternatives. In this, curiously, his approach is not quite discursive, as one would expect it to be. He does not *argue* for the propriety of the choice he makes, treating, as he should have, the alternatives he rejects as *pūrvapakṣas* which must be shown as inadequate through a proper reasoning. The intellectual tradition of the *śāstras* such as *alaṅkāra* in which he was obviously trained, not to speak of the *darśanas*, do indeed follow an articulate argumentative path for arriving at conclusions. But Śārṅgadeva does not take this path. And yet Śārṅgadeva does make a choice, a choice which, among all the alternative theories he had at hand, most suitably matches his larger picture of music-making as an activity of a free and creative agent, a *vāggeyakāra*. In the theory he finally accepts, the process of *nādotpatti* emerges as a causal, physical process which a person desirous of singing can freely use.

Intriguingly, it also appears that Śārṅgadeva was being pulled in two different directions. He seems, on the one hand, to be *selecting* an appropriate scheme from among those he had before him, but at the same time one also feels that he wanted to present the different schemes, which do not really mesh with each other, as forming a large coherent whole into which the exiguous process of the production of tones in singing fits as a part. Noteworthy is also the fact that the two schemes he 'rejects' and which he takes up in some detail, clearly contain elements he could have used or adapted with advantage in order to formulate a process more in accord with his purpose. Such a procedure would, indeed, have given him a theoretically more satisfying scheme. But he does not follow this course. The process he actually ends up by adopting is, in comparison with what he rejects, or rather ignores, sketched quite cursorily.

Fortunately, for details concerning what Śārṅgadeva actually says I can refer the reader to the English translation of the *Saṅgītaratnākara* by R.K. Shringy and Prem Lata Sharma (vol.I, *adhyāya* 1, *prakaraṇas* 2 and 3).[1] This will allow us to be reasonably brief and save us from lengthy textual references. Although I find that I must reproduce some details for my own critical reflections on the text.

The two, what might be called, 'larger' schemes, skethced at a greater length, which Śārṅgadeva gives us, are outlined in a single chapter which he terms *piṇḍotpatti*, 'the birth of the body'. This chapters is, in a significant sense, the first in the text: it

[1]*Saṅgitaratnākara* of *Śārṅgadeva, Text and English Translation*, Vol.1 by R.K. Shringy and Prem Lata Sharma, Munshiram Manoharlal Publishers Pvt. Ltd., New Delhi.

follows a preamble which is just a list of contents of the *Saṅgītaratnākara* as a whole. *Piṇḍotpatti* deals not only with the birth of the body, as the name implies, but also its structure. Of the two distinct schemes it contains, the first is a picture sketched in some detail of bodily processes as they had been mapped in the discipline of medicine known to Śārṅgadeva, the *āyurveda*. Śārṅgadeva gives us quite a detailed picture which he had, in fact, studied in even greater detail, writing an independent book on the subject. He refers us to this book for further information. The book, which he had, interestingly, named, *Ādhyātmaviveka* — 'Distinguishing the Self' — is, unfortunately, no longer extant.[2] But we know that he was an expert in the subject, and he tells us that he was also a practising doctor.

In the picture of the 'self' — clearly, in this context, the body as an embodied self — visualised here, the human frame is conceived as a psychosomatic entity, a whole, a 'person', which combines entities and properties that may otherwise be distinguished as material, organic *and* conscious or mental. Processes which are inner or psychic, whether of thought, emotion or resolve, are part of the 'body', which is conceived as emanating from *brahma* itself, and is part of a cosmic scheme founded on the idea of a single 'spiritual' stuff which manifests itself in entities both physical as well as psychic. *Jīvas*, individual souls, emerge like sparks from a fire out of the ultimate spiritual reality, *brahma*. Shrouded by *avidyā,* and propelled by *karma*, they assume physical form, doing so again and again, till they attain *brahma*-hood and *mokṣa*.

This is not an unfamiliar picture in the tradition of Indian ideas about creation. What is important for our purpose here is a glimpse into the actual mapping of the human body that the picture envisages.

Right from the moment the *jīva* enters the womb, to be born

---

[2]*Saṅgītaratnākara,*1,2,118 *: iti pratyaṅgasaṅkṣepo vistarastviha tattvataḥ / asmadviracite' dhyātmaviveke vīkṣyatāṁ budhaiḥ//*
The book is not available if we are to believe the *New Catalogus Catalogorum*, which only refers to the work without reporting any manuscript of it.

as a human person, it begins to acquire the extremely complex psychophysical characteristics that will make him an embodied soul, a 'person'. The properties the embryo begins to acquire, have been analysed into six different *bhāvas* — 'states of being', which include a collection of very different things: such as, living organs, functions, propensities and downright physical things. The six *bhāvas* are shaped by, and named after, six distinct sources or causes: mother, father, *rasa*, *ātmā, sattva* and *sātmya*. It will be useful to have before us some idea of how they are composed.

Important is the fact that each *bhāva* is in itself a complex mosaic of plural characteristics, containing a mixed bag of elements which we today would separately class as psychic, organic and material. Intriguing, and in a profound sense fitting, as this way of understanding the human body as a psychosomatic entity is, the logic behind the mix is not easy to see, and often appears confusing. Let us have look. The *bhāva*, which is said to be 'born of the mother' (*mātṛja*), is obviously thought of as one 'single' *bhāva*, because the apparently very different entities which 'belong' to it share a common quality: that of 'softness' or 'delicacy' (*mṛdu*). The entities, which share this quality are also said to share the same source, namely, the mother; they are mainly organic entities such as blood, fat, the navel, the heart etc. But, true to the psychosomatic complexity of the picture, the heart is not just a physical organ, it is, as we shall later see, also the seat of consciousness. *Bhāvas* born of the father have, on the contrary, and quite expectedly, the property of being 'hard'; they consist of veins, arteries, body-hair, beard, teeth as well as semen. Veins and arteries play a vital role in the functioning of the body, as envisaged in this scheme, which they would, indeed, in any scheme with any empirical bias as this one also has, but veins are here instrumental not only in aiding organic functions, but also as carriers of the stuff of consciousness. '*Rasa*', which is another *bhāva,* stands, as the word suggests, for fluids which nourish the body and make it grow (*śarīropacaya*); but it is also responsible for a sense of satisfaction (*tṛpti*), absence of greed (*alolupatva*), and a continuing strength of resolution (*utsāha*: a word which in this context may also be taken as suggestive not of a property of the will but a general sense of optimism and 'pep' arising out of sheer good health). In any case, what we have is plainly a motley of very different things carrying the single label '*rasa*'. There is however, no common 'source' in this case. *Ātmā*, as can perhaps be expected, consists of somewhat more clearly distinguishable features associated with consciousness. Like the Nyāya *ātmā* it contains pleasure, pain, desire, effort and memory (*bhāvanā*: the word being evidently used in the Naiyāyika's, and not the Mīmāṃsaka's, the sense), as well as knowledge. But this *bhāva*, too, unlike the *ātmā* as pictured in Nyāya, is not free of a what seems a peculiar mix. *Ātmā*, thus, besides its bag of psychic qualities, is also the source of the sense organs — the *indriyas* — and is responsible for the age to which a body survives (*āyu*). The word '*indriya*' here indicates both *jñānendriyas*, the senses through which one perceives, or 'knows': the senses of sight, hearing, touch and the like,; as well as the *karmendriyas* or the 'senses' of action, the motor organs. These are: the organs of speech, the hands, the feet, the anus and the reproductive organs. There are also two internal organs, two distinct *antaḥkaraṇas*, associated with *ātmā* as parts of it. These are *manas* and *buddhi*. Pleasure and pain are the functions of *manas*, while the functions of *buddhi* are, expectedly, memory and conceiving (*vikalpa*); but, curiously with another odd mixture of categories, it is also the bearer of 'the sense of fear' (*bhīti*).

Manas and *buddhi* are important for our reflections here, since this is where one would expect Śārṅgadeva to locate 'agency' in man, as the producer of *nāda* and the user of *svara* in making music. But if we look for how Śārṅgadeva has pictured their active role in his scheme, and his understanding of the process of *nādotpatti* and *svarotpatti*, we face problems. How, to begin with, we might want to know, are they related to desire and effort ? Are desire and effort included under *vikalpa*, noted as a function of the *buddhi* ? — Śārṅgadeva is strangely unconcerned regarding how his *ātmā* could, in his scheme, be an agent. We find no relation in his picture between desire and effort, and *buddhi* and *manas*. *Saṅkalpa* is what we look for, but it is plainly quite different from *vikalpa*, which we have. Perhaps a cogent connection can be made between desire and effort and voluntary activity through the *indriyas*, especially the *karmendriyas,* which are part of the *bhāva, ātmā*. This is an idea which not only seems fitting but looks plausible in Śārṅgadeva's scheme. Of the *indriyas,* Śārṅgadeva speaks of two contrary views. Some regarded them as physical (*bhautika*) but others considered them to be non-material or 'spiritual' (*brahmayoni*). Indeed, they do seem to share properties which are both conscious as well as material. They could be made to form a bridge between the body and more 'disembodied' entities like desire and effort. But there is nothing in Śārṅgadeva that might lead us to think that he envisaged any such connection. He also speak of the heart, described as a lotus-shaped physical organ, as the seat of consciousness. This, too, we shall see, has possibilities which could have lead to a cogent picture of *nādotpatti* as an agent-produced activity but Śārṅgadeva does not follow the lead.

Sattva is another *bhāva*. It has three different 'aspects' or 'modes of operation' which are, in this case, conceived in terms of the three Sāṅkhyan *guṇas: sattva, rajas* and *tamas*. These are in their distinct capacities responsible for inner properties such as faith (*āstikya*), altruistic propensities (*śukladharmāḥ*), lust, anger, sleep, laziness etc. It is difficult to see why *sattva* was needed as a distinct *bhāva* and why its properties could not be subsumed under *manas* and *buddhi*. And again we do not know where to place this *bhāva* as a 'part' of the body and relate its functioning with the body as a physical entity. A doctor would have to ask this question if he were to administer medicine to the body in order to treat a malaise relating to this *bhāva*. Or is it perhaps simply a theoretical notion unrelated to the functioning of the body and included merely for the sake of completing the picture of 'man'. In which case why call it a *bhāva,* since it does not really appear to be related to the other *bhāvas* in any interconnected and organically meaningful sense ?

Sātmya, the sixth *bhāva*, is an even stranger entity. It cannot be said to be an organ. But neither is it described as another *antaḥkaraṇa*, though perhaps it could have been classed as such since it is certainly not a material thing. It is said to be the source of good health, clarity in the functioning of the *indriyas*, and absence of laziness. It is difficult to see why its functions, too, could not be included in another *bhāva*.

The body, like any physical entity, is made up of the five *mahābhūtas*, and imbibes properties from them, too. These again are a mixed bag. *Ākāśa* imparts to it sound, the power of hearing (*śrotra*), hollownesses (*suṣiratā*), and interestingly, a distinct identity in space (*vaiviktya*). But it also imparts a conscious property: subtlety of understanding. *Agni* is responsible for the eyes, form and colour, the quality of 'ripeness' or 'maturity', the state of being 'cooked'(*pāka*); though it is not clear whether the *pāka* spoken of here is a quality of organic entities, or also of 'subtle' *antaḥkaraṇa*-like entities such as *manas* and *buddhi*. *Agni* also causes bile as well as the property of making manifest (*prakāśatā*) — a property which is patently a property of consciousness — as well as heat, sharpness and energy. It is also the source of other inner qualities: bravery and anger and intelligence. *Vāyu* or air is responsible for the awareness of touch and the *karmendriya* of touch. Besides, it is also responsible for the various movements of the body. Ten modifications of *vāyu* (*vāyuvikṛtayaḥ*) reside within the human frame and are responsible for various bodily movements and functions. These include the well-known *prāṇa, apāna, samāna, udāna* and *vyāna*, which are the five major *vāyus*. There are five others with a more minor role. The ten *vāyus* help in carrying out various functions with and within the body, functions both voluntary and involuntary. *Apāna*, for example, expels urine and excreta. *Vyāna* is stationed in the eyes, the ears, the nose, as well as the ankles and the waist. Its role is not quite clear from Śārṅgadeva's account. Perhaps it helps other *vāyus* in carrying out functions such as smelling, hearing, batting of the eyes (for which one of the five minor *vāyus* is said to be responsible), functions which, like the function of the *indriyas* have in some sense both the aspects of being intentional and unintentional. But its functions in the ankles and the waist, whatever they are, are in no way within our control. *Samāna* performs functions which are purely organic and involuntary. Moving all over the body through *nāḍīs* or arteries numbering 72000, it distributes the juices resulting from food and drink.

The chief of the *vāyus* is *prāṇa*. From its station below the navel, it moves to the navel, the nose and the heart. It is responsible for breathing in and out, coughing and emitting sound.

A question to my mind arises as to why the *mahābhūtas* were needed in addition to the six *bhāvas* which together presumably form a complete picture. How are the *mahābhūtas* related to the *bhāvas* ? They might be said to constitute the purely material elements which make up the body. But then we have seen that they are not quite material in nature, being as complex as the *bhāvas*. This makes it even more difficult to understand why their functions could not have been included in the *bhāvas*.

And yet despite questions that might arise, the *piṇḍotpatti* presents us with a fascinating picture which is not merely conceptual in content but clearly takes detailed observations into account. We cannot but be impressed by it and its complexities which display the object needing a doctor's attention as not only a body but also a soul. But, to come back to our present purpose, how is *piṇḍotpatti* relevantly tied up with the process of *nādotpatti* ? Śārṅgadeva himself does not try to make the connections. For him it is only a general picture of the structure of the body as a whole. For the more specific processes of *nādotpatti* and *svarotpatti,* he paints a separate picture. One would have expected him to have shown how these specific processes are related to the general structure of the body as a whole, but Śārṅgadeva does not make such a move. This is puzzling, since it is not difficult to see that he could have done this with slight additions and modifications in the structure of the body as understood in the *piṇḍotpatti* picture. We have had a glimpse of an earlier of a possible move he could have made by relating the *prāṇa* to *manas* and *buddhi* through something like *saṅkalpa*. There was, as far as one can see, another potent possibility in the notion of the heart. The heart is plainly described as both an organ as well as the seat of consciousness. It is further described as forming the center of important arteries (*mūlaśirā*) which are carriers of force or energy (*oja*). Many of these arteries are indeed channels of communication between the heart and various organs, and responsible for functions such as smelling. Two of these, connected with the tongue, are said to have a role in the act of speech. There are also other arteries, called *dhamanīs*, which emanate from the navel as the center like spokes from the nave of a wheel. Some of these are connected to the heart from where they move into different directions creating channels through which awareness of sound, form and colour, taste and smell are conveyed. Two such arteries are responsible for the making of sound and speech (*bhāṣaṇa, ghoṣa*).

The picture obviously has elements which could have been suitably moulded to construct a model for explaining the process of *nādotpatti*, if not *svarotpatti*, which could meaningfully include the role of an agent. For *svarotpatti*, it would have needed further modifications in the picture to accommodate an organ that could produce different tones — such as an artery with appropriately placed holes which could function like a flute. Why did Śārṅgadeva not suitably modify the picture? Śārṅgadeva, himself has nothing to say. For him the picture of *piṇḍotpatti* seems to form a kind of larger basis which can serve as the ground for understanding the more specific process of *nādotpatti* and *svarotpatti*. But he makes no effort to actually tie up the picture presented in *piṇḍotpatti* with *nādotpatti* and *svarotpatti* in any significant manner.

What held him back? What kept him from remodelling the *piṇḍotpatti* picture in order to envisage *nādotpatti* and *svarotpatti* within it or at least tying it up in a relevant sense with it ? — since without this, *piṇḍotpatti*, fascinating as the picture it presents, is, yet remains an attractive but only loosely attached appendage to the rest of the text, constituting a major *doṣa* in the *śāstra*. Śārṅgadeva is silent. But, perhaps, *we* can speculate about possible reasons.

There are, I think, two major reasons why Śārṅgadeva did not tamper with the *piṇḍotpatti* picture in order to modify it in any way. One seems to be the fact that he considered the picture as complete and fixed and so unchangeable in principle. No doubt, to begin with, the science of medicine had strong elements of being an empirical science, needing observation and critical examination (*parīkṣā*) by its practitioners. It also, evidently, allowed for a plurality in its interpretations of the human body as a person. The two pictures, we have concerning this matter from Caraka and Suśruta, both ancient and foundational authors, are divergent in important ways: The Caraka picture is more Nyāya-like while the Suśruta picture leans much more obviously and significantly on Sāṅkhya. The two distinct views regarding *indriyas*, which Śārṅgadeva speaks of, one believing them to be material and the other putting them in the category of the conscious, also points at an important difference in Caraka and Suśruta. Suśruta calls them *bhautika* while Caraka takes them as distinctive of beings that are *cetana* — living and conscious.[3] Yet despite disagreements between them, and their acceptance of theoretical plurality in practice, Caraka and Suśruta, agree in considering their science as revelatory and unchangeable. Changes and new insights were no doubt incorporated within the *śāstra* during its long history, but, paradoxically, the myth of unchangeability was carefully maintained. Significant intellectual opinion in the days of Śārṅgadeva seems to have regarded *āyurveda* as no less than a revelation, considering it a transcendental and not an empirical

---

[3] Suśruta, *śarīrasthānam*, 1,10 : *bhautikāni cendriyāṇyāyurvede varṇyante tathendriyārthaḥ.*

Caraka, *sūtrasthānam*, 1,48 *sendriyaṁ cetanasthānaṁ nirindriyaṁ acetanam.*

science. This may be confirmed from the strongly expressed views of the famous and influential philosopher, Vācaspati Miśra (9th century; Śārṅgadeva wrote in the 13th). The *śāstra* of *āyurveda*, says Vācaspati, like the Vedic *mantra* is authored by God himself; its truth is evident from the success of its operation, but it is not a *śāstra* that could be conceived as being created by the exercise of merely human observation or reason; neither is it a *śāstra* which can be thought of as the result of a growth of knowledge in a *śāstric* tradition where subsequent works build on what had preceded.[4] By Śārṅgadeva's time, the science, then, seems to have acquired a kind of sacrosanct nature, resisting modification. In this it was different from *saṅgīta-śāstra* which allowed for changes both in theory and practice — *lakṣya* and

---

[4] See Vācaspati's *ṭikā* on the *Vyāsa-bhāṣya* on Patañjali's *Yogasūtra, samādhipāda, sūtra* 24. Vyāsa says that the *yoga* as a *śāstra* was composed by a transcendental supreme being (*prakṛṣṭa sattva*). Commenting, Vācaspati adds that the *śāstra* of *āyurveda* belongs to the list of such divinely-composed *śāstras* as the Veda, with the words : *ayamabhisandhiḥ : mantrāyurvedeṣu tāvadīśvarapraṇīteṣu pravṛttisāmarthy-ādarthāvyabhicāraviniścayātprāmāṇyaṁ siddham. na cauṣadhibhedānāṁ tatsaṁyogaviśeṣāṇāṁ ca mantrāṇāṁ ca tattadvarṇāvāpoddhareṇa sahasreṇāpi puruṣāyuṣairlaukikapramāṇavyavahārī śaktaḥ kartumanvayavyatirekau. na cāgamādanvayavyatirekau tābhyāṁ cāgamastatsantānayoranāditvāditi pratipādayituṁ yuktaṁ* .... . This may be translated as: 'This is what is meant (by Vyāsa). (In *śāstras* like) *Mantra* (that is, *Veda*) and *Āyurveda*, which are created by God, the *prāmāṇya* (their 'authentication', 'proof' but also 'true understanding') lies in the fact that what they say actually works, and is true; to understand and interpret them correctly is to authenticate them (there is no extrinsic proof apart form this). It is not possible to know all the different medicines and their combinations through any *laukika pramāṇa* (human means of true knowledge). (Just as it is not possible) to arrive at the true order of syllables (*varṇas*) in (Vedic) *mantras* by any process of (selection) through hypothetically choosing and rejecting syllables one by one (*āvāpaodhāra*), even if this process be repeated thousands of times by human beings using their pragmatic, inferential reasoning and other human means of authentication, through *anvaya* and *vyatireka* (projecting and rejecting empirical hypotheses in order to arrive at the truth). Neither can it argued that such a process of empirical inference (*anvayavyatirekau*) is something that is *initiated* by (a primal and) revealed *śāstra* (*āgama*), but, then, it is carried forward (by human agency and gives rise) to (newer) *āgama* on its own, because not only the *āgama* but its true transmission (without change) is a beginningless process...'.

lakṣaṇa. The category of the *deśī* as opposed to the 'given' and 'fixed' *mārgī* is one evidence of it: new musical forms could be freely created. And that such a development actually took place can be seen from the long list of *adhunāprasiddha rāgas* — 'modern' as opposed to 'traditional' forms — that Śārṅgadeva himself notes and describes. Kallinātha, commenting on Śārṅgadeva, not much after him, explicitly states that a description of these *rāgas* required basic changes in the theoretical structure of the *śāstra* — its *lakṣaṇas* — in order to mesh with the new material — the changing *lakṣya*.[5]

The second reason why Śārṅgadeva did not remodel the given picture he had for his purposes seems to be connected with the purpose behind the picture. The body in the *āyurveda* model, which is seen as conscious and incorporating volition as an important element in it, was yet also seen as an object to be acted upon, a net-work of causally linked entities that could be administered to and were thus passive. It was not a model designed to reveal the workings of human agency, and the role played by the body in it as an instrument of agency.

The second picture of *nādotpatti* which Śārṅgadeva gives us is also included in the *piṇḍotpatti* chapter. It does seem to be drawn with the role of an agent in view, but the agency it has in mind is a kind of yogic, 'spiritual' agency, and not the ordinary volition used in acts such as singing. The picture is a *kuṇḍalinī* map of the body, a map familiar enough from popular writings on *yoga*. The body is believed to have a number of 'centres' — *cakras* — through which the yogic energy called *kuṇḍalinī* passes on its path to the highest center at the apex of the head where immortality resides. The home of the *kuṇḍalinī* is at the base of the spinal column in the lower-most *cakra*. Awakened through *yoga*, the *kuṇḍalinī* begins to flow upwards through a *nāḍī* called *suṣumnā*, which is one of a vast network of *nāḍīs*. As

---

[5] *Saṅgītaratnākara*, 2,2,161-194. Note Kallinātha : *idānimadhunāprasiddharāgāṅ-gādīnāṁ lakṣye pratītānāṁ lakṣaṇavirodhanāṁ virodhaparihārārthamudyamaḥ kriyate*.
He proceeds to give us a formidable list of *virodhas*.

it reaches a new, higher *cakra*, pictured as a lotus with a certain number of petals, it can avail itself of the 'fruits' of that *cakra*, which lie as 'powers', on the petals of the *cakra*. The sixteen-petalled *cakra* at the throat is the home of Sarasvatī, where the music of the *sāma* resides. The seven *svaras*, the musical tones, also reside there. One who can move his *kuṇḍalinī* to that *cakra* can be a musician, as Śārṅgadeva says.[6] If the *kuṇḍalinī* can be made to reach up to the highest *cakra*, then one can, as is to be expected, achieve a very superior proficiency in music.[7]

Clearly this picture focuses on the role of the agent. But the agent here is a spiritual *sādhaka*, not a musician. The picture is not designed to explain the ordinary, every-day act of singing. It does not aim at explaining the physical processes of *nādotpatti* and *svarotpatti.* And so, Śārṅgadeva gives us a third picture, moving now to a new chapter for the purpose. This is the final picture he gives us, the one he seems to silently favour and after which he moves on to other things. This picture, where the body is envisioned as an instrument, does have elements, in Śārṅgadeva's description, which seem to tie it to the *kuṇḍalinī* picture also, but the cementing is done half-heartedly and does not really succeed. Yet the picture is fascinating. The description begins with a well-known *śloka* which is worth a look. Let me quote:

ātmā vivakṣamāṇo' yaṁ manaḥ prerayate manaḥ /
dehasthaṁ vahnimāhanti sa prerayati mārutam //

(*Saṅgītaratnākara*, 1,3,3).

"The *ātmā* desirous of saying something impels the *manas* which in turn strikes at the fire contained in the body. The fire then propels the air [to produce speech]."

We notice that Śārṅgadeva says: *ātmā vivakṣamāṇo' yam* — "the soul desirous of saying something ..." when he should — and easily could — have said, *ātmā jigāsamāno' yam*: "the soul

---

[6] *Saṅgītaratnākara*, 1,2, 141 : *viśuddherasṭamādīni dalānyaṣṭau śritāni tu / dadyurgītādisaṁsiddhim ...*

[7] Do. 1,2,143 : *brahmarandhrasthito jivaḥ sudhayā sampluto yadā / tuṣṭo gītādikāryāṇi saprakarṣāṇi kārayet.*

desirous of singing ...".[8] The reason for Śārṅgadeva's not quite appropriate phrase is not difficult to see. He has borrowed it from an older theorist who had used it in describing a process for the production of speech, rather than song. The *Pāṇinīya Śikṣā* begins its description of the process of how speech arises in the body with the words:

ātmā buddhyā sametyarthānmano yuṅkte vivakṣayā /
manaḥ kāyāgnimāhanti sa prerayati mārutaḥ //

(*Pāṇinīya Śikṣā* 6)

"Wishing to speak, the *ātmā* approaches meanings through the *buddhi* and harnesses the *manas* for the purpose. The *manas* strikes the fire in the body which in turn propels the air [to produce speech]."

Here obviously lies the source of Śārṅgadeva's own *śloka*. The date of the *Śikṣā* is not certain but it is certainly many centuries older than Śārṅgadeva. It was an important text for any one who learnt Sanskrit grammar, and every educated person had to do so. Or, perhaps, Śārṅgadeva had before him another text parallel to this *Sikṣā*, since the doctrine it espouses was ancient knowledge born in the traditions of Vedic learning and the transmission of the spoken Vedic vocables, and more than one text was written about it. We also find a step missing in Śārṅgadeva's account. *Buddhi* has no role there. The reason is apparent. The function of *buddhi* in the *Śikṣā* account, is to pick out the right words for what the *ātmā* wants to say. But singing is not speaking and so this function is not needed. But then what replaces *buddhi* ? Or does *ātmā* pick out the tones directly without a go-between which it needs for *vivakṣā,* but not for *jigāsā* ? But if so, the *ātmā* in this conception must be significantly different from that of the *Śikṣā* picture. Where lies the difference ? Śārṅgadeva provides no answers. He did not reflect on the matter. And yet, a borrower as he was, Śārṅgadeva

---

[8] An interesting discussion had taken place on this expression and scholars wondered if Sanskrit has an independent word for, 'the desire to sing'. I am thankful to Dr. Prem Lata Sharma for drawing my attention to the word '*jigāsā*' which, she points, has been used by Abhinavagupta.

could not help retaining the word '*vivakṣā*'.

There are also other modifications in Śārṅgadeva as we can see in the details of the process of *svara*-production he describes. These are, however, modifications not made by him — he seems to have been too tradtion-bound in this matter for that — but accepted by him from older *saṅgīta-śastras*.

The *Śikṣā* account of the process of speech production describes it in some detail. Low and high pitches arise as the fire-heated air moves to different regions of the human frame, the chest, the throat and the head. Different syllables are produced in the cavity of the mouth on the basis of *svara* (pitch), *kāla* (time taken in utterance), *sthāna* (chest, throat and head where different registers of a gradually higher pitch are produced) and *prayatna* (the nature of the effort). Further details of these categories and the distinct roles in the production of different syllables are also noted with care by the *Śikṣā*; but we need not enter into these here. It is an impressive account based on careful observation.

Śārṅgadeva's account of *svara*-production is somewhat parallels this account, though its basis is imagination rather than observation. He speaks of a harp-like *vīṇā* placed within the human frame. This was an old idea. The ancients called this *vīṇā* the *śarīra-vīṇā*, the 'body-harp', to distinguish it from the normal harp made of wood. It was this body-harp which was said to produce the musical tones in singing. The body-harp account of the production of tones shares the concept of *sthāna* with the *Śikṣā*. As in the *Śikṣā* scheme, different *sthānas* produce different octaves. The *Śikṣā* scheme also spoke of the seven *svaras*, but *svaras* there are only meant as general areas of pitches used in producing the different Vedic accents (*Pāṇinīya Śikṣā*, 12). They are not distinct tones for musical rather than verbal expressions. In singing, according to Śārṅgadeva, these distinct tones are produced by different 'strings' of the body-harp. These 'strings' are *nāḍīs* stretched across the various *sthānas* with a gradually decreasing length so that the higher the position of the *nāḍī*, the higher its pitch. Each *sthāna* has twenty two such *nāḍīs* which account for not only the seven *svaras* but also the *śrutis*, the shades of minute tonal distinctions that are audible to the human ear, and can, according to later *saṅgīta-śāstrīs* such as Śaṛṅgadeva, enter musical expression. The heated air from the base of the spinal column as it moves over these strings causes them to sound.[9]

This was a picture which Śārṅgadeva had inherited from older musicologists. He intended, apparently, to place it in the larger 'anatomical' perspective of the two other pictures that he draws for us. But the connection, as we can see, between the harp picture and *piṇḍotpatti* cannot be established in any meaningful sense, and any connection that we might think of — such as the common notion of the *nāḍī* — remains, to say the least, very shadowy. The body-harp can hardly be said to fit as a part in the larger *piṇḍotpatti* picture. The *nāḍīs* of the *piṇḍotpatti* picture have a nature and purpose entirely different from the harp *nāḍīs*. Neither does Śārṅgadeva attempt to connect the two.

He does, however, attempt to connect the harp picture with the yogic mapping of the *kuṇḍalinī*. He speaks of *five sthānas* including two others besides the three already mentioned. These two extra *sthānas*, his own additions, produce sounds which are *atisūkṣma* — very subtle — and *sūkṣma* — subtle — and are connected with the *brahmagranthi* and the *nābhi*, two yogic centres. But these subtle sounds, Śārṅgadeva adds, lie outside the range of musical sounds: they are not related to the *vyavahāra* — the actual practice — of the art. They are also not provided with *nāḍīs* which could manifest them. Their role lies purely in the realm of theory. The idea seems to be to connect the musical sounds needed in *vyavahāra*, the so-called *āhata* or 'struck' sounds which we can actually hear and produce for the ordinary purposes of speaking and singing, with the transcendental —

---

[9] See also, in this connection, the essay, 'Music in the *Ṭhāṇaṁga Sūtra*', for a more *Śikṣā*-like picture of the production of different *svaras*. The picture, however, is obviously off the mark, and nothing but a feeble, inadequate attempt to explain *svara*-production as a process identical with that of producing *varṇas*, or spoken syllables.

pāramārthika — *anāhata* or 'unstruck' sound of the *yogīs*. *Anāhata nāda* forms part of the *kuṇḍalinī* picture.[10] The two extra *sthānas* where Śārṅgadeva locates his 'subtle' sounds were obviously suggested to him by the *kuṇḍalinī* map. Śārṅgadeva himself tells us that the *anāhata* sound is of no real use to him as a musicologist. He says, 'since it is devoid of all 'colour' and cannot please men; therefore, I shall speak only of *āhata* sounds, which when produced in the form of the *śrutis,* produce song.'[11] Yet he did feel obliged to somehow create a cogent bridge between the harp picture and the *kuṇḍalinī* one, and did not mind bending it to his own ends. One wonders what made him feel more free with the *kuṇḍalinī* picture than with the *āyurveda* one.

The notions of *sūkṣma* and *atisūkṣma* are, for Śārṅgadeva, stages that connect the *anāhata* with the audible *āhata* sounds. These notions are however empty of any real content in his scheme. The bridge he builds between the yogic and the musical picture of sound production has no real function and is not spoken of later in his *śāstra.*

Another thing before I close. The concept of the body-harp, interesting as it is, is yet somewhat incomplete in comparison with the *Śikṣā* picture of the production of speech. The *Śikṣā* picture goes into the details of how every distinct syllable is produced, noting the exact placement of the tongue in the cavity of the mouth and the kind of distinct effort required. In the harp picture different tones are produced when the air arising from the navel strikes different *nāḍīs*. But where is the means, the tool, one cannot help asking, by which it is ensured that a particular chosen string is struck when required and not just any of them. Where, in other words are the 'fingers', or the 'tongue', evidently needed to play upon this harp ?

[10] *Saṅgītaratnākara,* 1,2,162-165.

[11] *op. cit.* 1,2,166-167.

17. REFLECTIONS ON THE LOGOS OF MUSIC

i. The Search for the *Apauruṣeya*, or Absolute in Music

Musicology, the 'logos' of music, its *prajñā*, as one might also call it, articulated as thought relating to music, can, I feel, be understood as thought with a meaning and significance much larger than is usually accorded to it. In this larger sense 'musicology' as an impulse of logos is a venture, or perhaps an adventure, of thought that sets out of music into all the rest that thought is about. Pythogoras was a great musicologist in this sense though we do not normally think of him as a 'musicologist'. Yet music, and the way he perceived it, was vital to his thought. As is well known, he saw a 'given', fundamental relation between *svaras* and numbers, such that *svaras* could be demonstrated on a string, and related to each other through simple mathematical ratios. He then extended this perception beyond music to a number-based 'ratio-nality' of knowledge itself with far-reaching consequences.

Let us also take Confucius. The relation of Pythagoras' thought with music is today a part of our general knowledge and picture of intellectual history. What is not so generally realised is that Confucius was also an equally great musicologist in a similar larger sense, although with a very different spirit.

But even though Confucius' role as a musicologist hardly figures as a living element in our image of the past today, yet he seems to have been much more of a musicologist than the Greek thinker. Unlike Pythagoras, he not only reflected on music in a larger sense but was also a musicologist in the usual narrower sense of the term, spending a great deal of his career as a devoted collector and archivist of music. It may be worthwhile then to sketch here, however briefly, his life as a musicologist and outline his thoughts about music.

Almost contemporaneous with Pythagoras, Confucius lived

in the sixth century BC, and is regarded in Chinese history not only as a great sage and thinker, momentous in the life of the nation for his ideas and ideals concerning man, society and polity, but also for his profound understanding of music. The logos he sought in music was related to his basic concern, the ideal life of man in polity and society. This also made him a deep student of ritual, since he saw an intrinsic relation between ritual and music, and related these two to the larger life of man. He believed that: 'The final goals of ritual and music and the criminal law and government are the same, namely, to bring about a community of the people's aspirations and to result in social and political order', as Lin Yutang quotes him to say.[1] It was with this thought in mind that Confucius is said to have compiled the ancient *Book Of Songs,*[2] revered in Chinese tradition as devoutly as a *Veda.* And he compiled it, it should be noted, not as a book of poems as it is often made out to be, but mainly as a book of music: of that ancient music which, for him, reflected the ideal of what music ought to be, namely the source of logos for the right man and the true rulers of men. So large did music loom in his understanding of man that at the comparatively advanced age of twenty-nine, he sought training in music from a renowned master and is said to have acquired commendable proficiency in it. Often in later life he is pictured as playing the lute and singing to his own accompaniment. In China, as in ancient Greece, music was an important part of an educated man's learning, but for Confucius its significance was much greater than Chinese tradition seems to have accorded it. Later Confucian schools were in fact considered exceptional and even peculiar for their

---

[1] *The Wisdom Of Confucius,* Lin Yutang, the Modern Library edition, Random House, 1938, Introduction, p. 12.

[2] For Confucius' life, I have mainly consulted Lin Yutang's famous and extremely readable *The Wisdom Of Confucius* , referred to in the previous footnote, which includes a biography by Szema Ch'ien (I give the name as Lin Yutang spells it), who lived from 145-85 BC, that is, about three hundred years after Confucius. Lin Yutang praises Szema Ch'ien for his critical, non-partisan, historical approach — his biography is, indeed, part of a work on Chinese history in general, the *Shiki* (p.53-54).

singular emphasis on music.

Confucius is believd to have edited the *Book Of Songs* when he was sixty-four. Before undertaking that important task, he carefully worked as a musicologist during the many years when he wandered over China, following his vocation as a statesman and political thinker. He lived, worked and taught in many different states which constituted the country during his days and one of his major activities during his wanderings was to collect the ancient songs which later went into the *Book Of Songs.*[3] Excercising his own aesthetic judgement, imbued with a high moral purpose, he made a critical and historical enquiry into the original melodies used for the songs, and arranged the texts of the songs in his *Book Of Songs* on their basis, thus organising the text on a musical rather than a textual or thematic principle. Like the *Guru-Granth*, the *Book Of Songs* classifies its material on the basis of melody.

But what makes Confucius really great as a musicologist is not his work as a scholar and collector of music, but his larger vision regarding the role of music in the life of man. Music, for him, reflected the deepest principle of harmony in the soul, a

---

[3] As is only to be expected, modern scholars, such as Arthur Waley, question the authenticity of the tradtional Chinese belief that Confucius himself compiled the *Book Of Songs*. Waley says that the 'songs are 'Confucian' in the sense that Confucius (who lived in *c*. 500 BC) used them as texts for moral instructions, much as Greek pedagogues used Homer'. See his *The Book Of Songs,* Grove Press, Ever Green Edition, New York, 1960, p. 18. Confucius, it should be remarked here, certainly *used* the *Songs* for his teachings, and, no doubt, for his own apprehension of things, and it is also true that the songs were known from before his times, though we do not know how they were put together into a single whole, if at all such a 'collection' had been made. But Cofucius' connection with the *Songs* was, evidently, much more than one of use alone. The Greek comparison made by Waley has a clearly inappropriate ring. Considering the strong traditional Chinese belief that Confucius did collect the *Songs*, and their inclusion among Confucian Classics, suggests a reasonably strong case for accepting Confucius as the collector. It is likely, however, as the traditional belief also suggests, that what Confucius did was to collect the *music* of the *Songs* and to arrange the text on a musical basis : See Lin Yutang, *The Wisdom Of Confucius*, pp. 15-16. Note, especially, his remark, 'it is said that after this job of editing, the different songs were first shifted and properly classified with respect to their music.'

principle that could serve as the ground for true order among men.

Plato, too, in his *Republic* shows a deep awareness of the power of music in moulding and socialising man, and is concerned about the kind of music that should be sung and taught in his ideal state. But music was peripheral for Plato. In Confucius' vision music is at the centre. The key to the order and harmony that Confucius sought, lay not in reason but in emotion, since human relationships are woven through a web of emotion rather than reason. Therefore, he sought a logos in music, which is directly tied up with emotions, and not in concepts or the realm of thought and philosophy. His logos is related to *svaras*, not words. Any order which rests on a deep mutuality among men, Confucius saw, has to lie in an order among their emotions and the path to this lay through music. Music alone could give that tranquil and joyous harmony to our world of feelings and affections, which could translate itself into an ideal harmonious polity and society. Confucius' vision was, in this sense, the perception of a unique *aesthetic* logos to be found in music, a logos centered in pleasure and joy. "In music", he says, "the sages found pleasure, and (saw that) it could be used to make the hearts of the people good. Because of the deep influence which it produces in manners and customs, the ancient kings appointed it as one of the subjects of instruction."[4]

I will, in my own way, try to articulate here Confucius's ideas concerning music, and the problems inherent in them. As is well-known, his thoughts did not move through well-reasoned and interconnected arguments. They are somewhat scattered, metaphorical and impressionistic, layed out in aphoristic sayings, interspersed with those of his pupils. Yet his meaning and purpose seem to clearly shine through. For my own purpose, I have used the *Yo Ki* section of the *Li Ki,* the Confucian classic. The *Yo Ki* or the 'Record Of Music' forms an important part of the *Li Ki,* which is a "collection of various records in the possession of

---

[4] The *Li Ki* as translated in the *Sacred Books Of The East*, second impression, 1926, tr. James Legge, vol. xxviii, part iv, book xvii, the *Yo Ki* , sec. ii, 7, p.107.

the Confucian school, and is definitely of extremely diverse origin" — as Lin Yutang puts it in his, *The Wisdom Of Confucius.*[5] It contains an essay on the concept of Central Harmony, ascribed to a disciple, mixed with large sections on funeral ceremonies, ceremonial robes and vessels of public worship. It is somewhat similar in this to our ancient writings on *dharma* and *yajña* in the *Brāhmaṇas*. The chapters on music also contain the ideas of the Confucian philosopher, Zse-hsia, a contemporary of the famous Mencius, who lived in the fourth century BC. Yet we certainly encounter a great and stimulating body of thought in the *Yo Ki*, and what we have of Confucius here is more authentically 'original' than the works of many other ancient thinkers. My articulation of Confucius' ideas concerning music is based on the translation of the *Li Ki*, by James Legge in the *Sacred Books Of The East.*[6]

Right in the beginning of the *Yo Ki* we have what can be significantly described as a formal 'definition' of music:

"Modulations of the voice", propounds Confucius, "arise from the mind and the various affections of the mind are produced by things (external to it). The affections thus produced are manifested in the sounds that are uttered... . The combination of those modulated sounds, so as to give pleasure, and the (direction in harmony with them of the) shields and axes, and of the plumes and ox-tails, constitutes what we call music".[7]

The reference to shields, axes, plumes and ox-tails is

---

[5] See Introduction, p. 43. The whole section in Lin Yutang, entitled, 'Sources and Plan Of The Present Book', pp. 36-47 of the Introduction is worth reading. It reveals that problems of getting to the Ur Confucius are as great as those presented by most ancient writings in any civilisation. Indeed, for those who are interested in the *thought* of a thinker, rather than a completely 'authentic' text, an insistence on first having a critical Ur text, can only mean a deprivation of meaningful thought. This is true not only of Confucius, but as we sometimes tend to forget, also of Plato and Aristotle, and even a host of later, more modern, writers, including those who have written within living memory.

[6] I have already given a reference to Legge's edition in a footnote above. The quotations that will follow are from the *Yo Ki*. Arranging the thoughts in my own way, I do not quote in a sequence that agrees with the text.

[7] *Yo Ki*, sec.i, 1, p.90.

intended, as Legge points out, to denote war-like ceremonial dances, what Lin Yutang in his own translation has called 'ritual'. Looking at *Yo Ki* as a whole, what seems intended is ceremonial dance or even a formal, ritual-like ceremony in general. The strange phrase,'modulations of the voice' is a queer rendering of what has been, more cogently, translated as,'air musical' by another translator, and which is explained by a Chinese commentator as, 'the five full notes of a scale'. This seems reasonable, since the passage we have quoted speaks of *combinations* of 'modulated sound' as giving pleasure, meaning, obviously, musical compositions containing combinations of the five *svaras* accepted in traditional Chinese music. Lin Yutang, in the book named above, translates it as simply, 'music'. The use of the phrase in the *Yo Ki* appears to contain echoes of all three meanings.

Dance, in a ritual-like, ceremonial form is bracketed with music into a single unit in this definition, and is evocative of the use of the word *saṅgīta* in a similar sense in our own tradition. But as in our usage of *saṅgīta,* dance is the lesser partner. Later in the *Yo Ki*, Confucius makes a crucial distinction between music and ceremony, characterising ceremony as the outer manifestation of the inner movement that is music. "The sphere in which", he says, "music acts is the interior of man and that of ceremonies is his exterior."[8]

[8]*Yo Ki*, iii, 25, p.126. Such a relation between ceremony and music is reiterated by Confucius in many ways. Confucius' thought in the *Yo Ki* can be felt to move in a kind of spiral-like manner : he keeps returning to his major ideas, but with a new thrust, and a movement forward, as we can see in the present instance.

In the very next paragraph, iii, 26, Confucius says : "Music springs from the inward movements (of the soul); ceremonies appear in the outward movements (of the body)." Earlier in the *Yo Ki* (i, 17, p. 98) we read : "Music comes from within, and ceremonies from without. Music coming from within, produces the stillness (of the mind); ceremonies coming without, produce the elegancies (of manner)." The 'inner', is by implication, also the 'higher', the transcendental, the *paramārtha*, in contrast to the 'outward' which belongs to this world, and has to do with *vyavahāra*, or, human behaviour; and thus going back to section one, we read : "Music is (an echo of) the harmony between heaven and earth; ceremonies reflect the orderly distinctions (in the operations of) heaven and earth." — *Yo Ki*, i, 23, p.100. Also : "Music appeared in the Grand Beginning

Confucius' definition of music suggests that he believed it to form a movement or aspect of consciousness integrally connected with affections, and yet distinct from it and independent of it. Affections are outward-bound, and produced by things (external to the mind), whereas music arises *from* the mind itself. Affections are passive and given, while music is an active principle which *combines* affections into aesthetic, 'pleasurable' wholes.

The picture we have here seems to have similarities with Bharata's notion of *rasas*. For, like Bharata's *nāṭya*, which is an active and creative process, music combines *bhāvas* or affections, which are 'given', as reflections of the world of things, and therefore essentially passive, into harmonious and pleasurable wholes. "All modulations of sound take their rise from the minds of man, and music is the intercommunication of them in their relations and differerences. Hence even beasts have sound, but not its modulations", says Confucius,[9] raising music, as a free and creative human propensity, into the differentiating property — like Greek reason — that distinguishes men from beasts.

But the similarity between Confucius and Bharata is deceptive; I think for two connected reasons. One, because Confucius, while equating music with reason, also, paradoxically, perceives the different affective wholes that music creates not as 'free' and self-sufficient, pleasurable and *rasa*-giving creations of the imagination, but as related causally with the kind of order ruling in the governance of a state where the music prevails. And, two, the real aim of music was, for him, not mainly aesthetic, lying in the exploration of *rasa*, but much deeper, since music could be a potent *instrument* of morality and true order among men.

(of all things), and ceremonies had their place on the completion of them." — *Yo KI*, i, 34, p.104-105. In music, as this last passage more vocally indicates, the pair of concepts, *paramārtha* and *vyavahāra*, in contrast to a great deal of Indian thought, are seen as essentially interlinked, the one fulfilling the other.

[9] *Yo Ki*, i, 7, p.95.

The first reason points at a strange contradiction in Confucius' thought. It is the inner 'ethos' of the polity reigning in a society which gives rise to a music matching it in form and spirit. And the world of polity, in the final analysis, constitutes the world of 'things' that cause affections in the mind. The 'things', or, in other words, 'the external world', which gives rise to the affections consisted, for Confucious, of *the human world as shaped by a polity.* Confucius did believe that every piece of music had an ethos of its own, but unlike *rasa,* the ethos of a musical composition, in his view, was not an independent *play* that creates pleasurable wholes at will. It was not an active and creative combination of *bhāvas*, as in Bharata — *bhāvas,* which even in Bharata reflect the human world — but a shadow of another order of human things, for it inevitably conformed to the ethos of the state, the polity, in which it was produced. He thus says: "The airs of an age of good order indicate composure and enjoyment. The airs of an age of disorder indicate dissatisfaction and anger, and its government is perversely bad. The airs of a state going to ruin are expressive of sorrow and (troubled) thought. There is an interaction between the words and airs (of the people) and the character of their government."[10]

Confucius, we find, conceives of a network of three-fold interrelations: between music, the world of our emotions and the social world shaped through polity. Polity, as we see in the above quotation, was the dominant, 'governing' factor in the network. Such a conception *can*, imaginably, lead one to a curious kind of aesthetics in which states going to ruin and those in which a sense of dissatisfaction and anger rules might be thought desirable because of the *aesthetic* quality of the music they produce: since sorrow, anger and dissatisfaction *as ethos in music* can be satisfactory as *rasas.* But this seems perversely unthinkable. Yet, it seems equally unthinkable on the part of a thinker who has elevated music to the level of the logos which defines man, to be, uncannily, making a move which denies

[10] *Yo Ki*, 1, 4, pp. 93-94

music a free and creative role. Indeed, the whole purpose of Confucius was to specify this role. For Confucius, not only saw music as an *index* of polity, but also as a free agent which could shape it, and this he did with a deeper conviction. His deepest aim was to discover the music that could be a profound mover in the *creation* of a desirable polity.

The contradiction, we see in his thought, can perhaps be better, more generously, described as a 'tension', and such tensions are, after all, present in all thought and can be found in the greatest of thinkers. The tension, is at its root, a tension between an aesthetic and a moral vision, present in almost all thinking about art. What is of interest, however, is how Confucius encounters and deals with the tension, and what he makes of it. For he was keenly aware of the independent value of music itself even as he asserted it as reflecting a moral state of things, and was profoundly intrested in exploring its potential as a moral tool.

We just spoke of a three-fold linkage in his thought between music, the emotions and the human order governed by a polity. The last link in the chain, namely, polity, appears to be intended as almost 'determining' the rest. But the linkage we do find in his deliberations is not as strong as to forge a smooth, unbroken hierarchy with polity at the topmost rung of the ladder. To forge any such chain, indeed, appears unrealizable in principle, and we can also see this in Confucius. The links between music and emotion, and between music and polity are different in kind, and cannot really be combined to form a straight and even chain, though Confucius seems to have desired to do so, at one level of his thought. The two relations, with music at the centre, clearly lead into quite different directions without a strong, convincing link: the directions of ethics and aesthetics. Confucius, indeed, shows awareness of the two directions as independent. We have quoted from a passage where he links the ethos of music with polity. There are other deliberations where an aesthetic of music emerges independently of polity, though Confucius apparently insists on a link. An intriguing passage establishes the connection between music and polity with detailed attention to considerations which are aesthetic, and can be detached from the political motive which seems almost imposed upon them:

"Hence, when a ruler's aims are small, notes that quickly die away characterise the music and peoples thoughts are sad; when he is generous, harmonious, and of a placid and easy temper, the notes are varied and elegant and the people are satisfied and pleased; when he is coarse, violent, and excitable, the notes, vehement at first and distinct in the end, are full and bold throughout the piece and the people are resolute and daring; when he is pure and straightforward, strong and correct, the notes are grave and expressive of sincerity, and the people are self-controlled and respectful; when he is placid, and kind, the notes are natural, full, and harmonious, and the people are affectionate and loving; when he is careless, disorderly, perverse and dissipated, the notes are tedious and ill-regulated, and the people proceed to excesses and disorder."[11]

This arresting passage, we can immediately feel, is very different in spirit from the one quoted earlier where the ethos of a piece of music is said to be determined by the state and the essence of its polity. The present passage, however, though also intended to be about kings and the quality of their rule, speaks of kings as *musicians*, judging their rule through the *aesthetics* of their music. It clearly says more about Confucius' understanding of music than of kingship; and the fact that he is actually speaking of kings, really seems a contingent and ulterior advisement, *added on* to insights related to music. Unlike the passage quoted earlier, it also implies that kings *create* a polity through their musicianship.

The tension in Confucius' thought between music as passively 'given' and actively 'created', is transparent here. Music in its relation to the emotions comes through as an active principle, composing *aesthetic* wholes; whereas music in its relation to polity is conditioned in its ethos, or in other words, its

---

[11] *Yo Ki*, ii, 9, pp. 107-8

aesthetic, by the latter. If our music passively expresses the ethos of a polity, we cannot actively create the music we want at will, since we are all creatures of one polity or another.

And yet, antithetically, Confucius also grants music an active and creative role, and a central one, too, in the very making of a state or polity. It is, indeed, a crucial element in his thought. Music for him, as we have seen, was related to ceremony, constituting its inner movement. The concept of ceremony is central for Confucius' understanding of human behaviour, since, in a profound sense, the whole social and political life of man, was for him, an extension of ceremony, or 'ritual', and 'formalised' action. It is *through* its relation to ceremony that music creates a polity, since the arena of ceremony extends itself to the state of society and polity as a whole. "Hence it is said', says the *Yo Ki,* quoting a maxim in order to advise a king, "carry out perfectly ceremonies and music, and give them their outward manifestation and application, and under heaven nothing difficult to manage will appear."[12] And therefore, to identify and produce the right music, with the right 'given' structure and ethos, was the central purpose of Confucius' musicology.

But we have also seen that Confucius has defined music in terms of pleasure right at the beginning of his discourse. This introduces another kind of problem: how to find the right morally desirable music? The pleasure-principle naturally leads to a pluralistic aesthetic, a multiplicity of *rasas*, since what pleases is naturally many. Also, of course, what pleases is not bound to be moral: *śreyas* and *preyas* do not go together. Music as pleasure seems obviously to lead *away* from Confucius's desired goal, rather than *towards* it. He seems to have deeply felt this 'contradiction', and his moves in trying to resolve it attract attention. One move appears to have led him to somehow deny the pleasure element in the music he desired. The move, natural in all thinking, was to discriminate between the 'real' or 'true' music from that which belongs to the sphere of pleasure, the

[12] *Yo Ki,* iii, 23, p.126.

merely 'sensuous' and 'apparent'. And so in a passage of the *Yo Ki*, we find a line being drawn between Music and 'pleasurable sound'.

Actually it is not Confucius himself who is said to make this distinction but a disciple, Sze-hsia (also spelled 'Hsentse'). But the move is inherent in Confucius' thought and, indeed, thought in general when trying to resolve similar 'contradictions'. Sze-hsia is quoted in the *Yo Ki* to have said to the marquis of Wei that "Now music and sound" (obviously, meaning 'pleasant sound') are akin, but they are not the same."[13] The translator deliberately spells the word 'Music' in this context[14] with a capital 'M', obviously, and rightly, to distinguish it from ordinary pleasure-giving music. 'Music', as distinct from 'music' is imbued with a moral spirit, and is radically different from the 'new', modern 'music', in Sze-hsia's words, which, he thought, was intended for mere pleasure or *rasa*. What we thus have is intriguingly analogous to the distinction that Plato made between knowledge and mere opinion.

Knowledge, unlike opinion, which is multiple by nature, can only be one. So should be 'good' Music. It has also to be 'given' to us in a vision that runs deeper than mere imagination. It may be bravely argued here that one *can* reasonably conceive of a multiplicity of 'good' political orders, each radically distinct from the other, and hence a multiplicity of 'good' and not just *rasa*-giving music, all sharing the property of being 'right' and morally appropriate. Indeed, in the passage where kings have been conceived as musicians, we do seem to have a plurality of 'good' music, implying a plurality of good polities, since we find Confucius giving his approval to more than one kind of music. Yet, he does not carry this move forward, and his search, predictably, leads him to look for *the 'one'* music matching *the*

---

[13] *Yo Ki*, iii, 9, p.117.

[14] See *Yo Ki*, iii, 10, p.118. This passage immediately follows the earlier one, and is linked with it. The ancient 'virtuous airs', which belong to 'true' music are contrasted with the new, 'modern' product, which is merely pleasant, and called, 'Music'.

'unique' and 'right' political order. The idea of any real multiplicity in the realm of the ideal polity and society has seemed to most thinkers as both irrational and immoral. Confucius apparently shared this spirit of thought. Perhaps in those moments when the *rasa* of music was dominant in his mind, he could imagine a *variety* of music which could all be described as 'good', but as a moralist, he looked, almost logically, for a *unique* principle of harmony, and hence a *unique* music. Interestingly, however, as we shall later see, Confucius does try to find a resolution, a balance, between the 'one' and the 'many' in as much as he conceives the music that is ideal for the right polity as a kind of *rāga*, which remaining 'one' has yet 'many' possibilities.

The source of true music, for Confucius, as for many other ancient thinkers, who looked for Truth and True Order, could only be a divine, transcendental intelligence or *pratibhā*. Such divine *pratibhā* was not to be found in the present. It had prevailed in the remote past, when moved by it, the *ṛṣis* of ancient China had instituted the ideal political order, and created the music that went with it. During this ideal age of the *ṛṣis*, "Heaven and Earth acted according to their several natures, and the four seasons were what they ought to be",[15] as Sze-hsia puts it. It was, in other words, the *kṛta-yuga* when *dharma* or *ṛta* reigned supreme, and when the music of *dharma* or *ṛta* could be created. It was during such an age, to quote Sze-hsia again, that "harmony was given to the five notes (of the scale), and the singing to the lutes and the praise-songs."[16] These songs were the "virtuous airs" constituting 'Music' as it ought to be.

Confucius, in this context, makes an interesting difference between two kinds of intellect: that of the creator and that of the transmitter. True, 'virtuous', music can *now* only be transmitted, since its creators were *ṛṣis*, who no longer exist. "Therefore they who knew the essential nature of ceremonies and music could

---

[15] *Yo Ki*, iii, 10, p. 118.

[16] ibid.

frame them; and they who had learned their elegant accompaniments could hand them down. The framers may be pronounced sage; the transmitters, intelligent. Intelligence and sagehood are other names for transmitting and inventing."[17] What Confucius means by 'inventing' here is obviously not the excercise of ordinary imagination but of divine *prajñā,* or *pratibhā*. But what about those, who like Confucius, could *identify* and *recognise* the right music even if they could not create it ? Such people are clearly necessary to oversee that transmission does not introduce distortions and "notes that are evil and depraved", as a later passage in the *Yo Ki* puts it. Such people cannot be mere transmitters, who are said to be no more than 'intelligent' in the passage above. They must be more like critics and theorists, and yet share something of the sage-like intellect, to be able to recognise sage-like music. They must have a kind of transcendental *bhāvayitṛ pratibhā,* a term, the famous 9th century Indian critic Rājaśekhara uses to distinguish the insight of the critic from the inventive and imaginative *kārayitṛ pratibhā* of the poet. (The first essay in this collection discusses these concepts.) Confucius does not quite explicate what he meant by the intelligence of the transmitter, but later tradition did recognise a sage-like intelligence in him, an intelligence which could distinguish the product of a sage's divine *pratibhā*, and teach us how to transmit it.

Confucius, too, though somewhat obliquely, does speak of a process by which the 'Music' of the sage could be recognised. The process appears to be a kind of *anumāna*, a process of inference; but at its heart it is the judgement of a profound music-critic. Sze-hsia, as we have seen above, speaks of a *kinship* between 'pleasurable sound' and 'Music' even as he sharply divides them: they are akin but not the same, he says, Confucius speaks of the necessity of recognising this kinship in order to be able to recognise "Music'. In a remarkable passage early in the *Yo Ki*, we find him saying, "We must discriminate

[17] *Yo Ki*, 1, 22, p.100.

sounds in order to know the airs; the airs in order to know the music; and the music in order to know (the character of) the government. Having attained to this, we are fully provided with the methods of good order. Hence with him who does not know about the sounds we cannot speak about the airs, and with him who does not know the airs we cannot speak about the music. The knowledge of music leads to the subtle springs that underlie the rules of ceremony. He who has apprehended both ceremonies and music may be pronounced to be possessor of virtue. Virtue means realisation (in one's self)."[18] Examples of the kind of 'musical' apprehension and discrimination Confucius had in mind clearly reveal a distinct *aesthetic* wisdom akin to that of a music-critic and *sahṛdaya*, although one who intensely feels that music does not belong to a world of self-contained sensibilities but is a part of man's total vision, character and behaviour. In the final passages of the *Yo Ki,* an odd demand is placed before a music-master: Sze-kung asks him to suggest the music appropriate to his (Sze-kung's) temper. The master suggests differnt pieces that suit the temper of different men — all these, however, being 'good' men in their own way. "The generous and calm, the mild and correct, should sing the Sung; the magnanimous and calm, and those of wide penetration and sincere, the Ta Ya ... The object of this singing is for one to make himself right, and then display his virtue. When he has thus put himself in a condition to act, Heaven and Earth respond to him..."[19]

Such a conception of *pratibhā*, or the true vision, might sound familiar, for it is found in most civilisations. What is remarkable about Confucius' transcendental vision is that it is

---

[18] *Yo Ki*, i, 8, p. 95. The last sentence, "Virtue means realisation (in one's self).", sounds plainly odd. What the translator has added, obviously to make the meaning clear, hardly serves its purpose. Confucius seems to be saying that virtue is not just an outward knowledge of how one should behave, and what rules one should follow, but an inner becoming, the attainment of a state of being from which virtuous behaviour flows spontaneously.

[19] *Yo Ki*, iii, 31, pp. 129-130

uniquely musical. It links human harmony with a true order among feelings, granting music alone the power to effect it. True music, correctly designed with an eye towards giving the right temper — or 'tone' — as well as proper organization and orientation to our emotions, could create the desired ethos among human relations, imparting its own balance and equipoise and sense of joy to man, polity and society. "Therefore," Confucius says "the ancient kings (in framing their music), laid its foundations in the feeling and nature of men."[20] Music, thus, was the rock on which a sure and constant harmony of feelings could be founded: "In music", he says, "we have the expression of feelings which do not admit of any change.[21]

This might appear to be a quaint belief not founded in experience, since the affect of music, notoriously, lasts only as long as the music lasts. But, for Confucius, music, or the *true* music, the music of the sage, was much more than we ordinarily understand by the term, though, to use his own phrase, 'akin' to it. Music, for him, seems to have been the source of a kind of *sādhanā*, a *yoga,* or more meaningfully and pointedly, a *karmayoga* in the sense of, '*yogaḥ karmasu kauśalam,* where *yoga* is understood as spiritual mastery over actions. Music could lead to a realisation which ran deeper than any ordinary aesthetic experience, though resembling it. It was certainly pleasure-oriented, but it could be a thing in which, "the sages found pleasure." And so it could lead to a state of the soul akin to that of a *sthita-prajña,* and yet not a withdrawn, emotionless state, but one imbued with a sense of spritual joy or *ānanda*, because the source was music which is pleasure-giving by nature; it was also impregnated with the emotional harmony and impulse for right action. "When", Confucius says in a remarkable passage, "one has mastered completely (the principles of) music, and regulates his heart and mind accordingly, the natural, correct, gentle, and honest heart is easily developed, and with this

---

[20] *Yo Ki*, ii, 10, p. 108

[21] *Yo Ki,* iii, 1, p.114

development of the heart comes joy. This joy goes on to a feeling of repose. This repose is long-continued. The man in this constant repose becomes (a sort of) Heaven. Heaven-like, (his action) is spirit-like. Heaven-like, he is believed without the use of words. Spirit-like, he is regarded with awe, without any display of rage. So it is, when one by his mastering of music regulates his mind and heart."[22]

This, I think, could be said to sum up the deepest *aesthetic* intent of Confucius' understanding of music. The *political* intent and purpose behind his vision of true 'Music', music as 'creating', 'regulating', 'causing' True Order, comes out in another striking passage which, evidently, intends to portray the *form* and *svara*-structure of the ideal music he had in mind. The music has obvious 'overtones' relating it to an ideal hierarchical social and political order. The music was to be formed with the five *svaras* of traditional Chinese music, and of these *svaras,* Confucius says, "(the *svara*) *kung,* represents the ruler; *shang,* the minister; *kio,* the people; *kih,* affairs; and *yu,* things. If there is no disorder or irregularity in these five notes, there will be no want of harmony in the state." *Irregularity* in a *svara,* he adds, will, naturally, cause disorder in the element connected with it. And, "if the five notes are all irregular, and injuriously interfere with one another, they indicate a state of insolent disorder; and the state where this is the case will at no distant day meet with extinction and ruin."[23]

Interestingly, the description that we have of the ideal music here has a *rāga*-like structure; indeed, it has a strong kinship with a certain metaphorical way of characterising the relation between *svaras* in a *rāga* which is often repeated in the texts of Indian *saṅgīta-śāstra*, where *svaras* are laid out in a scheme of hierarchy in terms of their importance within a *rāga,* and described as king, minister, followers and enemies. We shall discuss this more specifically a little later. The crucial difference

---

[22] *Yo Ki*, iii, 23, p.125.

[23] *Yo, Ki*, i, 5, p. 94.

between Confucius and the musicology of *rāgas*, however, is that *rāgas* are conceived as many by nature: different *rāgas* have a different scheme of hierarchy among *svaras*. The 'king' of one *rāga* can be a mere 'follower' in another, or even, perhaps, an 'enemy'. What Confucius had in mind was a *unique,* unchanging, *rāga.* But being *rāga*-like his structure characterises the desired relation between *svaras qualitatively* and not quantitatively in such a way that the structure cannot be reduced to a single form, and thus it cannot, in principle, be mapped through a musical score or notation;[24] or, to put it in other words, it can be scored in innumerable ways, provided different renderings maintain the given *quality* of the relation between the *svaras.* It is like an ideal *concept* of polity expressed as music, an *idea*, which can be expressed through very different words, and in many different ways, provided the *qualitative relation* between concepts which constitute the idea, remain the same. It also seems, curiously, that in Confucius' *rāga*, his two ideals, pulling him in two contrary directions, the moral, seeking a unique goal, and the aesthetic, bent towards plurality, achieve a kind of musical togetherness.

In our own country, during ancient times, much more anterior to that of Confucius, the transcendental in music was nurtured more pronouncedly as a path to spiritual realisation. The intent was also more singularly *ādhyātmika,* rather than social and action-oriented. It did have a kind of action-orientation, but this was purely ritualistic, since music was

---

[24] It may be interesting to note here that the emergence of the *rāga* form took place in a milieu which did notate musical structures. The Vedic people had been using a system of notation for ages before the *rāga*-form took shape. Yet the musicology of the *rāga* never thought of defining or characterising a *rāga* through notations. On the contrary, it broke away from the *sāma* system which practically *defined* its musical structures in notational terms.

Notations, however, have been used for centuries, down to our present times, for *indicating* possible or generally-made movements within a *rāga,* or pointing out dominant *parts* of a *rāga*-structure, but a *rāga,* as a whole, is not thought to be a kind of structure that can be notated. Such an attempt would amount to what can be called a confusion of categories.

integral to the *yajña*-ritual. Plato and Confucius can be said to have been looking for a music of *dharma*. In India such an association with music is difficult to find. But since the early Vedic period music was made part of a spiritual vision and *sādhanā,* giving rise to a distinct spiritual tradition and stream of thought.

Indian culture, in fact, is the only culture where transcendental revelation has taken the form not only of words but also of music: pure music undiluted by words. The Vedic music, called *sāma*, to which the texts of many Vedic *mantras* are sung, is *apauruṣeya* (or transcendental) *in its own right* and not *through* the *mantras,* and as subsidiary to them. *Sāma*, indeed, was thought to have a revealed transcendental logos of its own, a logos considered in *sāma*-singing circles as higher than the one manifested through the 'word'. This singular esteem for the *sāma* finds an echo in the *Gītā*, too, when the Lord Himself says: "*vedānāṁ sāmavedo'smi* — Among the *Vedas*, I am the *Sāmaveda.*"

The literature especially devoted to *sāma* is vast, and includes a significant body of texts which are obviously musicological in the narrower sense of the term, analysing, describing, arranging and notating the music. But more outstanding and profound is the independent tradition which reflects on the deep ritual and the deeper spiritual logos of *sāma*. This tradition, evidently, took root in Vedic circles from very early times. The *Jaiminīya Brāhmaṇa* and the *Jaiminīya Upaniṣad Brāhmaṇa* are quite early (dating, perhaps to the period between 1000 and 800 BC), and already remarkable examples of this literature. One of the essays collected here, 'Ancient Music And The Concept Of Man', can provide the reader with an idea of this vein of thought, its uniqueness and independence from the revealed word, and its feeling for *sāma* as an *upāsanā*, a pathway to the spirit. The well-known *Chāndogya Upaniṣad*, 'the *Upaniṣad* of the singers of *sāma*', is a key text of this tradition of thought, but the others that we have named, are in many ways even more distinctive. My essay in this collection makes some detailed use of the otherwise lesser-known, *Jaiminīya Upaniṣad Brāhmaṇa.* The Vedic *ṛṣis* of this tradition, evidently, believed that *sāma,* having descended *from* the spirit could also *lead to* the spirit. Echoes of this ancient spiritual logos according a unique value to the discipline of music, can be discerned in throught concerning music throughout the history of Indian culture, down to our own times.

Music, however, is not usually *isolated* from a sung text, especially in a liturgy such as *sāma* also was. But the *sāma*-tradition pointedly does this. No wonder, then, that there is an ancient controversy in India on the issue of the independence of *sāma.* The controversy is punctuated by the position taken by Mīmāṁsakas, the proclaimed arbiters of correctness concerning Vedic ritual, who believe that *sāma* is *subsidiary* to the *mantra* text. Given this issue, it might be interesting to take up the case of the *independence* of *sāma* in some detail here. I will do this in the context of Professor Daya Krishna's comments on the article in this collection, referred to above, 'Ancient Music And' The Concept of Man'.

Professor Daya Krishna is a distinguished philosopher who has raised many new and significant questions concerning Mīmāṁsā and other schools of Indian thought, as well as the Vedic corpus in general. Many of his articles, concerning this aspect of his interests, have been collected in his book, *Indian Philosophy, A Counter Perspective.* One of the articles is entitled, 'The Vedic Corpus: Some Questions'. It raises searching questions regarding the ancient notions of *anṛca* and *aśarīra sāma,* conceived in the *sāma*-singing tradition, as it has been articulated in the *Jaiminīya Upaniṣad Brāhmaṇa* and described in my article. These notions, I have argued, reveal the idea of *sāma* as independent of the sung *mantra.* Prof. Daya Krishna's comment (pp. 71-73 of his book) on my formulation deserves reflection.

The relevant passage which he quotes from my article reads:

"*Sāma* was a revealed form in its own right, just as the *ṛcas.* Further, in many cases, *sāma* was valued for music alone. An example is that of the *anṛca-sāma. Anṛca-sāma* was a form of *Sāma* that had no *ṛk* base and was sung to meaningless syllables."

The *anṛca-sāma,* mentioned in this passage, is described in the *Jaiminīya Upaniṣad Brāhmaṇa*, where another interesting word, *aśarīra-sāma,* also occurs. In my article, I have taken these two words to be synonyms, meaning the same forms of *sāma*, consisting of pure music without words. (Though, as we shall see, a meaningful distinction *can* be made between *anṛca* and *aśarīra sāmas.*)

Quoting this passage, Professor Daya Krishna remarks: "The term *anṛca*, literally speaking, can only mean a melody which is not sung to a *Ṛk mantra*. Dr. Lath has, however, taken it to mean a melody which is sung to no text whatsoever. This is an arbitrary interpretation, the justification of which is supposed to lie in the *Jaiminīya Upaniṣad Brāhmaṇa* where, in the *Prathama Khaṇḍa* of the fourth *Anuvāka* of the first *Adhyāya*, it is said that *Samnānṛcena svargaṁ lokaṁ prayāteti*; and in the second *Khaṇḍa* of the sixth *Anuvāka* of the third *Adhyāya* it is said that *sa me'śarireṇa sāmnā śarirāṇyadhunot*. The identification of *Anṛca* with *Aśarīra*, though not entirely unjustified, rests on the assumption that *Ṛk* alone can be the body of *Sāma*. But this obviously is a questionable assumption."

There are two questions here. One, whether *anṛca* could mean *sāma* with a text other than a *ṛk*; and, two, whether *anṛca* and *aśarīra* can be identified, if so with what justification. As to the first question, as Professor Daya himself remarks, there was an assumption — an assumption rooted in Vedic culture and the milieu of *yajña*, of which *sāma* singing was an integral part — that *sāma* could be sung to *ṛk* alone. The passage in the *Jaiminīya Upaniṣad Brāhmaṇa* which speaks of the *anṛca*, describes it as leading the gods to heaven *in contrast* to the *sāma* which was sung to *ṛk.* It is also said in the passage — in a line not quoted in the article, as I had written it originally, assuming that *ṛk* alone could be a text for *sāma* — that: "They (the gods) shook off *ṛk*-words, the bodies (*śarīrāṇi*) [of the *sāma*] as they proceeded [towards heaven], and they became victorious over the world of heaven: *ta etāni ṛkpadāni śarīrāṇi dhunvanta āyan. te svargaṁ lokamajayan*" (*Jaiminīya Upaniṣad Brāhmaṇa*, 1,4,1.).[25] We notice immediately that *śarīra* here is clearly equated with *ṛk*. The implicit assumption in this passage patently is that the text of a *sāma* could not but be a *ṛk*, and that the *ṛk* alone formed the 'body' of the *sāma*. So deep-rooted was the assumption that it seems to have needed no explicit statement. The *Jaiminīya Upaniṣad Brāhmaṇa* speaks of the 'shaking off' of *ṛk* words (*ṛkpadāni*) from *sāma*. But if *ṛk* formed *the* text of *sāma*, the *sāma* would then have no text left. And hence an *aśarīra sāma* was the same as an *anṛca sāma*: without any text whatsoever. But one might reasonably argue here that by '*śarīra*' the *Upaniṣad Brāhmaṇa* really meant a 'meaningful' text, since no singing can, after all, avoid using some 'text', meaningful or not. An *aśarīra sāma*, hence is a *sāma* using meaningless words, but words all the same.

This is how Dayaji does understand *śarīra,* for he further comments, "he (Mukund Lath) seems to assume that only meaningful words and/or sentences could be said to form the body or *śarıra* of music. But there is no reason for this assumption. The term 'body' here merely means *āśraya* or base and that could be provided by anything, meaningful or meaningless".

I would like to discuss the implications of the notion of *āśraya* in Dayaji's usage, and whether a meaningful and a meaningless *āśraya* can be the same thing. The first consideration is, I think, obvious: we obviously do not need words, meaningful or meaningless, as *āśraya* for instrumental music, unless we stretch the meaning of 'words' to absurd limits. The matter, however, can lead to interesting reflection.

Playing on the *sitār*, the *sāraṅgī,* the flute or any other instrument, requires a friction in order to produce sound of

[25] The edition I refer to, as in the article discussed here, is the Kendrīya Sanskrit Vidyāpīṭha, edition of the text : ed. Billikoth Ramachandra Sharma, Tirupati, 1967.

which a variety is available to the musician, depending on the instrument, the techniques available and the kind of music desired. Music needs sound, and this is what Indian musicology knows as the *āhata-nāda,* or 'friction-born sound'. When the instrument for producing the *āhata-nāda* is the throat, the sound produced is conditioned by what the throat can do. But the *āhata-nāda* in the throat also produces sounds which are put together as words rather than music. Further, these sounds can be put together *both* as words and music. This possibility of combining in the human voice *svara* with the production of words is, indeed, what makes it possible for us to sing with words, as no other instrument can do. But it would be wrong to speak of an *āśraya-āśrayi-bhāva* here, with words as the *āśraya* and *svaras* as based on them. As we utter words, the voice spontaneously travels over the octave, and if we pay attention, tonal relations can be identified. In dramatic speech attention is, in fact, paid to the tone accompanying the voice, as Bharata clearly recognised long ago, indeed, he articulates the rise and fall of dramatic speech on the basis of *svaras*, specifically naming them in describing the process.[26] Dramatic speech is emotion-laden speech, and we can see that Bharata, like Confucius, recognised the essential relation between *svara* and the 'affections', using the relation to his own *rasa*-producing ends. But *svaras* in speech, even dramatic speech, remain vague and subsidiary; unrecognised as *svara,* though when we speak of certain voices as musical, one reason is the clarity with which they naturally enunciate *svara*.

Given this natural relation in the human voice of *svara* and speech, either of them can, in a sense, be spoken of as the *āśraya* of the other and we might call them, *paraspara-āśraya*, sharing a mutuality of *āśraya*-hood. But the *āśraya* of *svara* in speech is *not*, really speaking, word, but friction-produced sound, *āhata-nada*. If by 'word' we are to understand any sound whatever,

---

[26] See *Nāṭyaśāstra*, the section on *pāṭhya,* where the concept of *kāku,* paraphrased above, is described: G.O.S edition, vol. 2, *adhyāya* 17, p. 385-399.

which accompanies a *svara* but can be distinguished from it in some sense, then to term 'words' as the *āśraya* of *svara* and music would become an empty truism. The question rather should be: can we think of the *āhata-nāda* arising in the human voice as being more naturally and essentially related to sounds that produce words and language rather than to *svara* and music ? For only in such a case can words be an *āśraya* of sung music in any worthwhile sense.

Let me try to further clarify. The *āhata-nada* or the friction-produced range of sounds in the human voice, as I have said, contains sounds of two distinct kinds: those that can be articulated as words and those that form *svaras*. Both these sounds are produced together in such a way that we can meaningfully speak of a relation of mutual or *paraspara āśraya* between those sounds that form words and those that form *svaras* . One or the other partner in this *paraspara āśraya* can be made to become dominant, a process leading either to speech or to music. The *āhata-nāda* in the throat, when articulating speech is dominated by *varṇas* or *syllables*: vowels, consonants and the like; but in making music, which, though it also uses *varṇas,* the main intention of using the voice is to turn itself into a musical instrument and articulate pitch and the web of *svaras* created by modulations of pitch. Modulations of pitch, however, are not *absent* in articulating *varṇas*. The question is what is more *natural* to the voice as *āhata-nāda, varṇa* or *svara* ? Or, in other words, in the given *paraspara āśraya* between *varṇa* (which forms words), and *svara* (which forms music), which is the *essentially* dominant partner ? Even on a simple reflection, we cannot fail to see that the relation between *svara* and the *āhata-nāda* in our throat has a much more essential quality than the relation between that *nāda* and words. The throat-born *varṇas* used in pronouncing words are also used in intoning music. The *varṇas,* however, appear as more naturally related to words and language than to music. We are tempted, therefore, like Professor Daya Krishna to call 'words' as *āśraya* of music. But the relation of the *āhata-nāda* with music is much stronger than it is with words. Because *āhata-nāda* as such, whether in the human voice or in animals, or even inanimate nature, has a natural *anuraṇana* or a sympathetic after-sound which makes it produce or echo other sounds at other pitches. This is what gives rise to *svaras*, and makes *svaras* something given in nature, a series of pitches, related to each other through what has been called a *saṁvāda* or harmony. It was this 'given' relation which Pythagoras, to his profound surprise, discovered to be governed by simple arithmetical ratios. There is no such natural relation between the *āhata-nāda* and the vowels and consonants, or *varṇas*, which are produced in the human voice alone and which we use for uttering words.[27] In fact, when we produce *varṇas*,

[27] This has been recognised in Indian scientific thinking for many centuries. The *Praśastapāda Bhāṣya* on the *Vaiśeṣika Sūtras* (*c.* 4th-5th centuries AD) recognises the peculiarity of sound as an object of the senses. Though sound is a *pratyakṣa*, Praśastapāda observes, that is, a 'sensible', or some 'thing' perceived, there is no 'thing' or object perceived in this *pratyakṣa*. Indeed, what is perceived is the end-product of a series of *waves*, each of which is destroyed immediately after giving rise to the next wave in the series till it reaches the ear. The series of waves which constitute sound, is born of friction between 'things' when they come in contact or break apart (*saṁyogavibhāgaśabdajaḥ*, the concept used by Praśastapāda for what in *saṁgīta-śāstra* is known as *āhata-nāda).* Sound, interestingly, is divided by Praśastapāda into two major categories : *dhvani* and *varṇa,* that is, sound in general, one might say, and phonemes or syllables. *Varṇas,* according to Prasastapāda, are units of speech such as the vowel, '*a*'; and *dhvani*, on the other hand, is produced by instruments such as the conch, the flute, etc, : *śabdo'mbaraguṇaḥ śrotragrāhyaḥ, kṣaṇikaḥ, kāryakāraṇobhayavirodhi, saṁyogavibhāgaśabdajaḥ, pradeśavṛttiḥ, samānāsamānajātiyakāraṇaḥ. sa dvividho varṇalakṣaṇo dhvanilaksaṇaśca. tatra ākārādirvarṇalakṣaṇaḥ, śaṅkhādinimitto dhvanilakṣaṇaśca.* (I quote from the Ganganath Jha Granthamālā edition of the text, ed. Bhagīratha Prasāda Śāstrī, Sampurnanand Sanskrit Vishvavidyalaya, Varanasi, 1977, pp. 692-93). I have made a precis of the text in the essay above, including only those points which were of interest here without translating the whole text, which has other points of interest, too, but which are not quite relevant here. *Varṇas*, in contrast to *dhvani*, Praśastapāda further seems to suggest, are produced through human effort : *tatra varṇalakṣaṇasyotpattirātmamanasoḥ saṁyogāt smṛtyapekṣād varṇoccārṇecchā, tadanantaraṁ prayatnaḥ* ... (ibid, pp 693-94). Although the examples given by Praśastapāda illustrating *dhvani imply* a similar human effort, he does not *speak* of such an effort in this case, and, patently, the concept of *saṁyoga-vibhāga* indicates that sound may be produced by friction

which are more contingent and conditioned sounds, through our voice, we at the same time, and more necessarily, produce *svaras*, too. Many languages, such as Vedic Sanskrit for example, indeed use *svaras* in forming and distinguishing words. So if we at all want to speak of an *āśraya-āśrayi-bhāva* between *svara* and words, *svara* seems to be a more reasonable choice as an *āśraya.*

There are other considerations in this context which we could also reflect on. A word, forgetting its loose sense as a combination of *varṇas*, cannot really be called 'word' without a meaning. A meaning, however, can have an entirely different string of sounds as *āśraya*, or an *āśraya* not in sound but in script. And, if we think of meaningful words as necessarily tied up with other words and with language as a whole, we would perhaps have to speak of a complex relationship of *paraspara-āśraya*, between language, meaning and sound, the sense of *āśraya* being different for each of the different relations. *Svara* may be said to be the *āśraya* of music in a sense analogous to the relation between a (meaningful) word and language: words depend on a language, within which they are words; similarly *svaras* in order to be significant and expressive for us and not mere sounds related in a certain natural way, assume music. How, one might ask, can the relation between *svara* and meaningless vocal sounds be characterised ? Is the relation the same

---

alone, without any human effort: these could only be sounds of the *dhvani* category. Other, later, texts make the distinction clear. The author of the *Śabdaratna*, whose views are summarised in the *Nyāyakośa*, differentiates between *śabda* which is knowingly and wilfully produced (*buddhihetukaḥ)* and that which is not so produced (*abuddhihetukaḥ),* and is 'natural': such as the sound made

by clouds: *sa ca śabdo dvividhaḥ buddhihetukaḥ abuddhihetukaśca. tatra abuddhihetuko meghādiśabdaḥ.* See *Nyāyakośa,* compiled by Bhīmācārya Jhalakīkar, pub. the Bhandarkar Oriental Research Institute, Poona, 1978, under '*śabda'*.

Intriguingly, though the distinction which Praśastapāda makes between *varṇa* and *dhvani*, is obviously made with language and music in mind, he does not take up the phenomena of *svara* and its relation to *dhvani* for any significant exposition, concentrating, rather, on the relation between *varṇa* and words or language. *Śabda* or language was for him important as a category of *pramāṇa* — to which he denied a separate category, including it under *anumāna* — but *svara* or music, clearly, did not interest him in its own right.

as that between a meaningful word and the sounds used to utter it? It does not seem to be so, unless one were to believe, like some do in the west, that a *written* musical score is as much or even 'purer' music than that which is sung or played; but the notion of the reducibility of music to writing strains our imagination beyond belief, and cannot be equated with the use of script in language. Music, which is made with *svaras* is necessarily friction-produced, or uses *āhata-nāda*, to employ the meaning-loaded ancient concept in the sense we have seen above. The *anāhata nāda* (sound produced without friction), another meaningful ancient concept, considered the transcendental ground of *āhata-nāda*, is not open to our senses and is not what music uses; though words, one could think, may be called *anāhata*, meaningfully, since they need not be heard. The relation of music to sound, indeed, specific sound, is much more intimate than the relation of meaning to sound, as is also clear from the fact that music is not translatable.

The *āhata* sounds in the human voice, have two given relations: one with *svara* and the other with words, through *varṇas*. This possibility of the same *āhata-nāda* to be related to both *svara* and words, makes it possible for us to *sing* words, something other musical instruments cannot do. *Svara*, we have argued, is more essentially related to *āhata-nāda*. Yet, since we use language more naturally, and in a sense more essentially than music, we tend to think of human sounds more basically as words rather than *svara* and music. This rather uncritically maintained idea, also seems the basis of Prof. Daya's assertion that music must have an *āśraya* in words, whether meaningful or not. Bharata, too, with a similar contention in mind speaks of *pada*, 'word', in music as either with or without meaning.[28] But as Bharata also makes us realise, the relation of music with the

[28] *Nāṭyaśāstra,* 32, 28 (G.O.S edition, vol, 4, p. 302) : *yat syādakṣarasambaddhaṁ tat sarvaṁ padasaṁjñitam* — 'whatever is [made up] through a correlation of syllables is termed '*pada*'.' Bharata says this in the context of describing the sung 'texts' of *gāndharva*, which included meaningless strings of syllables, besides meaningful ones. He has, for his own peculiar purpose, stretched the meaning of '*pada*' beyond the limits acceptable to both ordinary and śāstric usage : for which *pada* was necessarily meaningful.

two kind of *padas*, meaningful and meaningless, has an entirely different intent, and cannot really be equated. When 'words' are meaningless, we are making music, not words, because there are really no words. What we *call* 'words', in such a context, namely vowels and consonants, or, in other words, *akṣaras* or *varṇas*, can, I think, be better described as *parts* of *svaras*, rather than their *āśraya*. Like strokes on instruments they help manifest the *svara* in a certain manner, becoming a *sāmagrī*, an integral ingredient, of its expressive quality, its intonation; and it is *svara* as expression that constitutes music. The role of *akṣaras* or *varṇas* is quite different in language. They are *parts* of speech, but they are not integral to meaning.

But when a song *has* meaningful words, we have a large and complex spectrum of possibilities. The relationship can be either word-dominated or music-dominated. One could evoke Bharata once again in this context. He describes two kinds of music, the one, pure, called *gāndharva*, the other theatrical or programmatic, called *gāna*, they lie for him at the two ends of the possible relations between *pada*, that is, meaningful words, and *svara,* music, with music dominating in *gāndharva* and words in *gāna*. Our own music today has examples of both the *svara* and the *pada*-dominated forms, with other forms lying more at the centre of the spectrum, and containing a more even balance between *pada* and *svara* such as in the *ṭhumrī* or the *jāvalī*. From Bharata we can also form an idea of how words usually get to be treated when music dominates: the syllables are pulled, pushed, drawn out, broken, distorted, and treated in ways that they would not be treated if conveying meaning was the purpose. The production of music takes over and vocal sounds become more like strokes on the instrument that is the voice, and hence closer to meaningless 'words'. In forms dominated by meaningful words, we can, perhaps, relevantly speak of words as the *āśraya* of music. The music 'rests' on the words, moulding itself to them. But in music-dominated forms, such a concept of *āśraya* seems meaningless, since words even when meaningful tend to become vocables.

This is what had clearly happened in *sāma. Sāma* is sung to both meaningful and meaningless words, with most *sāmas* having words that are meaningful. *But* the words are treated as if they are not words but tools to make music with. They are distorted and pushed around in various ways, the distortions are obviously made with music and not meaning in mind.

The passage I had quoted above from the *Jaiminīya Upaniṣad Brāhmaṇa,* speaks of the '*śarīra*' being shaken off from *sāma,* this *śarīra* being the *ṛk.* It also suggests that this was done without loss to *sāma*, making it, on the contrary, 'lighter' — more subtle and pure, and hence, fit for being 'uplifted' to heaven. But if the *śarīra* could be dispensed with, it cannot really be taken to be synonymous with '*āśraya'*, if *āśraya* is to be understood as the indispensable base for the music.

Sāma, thus, was clearly music-dominated, though this is not generally realised, because our thought is dominated by the Mīmāṁsā view of *ṛk* as the ruling partner. But the *ṛk* as sung in *sāma* almost invariably undergoes extensive distortions, obviously made for the sake of music, with meaning plainly becoming a casuality.[29] These distortions are called *sāma-vikāras,* 'the modification/mutilation a text undergoes in singing *sāma'*. The Sāmavedins have carefully studied this musical phenomenon, which is, in fact, common, in a lesser or a greater degree, depending on the musical intent, in singing any text. The *vikāras* have been analysed in detail and classified into, mainly, six types. The exercise is unique in the history of musicology, important not only for *sāma*, but for understanding of texts in general as *sung*. Unfortunately, the idea of *sāma-vikāra* is little-known outside *sāma* circles, even to modern Indian music-critics and musicologists, who are otherwise quite preoccupied with the

[29] There are, of course, those who think of the *ṛk mantra* primarily as a *varṇānukramī,* a fixed string of syllables. For those who believe so, it is even more difficult to demonstrate the dominance of *ṛk* in *sāma* singing as has been pointed out by Sāmavedins. Because, *sāma-vikāras,* as we shall see, inevitably change the *ṛk varṇānukramī* and hence what is sung can no longer be called a '*ṛk' mantra.*

relation of text with music. (There is a short article in this collection, 'Words And Music', which makes some use of the notion of *sāma-vikāra* in a modern context). It may, therefore, be useful to illustrate the phenomenon from the *Sāmaveda.* I will quote the example that Satyavrata Sāmaśramī has given in his edition of the *Sāmaveda*, with Sāyaṇa's *Bhāṣya.*

Before proceeding, let me point out that the notion of *āśraya* or its synonym, *ādhāra*, was also used by the Sāmavedins. The sung *ṛk* was thought of in two ways: either as the *yoni*, the 'source', of the *sāma*, or as its *āśraya,* or sometimes as its *mūla*, 'root', meaning the same as 'source'. The two notions, of *yoni* and *āśraya,* are obviously not the same. The notion of *yoni*, clearly, does not imply the idea of a base as does that of *āśraya.* But the Sāmavedins do not seem to have made any real distinction between the two notions, taking them both in the same sense as '*āśraya*' or 'base'. This concept, we shall see, leads them into strange, almost absurd, directions, when the sung text was not *ṛk* but a meaningless string of *varṇas* to which *sāmas* were also sung.

The *ṛk āśraya,* or *yoni,* of the *sāma* to be illustrated for *vikāras* is as follows:

agna āyāhi vītaye gṛṇāno havyadātaye/

'Agni, come for the libation, sung by us, carry the offering'.

nihotā satsi barhiṣi.

'You are the priest, sit on the grass-mat'.[30]

(I have given a rough literal translation, following the word-order of the original, so that the *vikāras* to be illustrated may be more clearly seen).

This *ṛk*, the first in the *chanda-ārcika*, the primary or basic collection of *ṛks* for *sāmas,* can be sung to three different *sāma* compositions, revealed to two different *ṛṣis*, to Gotama, who sang two of them, and to Kaśyapa. In the first version, which is

---

[30] All our reference to the *Sāmaveda Saṃhitā* are to the Bibliotheca Indica, Calcutta, 1871-1878 edition, editor, Satyavrata Sāmaśramī Bhaṭṭācārya; reprinted by Munshiram Manoharlal Publishers Pvt. Ltd., New Delhi, 1983. For the present passage see Vol. I, p. 94.

by Gotama, the *sāma* has the following 'text' (the oblique marks in the 'text' to follow indicate punctuations in the music, not the meaning. I omit the musical notations which accompany the *sāma.* Though a necessary part of the song, indicating how it should be sung, they are not really needed here to understand the notion of *vikāras*, and will only clutter the text):

ognāyi / āyāhi / viyitoyāyi / toyāyi / gṛṇānoha / vyadāto yāyi / toyāyi / nayiho tasa / tsāyi / vā au hovā / hisi /[31]

One can plainly see that the *ṛk* now is unrecognisable. The *vikāras* have transformed it, so much so that the meaning can no longer be grasped without reference to the original. Satyavrata Sāmaśramī identifies and names the various *vikāras* the *ṛk* is considered to have undergone. The words, *agni*, *vītaye, ā yāhi*, have undergone the *vikāra* termed *vikṛti*, that is, 'distortion' or 'modification' of individual words (the general term *vikṛti*, a synonym of *vikāra*, being used here in a particular sense). The word *vītaye* has undergone other *vikāras* besides *vikṛti.* One is *viśleṣa,* or separation, in that a part of it, an already *vikṛta* part, *toyāyi*, has been detached from it. The word has also been 'pulled', that is, subjected to *vikarṣaṇa*: dragged out into a *yāyi* at its end. We further see an *abhyāsa* or a 'repetition' of a part of the already distorted word: in */vīyitoyāyi / toyāyi /.* There is also a *virāma* to be seen in this *sāma*: *virāma* being a pause which goes against the meaning. In this instance, it breaks the words, *gṛṇāno havyadātaye* into two meaningless segments: *gṛnānoha / vyadāto yāyi/,* the *virāma* here coming at '*ha*', instead of '*no*' where it should. We also see a *lopa*, or an 'omission': of the syllable '*r*' (the *repha*) in the *sāma* form of the last word in the *ṛk*, namely, *barhiṣi.*[32]

Another important thing that has happened is the *addition* of extra syllables, which are not in the *ṛk.* Such an addition is a

---

[31] Ibid. The *vikṛta sāma* form given here is recorded just below the *ṛk*, in the book we quote from.

[32] See Sāyaṇa's *avataraṇikā* or introduction to the *Saṁhitā*, vol. 1, p. 12. Note, especially, Satyavarata Sāmaśramī Bhaṭṭācārya's footnote (on the same page), where he illustrates the *vikāras*. Our example and exposition follows him.

marked characteristic of a great deal of singing, whether Vedic or not. The added syllables in the above *sāma* are, / *vā au hovā* / . Such added syllables were known as *stobha*. The phenomenon of *stobha* is important for understanding the *notion of anṛca* and the *aśarīra sāmas*. A *stobha* has been defined simply as: 'extra syllables not in the *ṛk' (adhikatve sati ṛgvilakṣaṇavarṇaḥ stobhaḥ),* but the notion is more complex than the simple, though suggestive, definition implies. We have seen that extra syllables have already been added through other *vikāras*. These, however, are considered as transformations, not additions. *Stobhas* are syllables not traceable to the *ṛk* through any *vikāra*. The concept of the *stobha*, as we shall see, reveals that in a deep sense, for *sāma*-singing, the only text that was really a meaningful text was a *ṛk*. The *vikāras*, mapped above, have shown that *sāma* treated the words of the *ṛk* more as vocables than as units of meaning. The illustration given here is not exceptional; indeed, the *ṛk* in most *sāmas* is equally unrecognisable, often to an even greater degree. Modern *khyāl*-singers, who obviously care more for music than for meaning, get chastised for a much lesser degree of *vikāra*-formation. *Stobhas*, we just saw, have been defined simply as 'syllables not in the *ṛk*'. This simple definition veils the fact that *sāma* could be independent of the *ṛk*, not only through the introduction of meaningless texts but also of meaningful ones, for syllables not in the *ṛk* need not be meaningless.[33] The truth is that there were *sāmas* sung only to *stobhas*, both meaningless and meaningful.

And this, appropriately, brings me to the point that Professor Daya Krishna has made about *anṛca sāma*. He is right, I must confess, in suggesting that *'anṛca'* need not mean a meaningless *sāma*. Non-*ṛk*, but meaningful words are found as the texts of quite a few *stobha sāmas*. Professor Daya's intention was, no

---

[33] For quite another kind of musical *vikāras*, where meaning is paid more crucial attention to see *The Hindi Padāvalī Of Nāmadev* by Winand. M. Callewaert and Mukund Lath, Motilal Banarasidass Publishers Pvt. Ltd. Delhi, 1989, pp.63-82 These we have called *geya-vikāras* to distinguish them from *sāma-vikāras*.

doubt, to make a logical or analytical point: '*anṛca*' can only mean 'having no *ṛk;* it *cannot* mean 'having no meaningful text'. But what he says is *actually* true, as I discovered on looking up the *Sāmaveda*, where there are a significant number of *sāmas* which are sung to a meaningful yet *anṛca* texts. These, in the present edition of the *Sāmaveda Saṃhitā,* are termed *stobha sāmas*.

Sāmavedins tell us that *sāma* is sung either to *ṛk* or to *stobha,* and, indeed, most often to both, as we have seen in the illustration above. *Sāmas* sung to *stobha* alone, the *stobha-sāmas*, intriguingly, include both meaningless *and meaningful* texts. Let me give examples. The *āraṇya gānas*, though placed in a '*pariśiṣṭa*' of the *chanda-ārcika* of the *Sāmaveda Saṁhitā,* are yet an integral part of the *Saṁhitā.* They include a number of songs sung to *stobha* alone. Among these we have examples of both meaningful and meaningless texts. Strikingly, the famous Vedic lines beginning with, '*aganma jyotiḥ amṛtā abhūma* — 'we shall find the light and become immortal', are sung as *sāma*. The *sāma* is described as a *stobha sāma* and is an *araṇya-gāna.* Its text as a *mūla*, that is what would otherwise be called its *yoni*-form, if it were a *ṛk*, is recorded in a curious manner, plainly different from the earlier example from the *Ṛgveda*; it is given as follows, and it is termed a *mūla* or *yoni*:

u / aganma / jyotiḥ / amṛtāḥ / a / mṛtāḥ / abhūma / antarikṣaṁ / pṛthivyaḥ / adhi / a / āruhāma / avidāma / devān / sam / u / devaiḥ / aganmahi /[34]

['We shall find the light and become immortal. From the earth we shall ascend to the skies, and from the skies to the heavens, and we shall know the gods, and walk with them.']

We have a clear example here of an *anṛca sāma*, which has a meaningful text. We could, perhaps, see a useful distinction in such instances between the ancient terms *anṛca* and *aśarīra*: for this *sāma*, though *anṛca,* need not also be described as *aśarīra* if

---

[34] See vol. II, pp. 465-466. There are some musical symbols written above many letters, these I have again omitted since the point I am making does not need their presence.

śarīra be taken as a meaningful text. We cannot say, however, whether the ancient *sāma*-singers had also thought of such a distinction between *anṛca* and *aśarīra*. If they did, *aśarīra,* for them, could have meant any *ṛk*-less *sāma*, whether sung to a meaningful or to a meaningless text. This seems reasonably imaginable, and it can, I think, be argued that what are now recorded as *stobha sāmas*, began in the earliest singing tradition as *aśarīra sāmas*, even though, as far as I know, such a connection has not actually been thought of.

To come now to the text of this *stobha sāma*, we notice that every word is segregated from the other; no running text is given in this instance, as it is when recording a *ṛk* as a *yoni:* we have seen this in the first example I gave of the *sāma, 'agna āyāhi vītaye'*. The text of the present song, as we can see from the manner in which it is written above — every word being segregated from the others with an oblique sign of separation — is not recorded as a continuous meaningful text containing words conjoined into phrases or sentences, but rather as a series of independent, disconnected string of syllables, or in other words, *stobhas* not really meant to be 'words'. This impression is strengthened if we take a look at the complete list of *stobhas* to be found at the end of the *chanda-ārcika* as another *pariśiṣṭa*:[35] this includes the meaningful words of this *sāma*, each recorded separately, along with words which in principle are considered meaningless, like the / *vā au hovā* /, of the earlier *ṛk-sāma.* We also notice elements in this *stobha sāma* which are not be found when a *ṛk* is recorded as *yoni* or, in other words, as a meaningful text without the *vikāras.* We have in the present case the additions of the meaningless '*u*' and the '*a*' sounds as *part* of the *mūla text* itself. We also have a repetition or *abhyāsa*, which is otherwise a *vikāra,* included as *part* of the text. It is an *abhyāsa* which, perversely, seems to turn the meaning around in a self-contradiction: / *amṛtāḥ* / *a* / *mṛtāḥ* /, turning '*a*' into a *stobha*, and separating it, and thus associating *amṛtāḥ* with its contradiction, *mṛtāḥ*.

---

[35] See *Sāmaveda Saṁhitā*, Vol. II, pp.519 to 542.

What is even more intriguing is that the above series of *stobhas* was not considered the form for actual singing but only a kind of basic text; it was subjected to further *vikāras* in actual singing. As *sung* this *sāma* had the following form (I again omit the *svara*-notations, except for those which appear to be recorded as *part of* the text):

Auhovāauhovāauhovā / aganmajyotiḥ / 2 / aganmajyotiḥ / amṛtāabhūma/2/amṛtāabhūmā/tarikṣampṛthivyāadhyāruhāmā/2/ tarikṣampṛthivyāa-dhyāruhāma / divamantarikṣādadhyaruhāma /3/ avidāmadevān/3 samudevairaganmahi/3/auhovāauhovāauhovā/ suvarjyotī /[36]

We again notice interesting changes which can only be called *vikāras*. There is, for one, the *addition* of both meaningful and meaningless syllables*: 'au, ho, vā' as well as 'suvarjyotī'*. This amounts, in the Sāmavedins' own terms, to adding *stobha* to *stobha* since what we have is already a *stobha sāma.* Even more interestingly, we have passages with only *svaras, / 2 /, / 3 /,* which I have not omitted, because they stand like *stobhas* as integral part of the the sung *text*, and not as notations *added* separately, as is done elsewhere in recording *sāma*, particularly those with a *ṛk yoni.* One wonders what vocable or vocables these *svaras* were sung to, for these *svaras* must have used some vocal syllables in order to be intoned. One also wonders whether such lone-standing *svara* signs are to be classed as *stobha.* If not, how are they to be categorised ?[37]

---

[36] The same textual reference as in fn. 34.

[37] In recording the text of a *sāma* as sung, a text whether composed of *ṛk* or of *stobhas*, the method usually employed in the available *Sāmaveda Saṁhitās* is to indicate the *svaras* above the *varṇas* : a^{1}ganma^{2}jyo^{1ra}tiḥ^{2}, the numbers pointing at *svaras* and '*ra*' indicating a prolongation by a *mātrā* of a syllable (see, *Kauthuma-śākhāyāḥ ūhagānam, ūhyagānam,* referred to in detail below, introduction, pp. 27-29 and 35-36). A *svara* is not separately given as in this and similar cases.

Prof. Daya Krishna recently pointed out to me an article by Prof. Wayne Howard where he describes a kind of *sāma*, sung by the Nambudiri *yājñikas*, called *anirukta sāma* : See 'The Music Of The Nambudiri Unexpressed Chant (*Aniruktagāna*)' by Wayne Howard in *Agni : The Vedic Ritual Of The Fire Altar,* ed. Frits Staal, pub Motilal Banarasidass, New Delhi, 1984 (Indian Edition), vol. II, pp. 311-342. But the *'anirukta'*, translated not too happily as, 'unexpressed',

Strange as the above conception of *stobha* added to *stobha* may appear, the additions, however, do come across as

---

by Howard, points really at no more than a special kind of *stobha* singing. Also it does not, as I had hoped, afford a clue to the meaning and use of lone-standing *svaras within* a text. We also find that the ancient term used to describe what is today known as *'anirukta'* among the Nambudiris, was, indeed, '*stobha*'.

What occurs in *anirukta*, as it is described by Howard, is that the meaningless syllables *o vā* or a series of *bhakāras* are substituted for *ṛk varṇas*. When *a bhakāra*, that is, the syllable '*bha*' is substitued for a *ṛk varṇa*, this is done in such a way that the *mātrā*, that is, the vowel value of the *bhakāra* corresponds with the *mātrā* of the original. Writing about two decades before Howard, Pandit A.M. Ramanath Dikshit in his introduction (in Sanskrit) to *Kauthumaśākhāyāḥ ūhagānam, ūhyagānam,* Kashi Hindu Vishvavidyalaya, Varanasi, 1967, had described the practice in some detail, referring in this context to a *brāhmaṇagrantha,* which he does not, however, name (see his introduction, p.45). The example Ramanath Dikshit gives, makes the phenomenon clear enough.To take his example, for the *ṛk* phrase, '*adugdhā iva dhenavaḥ iśānamasya jagataḥ*', the following series of *bhakāras* are substitued : *bha-bhu-bhā bhi-bha bhe-bha-bha bhi-bhā-bha-bha. bha-bha-bha,* the *bhakāras* thus retain the *mātrā*-structure of the original. Though Dikshit has not named any specific *Brāhmaṇa* work here, I found a description of the phenomenon in one of them, the *Saṁhitopaniṣad Brāhmaṇa*, pub. Kendriya Sanskrit Vidyapeetha, (Tirupati series nos. 2-4), Tirupati, 1983, ed. Bellikoth Ramachandra Sharma, with the commentaries of Sāyaṇa and Dvijarāja Bhaṭṭa. This interesting *Brāhmaṇa,* which seems a relatively later text, classes the phenomenon as *stobha.* It is written in *sūtras. Sūtras*, 18 and 19 of the second *khaṇḍa* read : *rathantare'nvakṣaraṁ bhakārān* (18), and *svaravanti vyañjanāni yathākṣaraṁ darśayet* (19)— 'in the *ratahantara sāma, bhakāras* [are substituted] for every syllable' (18), and 'the [*bhakāras*] should [take the place of] the consonants [in the original] and should have the [same] vowels'(19). I have followed the commentator, Dvijarāja, in making my translations, (Sāyaṇa's commentary does not exist for this part of the text), but the *Brāhmaṇa*, as one can see, is unambiguous enough. The next three *sūtras* (nos.20-22) promise and argue for a special merit accruing to both the singers of such *bhakāra rathantara sāmas* as well as to their *yajamānas*. In *sūtra* 23, the word '*stobha*' is plainly used in a manner which suggests that these very *bhakāras* are being named : *rathantarasya stobhā svaravantaḥ prayoktavyāḥ* — 'the *stobhas* of the *rathantara sāma* should be rendered [in singing] with the [right] *svaras*'. The context clearly implies that *stobhas* referred to are the *bhakāras*, and this is how the commentator, Dvijarāja, understands the text, commenting: *rathantarasya bhakāralakṣaṇā stobhā svaravantaḥ prayoktavyāḥ*.

There are some notable differences between the modern Nambudiri singing of *anirukta sāmas* and what is described by Dikshit and the ancient *Brāhmaṇa* : the latter do not speak of a modification in musical structure, and the alternative substitution of *o vā,* for example, but, essentially, the phenomenon *can* be reasonably classed as *'stobha'*, and the *Brāhmaṇa,* indeed, does so.

additions, because the original *stobha sāma* contains meaningful units of syllables. But here now is a really queer example. Look at the following *stobha sāma* in its what is termed the *yoni*-form:
hu // 2 // 1 / / 5
This *stobha-sama* when sung, was given the form:
hau / 3 / ū / 3 / huū / iyāhau / 2 / iyāhau / vā / iṭiḍā // [38]
The original contains four segments: a meaningless syllable and three *svaras;* in what sense it is the *yoni* or *āśraya* of what is actually to be sung is difficult to imagine. In any case, if only a *ṛk* can be the textual *āśraya* — as the Sāmavedins say — of a *sāma*, the notion of *vikāra* in singing seems meaningful only with *ṛk*. The *ṛk*, moreover, has a fixed textual form independent of the *sāma,* which is plainly recognisable as such. But in the other cases, especially the last one, the very conception of an 'original', a *yoni,* that is, an *āśraya*, is puzzling in the extreme. The 'original' here seems to be a pure *abstraction* made from what was actually sung. Why was it felt necessary to take this step, we do not know. The relation between the *sāma* and its 'abstract' *yoni* seems transparent in some forms: We can accept '*hu*' as the *yoni*, in some sense, of '*hau*', *'huu'* and *'iyāhau':* we can even think of '*vā*' and '*iṭiḍā*' as *stobhas*, further added to the 'original'. But no stretch of imagination can lead us to think of the *svaras*, /2 /, / 1 /, */ 5 /,* as *yonis* of the *svaras*, / 3 /, / 3 / and / 2 /, occurring in the sung text. Perhaps, one might argue that it was thought necessary that every *sāma* should have a *yoni* or *āśraya* analogous to the *ṛk.* But if this was so, it certainly led to queer results, revealing the oddity of thinking in terms of an *āśraya* in cases where the sung 'words' were meaningless.

We have quoted, as I said, the above *sāmas* from the monumental work of Satyavrata Sāmaśramī Bhaṭṭācārya, the famous Sāmavedin who edited the *Sāmaveda Saṁhitā* with Sāyaṇa's commentary more than a century ago. He records the above *sāma* with an editorial comment: "*asya mūlaṁ na ṛk api tu*

---

[38] *Sāmaveda Saṁhitā*, vol II, p. 487 (*grāme araṇyagāne pañcama-prapāṭhaka).*

stobhaḥ — the base (*āśraya, yoni)* of this *[sāma]* is not *ṛk* but *stobha.*"

We find that the *Sāmaveda Saṁhitā*, its *bhāṣyas* and its modern edition, do not use words such as *anṛca* or *aśarīra* for the *ṛk*-less *sāmas*. The concepts of *anṛca* and *aśarīra* were developed in the early esoteric circles of ancient *sāma*-singers who were inspired by a purely musical vision and felt the words to which they usually sang their *sāma* as a burden. This seems to have been for them a revolutionary move, since as priests and ritualists they must have felt *ṛk* to be inseparable from *sāma*. It was their deeper, *ādhyātmika* or spiritual quest which freed the revealed *svara* from the revealed word. Their literature, thus, shows an ambivalent attitude towards *ṛk*; a rejection of *ṛk* is bracketed with a respect for *ṛk* even as they extol *sāma* for itself, and glory in the independence of *sāma*. In the *Upaniṣad Brāhmaṇa* story, after the gods are said to have shaken off the *ṛk* from the *sāma*, Prajāpati, the Creator Himself, collects them as they lie scattered in the firmament and offers them His devotion (*tanyā divaḥ prakīrṇānyaśeran. āthemāni prajāpatirṛkpadāni sañcityābhyarcat: Jaiminīya Upaniṣad Brāhmaṇa,* 1, 4, 1, 6). The *ṛk* is identified with *śrī,* 'wealth', 'prosperity', 'well-being', which the gods lose since they had shaken it off, and the *asuras* gathered it. In order to win back the lost *śrī*, the gods restore *ṛk* to *sāma*, singing the *sāma* to the *ṛk* (Ibid. 1, 4, 2, 1-5). Apparently, for the ancient *sāma* singer, the *sāmas* in which he could realise the luminosity of music in itself was a mystic area, inviting exploration, and yet, somewhat forbidden.

However, the impulse to *svara* was basic in *sāma*. The association of *ṛk* with *sāma*, even in *ṛk-sāmas* was, as we have seen, such that meaning was distorted in multiple ways for the sake of music; this seems to have invited the singer to give up meaning altogether. He also, in a step he seems to have felt as equally radical, gave up *ṛk*, choosing new words for his *sāmas*. The use of *stobha* in the existing literature for *both* these moves reflects, I think, the fact that for the ancient *sāma*-singer the tyranny of meaning, the tie to an *āśraya* in words outside music, was associated primarily with *ṛk*, and once he felt free of *ṛk*, he could give up meaning altogether, as a step in the same direction. The surviving use of the term *stobha* for both an *anṛca* and a meaningless *sāma* seems to echo this ancient feeling. Associated with this move to make music free of its *ṛk* — body — *śarīra* — was a move towards a profound internalisation of music as something spiritual, as truly *'aśarīra'*, one might say. This was a counterpart in music of the same internalisation of meaning which was taking place in the realm of ritual as a whole, translating it from the physical to the inner symbolic world, as we see in the *Āraṇyakas* leading to the *Upaniṣads*. No wonder, then, that the *stobha sāmas* we have, have been preserved as forest-songs, *araṇya-geya-gānas*. It is not unlikely that the surviving *stobha sāmas* are only a portion of a much larger corpus. For the *sāmas* that survive are geared mostly to ritual, the inward turn having become peripheral: the *stobha*-songs are recorded as *pariśiṣṭa*, an 'appendix' to the *chanda-ārcika* consisting of *ṛks*.

We do not know how long the tradition of *sāma* as *upāsanā* — worship — and as spiritual *sādhanā* continued. But unlike the *sādhanā* inspired by the other *Vedas*, through their *Āraṇyakas* and *Upaniṣads*, and proliferating into and becoming part of the many pathways that spirituality took in India, the *sāma*-inspired, music-oriented *sādhanā* does not seem to have remained fertile for long. Its spiritual motivation seems to have passed into the new music of *gāndharva*, sung to *jātis*, progenitors of the *rāgas*. Like the *sāma*, of which we have spoken, the *gāndharva* was imbued with a spiritual purpose, and was similarly dominated by music rather than words.[39] *Gāndharva* does not survive today. *Sāma* does. But it seems to have lost not only its independent spiritual intent but also its musical impulse. There seems to be no real regard for musicianship, no *svara-sādhanā*, in the traditions of *sāma*-singers. *Sāma*, for which The *Bṛhadāraṇyaka Upaniṣad*

[39] Readers interested in more details concerning *gāndharva* may see my *A Study Of Dattilam : The Sacred Music Of Ancient India*, pub. Impex India, New Delhi, 1978.

says: *tasya vai svara eva svaṁ*[40] — 'its self is the *svara'*, has, sadly, lost its *svara.* The *bhakti* movement brought back the spiritual motive in music, considering *kīrtana* as part of *sādhanā*, but music in *bhakti* is dominated by the word and not *svara.*

[40] The whole passage is worth quoting : *tasya ha etasya sāmno yaḥ svaṁ veda bhavati hāsya svaṁ tasya vai svara eva svaṁ tasmādartvijyaṁ kariṣyanvāci svaramiccheta tayā vācā svarasampannayārtvijyaṁ kuryāttasmādyajñe svaravantaṁ didṛkṣanta eva' atho yasya svaṁ bhavati bhavati hāsya svaṁ ya evametatsāmnaḥ svaṁ veda // 25 // tasya ha etasya sāmno yaḥ suvarṇam veda bhavati hāsya suvarṇam tasya vai svara eva suvarṇaṁ bhavati hāsya suvarṇaṁ ya evametatsāmnaḥ suvarṇaṁ veda //26//*: *Bṛhadāraṇyaka Upaniṣad*, 1,3, 25-26. Even the *ṛtvika*, concerned with *ṛk* in the rituals, is advised to imbibe *svara*, which is described as the province of *sāma*. The *suvarṇa* of *sāma* — its 'gold', but also its 'right' or 'proper' syllables — are also, significantly, said to be *svaras.*

ii. The *Pauruṣeya* Logos, Immanent in Human Seeking

The *sāma* is considered in the Indian tradition to be the progenitor of all later music, as the ancient musicological texts repeatedly tell us. From the *sāma*, they say, was born the *jāti*, the generic name for the *svara* forms of *gāndharva*, and from the *jāti*, was born the *rāga*: thus goes the received genealogy recorded in the *saṅgīta-śāstra*. Noteworthy, however, is the fact that the *jāti* music, which still continues in spirit through the *rāga*, was quite different from its parent, *sāma*, both in form and spirit, though it traces its origin to *sāma*. It had a uniqueness, a logos, of its own, for although like *sāma*, it was considered revealed, and thus 'fixed', it yet had space, in principle, for free improvisation.

I have been trying in the last section of these 'Reflections', in speaking of Pythagoras, Confucius and the ancient singers of *sāma*, to formulate an idea which, I think, may be described as the different logoi of music perceived in three great ancient cultures. There is, it also seems to me, a vision they share in common: the logos they intuit, is a transcendental logos, looking *beyond* music for an Absolute with music as its centre. The logos, so to say, ventures out of music into things *without* it. Pythagoras seeks the unchanging principle for understanding the essence of nature, and Confucius strives after the essential music for harmonious order in man, society and polity. The *sāma*-singers sought the Transcendental for itself, as an inner realisation, for which the *sāma* provided a path of *sādhanā* and *upāsanā*. But in the conception of *rāga* and in its history we seem to perceive a logos very different in intent, a logos that can be felt *within* music itself, as it develops and unfolds. I will try to envision it before you, in brief, in the light of Indian musicology and its evolution. Interestingly, the musicology of the *rāga* shows an awareness of this, and articulates it self-consciously. The logos of the *rāga* is, indeed, itself a logos of evolution and continuing potentiality; it is *historical* in its very essence, with a dialectic of growth that can perhaps be seen to have a parallel in the process of culture itself. For, like culture, it begins with the constraints of a 'naturally given', which it then continuously transforms through its own creative workings, producing a *cultural* 'given' at every stage of its progress, its logos being one of *process,* so to say.

Music, it is almost axiomatically believed, is made with a 'naturally given' set of tones; even though what is perceived as self-evidently 'given', differs in different cultures. In China, as we saw, the 'given' was a set of five *svaras*. The name in ancient Indian musicology for the set of seven *svaras* considered given, was '*svara-maṇḍala*'. The term *svara-maṇḍala* belongs to the musicology of *gāndharva* and its *svara*-forms with the generic name, *jāti,* and not *to sāma*; yet the *set* of *svaras* in the ancient *svara-maṇḍala,* was more or less common to both, with the important difference that the *jāti svara-maṇḍala* admitted two extra *svaras*, augmented positions of the third and the seventh (*ga* and *ni*), though considering them only as kind of semi-*svaras.* The texts of ancient musicology, which are concerned with the *jātis,* and which still have strong echoes in our own thinking about music, recognised twenty-two tonal distances in an octave, which they thought the ear could distinguish. These were called the *śrutis*, or the 'audibles'. The seven *svaras* of the *svara-maṇḍala* were fixed at tonal distances made up of two, three or four of these 'audible' micro-tones. The *śrutis* in themselves were *non-svaras*; so were other possible groupings of *śrutis*, not contained in the 'given' *svara-maṇḍala. Sāma* thinkers do not seem to have had the concept of the *śruti*, but the idea of the intrinsic givenness of the seven *svaras* was common to *sāma,* and *gāndharva* and its *jātis.*

The 'givenness' of a *svara* has two different dimensions, which can be seen as distinct: there is, on the one hand, a natural harmonic relation existing between pitches; Pythagoras, in fact, tried to spell out and draw upon this *givenness* in mathematical terms. But, on the other hand, there is the *felt* givenness of certain tonal distances as *musical,* and hence constituting *svara*: defined, indeed, as 'that which pleases', *svato rañjayati.* The relation between these two elements of the 'given' are complex, and can be problematic, as we shall further see in the light of Indian musicological thought. Actual music-making reveals an interesting tension between the *svara* as given in nature and given in consciousness. This tension dynamically comes across to us at the articulate level of thought in Indian musicology, especially in the thought concerning the *rāga*-form, becoming more acutely articulate as we reach our own times.

Articulating the concept of fixed *svara*-points in the *gāndharva svara-maṇḍala*, Dattila stipulates that *svaras* are fixed at given distances within a scheme of measurement: they are, as he puts it, *vyavasthita-antara,* spaced-out in an ordered arrangement measured in terms of *śrutis*, and form the *svara-maṇḍala,* so that he who knows the measure of their spacing knows the *svara-maṇḍala.*[1] Dattila, and other ancient Indian theorists, measured the said distances, as we have said, through *śrutis*; but unlike Pythogoras, who noted with profound insight that the relations between *svaras* in a *svara-maṇḍala* can be expressed in terms of simple arithmetic ratios, the *śruti*-measure had no mathematical basis, and was ultimately perceived through the ear. This made the *śruti*, in the final analysis, not only a loose measure, but essentially dependent on a *felt* musical perception, even though it was *considered* as fixed and 'given', and existing on its own, out there. The importance of musical perception in fixing the place of *svaras,* perhaps helped in the later loosening of the idea of the fixity of *svaras*, a loosening, as we shall see, which developed as a distinctive feature of the history of the *rāga*. It is perhaps because of Pythagoras and his mathematical notion of *svara* that the idea of its predetermined givenness remained relatively more intrinsic to western musical culture than to

---

[1] *A Study Of Dattilam,* by Mukund Lath, *op.cit.*, verses, 12-15, p. 318.

the tradition of *rāga*-making. Pythagoras' 'musicological' vision sought a *nitya* and *apauruṣeya* logos, an unchanging 'given'. The logos of the *rāga* is, on the contrary, essentially and strongly *pauruṣeya* or 'human' in intent, creatively *seeking* its own basis and an ever-new 'givenness', which it keeps modifying; striving for a meaningful ground rather than assumimg it as fixed and 'given' once and for all. In this, it is also obviously very different from what Confucius or the ancient Sāmavedins sought in music. It is the logos of a *puruṣārtha,* a *human* seeking, which looks beyond what *is*, namely, the given, even as it keeps formulating and reformulating it in an on-going process.

The seed of the *pauruṣeya* logos inherent in the *rāga,* lies, I would like to suggest, in two distinct but related grounds or principles: the first could be termed the principle of improvisation, and the second — quite contrary, interestingly, to the Confucian ideal of what music ought to be — the motive or principle of pleasure: ordinary human pleasure, and not that of a *sthita-prajña* sage. The principle of improvisation is already to be found in the *svara*-forms of *gāndharva*, namely *jāti.* We have in *gāndharva*, a concept of *svara*, not only as a set of *given* relations of *śruti*-distances, but also as a web of *created* relations called *vādī*, *saṁvādī*, *anuvādī* and *vivādī.* These relations are not given in nature, though they have a basis in natural harmony. They, fundamentally, consist of relations which *we* give to *svaras*, a relation of hierarchy, making one dominant, others subservient or dissonant. They also form the foundations for *rules* with which to construct structures, rules which assume improvisation. The *svaras*, as Pythogoras showed us, may be given to us in 'nature' — or what amounts to the same basic intention — in mathematically measurable ratios, yet, clearly, *the use* of *svaras*, consciously combining them into *music,* as Confucius stressed, is not a given thing. Music, like language, uses, in its own distinct way, a set of given sounds, in order to create patterns of meaning. Sounds are given to language as well as music as *āhata- nāda*, to create their own distinct patterns of significance, though, admittedly, the relation of language and music *to nāda,* as we have noted earlier, are very different. Music, as we had also noted, seems more fundamentally attached to *svara* as *nāda*, and, for this reason, to be much more obviously rooted in nature and the 'given', than language. This makes the history of *rāga* a revealing pursuit, for it displays *svara* to be as much a creative function of the culture of music, and what might be called its 'thought' or its logos, as of the 'given' in nature.

Dattila, who wrote his treatise, the *Dattilam*, in order to describe the sacred *sāma*-born form called the *gāndharva,* can be taken as a good starting-point for a greater familiarity with the notions of *vādī*, *saṁvādī, anuvādī* and *vivādī,* and thus initiating the history we have in mind. Dattila will also, interestingly, take us back close enough in time to Pythagoras, since Dattila was a musicologist who perhaps lived not much after Pythogoras; and even though we may not be able to place him quite as early as the Greek musicologist, it is evident that Dattila had received many of his ideas as an heritage from an older tradition of theory-making, which does seem to go as far back as Pythagoras.

Knowledge of music, Dattila suggests, involves two distinct kinds of *jñāna* — 'cognition', 'knowledge', 'understanding'. A man who knows the *svara-maṇḍala*, as we have already quoted him to say, is the man who knows the fixed and given relation between pitches that make the gamut of *svaras* forming the *svara-maṇḍala*. To give his very words: *dhvaniviśeṣānyaḥ sarvān ṣaḍjādisaṁjñitān / vyavasthitāntarān vetti sa vetti svaramaṇḍalam.* (*Dattilam*, 15). But this is not enough to be a *svara-yoga-vit,* 'a man who knows the *use* of *svaras'* — 'and the ways of combining them', one might add, since the word *yoga* here can suggest both *pra-yoga* as well as *saṁ-yoga* — knowing the *svara*-positions in the *svara-maṇḍala* alone will not make one a musician. Or, in other words, the *svara-maṇḍala* and its 'given' relations are not *enough* for music. There is another set of relations, equally foundational, which allows us to make music, providing, as it does, space for the *use* of *svaras*. The man who knows the *use of svaras*, says Dattila, should know that there is a certain relation of dependence between *svaras*, which serves as the ground for their *usage*.[2] Although *this* relation presupposes the 'given' *svara-maṇḍala* relations, yet it is independent of them, and is imparted by *us* upon the natural foundation, in order to create the possibility of *making* music. This is why Dattila distinguishes this created relation of *dependence* as concerning the *usage* of *svara* — *svara-yoga* — and speaks of it *after* he speaks of the *svara-maṇḍala*. The usage that Dattila had in mind was the singing and playing of *jātis*, the *gāndharva svara*-forms, progenitors, as we have noted, of our *rāga*, and was continued in the *rāgas*.

The *svara* used most profusely (in a *jāti*), Dattila says, is its *vādi*. The *vādi*, we should add here, was also the tonic, the *aṁśa*, which was roughly, though not exactly, equivalent to what we today call the *sā* in Hindustani music, or the *ādhāra-śruti* in Karnatak. However, it was *not*, unlike present practice, the foundational pitch, the basis on which all other *svaras* stand and acquire their individual place and character. Yet, like our own *vādī*, it was the *svara* to be most profusely used in order to establish the characteristic form of a *jāti*. *Svaras* related to the *vādī*, through a certain given *śruti*- distance in the *svara-maṇḍala*, were known as *saṁvādīs*. *Saṁvādīs* were *svaras* related through the 'given' harmonious relation of the fourth and the fifth. (Our own practice, one might notice here, no longer quite insists on the *saṁvādī* being in *saṁvāda* or harmonic relation to the *vādī*, even in those *rāgas*, such as Mārvā, where the *vādī-saṁvādī* relation can still be said to be a ruling factor in forming a *rāga*). Other *svaras* of the *svara-maṇḍala* were *anuvādīs*, *svaras* that could be used without conflict with the *vādī* and *saṁvādī*. *Svaras*, which created a conflict, a dissonance, were *vivādīs*, which, in *gāndharva*, were marked by a given pitch-relation with the *chosen vādī* (*Dattilam*, 18-19). The *vivādī* in *gāndharva* was a *svara* believed capable of 'destroying' a *jāti*. Yet the *svara* was not altogether avoided, and was used, though sparingly and only in the passing, in order to create a much

[2] ibid. verse, 19.

needed sense of tension in a melody, which can pall if it is too smooth. Later, in *jāti*-born *rāgas*, the use of *vivādī* became more profuse; what was earlier understood as destroying a structure, became the source of a great dynamic tension and a pleasingly oblique charm.[3]

It can be argued that the *vādī-saṁvādī-anuvādī-vivādī* set of relations, contrary to our contention, can be understood as purely analytical categories which may be used for understanding *any*

---

[3] There is more discussion on this later in the essay. In a sense, the whole development of later music, the *rāga*-music, can be said to be a loosening or slackening of the concept of *vivādī*. In *gāndharva, vivādī* is defined in terms of a fixed *svara-maṇḍala* : certain *svaras* of a given *śruti*-measure are *vivādī* in nature. In *rāga*-music, and as we also understand the notion today, a *vivādī* is defined not in terms of a *svara-maṇḍala,* with a given scheme of *svaras,* but in terms of *rāgas* : a *svara,* which is *not* considered or stipulated as part of the structure of a *rāga* is a *vivādī for that* rāga. Unlike the ancient system, *svaras* are not *vivādīs* in themselves. A *vivādī* is a *svara* belonging to *another* rāga. But like the ancient *vividī*, it has its use. Śārṅgadeva, writing in the 13th century, uses the notion of *kāku*, which, in the context, may be translated as 'oblique charm', in speaking of the phenomenon we have in mind, though he does not use the word '*vivādī*' to describe it. In describing possible *parts* of a *rāga, rāga-avayavas* or, what he also calls *sthāyas*, he speaks of the use of *svara-kāku* and *anya-rāga-kāku.* A *svara-kāku* consisted of the scintillating use of a *śruti* from an alien *svara*, and *anya-rāga-kāku* consisted of the use of the semblance of an alien *rāga* in rendering the *rāga* one had chosen. *Anya-rāga-kāku*, it is true, need not imply the use an alien *svara*, but only the *semblance* of an alien *movement* with the same *svaras*, as the commentator, Kallinātha, does understand this notion, but the notion does not *forbid* alien *svaras*. There is, however, another concept in Śārṅgadeva, similar to that of *anya-rāga-kāku,* which seems to make a more clear space for the use of alien *svaras*: this the notion of '*rāgāntarasyāvayavo rāge'ṁśaḥ*, or 'incorporating a *part* of an alien *rāga* in the *rāga* being rendered'. This could be done in various ways, most of these consisting in the use of more or less similar *rāgas*; but the more daring could also use the path which consisted in the use of a part of a *rāga* which was totally dissimilar (*atyantaṁ visadṛśa*) to the *rāga* being rendered. Certainly, this would imply the use of an alien *svara*.The notion of *svara-kāku*, as we have seen above, even more clearly implies the use of an alien *svara.* To quote Śārṅagadeva:

śrutinyūnādhikatvena yā svarāntarasaṁśrayā // svarāntarasya rāge syāt svarakākurasau matā / ..sā tvanyarāgakākuryā rāge rāgāntarāśrayā / ... rāgāntarasyāvayavo rāge'ṃśaḥ sa saptadhā / ... sādṛśyaśūnyayoraṁśo'tyantaṁ visadṛśāṁśakaḥ / Saṅgītaratnākara, 3, 121-138.

musical structure, whether *rāga*-like or not, and hence improvisation-oriented or not. But in the Indian tradition, it was made the basis of creating a structure through improvisation. We can see this in the manner in which the *vādī-saṁvādī-anuvādī-vivādī* principle was elaborated: it was made the basis of rules for the building of *jātis*.

Interestingly, these *rules* are called *lakṣaṇas*, that is, 'descriptions' or 'defining characteristics' of the *jātis,* and are termed *'jāti-lakṣaṇas'*. But they are 'descriptions' of the *procedure* with which *svaras ought to be* related to each other in order to build the patterns that form a *jāti.* Or, in other words, they are rules. The *śāstras,* such as that of Dattila, formally list ten *jāti-lakṣaṇas,* but a few others are informally spoken of and assumed.[4]

The *lakṣaṇas* are simple enough. The first pair is, clearly, the most crucial: these are the *lakṣaṇas* or rules of *alpatva* and *bahutva*. *Bahutva*, was the rule of 'profusion', to be applied, expectedly enough, to the *svara* taken as the *vādī*. *Svalpatva* was the opposite; it was the rule of 'enfeebling' a *svara* or *svaras.* It applied to *svaras* that were to be made especially weak. There were, besides these quite general rules, others designed to articulate a structure in more specific details. One such was the *lakṣaṇa* laying down initial *svaras*: these consisted of the *svara* with which the structure as a whole was to be begun and other *svaras* placed at the beginning of parts, greater or smaller, within the structure (the *svaras* were known as, *graha, nyāsa,* and *apanyāsa*). There was also the rule of dropping *svaras*, and forming scales of five or six *svaras* (*auḍava, ṣāḍava).* Another rule was a rule of 'limitation': it prescribed the range in the lower and higher octave within which a structure was to be confined, (it was known as the rule of *mandra* and *tāra).* There were other, more special, rules of 'associations' (*saṅgati)* between specific *svaras*, and of distinct movements (*sañcāra, antaramārga)*, characterising individual *jātis*. And, in addition,

---

4 *Dattilam*, verses 55-56.

there were certain general constraints, applying to *jātis* as a whole which limited the possibilities opened up by the *lakṣaṇas*. These were *niṣedhas*, in contrast to the *lakṣaṇas* which can be called *vidhis*, or rules that create the basis of generating structures.[5] (The reader might also like to see, in this context, the essay entitled, 'Taṇḍu, the first theoretician of dance', included in this collection, where a similar, or even a more open *vidhi* for the generation of the pure dance-form, *tāṇḍava*, is discussed.)

In later music, the *jāti-lakṣaṇas* became *rāga-lakṣaṇas*. The earliest writer on *rāga*, Mataṅga, engaged in defining *rāga* rather than *jāti*, in fact, equates the two. The *rāga-lakṣaṇas*, he says, are the same as the *jāti-lakṣaṇas*.[6] The principle of improvisation which the *jātis* initiated was carried over into *rāga*.

These *jāti* and *rāga lakṣaṇas*, one can see, are qualitative in principle and are not capable of being measured and quantified. We cannot say that in order to apply *bahutva* to a *svara*; or to apply the rule of *alpatva*, or any of the other rules mentioned above, a *svara* must be made to occur so many times and for such durations. The relations obtained through the *lakṣaṇas* are not only basically qualitative, they also have plural possibilities of realisation. *Jātis*, and *jāti*-born forms, the *rāgas*, which are described through these relations, cannot, therefore, be notated, in principle. Notations can only serve a subsidiary purpose to describe parts of a *rāga*, or indicate possibilities of movement in it. Even if one were to, conceivably, notate a *jāti* or a *rāga*, and achieve a 'complete' rendering of it, it would remain only one

---

[5] *Dattilam*, verses 55 to 61. For details and an exposition of the text, see *A study of Dattilam*, pages 268 to 278.

[6] See the *Bṛhaddeśī* of Mataṅga, Trivandrum Sanskrit Series, Trivandrum, 1928, *vṛtti* following verse 363, p. 103. What is it, Matanga (or the author of the *vṛtti*, if the two are different, which appears likely) asks, that distinguishes a song in general from a *rāga* . The reply is that when a song is charactarised by the ten *lakṣaṇas*, it is called a *rāga*: *nanu gītarāga (yoḥ ko) bhedaḥ. ucyate. daśalakṣaṇalakṣitaṁ gītaṁ rāgaśabdābhidheyam. The* ten *lakṣaṇas* are given by Mataṅga earlier in his work in describing the *jātis*, delineated as a prelude to the *rāgas*, which are Mataṅga's express occupation. In describing the *rāga* forms, he thus assumes the ten *lakṣaṇas* as known.

possible rendering, and would not exhaust the *rāga* itself. And in a deeper sense the form thus achieved through notation, would no longer be a *jāti* or a *rāga* at all, but only a shadow of it, like film-songs composed in a *rāga* or like *rāga*-based Tagore songs, for example. These are, indeed, forms that can be reduced to a notation. But singing or playing a *jāti* or *rāga* on the basis of a notated score would not give us a *jāti* or a *rāga*, since this would not *create* the relations between *svaras* that make the form, but would assume them as given in an already created structure. This is not the idea behind the *lakṣaṇas*. The qualitative relations between *svaras* that make a *jāti* or a *rāga* are to be *imparted* in actual living *usage*, that is, performance. This makes the *jāti*, and its progeny, the *rāga*, also very different from the *sāma* which could be and was notated.[7] The musician in rendering a *jāti* or a *rāga* is not just a transmitter, to use Confucius's telling term. His function is not the re-rendering of something already created, and, hence, 'given'. Involved here is the principle of improvisation which unlike transmission, has a natural tendency towards invention, to use another Confucian term.

Later theorists, also gave a political metaphor for the *vādī-saṁvādī* relation of dependence between *svaras*. The metaphor is similar to the one given by Confucius, where he speaks of the musically correct hierarchy between the five 'given' *svaras* of his tradition, identifying the 'king'-*svara*, the 'minister'-*svara*, the 'people'-*svara,* the 'affairs'-*svara* and the *svara* representing 'things'. In India, this metaphor has a somewhat different form,

---

[7] We have given an illustration of how this is generally done in the *Saṁhitā* editions available today in an earlier footnote in the previous section of this essay; see fn. no. 37. The earliest system of notating *sāma* was a non-written method using the pores of the fingers as marking different *svaras*. Later, as we still find in the written *Sāma Saṁhitā*, more than one method for *writing* the *svaras* along with the text was used. For a description, see, introduction to *Kauthumaśākhāyāḥ Ūhagānam, Ūhyagānam*, edited by Pandit A.M. Ramnath Dikshit, Varanasi, 1967, pp. 27 to 36. As far as I know, no one has really tried to investigate the history of the written *sāma* notation, and unearth the earliest examples. Intriguingly, the *sāma* system of writing *svaras* is very different from that of the musicological texts devoted to *jāti* or *rāga*.

and it seems to have readily caught on; it became very popular in the musicology devoted to describing *rāga*, because of its aptness and also, it would seem, its picturesqueness. The first musicological work in which the metaphor appears is the *Bṛhaddeśī* of Mataṅga, which is also, as we said, the first work devoted to describing *rāga*. It is usually dated to the eighth century, though it may be earlier. The metaphor itself might be older than Mataṅga, but after Mataṅga it became a commonplace in musicological literature. The *vādī*, in the metaphor, was compared to the king, the *saṁvādī* to his minister, the *anuvādīs* to his retinue of followers, and the *vivādī* to his enemy.[8] The presence of the 'enemy' as an integral part of the picture is interesting both musically and politically. Musically, the *vivādī*, as we have pointed out, creates a much-needed tension. Politically, the picture made sense because according to Indian political thought, a state is only one among a plurality of states which are, in various degrees, potential enemies, but which can be turned into temporary friends. The notion of a *vivādī*, as pictured in this metaphor, is therefore a relative one, the *vivādī* of one *rāga* can be the *anuvādī* or even the *vādī* of another, as we still find in our musical practice. The idea of the *vivādī*, we notice, is missing in Confucius, who seemed to have cared for pure and absolute harmony with no discordant note. Also, the intent of the metaphor for Confucius and for *rāga*-theorists was radically different. For *rāga*-theorists, it was a metaphor for open pluralism. But Confucius' transcendental vision had hardly any room for real pluralism. His vision, though seeming to picture a *rāga*-like structure, as we had remarked earlier, pictures the *rāga* as one and unique.

---

[8] See *vṛtti* on verse, 63a : *idanīmavasaraprāptaṁ caturvidhyaṁ svarāṇāṁ darśayāmi. tadyathā — vadanād vādī svāmivat. saṁvadanāt saṁvādī amātyavat. anuvadanādanuvādī parijanavat. vivadanād vivādī śatruvat* — 'Having come to the subject of the four kinds of *svaras*, I shall show them. The *vādī* is like the king, for it commands. The *saṃvādī* is like the minister, for it is in accord [with the *vādī*]. The *anuvādī* is like a follower, for it echoes [the *vādī* and the *saṁvādī*]. The *vivādī* is like an enemy, for it is in discord [with the *vādī*, *saṁvādī* and *anuvādī*].

The reason for the difference between the ways in which the *rāga*-theorists and Confucius took the metaphor, seems to lie in the fact that the musicology of the *rāga*, which originated the metaphor in India, thought of music as pleasure and not as the means for attaining absolute harmony in life. Indeed, a major characteristic by which *rāga* as a form is defined and distinguished by Mataṅga in his *Bṛhaddeśī*, is its pleasure-giving quality, '*rañjanājjāyate rāgaḥ* — *rāga* is *born* of pleasure', another notion which became standard fare for subsequent musicology in India, and is still found meaningful.

For Mataṅga, this pleasure motive or principle, as we have called it, not only defines *rāga*, but also distinguishes *rāga* from the earlier *jāti*, its parent.[9] The *jāti*, though structurally conceived on the same lines as *rāga*, was not for pleasure; it was, like *sāma*, a sacred, revealed form.

We should remark here that Mataṅga, evidently, intended his Confucius-like political metaphor for *both jāti* and *rāga*. For him, the metaphor articulated a structural principle they both shared; the difference being one of degree, despite the distinct

---

[9] *Bṛhaddeśī*, verses 278-284. Mataṅga, having finished his exposition of the *jātis,* moves to distinguish the *rāgas* from them. He makes an imaginary interrogator ask the question : *kimucyate rāgaśabdena kiṁ vā rāgasya lakṣaṇam / vyutpattilakṣaṇaṁ tasya yathāvadvaktumarhasi* (verse, 278) — 'What is it that is said through the word '*rāga*', and how is *rāga* to be characterised ? Please expound the right manner in which the word should be etymologically understood [in this context]'. Mataṅga, in reply promises to speak of the *rāga*-form, giving details which are not to be found in ancient writers such as Bharata (or Dattila, for that matter, whom he, however, does not actually name in this context) : '*rāgamārgasya yadrūpaṁ yannoktaṁ bharatādibhiḥ / nirūpyate tadasmābhiḥ lakṣyalakṣaṇasaṁyutam.*' His intention also was to distinguish the *rāga* from the music which Bharata does describe in detail, namely the *jāti*, and of which he, too, had been speaking hitherto. The basic distinguishing mark that he speaks of in the *rāga* is its quality to please. He says : 'The wise call that *svara*-form a '*rāga*' which pleases everyone' — *svaravarṇaviśeṣeṇa dhvanibhedena vā punaḥ / rajyate yena yaḥ kaścit sa rāgaḥ sammataḥ satām //* (verse, 280). Then he reiterates almost verbally the same statement in the next verse, stating that *rāga* pleases people : *rañjako janacittānāṁ.* Then, just a little later, he puts forth the same matter in terms of etymology : *rañjanājjāyate rāgo vyutpattirsamudāhṛtā* (verse, 283).

motivations of the two forms, rather than one of kind. The metaphor, however, could not have been applied to *sāma*, from which they both thus differed in kind. Rendering *sāma* was an act of transmission, not innovation, to use Confucius' words again. To help the process of correct transmission, *sāma* was preserved through a system of indicating *svaras* on the fingers — known as the *hasta-viṇā* — and later through written symbols, indicating notes.

The pleasure motive also implied a great difference between the approach to structure in *jāti* and *rāga.* The *rāga* was much more open and freer with the rules, even ignoring, flaunting and changing them in its development. The difference between the two thus lay not so much in the approach to *vidhi* as to *niṣedha*. The strictures and limitations which, in the *jāti,* restricted free play of possibilities created by the *lakṣaṇas*, were loosened in the *rāga* as a form, by the impulse to pleasure, creating more space for movement, and inspiring the creation of ever new *rāgas*. Thus the word *'ālāpa'*, used for the first time by Mataṅga, becomes another 'defining' character of *rāgas*, and *rāgas* began to increase in number, and are in later texts described as, 'innumerable'. This great increase in space for innovation was possible because of a radical change in telos.

This new telos was to make even more radical changes as the tradition of the *rāga* evolved. The ancient *jātis* had a fixed set of *svaras*, 'given' in the *svara-maṇḍala.* One could not *create svaras*, but only *relate* them with a set of *lakṣaṇas* or rules in mind. This, to give a more familiar analogy, was like being given a harmonium or a multi-stringed instrument such as the pre-tuned *svara-maṇḍala* (the instrument, not the concept)[10] on which a number of *svaras* have been fixed once and for all. These are ready-made entities we cannot change; though we can put them to our own use, combining them into various forms.

---

[10] Though the two are clearly related, and the *svara-maṇḍala* as an instrument is similar to the ancient Indian harp-like *viṇā*, which, in fact, played an important role in theorising about *svaras* and in giving rise to the concept of the *svara-maṇḍala*.

There is much in ancient Indian musicology that reinforces this picture of a set of unalterable, 'given', *svaras.* The ancient *vīṇā* was similar to the modern *svara-maṇḍala,* on which the *svaras* were fixed. Interestingly, however, the *svaras* were 'given' not only on the *vīṇā* — where they could be altered, at least in principle, — they were also thought of as 'given' within us, within our body: the human frame was believed to contain a *vīṇā* similar to the instrument that was played, and on which the *svaras* were fixed. The *svaras* thus had a set of predetermined *svara-sthānas* within us, arranged at proper *śruti*-distances. (The article, 'The Body As An Instrument', in this collection, reflects on this notion, giving more details.)

The distance between *svaras,* as we have noted, was measured through *śruti.* A *śruti*, let us remember, could be *heard*, but it *could not* be musically used. Only certain *śruti*-groupings were 'given' as *svaras*. Others were *not* permitted, since they were *not svaras*. All this was to undergo a revolution in later thinking. Later musicians, in exploring the realm of pleasure, or *rañjana*, through the *rāgas*, seeking aesthetic innovation, seem to have quickly realised the musical potential of the 'unuseable' *śrutis*. In *rāga*-music, any *śruti* could be used provided one could create a desired aesthetic effect. Abhinavagupta, the famous Kashmīrī philosopher and musicologist, writing in the period spanning the end of the 10th century and the beginning of the 11th, speaks of the effect created by musicians through the use of *śruti-vaicitrya*: the free and brilliant use of *śrutis* which were denied to the *jāti.*

The ancient *svara-maṇḍala*, as we remarked earlier, did allow two augmented *svaras* besides the regular seven. These extra *svaras* lay *between* two regular *svaras*, and were, hence called, *antara* (in-between) *svaras.* They were also called *sādhāraṇa*, that is 'common' *svaras*, because they occupied a space that separated two *svaras* and was thus 'common' to them. But if the 'common' space between two *svaras* could have positions that were themselves '*svaras*', however 'irregular' they may be, in the sacred *jāti* form, the idea could certainly be extended to common spaces between other *svaras,* too. And this was done in the more free-flowing *rāga* music; there was no sacred rule of limitation to stop it, and one could be guided by the impulse to pleasure. Indeed, the idea of 'common', in-between *svaras* was extended even further, and taken to what could be called its logical extreme. *All* the *śrutis*, which were earlier denied *svara*-hood, were now seen as *sādhāraṇa*, since they all did, in fact, lie in the spaces between *svaras*. And hence they were allowed *svara*-hood. Abhinavagupta has outlined the above extension of the notion of *sādhāraṇa;* and after having done so, he observes: "the displacement of a *svara* from its primary position, and its thus acquiring a distinctivenss *(viśeṣo vailakṣyaṇyātmā)* is what obtains when a *svara* becomes *sādhāraṇa* in musical usage. This implies that *all* [otherwise accepted as fixed] *svaras* can shift to positions above or below [their fixed places] when a pleasing diversity is sought in musical expressions. The rule limiting a *svara* to a single *śruti*-position — on which it is permanently fixed — obtains only in *gāndharva* (that is, the *jāti*-system); in *rāgas* and *bhāṣās* (which were also *rāga*-like forms, described as 'born of the *rāgas'*), it can be seen that musical usage permits a diversity [of *sādhāraṇa* positions]."[11]

This 'diversity', which was, in effect, introduced in the *svara-maṇḍala* itself, transforming it, and allowing any in-between *śruti* to function as a *svara,* had occurred much earlier than Abhinava, who himself quotes an earlier authoritative text, in this context, to support — and justify — his own observation.

[11] Hardly any passage from the *Abhinava Bhāratī*, Abhinava's commentary on the *Nāṭyaśāstra*, is entirely free of textual problems, the readings being often corrupt. The passage translated above also has words and expressions which are not entirely clear. Yet the meaning, I think, is unmistakable. Here is original from the G.O.S. edition of the text: *svarasvayaḥ* (*svarasya yaḥ*) *prāktanarūpādviśeṣo vailakṣyaṇyātmā sa eva svarasādhāraṇatāyāṁ prayogaḥ. anena caitatsūcayati sarveṣāṁ svarāṇāmuccanicatvavaicitryoktiviśeṣāt kevalaṁ gāndharve niyamaṁ(mā)adṛṣṭasiddhyai ekaśrutitvaṁ svarāṇāṁ darśitaṁ, vaicitryāntaraṁ tu rāgabhaṣādau lakṣye dṛśyata eva. Ahinava Bhāratī* on *Nāṭyaśāstra* 28, 35.

The text he quotes, is attributed by him to a musicologist named Vṛddhakaśyapa whose writings are not otherwise available, and whose date is difficult to determine. A reasonable conjecture, I would think, might place him roughly in the same period as Mataṅga, or perhaps a little after. The Vṛddhakaśyapa passage, which Abhinava quotes, is, I must confess, not entirely clear to me, but its general intention, for our purpose, can be readily sensed. The first part of the passage, with which we are concerned here, is, fortunately, clear enough. Vṛddhakaśyapa says:

"In *rāgas* and *bhāṣas*, all *svara*-distances, whether comprising of one, two, three or four *śrutis,* can be taken as *kākali* (another name for *sādhāraṇa*) or as *antara* (still another name for the *sādhāraṇa*), and should be freely (*sarvathā)* used".[12]

---

[12] The Vṛddhakaśyapa passage comes immediately after the lines from the *Abhinava Bhārati* quoted in the footnote above. The lines which I have translated read :

kākalyantarayogena catustridvyekataḥ śrutin /
svarānsarvānprayuñjita rāgabhāṣāsu sarvathā //

This is followed by two more *ślokas* where Vṛddhakaśyapa seems to be saying that in the *jāti* there are fifteen distinct *svara*-positions. This is so obviously against the position of the *gāndharva śāstras,* that I do not quite know what to make of it :

svarāḥ ṣaḍjādayaḥ sapta tathā cotkṛṣṭapañcamaḥ /
atha dhaivatatascānyaḥ kākalyantarasaṁjñakau //
ṣaḍjamadhyamagāndhārāścatvāraḥ iti sarvathā /
jātiṣvete prayoktavyāḥ svarāḥ pañcadaśaiva tu //

Vṛddhakaśyapa quite unambiguously appears to speak of fifteen *svaras* in the *jātis* (*jātiṣu*). There can be no mistake about this if the reading is correct, and there seems nothing wrong with it. With what grounds, or with what purport in mind he says so is another matter, which is to me a puzzle. Another puzzle, though not such a perplexing one, is the identification of the fifteen *śrutis* he recounts as *svaras* here. I have been able to identify only the following : the seven regular *svaras, ṣaḍja* etc., the two augmented *svaras* (*antara ga* and *kākali ni*), and the two 'displaced' *pa* and *dha* of the *madhyama-grāma* as relative to the *ṣaḍja-grāma.* This makes eleven *svaras*, and this seems quite in order within the *jāti* system, except for the curious fact that the distinct *pa* and *dha* of the two *grāmas* have been 'counted' as *independent svaras.* This in *gāndharva* was never done, because the *svaras* of one *grāma* could not be confused with those of the other. In counting them as *svaras*, Vṛddhakaśyapa seems to be discounting the ancient, quite categorical, *grāma* division, and taking the two *sthānas* as though they were given as *svaras* within a single

We find that the pleasure-oriented aesthetic of the *rāga* has opened the door for *śrutis* and their possible groupings into tones, which were earlier left out of the system as non-*svaras*. The *rāga,* consequently, had room in its music for all the *śrutis.* Vṛddhakaśyapa speaks of *every* single *śruti*, and every possible grouping of two three or four *śrutis* as *svaras*. In effect, now, since single *śrutis* were permitted as musically usable, any 'audible', pitch-distinction was a possible *svara.* This was unthinkable in the earlier *jāti* music. Indeed, the very notion of *śruti* seems redundant in the new *rāga svara-maṇḍala*, if one were to still use the ancient term. The only condition for a *śruti* to function as *svara* was that it should produce a desirable, expressive effect as part of a *rāga.*

Expectedly, however, though the new music declared all *śruits* as *svaras* in practice, yet the *theoretical* position still sanctioned only seven positions as *svaras*, the other *śruti*-positions lying between them were understood to be *sādhāraṇa svaras:* Vṛddhakaśyapa compares them to the earlier *antara* and *kākali svaras,* and, evidently, like these traditional 'semi-*svaras*', they were still *thought* to be somehow subsidiary or displaced in status.

It is clear, though, that the change in the notion of *svara*

---

scale. Perhaps this is symptomatic of the loosening of the strict *grāma* division during Vṛddhakaśyapa's days, but it cannot be a reckoning that fits the *jāti*-system. Then, there is a phrase which identifies more *svaras*: '*ṣaḍjama-dhyamag-āndhāraścatvāraḥ*'. This I have not been able to understand. According to Vṛddhakaśyapa's count, we already have elven *svaras* and need four more. And these are what the phrase, one would think, intends to give us. But, what are they? They are, presumably, four extra places which the three regular *svaras, sa, ga* and *ma*, occupying 'displaced' *sthānas* on *śrutis* that lie between them and the preceding or following *svara*. But which *śrutis* can these be ? There are no such 'displaced' *svara*-positions in the *jāti svara-maṇḍala.* And which of the three *svaras* is to have two positions, and where ? What, moreover, about the other *svaras, ri, pa, dha, ni,* are they not to have more positions, and why not ? These and other questions are bound to bother one in trying to get at what might have been meant. An answer can, perhaps, only be found if we could discover more of Vṛddhakaśyapa's work, which, at present, seems a remote possibility.

However, The first *śloka,* which is about *rāgas* and *bhāṣās,* and not about *jātis,* presents no such difficulties.

hinges on the new music of the *rāga*, its new orientation, new demands, and its openness towards new possibilities of tonal expression. A radical transformation in the logos of music seems to have happened, even though not so radically articulated: the *rāga* has become the key for discriminating between the *svara* and the non-*svara*. Instead of *svaras* being the basic 'given', and then being taken as the building blocks for making music, we now have the situation where the *rāgas*, which are not given but humanly created, *pauruṣeya* things, become themselves the creators of *svaras*: a *svara* is a tone which a *rāga* uses to make itself.

The musical situation clearly called for a new theoretical vision, or revision, which, as we shall see, was developed in the 16th century, becoming sharper and more radically self-articulate in the 17th. We find a new understanding of *svara* taking a meaningful shape in a remarkable 16th century musicologist, Puṇḍarīka Viṭṭhala. He has written a number of tracts on the *rāga*, the most ambitious being the *Sadrāgacandrodaya.* But he also has other works devoted to the *rāga*, which were written later and are comparatively smaller in size; one of these is the *Rāgamālā*, a work especially interesting for our purpose. Unlike Vṛddhakaśyapa, Puṇḍarīka, in his *Rāgamālā*, identifies only eighteen *śruti*-positions as possible *svara*-positions. The fifth, the sixth, the eighteenth and the nineteenth *śrutis*, he says, right in the beginning of the *Rāgamālā*, are never *svaras;* the others can all be: *śeṣā aṣṭādaśaiva syuḥ śrutayaḥ svarabodhakāḥ* (*Rāgamālā*, 16). Those *śrutis* which can be cognised as *svaras* (*svarabodhakāḥ*), are still cognised in terms of the conventional seven *svaras*, but with the radical difference that each of the seven *svaras*, except *sa* and *pa*, have no longer a single fixed position: they have two more possible positions on neighbouring *śrutis,* occupying the 'non-*svara*' space between *svaras*; *ga* having three such positions.

Puṇḍarīka is aware that he is talking of a *svara-maṇḍala* quite different from that of traditional musicology, and he remarks that 'Bharata and other [ancient authorities] have spoken of only a single *śruti*-position for a *svara* which [in my scheme] is its first or initial position: *ṣaḍjādīnāṃ sthitiḥ proktāḥ prathamāḥ bharatādibhiḥ.'* This may also be translated as: 'This, (that is the sequence of *svara*-positions conforming to the ancient mapping and described by Puṇḍarīka just before the present passage), is the position initially enunciated (*prathamā sthitiḥ*) by Bharata and others.'[13] But whichever of these two

---

[13] *dvāviṁśatiḥ śrutisthānaṁ sopānākāravat kramāt //*
vāyupūraṇatastāstu tāvatyuttarottaram /
prabhavantyuccoccatarāḥ śrutayaḥ śravyamātrataḥ //
rāgādivyavahārāya tāsu sapta svarāḥ sthitāḥ /
ṣaḍjaśca ṛṣabhaścaiva gāndhāro madhyamastathā //
pañcamo dhaivataścātha niṣādaścetyanukramāt /
teṣāṁ saṁjñā sarigamapadhanityaparā matā //
vedācalāṅkaśrutiṣu trayodaśyāṁ śrutau tataḥ /
saptadaśyāṁ ca viṁśyāṁ ca dvāviṁśyāṃ ca śrutau kramāt //
ṣaḍjādīnāṁ sthitiḥ proktā prathamā bharatādibhiḥ /
Rāgamālā, 8-13

I quote in detail; also because the only reliable critical edition of the texts of Puṇḍarīka Viṭṭhala is available in a collected edition printed in Kannada letters with a Kannada translation, comments and annotation. The author of this laudable work of scholarship is Dr. R. Satyanarayana. The work is published as *Puṇḍarīkamālā*, pub. by the Goverment Of Karnataka, (Karnataka Sangeetha Nritya Academy and Directorate of Kannada And Culture}, Banglore, 1986. The Sanskrit text of the *Rāgamālā* covers pages 170 to 202 of this work. The quoted passage is on p. 172. Not knowing Kannada, but only its script, I have, unfortunately, not been able to see Dr. Satyanarayana's translation. I offer my own : 'There are twenty-two *śrutis* (each on a separate string-like artery within the human frame) arranged in a ladder-like sequence. When the air (which arises from the base of the spinal column) strikes them, they produce, in a gradually rising sequence, the gamut of *śrutis,* each of which has a pitch higher than the preceding [*śruti*], [the pich-difference consisting of the] smallest distinction that is audible. For [rendering] the [musical] forms like *rāgas*, there are seven *svaras* which are stationed on them. These are, in their sequence, named, *ṣaḍja, ṛṣabha, gāndhāra, madhyama, pañcama, dhaivata* and *niṣāda*, an alternative set of terms for them being, *sa, ri, ga, ma. pa. dha* and *ni.* The seven *svaras*, *ṣaḍja* and the others, are, in squence, stationed on the [following] *śrutis* : the fourth (which is the place of *ṣaḍja*), the seventh, the ninth, the thirteenth, the seventeeth, the twentieth, and the twenty-second. Such is the original position initially [mapped] for them by Bharata and other [ancient theorists]'.

One might notice that the positioning of the various *svaras*, *on the fourth śruti* and so on, is not how the ancients proceed, but the resulting *svara-maṇḍala*, remains essentially the ancient one.

ways in which we may choose to translate Puṇḍarīka, it is unmistakably implicit in his statement that he felt a conspicuous gap between the ancient system and his own.

What is even more revolutionary in his musicological thought, is his statement that the basis on which a *śruti*-position becomes a *svara* is not a given *antarāla* or distance from another *śruti*-position, but the *rāga* being rendered: In a remarkable passage he says:

'A (*svara*) shifts its position, depending on the demand of the *rāga* being rendered: *yadyadrāgopayogaḥ syād tattadicchā-gatirbhavet.*' (*Rāgamālā*, 14)[14]

In his earlier work, the *Sadrāgacandrodaya*, Puṇḍarīka had recognised only fourteen and not eighteen *śruti*-positions as possible *svara-sthānas*,[15] but he added an interesting, though short and not fully developed, argument in order to justify his radical departure from traditional musicology regarding the relation between *śruti* and *svara*. He, obviously, thought that he was making a fundamental break from an almost self-evident orthodoxy, and this needed justification. The defence he gives, leads to a basic reflection on the very nature of *svara*.

Musicological thought in India has conceived *svara* on two distinct bases, which, supposedly, should lead to an identical cognition, but which can be seen to have parted ways with the dominance of the *rāga*. The distinction, which we have earlier described in terms of *svara* as given and *svara* as felt, becomes, in the hands of Puṇḍarīka, an opposition. This opposition can be significantly understood in the light of two *svara-lakṣaṇas*, or 'definitions' of what constitutes the *svara*-hood of a *svara*, which have been articulated in musicological thinking. It is also, one might notice, a fundamental opposition concerning

---

[14] *op. cit.*, p. 172.

[15] I *assume* it to be earlier, for the reason of its greater conservativeness, and also because Dr. Satyanarayana gives it before the *Rāgamālā*. Unable to understand Kannada, I have not been able to follow his discussion concerning the dates of Puṇḍarīka's works. However, for my purpose, their relative dating is only of passing importance.

cognition, and is to be found not only in the logos of music, but in a sense in logos itself.

The first, and as it appears, the more ancient, of the two *svara-lakṣaṇas* can be expressed as, *'antarāla niyamo svaraḥ* — svara is an [unbending] *rule* which fixes distance [between pitches]'; this, as we have seen, was enunciated many centuries ago by Dattila in describing the *svara-maṇḍala* of the ancient *jātis*. Pythagoras' vision, more mathematically oriented, follows the same path. The attempt is to cognise and 'measure' something in itself, as it were, without reference to the cogniser.

The second *lakṣaṇa*, places the cogniser, or consciousness at the centre: '*svato rañjayata iti svaraḥ* — it is that [distinct pitch-position] which pleases in itself'. It is, in other words, *svara* as it is evident to our awareness when we make music and seek an aesthetic pleasure, or in other words a musical meaningfulness. This *lakṣaṇa*, relies on the etymology of the name, '*svara*' itself, and was believed by later musicologists to be inherent in the very concept of '*svara*', if it was to be the basis of music and not just an object out there in nature. There is also, not surprisingly, a definite connection between this music-oriented *lakṣaṇa* of *svara* and the *lakṣaṇa* of *rāga* itself. Like *'svara', 'rāga'* is defined by later musicologists as 'that which pleases — *rañjayata iti rāgaḥ'*. In the ancient system, which also had the second *lakṣaṇa* in mind, though not so explicitly, there was no quarrel between the two *lakṣaṇas*. Indeed, as for Pythagoras, they were believed to coincide. The *lakṣaṇa* of *svara* as *svayambhū*, 'self-born', is old and may be construed to represent this accord between the inner and outer, *svara* as given in nature and *svara* as felt, since *'svayambhū'* does not incline towards either senses, and can embrace both. For Pythagoras, the fact that the 'felt', 'perceived' *svara* coincided with a 'rational', mathematical equation was a profound discovery, the discovery of a *'pramāṇa'* a 'measurable criterion' through which consciousness could not only be aware of things, but 'know' them as they were in themselves, and not merely as they appeared. This was the seed that has found its fruit in the modern scientist's assertion that mathematics is the language of nature herself. But music is not a 'natural' object, though it uses what is given in nature. In fact, even the *svara* as given in nature, has obviously to be 'felt' as integral to music in order to be part of musical usage: hence the difference in what is 'given' as *svara* in different musical cultures. The history of the *rāga* significantly and articulately reveals that *svara* as a felt entity can also find those sounds meaningful which are 'discordant' with those 'given' in nature. The world of music, like all human, *pauruṣeya* worlds created in culture, is the product of a tension between the given in nature and the creative human consciousness with *puruṣārthas* of its own, one of the *puruṣārthas* being the exploration of aesthetic possibilities. The opposition or discord between *svara* as given in nature, and as given in our musical creativity, is *not*, as one might be tempted to conclude, between a 'real' and an 'apparent' or merely imaginary entity. The *antarāla*, or tonal distance, which was *rejected* earlier because it was thought to be self-evidently given as a *non-svara*, and also *felt* to be so — on the ground of being *not svayambhū* — is now, in exploring the possibilities of the *rāga*-form through the pathways of improvisation, and of seeking new pleasures, discovered to be a *svara*. The deeper tension here is between the changing 'given' in the world of music and what is believed to be the really and uniquely given, either as essence or law in Nature, or the Transcendent.

In Puṇḍarīka's musicology of the *rāga*, we can find an interesting reflection on the opposition between the two ways of conceiving *svara*, and a defence of the second of the two *lakṣaṇas*. His definition of *svara* unmistakably leans towards the second *lakṣaṇa*:

"That which is produced immediately after a *śruti*, and is smooth, and gives rise to a [sympathetic] after-sound, and is [also] self-resplendent, [such a sound] is termed by the knowledgeable, a *svara,* because it pleases the mind of a listener by itself."

This definition is to be found in the *Sadrāgacandrodaya.*[16] Puṇḍarīka begins the work with a description of *svara* which assumes the ancient *svara-maṇḍala* and the fixed position of the seven *svaras* at specific *śruti* — positions.[17] But in this he was merely paying lip-service to the tradition of the *śāstra* and its conventions. For, he quickly changes his stance, and controverts the old *svara-maṇḍala*, and states that *śrutis* can also be *svaras*, implying that *any śruti* can be a *svara.* He also realises the evident contradiction in his statements, and poses it as a *pūrvapakṣa:* 'You have', he says, voicing the *pūrvapakṣa*, '[earlier] made a distinction between *śruti* and *svara,* but that distinction contradicts what you are saying now [in equating the two] — *nanu svarasya śrutitaḥ pṛthaktvaṁ tvayā yaduktaṁ na tathā'tra yuktam* (*Sadrāgacandrodaya*, 1, 31).

In reply, he gives a short statement, trying to make short work of the above charge. He says: '*śruti* is [that sound] which is heard before [a pitch-position] is actually struck; *svara* is the after-sound that it produces. [This should suffice as an answer to the objection] which is, indeed, trifling.' This statement is not entirely clear to me: what does he mean by a sound heard before it is struck ? It obviously assumes a discussion which was part of the thinking current in the new musicological milieu in which Puṇḍarīka was writing. However, the thrust of Puṇḍarīka's counter-argument is not difficult to guess. It banks upon the distinction between *āhata* and *anāhata* sound, and takes an *anāhata* — unstruck — sound to be the potentiality of a sound and not an actual sound; this potentiality he calls *śruti.* An *āhata* sound is the realisation of that potentiality, and is distinguished as *svara*. Resultingly, no pitch-position that can be sounded and heard is, in this view, a non-*svara.*

Puṇḍarīka then gives another argument in his support. This argument assumes a latter-day understanding of *śrutis* in terms

---

[16] *śruteśca nairantarabhāviko yaḥ snigdho'nuśabdātmaka ojasātmā / śroturmanorañjanakārakatvātsvatastu tajjñairuditaḥ svaro'sau//*
Sadrāgacandrodaya, 1, 24. *op.cit.*, p. 79.

[17] Ibid, 1, 22-23.

of *śruti-jātis*, a concept, which appears only in medieval texts, in a period when *rāga*-music had become the generally accepted form of what music should be. It is not to be found in ancient *jāti*-oriented musicology. The concept of *śruti-jātis* classifies all the *śrutis* into five kinds, on the basis mainly of their *expressive* quality, and not their position in the *svara-maṇḍala.* These five kind of *śrutis* are named: *dīptā* ('bright', 'shining'), *āyaytā* ('expansive'), *karuṇā* ('having pathos'), *mṛdu* ('soft') and *madhyā* ('middling', 'neutral').[18] All except one, the *madhyā*, indicate an aesthetic function. Elaborating his short argument, discussed above, in favour of considering any *śruti* a *svara,* Puṇḍarīka now refers us to the authority (*pramāṇa*) of those who speak of the five *śruti-jātis.*[19] What this *pramāṇa* is, Puṇḍarīka does not tell us, and I have not been able to discover it elsewhere. But one can guess its purport: If *all śrutis* have an *expressive* quality of some kind; they are, clearly, all of them, possible *svaras* , whatever their comparative pitch-position in a *svara-maṇḍala*, since being expressive is a basic characteristic of being a *svara.* This view, obviously, makes the cogniser's sense of music the *'pramāṇa'*, the criterion, for *svara*-hood.

In Ahobala, a more adventurous thinker, who wrote his *Saṅgīta-pārijāta,* a century after Puṇḍarīka (in 1665), the radical ideas found in Puṇḍarīka achieve their logical culmination, and also a much greater sense of self-assurance. They are no longer a matter of doubt and questioning, but are taken as a new 'given',

---

[18] A relatively old text where the idea occurs is the *Bharata Bhāṣya* of Nānyadeva, written perhaps between 1097 and 1133 A.D., the period of Nānyadeva's rule over Mithila. This line of thinking about *śrutis* had indeed named all 22 *śrutis* on expressive lines. Nānyadeva, in his chapter on *śruti,* after expounding and discussing the ancient views on the subject, where he speaks of the twenty-two *śrutis,* says : 'there are in [all] the *grāmas, only five śrutis* to be always found, *dīptā, āyatā, karuṇā, mṛdu,* and *madhyā'* — *dīptā'yatā ca karuṇā mṛdu madhyeti nāmataḥ / pañcaiva śrutayaḥ proktā jñeyā grāmeṣu nityaśaḥ //* See *Bharata Bhāṣya,* edited with notes by Chaitanya Pundarika Desai, pub. Indirā Kalā Saṅgīta Viśvavidyālaya, Khairagadh, 1961, vol,1, *śrutyādhyāya*, verse 83, p.94.

[19] *yairjātayaḥ pañca matā śrutināṁ te tu pramāṇaṁ pravadanti tatra. Sadrāgacandrodaya, op. cit.*, 1, 33.

which can be meaningfully described as a cultural, 'given': Ahobala's *pramāṇa* are musicians and the knowers of music.

There is a tendency, with the great cultural prestige of 'science' ruling our minds, to decry such a 'given' as merely 'subjective' as opposed to the 'measured' and the 'given in nature' as being truly 'objective'. But all cultural things are founded on the tension between the 'measured' and the 'perceived'. Their 'objectivity' is never free of the 'subject; it lies in inter-subjectivity. What Ahobala does is to articulate the inter-subjectivity of music, in other words, its culture-dependence.

He unreservedly states:

'*Śrutis* are not different from *svaras,* because [like *svaras*], they [too] are audible. Their difference, according to the *śāstras*, is similar to that between a snake [in its usual straight, oblong form] and its [special] coiled state. All *śrutis* can acquire the state of *svara*-hood, in different *rāgas*. Because they are bases of *rāgas*, therefore are they rightly called *śrutis. Śrutis* are many, separated from each other by the breadth of a hair; this can be perceived on the *vīṇā* as well as the voice: such is the view of those who know music.'[20]

The confidence we notice here, that what Ahobala has to say is truly based on the *śāstras*, is remarkable, even if not correct, if the reference *saṅgīta-śāstra.* The *śāstra*, referred to cannot be any prestigious work of the *saṅgīta-śastra*, as one might be likely to presuppose. The *śāstra* Ahobala has in mind seems to be the *darśana-śāstra,* and his metaphor for equating *śruti* and

---

20 *śrutayaḥ syuḥ svarābhinnāḥ śravaṇatvena hetunā /*
ahikuṇḍalavattatra bhedoktiḥ śāstrasammatā //
sarvāśca śrutayastattad rāgeṣu svaratāṃ gatāḥ /
rāgahetutva etāsāṁ śrutisaṁjñaiva sammatā //
keśāgravyavadhānena bahvyo'pi śrutayaḥ śritāḥ /
vīṇāyāṁ ca tathā gātre saṅgītajñāninām mate //

Saṅgītapārijata, 38-40 (as quoted in the notes on *Bharata Bhāṣya* by Caitanya P. Desai, *op. cit.*, vol. 1, p. 102. See also *Saṅgītapārijata* with a translation into Hindi by Kalind, pub. Saṅgīt Kāryālay, Hathras, 1971 verses 38 to 41, pp. 18-19).

svara appears to be taken from a work of a *bhakti* school of philosophy, arguing against *advaita* and its *māyāvāda*. But, as he himself later adds, his confidence is really based on the belief that his views accord with those who really know music. Relying on the perception of musicians and music-knowers, he breaks away not only from the *antarāla niyama* of the ancients, but even from the ancient and strangely continuing myth that there are only twenty-two audible tonal *antarālas* in an octave. Intriguingly, Ahobala also argued, in the lines which follow the above passage, that the twenty-two *śruti svara-maṇḍala,* which he finds inadequate was constructed by the process of *ṣaḍja-pañcama-bhāva:* arriving at pitch positions through the harmonics of the fifth (making *pa* the *sā* gives *re*; with *re as sā* we have *dha* and so on).[21] So, in effect, Ahobala seems to reject the harmonic principle itself on which the 'natural' givenness and mathematical measurability of *svara* is based. This is a revolutionary move, indeed.

What I have said above regarding the dynamic, evolving and integrally inter-connected, relation of *svara* and *rāga* is, in fact, true, I believe, of the relation between *svara* and the music of any rich and enterprising musical culture. The example of the *rāga* is, surely, only an instance of a more universal cultural phenomenon. The specific ways in which the relation between *svara* and music develops, will certainly differ with the individual history of a culture, yet one would think that tensions similar to the one outlined above would be common. What I have done is to describe the phenomenon as I see it in the history of Indian music. This will, I hope, also serve a cautionary purpose, and dispel the myth that Indian music or its musicology is basically ahistorical.

Paradoxically, the *saṅgīta-śāstra*, in more recent times, has tried to get back to the assurance of the *svara-sthānas* as somehow 'given' even as it has become more historically

---

[21] *madhye pūrvottarabaddhavīṇāyāṁ gātra eva ca /*
ṣaḍjapañcamabhāvena śrutirdvāviṁśatirjaguḥ //
ibid, verse, 41.

oriented. But the essence of the idea that Ahobala so daringly propounds, continues among the *sampradāyas* of music, both musicians and *guṇījans* — the 'knowers of music'. Indeed the idea, I think, can be carried still forward. In all musical thinking the belief — or rather the rooted *saṁskāra* — that *svara* is a *position*, has continued, and is still with us. It is there even in Ahobala. But if we go by what we actually do in practice, as Ahobala bravely does, the idea cannot but be challenged. If *rāgas* decide *svaras*, as has been believed for a few centuries now, then a *svara* need not be a static *position*, that is, a *sthāna*. We also have *āndolita svaras* in many *rāgas*, such as the *Miyān kī Malhār* and *Ḍarbārī*, where a *svara* to be a *svara in the rāga* has to be a swing, a particular movement over *sthānas*, which is what an *āndolana* is, and not a static *position*.

Many of the larger visions and reflections of the great musicological thinkers discussed above are denied today in musicology or even in what we know in our own culture as *saṅgīta-śāstra*. The discipline is understood as a descriptive science, or a *lakṣaṇa śāstra*, with prescriptive undertones — or overtones — that such a 'human' science or *śāstra* is bound to have, but the spaces of thought beyond this, leading out of music or deeper within it, are considered out of bounds. It is forbidden to take 'speculative' leaps of the kind that ancient thinkers like Pythagoras, Confucius or the singers of *sāma* like Yājñavalkya — to mention only one of them—took. These, it is believed, were thinkers who had not yet been able to shake off their non-scientific, mythological and mystical moorings. One might wonder if the visions of Pythagoras, Confucius and Yājñavalkya can be dismissed as merely 'mystical' and 'mythological', even though one might agree with the thrust of thought which distinguishes between myths and mystical statements and those produced by what is called the cognitive enterprise. The musicological enterprise, as we have tried to look at it above, has clear roots in 'reason' or a 'rational logos' in the larger sense of the term. What it tries to do is to explore the manifestation of 'cognition' or 'knowledge' in music itself. It is thus truly a 'science' or the 'logos' of music. What we find, I think, are visions which life and thought can feed on creatively.

I say this also as a kind of self-justification for my own venture into fields outside the '*lakṣmaṇa-rekhā*' of what can be called 'traditional' musicology, using the term 'tradition' in its sense as 'the accepted convention' regarding the domain of the discipline. But a reader might ironically note, however, that the present collection of essays does not really fall outside the field of convention. This is true. If, as I would fondly like to believe, I have really done any substantial stepping-out, it is more in a long Hindi essay, a venturesome project, entitled, *Saṅgīt Evaṁ Cintan,** published separately as an independent work, and not collected here. This Hindi essay seeks to understand thought itself, its nature and creativity as a human, cultural enterprise, through the eyes of music, especially the *rāga*. The present essay too, has acquired an analogous, if not an identical, thrust.

But something more can be said here concerning the notion of stepping-out, which, I believe is relevant to those who do musicology in India. I would like to point out that musicology as *saṅgīta-śāstra* is an old and hoary discipline in India. The *śāstra* had its own traditions and its traditional boundaries, its *maryādā,* which was not quite fixed, as it never is in any long tradition of thought on a subject — and as I hope the survey above also reveals — yet it did move within discernibly marked limits. A remarkable stepping out of *saṅgīta-śāstra* took place in the 19th century with our encounter with of west. Musicology in the west has interests quite different from traditional *saṅgīta-śāstra*, and though it too is a *lakṣaṇa-śāstra* of its kind, its notion of *lakṣaṇa* in the context of music is quite different from ours. It has, for one, a pointedly 'contextual' orientation and gives much more value to the history of music and the circumstances under which music is created than our *saṅgīta-śāstra* does — or, for that matter, any of the other Indian *śāstras* connected with the arts,

---

* Delivered as a series of lectures under the auspices of the Hiranand Shastri Vyākhyānmālā, organised by Vatsal Nidhi and published by Prabhat Prakashan, New Delhi, 1994.

including the richest of them, namely, *alaṅkāra-śāstra,* do. A contextual, historical approach is, in the west, considered not something contingent, but a central part of the *lakṣaṇa* of these arts. We have also learnt to follow the west in this regard, and, consequently, all our *śāstras* regarding the arts, including *saṅgita-śāstra*, have stepped out, so to say, from their earlier confines. Indeed we can no longer even think of these *śāstras* in purely traditional Indian terms, so much has the western śāstric tradition taken hold of us. But, looking at the *pauruṣeya* logos of the *rāga* and its essentially *historical* spirit, the addition of history to our *saṅgīta-śāstra*, need not be considered an entirely alien implant.

The case of modern *saṅgīta-śāstra* is, in an important sense, different from other *śāstras*, say *alaṅkāra-śāstra* or *vāstu-śāstra.* In these *śāstras*, unlike *saṅgīta-śāstra*, we have not added something new to an already rich tradition, but, literally, stepped-out of the Indian tradition and its own *maryādā* into a new tradition, the western, and its different confines. This has been a kind of total stepping-out almost similar to what happens with people at the end of a civilisation, to which they had been long heir. *Saṅgīta as well as saṅgīta-śāstra* have been an exception. Stepping-out here has been more of a reaching out, a broadening of frontiers. We have come to acquire a 'contextual' interest without losing our moorings in the earlier approach and the central concepts of what constitutes *lakṣaṇa* in music.

Appendix I

Some time back Professor Bansidhar Bhatt of Munster, Germany, was kind enough to send me a paper he had written, entitled, 'Study of the word, *nikṣepa* and other derivatives in the Śvetāmbara Jain Canon' (published in *Akten des Melzer — Symposiums 1991,* ed. Walter Slaje and Christian Zinko, Leykam, pp. 15-53). Prof. Bhatt has serious and radical objections to my understaning of *ruiya-joṇīyam* (*rudita-yoni*) as meaning that the source of song is lament, or the sentiment of *karuṇa* in man. This, he says, is a merely a 'poetic' statement and can hardly be expected of a work devoted to the 'scientific' discipline of musicology which seeks 'universal theories' (p. 47).

No one, I should think, would really deny that the statement in question, as I have understood it, does, in fact, make a 'universal' or general claim; it can also be certainly called a 'theory' concerning what makes man sing. Lament, the theory claims, is the cause of song. There is, of course, no attempt in our text to adduce arguments in favour of the 'theory', nor should this be expected from the kind of text that we have, which deals only sketchily with its subject. As to being 'scientific', what one may ask, is wanting here ? The theory is certainly 'scientific' in being 'causal'; it speaks of a causal relation between lament and song. But what is lacking , perhaps, is that such a theory, even though apparently causal, cannot really be a matter of factual, experimental examination; and so it is unscientific. One might even add that the very enquiry, as to the basis of song in human nature is unscientific in principle since it cannot lead to any proper empirical examination. But then would it be proper to be only 'scientific' in an enquiry concerning music ? Are suggestive and intuitive statements to be totally avoided, even if they add to the wealth and depth of our understanding ? Should one not be speculative in understanding music, since music, it can be meaningfully said (to make another 'theoretical' point, so to say) is itself born of the speculative spirit. Music is also an aesthetic activity, and statements concerning aesthetics, though obviously central to musicology, cannot be termed 'scientific' in the sense of being purely descriptive. Take the statements we have in our text regarding *guṇas* and *doṣas*. Their intention is obviously prescriptive and not descriptive as demanded by a 'science' of the kind which Prof. Bhatt appears to have in mind. But the question really is, should such a demand be made a prescriptive, or imperative, demand for the science or the knowledge, the *vidya, śāstra* or *veda*, of music ?

Prof. Bhatt's own understanding of '*ruiya joṇīyam*' is interesting. '*Ruiya*', he has tried to show, is really a misreading for '*ruinda*', a word which stands for '*rovindaka*', a *gītaka* sung in *gāndharva*, a distinct form of ancient music; and '*yoni*', means 'a basic stanza'. Thus the phrase, '*gīyaṁ ruiya-joṇīyaṁ*', should actually be read as, '*gīyaṁ ruinda-joṇīyaṁ*', and it means, 'the *rovindaka* is a basic stanza (a form) of *gīta*'. This, I think, is not only extremely far-fetched, but seems to make no sense. I have not been able to understand the phrase, 'a basic stanza (a form) of *gīta*'. In what sense is a stanza intended as a *form* of *gīta* ? A stanza, one would think, is a *part* of a *gīta*, which is usually a larger unit. Indeed, the *rovindaka*, as the reader can see from the *Dattilam* and the *Nāṭyaśāstra* (or from my exposition of *rovindaka* in a *A Study Of Dattilam*, especially pp. 406-410) was a large and complex form containing many stanzas, and can hardly be equated with *a* stanza, even 'a *basic stanza*', however the term 'basic' might be understood here.

The notable thing in Prof. Bhatt's article, in the context of our Jain text, is that he shows us through references that *rovindaka* was known to ancient Jain circles, thus adding meaningfully to our knowledge concerning ancient, and what might be termed, 'non-*saṅgītaśāstric*' references to the *gāndharva* and its forms.

Appendix II

Ṭhāṇaṁga Text on Music

(Major variant readings are given from the Aṇuôgaddāra text published in a critical edition by Sri Mahavira Jain Vidyalaya, Bombay).

सत्त सरा पण्णत्ता, तं जहा—

सज्जे रिसहे गंधारे मज्झिमे पंचमे सरे।
धेवए चेव निस्साए सरा सत्त वियाहिया॥ 1॥

एएसिं णं सत्तण्हं सराणं सत्त सरट्ठाणा पण्णात्ता, तं जहा—

सज्जं च अग्गजीहाए उरेण रिसएं सरं।
कंठुग्गएण गंधारं मज्झजीहाए मज्झिमं॥ 2॥

नासाए पंचमं बूया दंतोट्ठेण य धेवयं।
मुद्धाणेणं[1] य णेसायं सरट्ठाणा वियाहिया॥ 3॥

सत्तसरा जीवणिस्सिया पण्णत्ता, तं जहा—

सज्जं रवइ मऊरो कुक्कुडो रिसएं सरं।
हंसो णदइ[2] गंधारं मज्झिमं च गवेलगा॥ 4॥

अह कुसुमसंभवे काले कोइला पंचमं सरं।
छहं च सरसा कोंचा नेसायं सत्तमं गया॥ 5॥

सत्तसरा अजीवणिस्सिया पण्णत्ता, तं जहा—

सज्जं रवइ मुयंगो गोमुही रिसहं सरं।
संखो णदइ[3] गंधार मज्झिमं पुण झल्लरी॥ 6॥

चउचलण पइट्ठाणा गाहिया पंचमं सरं।
आडम्बरो धेवइयं महाभेरी य सत्तमं॥ 7॥

---

1. भमुहवक्खेवेण।
2. रवइ।
3. रवइ।

एएसिं ण सत्तण्हं सराणं सत्त सरलक्खणा पण्णत्ता, तं जहा—

सज्जेण लहई वित्तिं कयं च न विणस्सइ।
गावो पुत्ता य मित्ता य नारीणं होइ वल्लहो ॥ 8 ॥

रिसहेण य एसज्जं सेणावच्चं धणाणि य।
वत्थ गंधमलंकारं इत्थिओ सयणाणि य ॥ 9 ॥

गंधारे गीयजुत्तिण्णा वज्जवित्ती कलाहिया।
हवंति कइणो पण्णा जे अण्णे सत्थपारगा ॥ 10 ॥

मज्झिमस्सरसंपन्ना भवंति[4] सुहजीविणो।
खायई पियई देई मज्झिमस्सरसस्सिओ ॥ 11 ॥

पंचमस्सरसंपन्ना हवंति पुढवीवई।
सूरा संगहकत्तारो अणेगगणनायगा[5] ॥ 12 ॥

धेवयस्सरसंपन्ना[6] हवंति कलहप्पिया।
साउणिया वग्गुरिया सोयरिया मच्छवंधा य ॥ 13 ॥

चंडाला मुट्ठिया सेया[7] जे अण्णो पावकम्मिणो।
गोघातगा य जे चोरा णिसायं सरमस्सिया ॥ 14 ॥

एएसिं णं सत्तण्हं तओ गामा पण्णत्ता, तं जहा—सज्जगामे मज्झिमगामे गंधारगामे। सज्जगामस्स णं सत्त मुच्छणाओ पण्णताओ, तं जहा—

मंगी कोरवीया हरी य रयणी सारकंता य।
छट्ठी य सारसी नाम सुद्धसज्जा य सत्तमा ॥ 15 ॥

मज्झिमगामस्स णं सत्त मुच्छणाओ पण्णत्ताओ तं जहा—

उत्तरमंदा रयणी उत्तरा उत्तरासमा[8]।
समोकंता य सौवीरा अवभीरु[9] हवइ सत्तमा ॥ 16 ॥

4. हंवति।
5. अणेगणरणायगा।
6. धेवयसरमंता।
7. मेता।
8. उत्तरायता।
9. अभीरू।

गंधारगामस्स णं सत्त मुच्छणाओ पण्णत्ताओ, तं जहा—

नंदी य खुड्डिया पूरिमा च चउत्थी च सुद्धगंधारा।
उत्तरगंधारा वि य पंचमिया हवइ मुच्छा उ॥ 17॥

सुद्धु त्तरमायामा सा छट्ठी नियमसो उणायव्वा।
अह उत्तरायया कोडिमा य सा सत्तमी मुच्छा॥ 18॥

सत्तसरा कओ संभवंति गीयस्स का हवंति जोणी।
कइ समया उस्सासा कइ वा गीयस्स आगारा॥ 19॥

सत्तसरा नाभिओ हवंति, गीयं च रुइयजोणियं[10]।
पायसमा ऊसासा, तिण्णि य गीयस्स आगारा॥ 20॥

आइमिउ आरभंता समुव्वहंता या मज्झगारंमि।
अवसाणे तज्जविंतो[11] तिन्नि य गीयस्स आगरा॥ 21॥

छद्दोसे अट्ठगुणे तिण्णि य वित्ताइं दो य भणिईओ।
जाणाहिइ से गाहिइ सुसिक्खिओ रंगमज्झम्मि॥ 22॥

भीयं दुयं रहस्सं[12]गायंतो माय गाहि उत्तालं[13]।
काकस्सरं अणुणासं च होंति गीयस्स छद्दोसा[14]॥ 23॥

पुण्णं रत्तं च अलंकियं च वत्तं तहा अविघुट्ठं।
महुरं समं सुललियं अट्ठगुणा होंति गेयस्स॥ 24॥

सरकंठसिरपसत्थं[15] गिज्जइ मउरिभियपदबद्धं।
समतालपडुक्खेवं सत्तस्सरसीभरं गीयं॥ 25॥

निद्दोसं सारमंतं च हेउजुत्तमलेकियं।
उवणीयं सोवयारं य मियं महुरमेव य॥ 26॥

समं अद्धसमं चेव सवत्थं विसमं च जं।
तिण्णि वित्तप्पयाराइं चउत्थ नोवलब्भइ॥ 27॥

---

10. रुन्नजोणीयं।
11. अवसाणे य झवेंता।
12. दुयमुप्पिच्छं।
13. उत्तालं च कमसौ मुणयव्वं।
14. छद्दोसा होंति गीयस्स।
15. विसुद्धं।

सक्कया पायया चैव दुहा भणिईओ आहिया।
सरमंडलम्मि गिज्जंते पसत्था इसिभासिया॥ 28॥

केसि गायइ महुरं केसि गायइ खरं च रुक्खं च।
केसि गायइ चउरं केसी य विलवियं दुतं केसी॥ 29॥

विस्सरं पुण केरिसी॥
सामा गायइ महुरं काली गायइ खरं च रुक्खं च।
गोरी गायइ चउरं काणा विलंबं दुतं च अंधा॥ 30॥

विस्सरं पुण पिंगला।
तंतिसमं[16] तालसमं पायसमं लयसमं गहसमं च।
नीससिऊससियसमं संचारसमं सरा सत्त[17] ॥ 31॥

सत्तसरा तओ गामा मुच्छणा एकवीसई।
ताणा एगूणपण्णासं सम्मतं सरमंडलं॥ 32॥
इह सरमंडलं समत्तं[18]।

16. अक्खरसमं।
17. In *Aṇuôgòddāra* this verse comes after verse 25 above.
18. *Aṇuôgaddāra* ends with से तं सत्तनामे।

Index

A Historical Study of Indian Music 199
A History of Indian Literature (see also, 'Winternitz, Maurice') 218fn, 223fn
A Study of Dattilam ii, 49fn, 63, 110fn, 305fn, 309fn, 315fn, 337
Abdul Karim Khan 55, 59, (same as, 'Abdul Karim')
Abhijñāna Śākuntalam (see, '*Śākuntalam*')
Abhinava (see also, 'Abhinava Gupta' and 'Abhinavagupta') 242fn, 245; and composite arts 95ff; and dance 75ff; on dramatic speech 99fn; on music in theatre 128fn, 135ff; on *nāṭya* 95ff, 133ff; on *viṇā* 201
Abhinava Bhāratī (see also, 'Abhinava Gupta') — 69ff, 85fn, 128fn, 169fn, 321fn
Abhinava Gupta (see also, 'Abhinava', 'Abhinavagupta', '*Abhinava Bhāratī*') 8, 18, 20, 37ff, 38fn, 69ff, 93fn, 95ff, 115, 168-169, 176fn
Abhinavagupta 127, 131fn
abhinaya (mime, acting) 70, 72-73, 81ff, 106ff; and *bhāva* 118
absolute; in music 267-306
actor 28, 100, 126
Adāraṅg 59
Adhyātmaviveka (of 'Śārṅgadeva') 249
affinity; between realms 120ff, 163ff
Agni: The Vedic Ritual of The Fire Altar 301fn
āhata 263, 329; *nāda* 289ff, 311
Ahobala 330ff
Ajanta 24, 57
Akten Des Melzer 336
alaṁkāra-śāstra 17-18, 118fn, 247, 335
alaṅkāra 103, 117; in music 103, 228fn
ālaṅkārikas 19, (see also, 'critics; literary')
ālāpa 51, 88ff, 221, 319
ālāta-cakra 97, 135
ālekhyavat (also, '*tulya*', '*prakhya*', '*kalpa*; a painting-like resemblance or *saṁvāda*); concept of and musical style 36: a kind of *saṁvāda* (see also, '*saṁvāda*') 24ff; subspecies of 27ff
Allaudin Khan 12
Altekar, A.S. 159, 191, 192fn, 199, 202
Amara 201
Amarakośa 70fn, 201
Amaru 21
Ames, Roy (see, 'Roy Ames')
Amir Khan 36, 53, 59
Amitabh Bacchan (an actor) 157-158
Amolak Chandra Surpuria 223fn
Amṛtamanthana 105
anāhata 263, 329; *nāda* 293
Ānanadavardhana 93; his concept of literary creativity 16ff; his concept of meaning 19-20; on *pratibhā* 20ff
Aṅga (a branch of Jain literature) 223, 232
aṅga (style) 38
aṅgahāra (a dance-whole) 73ff, 83, 115

aṅgavidyā 243
Aṅgavijjā 243-244
anirukta; *sāma* 301fn
anṛca; *sāma* 46ff, 286ff
antarmārga 35; of a *rāga* 32
anukaraṇa (mimesis) 95, 101, 105ff, 114, 118-119, 128fn
Aṇuôgaddāra 223-224
anuvādī 312ff
Aparājitapṛcchā 180
Āpastamba Gṛhya Sūtra 195fn
apauruṣeya; music 267-306
Āraṇyaka; texts 44, 305
architect 17,
architecture (see also, '*vāstu-śāstra*') 4, 5, 40-41, 334; vis-à-vis music 14, 58,
Aristotle iii, 271fn; and Bharata 94-95, 111
Arjuna; as a musician 186
art; forms, composite 52, 93-122 (see also, 'arts the association of'); history of 15, 58
arteries; and the production of speech and *svara* 255ff
artists 7, 15, 56; their activity of transformation 17
arts; affinity of 120; formal 16, 122, (see also, 'form; non-representative'); non-representational 101, 118-119; performing 58, 99; the association of 52, (see also, 'art-forms, composite') traditional and modern 4ff
aśarīra (see also, '*sāma*'); *sāma*; 46ff, 287ff
Ashok Kumar (an actor) 158
āśraya (base); of music 288ff
auditorium 139 (see also, '*nāṭya-gṛha*')
Āyāra (*Āyāraṅga*) 223fn
āyurveda 263; as revelation 256ff; birth of the body in 248ff.

Bach 59
Bade Ghulam Ali 91
Bahār (a *rāga*) 89, 91, 169
Baiju Bāvarā (see also, 'Nāyak Baiju') 214
Bāṇa 187, 198
bandish 90 (see also, '*chiz*' and '*kṛti*'); its replication 32
bānī (see also 'style') 62
Basant (a *rāga*; see also, '*Vasant*') 167
Beethoven 184
Begum Akhtar 53, 104, 105
Bhāgavata; painting 184
Bhagīratha Prasāda Śāstrī 291fn
Bhairava (a *rāga*); painting of 185
Bhairavī (a *rāga*) 33; and *rāga*-time association 167
Bhaktamāla 214
bhakti 49fn, 306
bhāṇas; music in 197ff
Bharata (see also, '*Nāṭyaśāstra*') 19, 21, 51, 53, 168, 199, 239fn, 318fn, 324-325; and Confucius 273, 289; and Hindi films 123-162; and his *Nāṭyaśāstra* 19, 130ff; and his theatre 92-122, 130ff; and Taṇḍu 69ff; his concept of *vṛtti* 111ff; his *saṅgraha* 98, 99 110; on dance 37, 69ff; on *pada* 293-294
Bharata Bhāṣya (see also, 'Nānya Bhūpāla) 65, 169, 231, 236fn, 330fn, 331fn
Bharata Nāṭyam 109, 112, 113
Bharatakośa 175-176fn
Bhāratīya Calacitra Kā Itihās 126fn
Bhāratīya Saṅgīta Kā Itihās (of Thakur Jaidev Singh) 70
Bhāsa 189
Bhatkhande; and musical institutions 14; on *rāga* and time 12, 164ff
Bhātkhaṇḍe Smṛti Grantha 168fn, 172fn
Bhatt, Bansidhara 336-337

Bhaṭṭa Nārāyaṇa 141
Bhaṭṭa Śobhākara 235fn
*bhāva (*in *nāṭya);* and *abhinaya* 118; and *rasa* 118, 273ff
bhāva (in *āyurveda*) 250ff
Bhavabhūti 242
Bhīmacārya Jhalkīkar 291fn
Bhimsen Joshi 59
Bihāg (a *rāga*) 36
Billikoth Ramachandra Sharma 288fn, 302fn
biruda (a limb of '*prabandha*') 216
Biwi O Biwi (a Hindi film) 155-156, 158
Bobby (a Hindi film) 142, 143
body; as an instrument 247-263; as embodied self 249ff; the birth of 248ff
bol (in percussion playing) 116-117
Book of Songs (Chinese) 268ff
Boy Friend (a Hindi film) 157, 158
Brāhmaṇa; texts 42ff, 225fn, 271, 285ff, 302fn
Bṛhadāraṇyaka Upaniṣad 306
Bṛhaddeśī (see also, 'Matanga') 62, 65, 168, 207, 215, 238fn, 315fn, 317, 318-319
Bṛhaddharma Purāṇa 177ff
Bṛhatkathākośa 198fn
Bṛhatkathāmañjari 195fn
Buddha 48, 196, 197
buddhi; and the body 251ff; and the process of speech-production 255, 260-261
Buddhist; ethos and music 49; literature, music in 187, 196-197 (see also, '*Jātakas*')

Caitanya 179
cakras (connected with the *kuṇḍalinī*) 259
Candragupta II 198; as a musician 190-191; as a playwright 191
Caraka 256
cārī (movement in dance) 76, 86
Caturbhāṇī 198fn
Caurapañcāśikā; paintings 185
Chaitanya P. Desai 170fn, 330fn
chālikya-gāndharva 186
Chāndogya Upaniṣad 285
Chari, V.K. 114fn
China; music in, 267ff, 307ff
chiz (composition) 61
civilization; traditional 3
classical (see also, '*śāstrīya*' and '*prabandha*'); forms 32, 55-56, 59, 87ff, 143; musicians 51 (also, 'musicians'); singing 51-53, 222
coinage; Gupta, *viṇā* in 186-204
composers (see also, '*vāggeyakāras*') 30, 59-60, 144, 206fn
composite; 94ff art and the concept of *uparañjana* 94ff
Confucius 289, 307, 310, 316-319, 333; as a musicologist 267ff; defines man through music iii, 273
content; vis-à-vis form 16, 31, 72-73
correspondences; cosmic 44-45
creation; as transformation 16-38
creative; transformation and style 32ff
creativity (see also, 'creation,' '*pratibhā*'); and plagiarism 24ff; and similarities 23ff; and the concept of *dhvani* 20-21; and the concept of *yoni* 25; and the structure of a poem 29; denial of 23; literary 16ff
critic(s) (see also, '*sahṛdaya*') 280; Confucius as 280ff; literary; 17ff
criticism (see also, '*sahṛdaya*'); in music, 1, 10ff, 218; in newspapers 14-15; in poetry 56; oral 10, 14

dādrā 90

Dāmodara Gupta (see also, '*Kuṭṭanimatam*') 145ff
dance 6, 16, 37, 52, 119; and Hindi films 123ff, 144ff, 154ff; and *nāṭya* (theatre) 72-73, 99, 105ff, 153; ceremonial 272; theory of, and Taṇḍu (see, 'Taṇḍu'); unit of 37-38, 71ff, 114ff (see also, '*nṛtta*; *mātṛkā*'); *yojanā* in 74fn, 84ff
Darbārī (a *rāga*) 333
Dasaveyāliya 223fn
Dattila (see also, '*Dattilam*') iii, 174fn, 237fn, 311ff, 318fn, 327
Dattilam (see also, 'Dattila') ii-iii, 65, 66, 176fn, 194fn, 224, 233fn, 237fn, 311fn, 337
Daya Krishna 286ff
deśī 86, 119, 217-218, 258
Deśi Toḍī (a *rāga*) 91
Devanand (an actor) 141, 149
Devardhigaṇi 224fn
devices; theatric 129, 132ff, 150ff
Dhaky, M.A. 180fn
dhamanī (see, 'artery')
dhamār 89
dharma 271, 279
Dharmendra (an actor) 149
dhātu 220
Ḍholā-Mārū; paintings 184
dhrupad 34-35, 38, 88ff, 102, 207; analogous to *gāndharva* 102; as a style of rendering *rāgas* 32ff, 88ff; its history 61-62, 215fn
dhruvā (theatrical songs; see also, '*gāna*', 'theatrical') 128fn, 242; and *gāndharva* 102ff, 115, 121, 144; *ātma-saṁstha* and *para-saṁstha* 142-143; types of and their uses 135ff, 156ff
dhvani; and the concept of *kāku* 100; theory of, and creativity 20-21
Dhvanyāloka (see also 'Ānandavardhana') 8fn, 18ff, 23fn
Dhvanyālokalocana (see also, 'Abhinavagupta') 18
Die Musikinstrumente Indiens Und Indonesiens 192fn
Dīghanikāya 196
Dikshit, Ramanatha A.M. 302fn, 316fn
Dilip Padgaonkar; and songs in Hindi films 127-128
Dīpak(a) (a *rāga*) 232; occult effect of 12
director; of films 126, 137-138
doṣa 10, 218, 227, 240ff, 337
drama (see also, 'theatre') 52, 128fn
dramaturgy (see also, '*nāṭya*') 130
dṛśya-kāvya (see also, 'theatre') 19
Druhiṇa 93fn
Dvijarāja Bhaṭṭa 302fn

Ebeling, Klaus 174ff, 183-184
education (see also 'music'); in music and improvisation 31, 60
emotions; harmonised through music 270; in Hindi films 137ff, 153ff, 160
Epigraphica Indica 187fn
ethnomusicologist i
Europe (see, 'European')
European; music 39ff
experience; universals of 23

Faiyaz Khan 59
Falke, D.G. 126
feeling (see, 'emotion')
film 52; and the *nāṭya* of Bharata 94-95, 102; documentary 129; Hindi, and dance 123ff; Hindi, and music 102, 105, 123ff; Hindi, history of 125ff
Film And Reality 125fn
film-songs; tradition of 123ff
Fleet, J.F. 186fn

folk; music 215, 217-218
form; archetypal 87; classical 30-31 (see also, 'classical'); generation of 71ff; musical (see also, 'music') 39, 63, 65, 66-67, 88ff, 104, 143, 215ff, 229; non-representative 71-73, 105ff, 114; of a *rāga* 87-91; vis-à-vis content 16, 31, 71
formal; arts 16, 101; influences on Hindi films 125ff
formalistic 18
formula 88, 124
Fox-Strangways, A.H. 166, 177fn

Gadyacintāmaṇi 198-199fn
gamak 38, 221
gāna (see also, '*dhruvā*', 'theatrical'); vis-à-vis *gāndharva* 102, 294
gāndharva 49-50, 53, 70-71, 101ff,121, 144, 193-194fn, 294, 305, 308ff, 321, 337; and *rāgas* 70; improvisation in 66-67; *tāla* 104; vis-à-vis *gāna* 102, 294
gāndharva śāstra 70, 322fn
geya-vikāras (see also, '*vikāra*') 298fn
gharānā 32, 56, 61, 62, 88
Ghasilal, Muni 224fn, 225fn, 227fn, 228fn
ghazal 30, 31, 53, 104, 105
Gītagovinda 63; and the tradition of music 205-222; paintings 184; vis-à-vis *Mānasollāsa* 207ff
gitaka (see also, '*gāndharva*') 105, 106, 337
gīti (see also 'style') ; and *rāga*-time association 169-170
Gotama (a *sāma* singer) 297
grāma 226, 229; number of 230-231, 238
grāma-rāgas 103-104, 168
Greek 2, 57, 60, 268, 269fn; music 39; musicology 267
guṇa 10, 218, 227, 240ff, 337; Sāṅkhyan 252
Gupta; kings and music 186ff, 200ff
Gupta Inscriptions 186fn
Gurjarī (a *rāga*) 222; legends about 12-13
Guru-Granth 269

Hara Prasada Sastri 207
haraṇa (see also, 'plagiarism') 25
Haricandra 188
Hariṣeṇa 188, 198-199fn
harmonics 332
Harṣa 188
hasta-viṇā 319
Hazra, R.C. 179
Hema Malini (an actress) 141
Hindi (see also, 'film'); films and dance 123ff; films and music 102, 105, 123ff; films, history of 125ff; plays 125ff
Hindustani; music (see also, 'music, Hindustani'); 14, 16, 32ff, 59-60, 65, 117, 206fn, 236, 312; music and the category of *pratibimba-kalpa* 30; styles 32ff; vis-à-vis Karnatic 163ff
Hiraṇya Śrauta Sūtra 195fn
history (see also, 'music'); and music 39ff, 54ff, 163-173 (see also, 'music, history of'); and the concepts of *vṛtti* and *rasa* 119ff; axial break in 2; milieu and style 34-35; of Hindustani music 16
History of Dharmaśāstra 187fn
Howard, Wayne 301fn
Hussain, M.F.; and *rāga*-painting 185

ideas; and music 39ff
identity; cultural 6; of a musical piece 31

imagination (see also, '*pratibhā*') : creative 16-38
Imān Dharam (a Hindi film) 158
imitation; and theatre 95, 128fn, 151 (see also, '*anukaraṇa*')
improvisation; and music education 31, 61; and *śāstriya* (classical) music 31, 62, 89-91; and style 32ff; in *gāndharva jātis* (see also, '*gāndharva*', '*jāti*') 67
India's Intellectual Traditions 107fn
Indian (see also, 'music'); music, drone in 40-41
Indian Philosophy: A Counter-Perspective 286ff
indriyas (sense-organs); spiritual or physical 252, 254
innovation (see also, 'creativity') 8, 319
instrument; body as 247-263 (see also, '*viṇā*')
international; and the 'modern' in art 2-3, 5
interpretation; in music 30, 59; vis-à-vis transformation 30
Isibhāsiyāiṁ (see, '*Ṛṣibhāṣita*')
itivṛtta (dramatic plot) 112ff, 160ff (see also 'plot')

Jagadekamalla 170, 176fn
Jaiminīya Brāhmaṇa 285
Jaiminīya Upaniṣad Brāhmaṇa 42ff, 285ff
Jaiminīya-śākhā 42
Jain; ethos and music 49; literature and music 188ff, 198, 201, 210-211, 223-246, 336-337
Jain, Panna Lal 198-199fn
Jātakas (see also, 'Buddhist; literature'); and music 187fn, 194fn, 196-197, 199
jāti (a *gāndharva* form; see also, '*gāndharva*') 63, 103, 230fn; and *rāga* (see also, '*rāga*') 66-67; *dhyāna* 176fn; improvisation in 67
jāvalī 294
Jayadeva (see also, '*Gītagovinda*') 63, 112, 113, 179, 205-222
Jayadeva Singh (Thakur) 70fn
Jijñāsā: A Journal of the History of Ideas And Culture 150fn
Jineśvara Sūri 210
Jīvandhara Campū 199fn
Johny Merā Nām (a Hindi film) 141, 149
Journal of The Asiatic Society 191fn

Kādambarī 188, 198
kaiśikī (a *vṛtti*; see also '*vṛtti*') 144ff
kāku (intonation); in dramatic speech 99ff, 102, 110, 289fn
Kalānidhi (see also, 'Kalliṇātha') 86fn
Kālidāsa 29, 139, 147, 187, 191, 212, 229fn, 238
Kalind 331fn
Kallinātha 86, 206fn, 213-214, 215fn, 216fn, 237fn, 258, 313fn
Kalpasūtra; miniatures 174, 183
Kāmasūtra 191
kambala-gāna (a *gāndharva* form) 63
Kāmod (a *raga*) 91
Kane, P.V. 187fn
Kanhupāda 207
Kapadia, H.R. 228fn
karaṇa (a unit in dance) 37ff, 73ff, 115ff, 119
Karnatic(ak); music 14, 60-61, 65, 164ff, 312
Kashmir (see also, 'Kashmiri') 142
Kashmiri 17, 142, 320; theorists 18
Kaśyapa; 138 on music in theatre 108
Kaśyapa (a singer of *sāma*) 297
Kathākoṣaprakaraṇa; music in 210-211

Kathāsaritsāgara; *viṇā*-playing in 195fn
Kaumudī (commentary on the *Dhvanyālokalocana*) 8-9fn
Kauthumaśakhāyāḥ Ūhagānam Ūhyagānam 302fn, 316fn
kavi (see also, 'poet') 8-9, 20, 117
kavi-karma (activity of the poet) 7
kāvya (see also, 'poetry') 17, 18, 29, 201; and *nāṭya* 117, 118; and *rasa* 19; *dṛśya* (theatre; see also, 'theatre') 19
Kāvyamimāṁsā (see also 'Rājaśekhara') 24fn; and plagiarism 24ff
Khamāj (a *rāga*) 33
Khāravela (see also, 'kings') 187, 188
khyāl 30, 31, 38, 52, 59, 60, 61, 88, 91, 103, 104, 207, 215fn, analogous to *gāndharva* 298; 102; as a style of rendering *rāgas* 32ff
kings; as musicians 186ff, 276, 278, 282
kirtan 53, 104
Kīrtidhara 86
Kohala 86, 238
Kṛṣṇa; as a composer 186
kṛti (see also, '*chiz*', '*bandish*') 60, 61
Kṣemendra 195fn
Kumar Gandharva 36, 59
Kumāragupta I 198; and music 186ff, 190, 202
Kumbha (see, 'Rāṇā Kumbha')
kuṇḍalinī; and *svara*-production 258ff
Kuntaka 9, 27
Kuṭṭanīmatam (see also, 'Dāmodara Gupta'); on theatre 133fn, 145ff

Lakṣamaṇasena 214, 219
lakṣaṇa; of *jātis* and *rāgas* 314ff: of *svara* 326ff; vis-à-vis *lakṣya* 258
lakṣya; vis-à-vis *lakṣaṇa* 258
Lalitavistara 187fn
Lallan Piyā (a composer of *ṭhumrīs*) 33
Lallan Piyā kī Ṭhumriyāṅ 33fn
Laṅkāvatara Sūtra 197
Laura-Candā; painting 185
Laxman Pai; and *rāga*-painting 185
Legge, James 2714ff
Li Ki 270ff
Lin Yutang 268, 271ff
linguistics (see also, '*Śikṣā*') 57, 100
literary (see also, 'literature'); creativity, concept of 16ff
literature 31, 57; Buddhist, music in 187 (see also, 'Buddhist'); critical awareness in 16ff; Urdu-Persian 21; vis-à-vis music 15, 63-64
Loafer (a Hindi film) 149
Locana; on *Dhvanyāloka* 8-9fn
logos iii-iv; of music 267-335
lokadharmī 82, 110, 130ff
lokasvabhāva 91, 95, 106, 112, 113, 114, 116
lyrics 51

Madan, J.F. 126
Madhubala (an actress) 156
Mahābhārata 124, 186, 187
Mahāvagga 187fn, 196
Mahāvīra 48, 231, 232
Mahimabhaṭṭa 9
Mālakosha (a *raga*) 90
Mālavikāgnimitram (see also, 'Kālidāsa'); and Hindi film 147-148
Malhār (a *rāga*) 167, 236; occult effect of 12
man; 39ff concept of and music 31ff
Mānāṅka (a commentator on *Gītagovinda*) 211fn, 219fn

manas (mind) 259-260; and the body 251ff
Mānasollāsa (see also, 'Someśvara') 65, 170, 206fn, 218fn; *prabandha* in 207ff, 215fn
mantra; pronunciation of 100; Vedic and *sāma* (see also, 'Vedic'; '*sāma*') 42, 64
mārga (see also '*mārgi*') 217-218
mārgi (see also, '*marga*') 258
Mārkaṇḍeya Purāṇa 223
Mārvā (a *rāga*) 312
Masterpieces of Jain Kalpasūtra Painting 174
Mataṅga (see also, '*Bṛhaddesi*') 168, 169, 207, 215, 217, 235, 238, 315, 317, 318-319, 322
mātṛkā (see also, '*nṛtta*'); approach to structures 115ff, 122; concept of, and *sthāya* 36ff; vis-à-vis *vṛtti* 115ff
mātu 220
mazmūn (poetic theme) 21
meaning; theories of 19-20
Meghadūta (see also, '*Kālidāsa*') 229fn; music in 197
Mīmāṁsā (see also, 'Mīmāṁsaka') 251
Mīmāṁsaka 251, 286
mind (see, '*manas*')
Misra, G.S.P. 142fn
Mithun Chakravarti (an actor) 155
modern (see also, 'modernity'); as international 2-3, 6; as opposed to traditional 1ff; music in Confucian thought 278ff
modernity (see also, 'modern'); and tradition 1ff; its absence in music and dance 4-5
mokṣa 48
Motichandra 198, 243fn
Mṛcchakaṭikam (see also, 'Śūdraka') 10-11, 197
mudrā (in dance) 119
Muhammad Shah 35
Mukherjee, Bratindranath 191fn
Mumtaz (an actress) 149
Muni Ghasilal (see, 'Ghasilal, Muni')
Muni Nathmal (see 'Nathmal, Muni')
music (see also, 'musical', '*saṅgita*'); absolute or *apauruṣeya* 267-306; *ādhyātmika* 284ff; aesthetic thought concerning 10ff, 227ff, 240ff, 270ff and ceremony 277; and cosmic correspondences 42ff; and dramatic speech (see also, '*pāṭhya*') 99ff; and film 123-162; and human harmony 270ff; and ideas 39ff; and polity 273; and style 32ff; and the analytical categories of poetry 31; and the category of *pratbimbakalpa* 31; and the concept of man 39ff; and the *kuṇḍalinī* 258; and the other arts 7ff, 52-53, 99ff; and the pleasure principle 318ff; and the *sanyasic* ethos 48; and theatre (see also, 'theatre', '*nātya*') 101ff, 118-119, 127ff, 152-153; and words 51-53, 101ff, 286ff; as *upāsanā* (see also, '*sāma*') 48; Chinese 267ff, 307-308; conceptual framework concerning 66ff; criticism in 1, 10ff, 14ff, 240ff; drone in 40-41; education 66, 87-88, 187-188, 268ff, 281; European (see also, 'west') 31-32, 59, 62; Greek (see also, 'Greek') 39, Hindustani (see also, 'Hindustani') 12, 16, 30, 32, 59-60, 117; history 15, 39ff, 45, 54ff, 120, 163ff, 307ff; ideal 268ff; lighter forms of 53; logos of 267-335; meaningless

syllables in (see also, 'syllables, nonsense') 46ff, 51, 216, 221, 290ff; miraculous effects of 12-13; monodic 40, 45; northern Indian (see also, 'Hindustani') 88; notation in (see also, 'notation') 61; real or true 277ff; recordings of 15, 55, 62; replication of (see also, 'transmission') 32; texts (see also, '*saṅgīta-śāstra*') 54-68, 168ff; vis-à-vis society 34-35.
musical (see also, 'music'); culture 54, 57, 66; education 31; lore 245; notation (see also, 'notation') 15, 54; texts (see also, '*saṅgīta-śāstra*') 54-68, 168ff
musician(s) (see also '*vāggeyakāra*') 17, 49fn, 66, 87-88, 90, 91, 110fn, 316, 331ff; and the *kuṇḍalinī* 259; classical 51, 166-167, 172, 193, 202fn; kings as 186ff; 276, 278, 282; occult power of 47
musicologist (see also, 'musicology') 67
musicology (see also, '*saṅgīta-śāstra*') iii, 296; as logos of music 267-335; history of 67, 308ff; practice of 67-68.

Nābhādāsa 214
nāda (see, '*āhata, nāda*')
nāḍī (artery) 254; and *svarotpatti* 255ff, 259ff
nādotpatti (the birth of *nāda* – sound – in the body) 247ff
Naiyāyika 151
Nalanda 141
Namak Halāl (a Hindi film) 154, 157-158
Nandī 223fn
Nānya (see, 'Nānyabhūpāla')
Nānyabhūpāla 169ff, 176fn, 217, 231, 235fn, 330fn
Nānyadeva (see 'Nānyabhūpāla')
Nārada 174ff, 186, 230fn
Nāradī (Nāradiyā, Naradiya) Śikṣā 64-65, 224, 230-231, 232fn, 233ff
narratives; in Hindi films 123ff, 153ff; the grammar of 150ff
Naṭasūtra 70
Nathmal, Muni (same as 'Muni Nathmal') 223fn
naturalism (see also, 'realism') 124ff
nāṭya (see also, 'theatre', '*Nāṭyaśāstra*'); and music (see also, 'music') 101ff; and stage-space 98-99; as a composite art (see also 'art') 92fn, 136fn; plot in 112-113; the *śāstra* of 92-122; vis-à-vis dance 72-73, 80ff
nātyadharmī 82, 130ff; as a transformed world 107ff, 118-119, 151ff, 159ff; *itivṛtta* as (see also '*itivṛtta*') 112-113
nāṭya-gṛha (see also, 'theatre-hall') 98-99
Nāṭyaśāstra (see also, 'Bharata') 38fn, 65, 66, 69, 72, 73fn, 74fn, 75fn, 76fn, 77fn, 79, 80, 81, 82, 83fn, 84fn, 85fn, 130fn, 161fn, 176fn, 194fn, 200fn, 201, 224, 228fn, 230, 231, 234fn, 289fn, 293fn, 321fn, 337; forms of theatre in 131fn; its authorship 92; its system and structure 92-122; music criticism in 241; *rasa* in (see also '*rasa*') 18-19, 93; theatric devices in (see also 'theatric, devices') 129, 150ff
nāṭyāyita 148ff
Nawab, Sarabhai (see, 'Sarabhai Nawab')
Nawab, Vidya Sarabhai (see, 'Vidya Sarabhai Nawab')

Nāyaka Baijū (see also, 'Baiju Bavra') 90
Nāyaka Gopāla; Kallinātha refers to 215fn
nāyikā-bheda; painting 184
New Catalogus Catalagorum 249fn
newspapers; musical criticism in 14-15
Nirukta 64
nirvāṇa 48
notation (see also, 'music') 15, 54, 59, 61, 65-66, 284fn, 301, 315ff
nṛtta (see also, 'dance', 'Tandu') 82, 105ff, 147fn; *hastas* 82-83; *karaṇa* (see also, '*karaṇa*') 73ff; *mātṛkā* (see also, '*mātṛkā*') 37ff, 73ff, 114ff; vis-à-vis *nṛtya* 37
nṛtya (see also, 'dance', '*nṛtta*'); vis-à-vis *nṛtta* 37
Nyāya 251
Nyāyakośa 292fn

Oḍḍisī 109, 112, 113
On The Art Poetry (see also, '*Poetics*', Aristotle') 94fn
oral; criticism (see, 'criticism; oral')

pada (see 'words')
Pādatāḍitakam 198, 199
Padgaonkar, Dilip (see 'Dilip Padgaonkar')
Padma Khanna (an actress) 149
Padmaprābhṛtaka 197
Padmāvatī; and Jayadeva 211, 212, 214, 169
painter 16
painting 4, 5-6, 39, 40, 41, 193; and *saṁvāda* (see also, '*saṁvāda*') 24; of *rāgas* 12-13, 174-185; vis-à-vis music 13, 58, 63-64
Pande, G.C. 212fn
Pāṇini 71-72; and theoretical activity in India 69ff
Pāṇiniya Śikṣā 260ff
Paraj (a *rāga*) 91
paramārtha; and *vyavahāra* 272-273fn; as essential meaning (see also, '*mazmūn*') 25
paramparā (see also, 'tradition'); as understood in the 'tradition' 7ff; and *rūḍhi* 7; and convention 7; criticism in 7ff; three elements of 7; and 'tradition' 7
parapurapraveśa-tulya (also, '*vat*'; transformation through change of context) 26ff; sub-species of 27-28
Pārśvadeva (see also, '*Saṅgīta-samaya-sāra*') 171, 176fn, 215fn, 217
Parveen Babi (an actress) 154-155
pāṭa (a limb of *prabandha*) 216, 222
Patañjali 257fn
pāṭhya (speech); and *kāku* 99ff; in *nāṭya* 99ff, 102
pauruṣeya: logos and music 307-335
Padmini Kolhapure (an actress) 155
percussion-playing; in Bharata 116-117
person (see, 'body; as embodied self')
phonetics (see also '*Śikṣā*') 100
piṇḍotpatti (birth of the human body) 248ff
plagiarism; creative and imitative 24ff
Plato 278; on music 270
playwright 7, 107
pleasure; the principle of, and *rāga*-music 318ff
plot (in a play; see also, '*itivṛtta*') 117
poem: its structure and creativity 29
poetic (see also, 'poetry'); tradition 56
poetics; Indian (see also, '*alaṅkāra-śāstra*') 18, 56
Poetics (see also, '*On The Art*

Poetry', 'Aristotle') 95
poetry 41; analytical categories of, and music 31, 35; and music 51ff, 104-105, 205ff, 220ff; and theatre 99, 117, 133-134, 152; creativity in 23ff; criticism in 56-57; practice of 23ff; Sanskrit 30; transmission of 29
poets 51; practice of 23ff
polity; and music 274ff
polyphony 40; and Vedic music 43-45
post-modernism 1
prabandha (a form of music) 170, 206fn, 207fn
Pracina Bhārata meṅ Saṅgīta 197fn
Pradyota (king of Avantī) 187, 188
prajñā; musical (see 'logos')
Prajñānānanda, Swami 179, 192fn, 199
Prakrit 218, 228
Pran (an actor) 158
prāṇa (vital breath); and the production of speech and *svara* 253ff
Praśastapāda 291fn
Praśastapāda Bhāṣya 291fn
pratibhā (the creative impulse) 8-9, 213 Ānandavardhana on 20ff; and imagination 8; transcendental 279ff; two kinds of 8-9, 14
pratibimbakalpa (also, '*tulya*' and '*vat*'; mirror-image-like transformation) 24, 25ff and Hindustani music 30-31; and *saṁvāda* (see also, '*saṁvāda*') 23ff; sub-species of 28-29
Pratṛda Bhalla (a *sāma*-singer) 47
pravṛtti (a concept in Bharata); and *vṛtti* 111fn
prayoga ii-iii, 94, 311; and *nāṭya* 94, 111, 113, 117fn; vis-à-vis *śāstra* (see also, '*śāstra*') ii-iii
prayoktṛ (the director of a play) 111fn, 114
Premnath (an actor) 149
Puṇḍalika (a Hindi film) 126
Puṇḍarīka Viṭṭhala 324ff
Puṇḍarikamālā 325fn
Purāṇa 49fn, 65, 124, 175, 177ff, 223, 229, 231fn, 232, 245, 246
Pūriyā (a *rāga*); *ṭappā* in 34
puruṣārtha ii, iii, 328
pūrvaraṅga 98, 105, 115
Pyārī Behnā (a Hindi film) 155
Pythagoras iii, 267, 291, 307, 309, 310, 311, 327-328, 333

qawwālī 30

rāga 62, 104, 206, 207, 219, 230fn, 232, 258; and association with time 11-12, 44-45, 163-173, 236, 240; and *jātis* (see also, '*jāti*') 66-67, 305, 307; and seasonal affinities 44, 166-167; and style 33ff, 61; and words 51ff; as deity 13, 181ff; auspicious quality of 169ff; compositions in (see also '*bandish*', '*chīz*') 60-61; description of 32, 87-88; *dhyāna* 12-13, 174ff, 236fn; 87ff form of 164ff; formulas in 88; hierarchy of *svaras* in 283-284; improvisation in (see also, 'improvisation') 87-91; its logos 307-305; *lakṣaṇa* 314ff; miraculous effects of 12-13; paintings 12, 174ff, 236-237; purity of 55-56, 59-60, 67-68; reproduction of 32; theorising about 70
rāga-dhyāna; and *rāga-mālā* painting (see also '*rāga-mālā*') 174ff
rāga-mālā; and *nāyikā-bheda* 184: paintings 174-185, 237; texts 13, 174ff
Rāgamālā (of Puṇḍarīka Viṭṭhala) 324ff

Rāgamālā Painting 174ff, 183
Rāgasāgara 174ff
Raghavan, V. 189fn
Raghuvaṁśa (see also, 'Kālidāsa') 187
Rājā Hariścandra (a Hindi film) 126
Rājapraśnīyam 201
Rajasekhara 27, 28, 29; his concept of creativity in poetry 16, 24ff; his transformational categories and music 31ff; on plagiarism 24ff
Ramakrishna Kavi 77, 175-176fn
Rāmāmātya 167
Rāmāyaṇa (of Vālmīki) 23, 124, 187, 196
Rāṇā Kumbha 176, 205fn, 219ff
Randhir Kapoor (an actor) 156, 158
Ranjit (an actor) 149
rasa 22, 45, 57, 104, 111, 113, 114, 139, 150, 155, 162, 273 274, 278; and *bhāva* 118; and history 119ff; and theatre 21ff, 95ff; and *vṛtti* 113ff as a *bhāva* in *āyurveda* 250-251; extended beyond theatre 18ff, 93; how aroused in *kāvya* 20ff; theory of, and music 13-14, 89
Rasikapriyā (see also, 'Rāṇā Kumbha') 63, 219ff
Ratnāvali; an ancient performance of 133fn, 145ff, 148
Ravīndra Saṅgīta (see also, 'Tagore; songs'); transmission of 29
ṛcas (see also, '*ṛk*') 46
realism; and Hindi films 125ff, 150ff, 159ff
realms; affinity between (see also 'affinity') 119ff
reciprocal; functioning, concept of 42ff
replication (see also, 'reproduction'); and transformation 30ff; in music 30, 31, 32
reproduction (see also, 'replication') 30fn
Republic (see also, 'Plato') 270
Ṛgveda (see also, '*ṛk*') 43
ṛk 43, 286ff, 295fn; vis-à-vis *sāma* 286ff
Roman 2, 60
Roopa-Lekha 192fn
Roy, Ames 125fn
ṛṣi(s) 279ff
Ṛṣibhāṣita 228
ṛta 43ff, 279
Rudradāman; as a musician 187

Śabdaratna 292fn
Sachs, Curt 192fn
Sacred Books of The East 270fn, 271ff
Sadāraṅg 59, 215fn
Sadrāgacandhrodaya 324ff
sahṛdaya (see also, 'critic', 'criticism') 7, 8, 14, 20, 23, 56, 72, 281
Saira Bano (an actress) 149
Śaivism 49, 70
Śākuntalam (see also, 'Kālidāsa') 113
sāma (see also, 'music, Vedic') 42, 43, 49, 101, 308; and mystic attainment 45ff, 285ff and the *kuṇḍalinī* 259; and the syllable '*Om*' 45; *anirukta* 301-302fn; *anṛca* 45ff, 286ff; as revealed music 46, 285ff; as *upāsanā* 46ff, 286ff; *aśarīra* 46ff, 286ff; attitude to, Vedic 45ff, 64, 67, 285ff; independence of 286; its parts and cosmic identities 44-45; literature concerning 285ff; meaningless syllables in (see also, '*aśarīra*, '*anṛca*', '*anirukta*') 46-47; notation in (see also, 'notation') 284fn; *vikāras* 52, 295ff; vis-à-vis *ṛk* 286ff

Sāmaveda (see also, '*sāma*') 42, 295ff; notation in 316; singers of iii, 286ff
Saṁhitopaniṣad Brāhmaṇa 302fn
sampradāya iv, 66, 182
Samudragupta; as a musician 186ff, 190, 193, 199, 202, 204
saṁvāda (harmony between *svaras*) 291, 332
saṁvāda (resemblance between poems) 23; kinds of 23ff
saṁvādī 311ff
saṅgat 110fn
saṅgīta (see also, 'music'): ii-iii, 67ff, 247ff, 261, 272, 283-284, 291fn, 307ff 332ff, 337; texts (see also, 'music, texts') 174ff, 212-213, 217, 218, 223ff; the defence of 49fn
Saṅgīta Cintāmaṇi 65
Saṅgīta Cūḍāmaṇi 170, 176fn
Saṅgīta Darpaṇa 172
Saṅgīta Evaṁ Cintan 66fn, 72fn, 87fn
saṅgītaka 52
Saṅgīta-makaranda 180
Saṅgītapārijāta (see also, 'Ahobala') 330fn
Saṅgītarāja (see also, 'Rāṇā Kumbha') 63, 176; and the *Gītagovinda* 220ff
Saṅgīta-ratnākara (see also, 'Śārṅgadeva') 62-63, 65, 86, 119, 171ff, 175-176, 193fn, 206fn, 207, 237fn, 238fn
Saṅgīta-ratnākara of Śārṅgadeva, Text And English Translation 248fn
Saṅgīta-samaya-sāra (see also 'Pārśvadeva') 65, 171, 175, 176fn
Saṅgītopaniṣad (see also, 'Sudhākalaśa') 175
Saṅgītopaniṣadsāroddhāra (see also, 'Sudhākalaśa') 174ff, 236fn; and the *Ṭhāṇaṁga Sūtra* 239fn
saṅgraha (see 'Bharata')
Sanjiv Kumar (an actor) 155-156
saṅkalpa; and the body 252ff
Śankara Miśra 219fn
Sāṅkhyan; *gunas* 252
Sanskrit 218, 228, 286; poetic tradition 16ff, 31, 205ff; poetry, anthologies of 10; Vedic, and *svara* 292
Sarabhai Nawab 174
Sarahapāda 207
sargam (see also, '*svara*, as a limb of *prabandha*'); singing of 216, 222
śarīra-vīṇā (see also, '*vīṇā*') 261-262
Sarma, K.V. 189fn
Śārṅgadeva (see also, '*Saṅgīta-ratnākara*') 175-176, 193fn, 206fn, 207, 217, 235. 238, 313fn and *rāga*-time association 171ff; and the concept of *sthāya* 36ff; on body as an instrument 247-263; on composers (*vāggeyakāras*) 28fn; on the process of sound production 247ff
śāstra (see also, '*śāstric*') ii-iii, 69ff, 119-120, 217, 247ff, 307ff, 332ff; and structure in relation to the Nāṭyaśāstra 92-122; as revelation 256ff; its relation to *prayoga* ii-iii, 69ff, 114, 256ff, 262-263; of speech 99ff
śāstrakāra 73, 80
śāstric 217; activity 69ff, 74; impulse; iii
śāstrīya (see also, 'classical'); as a transformational form of music 31
Śatapatha Brāhmaṇa 225fn
Satyanarayana, R. 325fn
Satyavrata Sāmaśramī Bhaṭṭācārya 296ff

Sāyaṇa 233, 302fn
scale (see also, '*thāṭ*', '*svara-maṇḍala*') 32
Schroeder 215
sculptor(s) 4, 16
Sekaśubhodaya 214
self; body as 249ff
Shammi Kapoor (an actor) 156-157, 158
Sharābi (a Hindi film) 158
Sharma, Prem Lata 34fn, 248, 260fn
Shashi Kapoor (an actor) 154-155, 158
Shelley 242
Shiki 268fn
Shorī Miyāṅ (a composer) 35
Shringy, R.K. 248
Śikṣā 64; as *śāstra* of speech (phonetics) 99ff, 245-246, 260ff
Śilālin 70
śilpa 98
Siṁhabhūpāla 215fn, 216
singer(s) (see also, 'musicians'); classical 51ff; women as; 228-229, 244-245
śirā (see, 'artery')
Skandagupta 191
Slaje, Walter 336
Smita Patil (an actress) 158
Smṛti(s) 49; *Yājñavalkya* 49fn
society; and music 34-35
Somadeva 195fn
Someśvara (see also, '*Mānasollāsa*') 170-171, 208ff, 217
song (see also, 'music'); and Hindi films 123ff, 150ff; and speech 101; in *Ṭhāṇaṁga Sūtra* 226ff; *viṇā* accompaniment to 193ff; virtuous, in Confucius (see also, 'Confucius') 279ff
soul; as embodied 247ff
speech (see also, '*pāṭhya*'); and music 101; in theatre 99ff, 133, 289; vis-à-vis *svara* 289ff
Śrī (a *rāga*); 12 occult effect of 10
śruti 263; *jāti* 329ff; vis-à-vis *svara* 320ff
Staal Frits 301-302fn
sthāna ('position' in dance) 68, 76, 79-80, 83-84, 86
sthāna (position of *svara*) 100-101, 200fn, 224, 228, 230, 232ff, 261-262, 320ff, 333
sthānaka (see, '*sthāna*' in dance)
sthāya; and *karaṇa* (see also, '*karaṇa*') 37-38; as a unit of musical style 36ff; concept of, and *mātṛkā* (see also, '*mātṛkā*') 37-38
stobha 298ff; *sāma* (see also '*sāma*') 299ff
stobhākṣaras (see also, '*stobha*') 51
story (see, 'narrative')
structure; of the *Nāṭyaśāstra* 92-122
Studies In The Upapurāṇas 179
style 11, 117; as transformation 32ff, 88ff; cultural 75; in music 11, 32ff, 59, 88ff; structural basis of (see also, '*sthāya*') 32ff, 35ff
Sudhākalaśa (see also, '*Saṅgītopaniṣadsāroddhāra*') 174ff, 236fn, 239fn
Śūdraka; as a *sahṛdaya* of music 10-11, 197-198
Sujātā (a Hindi film) 143
Surpuria, Amolak Chandra 223fn
śuṣkākṣara (see also, 'nonsense') 51
Suśruta 256
sūt 38
svara 177ff, 272, 301, 303; and speech 99ff, 289ff and *śruti* 320ff; as a limb of *prabandha* 216, 222; *āśraya* of 288ff; in Confucius 283-284; its correlation with colour etc. 234ff; *lakṣaṇa* 244, 326ff; *maṇḍala* 229, 308ff, 320, 327, 329, 330; production, physiology of

233-234, 247ff; *sādhāraṇa* 320ff; the logos of 270ff; vis-à-vis *pada* (words) and *tāla* (see also, 'music' and words') 102ff
Svaramela-kalānidhi 167
svarotpatti (the process of *svara*-production) 247ff
svayambhū; *svara* as 327
svīkaraṇa (creative assimilation) 25
Swami Prajñānānanda (see, 'Prajñānānanda, Swami')
Śyāma-kalyāṇa (a *rāga*); representation of 183
Śyāmilaka 198, 199
syllables (see also, 'music, meaningless syllables in') 290ff; as *āśraya* of music 288ff; nonsense (see also, 'nonsense') 51ff, 102; of Sanskrit speech 233-234, 257fn
system; combining multiple structures 96, 92-122
Sze-hsia (Hentse) 271; on music 278ff
Szema Chi'en 268fn

Tagore; songs (see also, 'Ravīndra saṅgīta') 316
Tāṇḍava 69ff, 106
Taṇḍu 106, 315; and his theory of dance 69-86
tānpūrā 40, 193, 203
Tānsen 47, 62, 214
Tāntrism; and rāga-*dhyānas* 181ff
ṭappā 88, 217fn; as a style of rendering *ragas* 32ff
tarānā 51
tena (see '*tenaka*')
tenaka (a limb of *prabandha)* 216, 220, 222
Tere Mere Sapne (a Hindi film) 142,
Texts des Purāṇa sur la Theorie Musicale 231fn
Ṭhāṇaṁga Sūtra 65; music in 223-246, 336-338
thāṭ (see also, 'scale') 32; *melakartā* system 40-41
The Canonical Literature of The Jains 228fn
The Coinage of The Gupta Empire 191fn, 192fn
The Gupta Gold Coins In The Bayana Hoard 192fn, 202
The Hindi Padāvalī of Nāmadev 298fn
The Music of Hindustan 166-167, 177
The Wisdom of Confucious (see also, 'Lin Yutang') 268fn, 269fn
theatre (see also, *'nāṭya')*; and dance 72-73, 80ff, 105ff; and music 101ff, 191; and *rasa* 18; conventions in 130ff, 151ff; indigenous, and Hindi film 125ff; Pārsī 129; popular 126, 129-130; traditional 129-130, 151
theatric; devices 130ff, 151ff
theatrical; songs (see also, '*dhruvā*', '*gana*') 53
theme 87
ṭhumrī 31, 31, 38, 88, 207, 217fn; as a style of rendering *rāgas* 33ff; its decline 34; words in 53, 294
Ṭhumrī Saṅgraha 33fn
Times Of India, *The* 127
tradition 17; as modernity understands it 1-7; of film-making 125ff; as it understands itself 7-8
traditional; and the modern 1ff; theatre 129ff, 151ff
transformation; and replication 30, 58ff; and *śāstrīya* music 31ff; as innovation 8; creative, and style 32ff, 59; creative, and the concept of *yoni* 25; its role in creativity 16-38; kinds of, in

poetry 20ff
transmission; of music 279ff, 319; of poetry vis-à-vis music 29
Tripura-dāha 72, 105
tulyadehitula (also '*vat*'; see also, '*saṁvāda*'); and style 35-36; as a kind of *saṁvāda* (resemblance) 23-24, 26 sub-species of 29
Tumburu 186
Tyāgarāj 60

Ubhayābhisārikā 198
Udātta-rāghava; music in 140
Udayana; as a musician 186-187, 188-189, 194-195
Upaniṣad(s) 305-306
Upapurāṇa; *Bṛhaddharma* 177ff
uparañjaka 102, 104, 110, 135-136
uparañjana 135-136; concept of, and composite arts (see also, 'arts') 95ff
uparañjanīya 135-136
upāsanā; *sāma* as (see also, '*sāma*') 46ff, 284ff
Urdu; plays 126
ustād 59
Uttuṅgodaya (a Kerala critic) 8

Vācaspati Miśra 257
vādī (svara) 310ff
Vādībha Siṁha Sūri 188, 198-199fn
vādya 110
vāggeyakāra(s) (see also, 'composers') 28fn, 213-214, 218, 248
Vaiśeṣika Sūtra 291fn
Vaiṣṇavism 49, 177ff, 205
vāk-karaṇas 116-117
Vālmīki 23, 196, 242-243
Vararuci 198
varṇa (syllables in speech; see also, 'syllables') 100; *mātṛkā* 116; *prakarṣa* 116; 103
vartanā (in dance) 84ff
Vasanta (a *rāga*; see also, '*Basant*') 91
Vasanta Vilāsa 185
Vasiṣṭha Caikitāneya; a *sāma* singer 46
vāstu-śāstra (see also, 'architecture') 335
Vasudeva Hiṇḍī 188, 198
Vātsyāyana 191
vāyu (wind); and the production of speech and *svara* 253-254, 260
Vāyu Purāṇa 231fn
Vedāṅga 64
Vedic 196; attitude to *sāma* 42ff, 66-67, 285ff; literature (see also, '*sāma*') 64-65, 195; *mantras*, relation to *sāma* 285ff; music (see also, '*sāma*') 41ff; 48-49, 64-65, 66fn, 67, 195, 285ff
Veṇisaṁhāra; music in 141
Victoria No. 203 (a Hindi film) 149, 158-159
Vidya Sarabhai Nawab 183fn
vikāras (distortion of words); in *sāma* (see also, '*sāma*; *vikāras*') 52
Vikramorvaśīyam (see also, 'Kālidasa') 133fn, 147fn
Vimānavatthu 199
viṇā; as accompaniment to song 186-204; *hasta* 319; in the human frame 261ff; *sapatatantrī* 199ff; *svara-maṇḍala* as 319-320; *svayaṁvara*, the motif of 188, 198
Viṇā-vāsavadattam 153-154, 189, 194-195
Viṣṇudharmottara Purāṇa 223
vivādī (*svara*) 310ff
Vohra, M.P. 180fn
vrātya(s) 45
Vṛddhakaśyapa 322ff
vṛtti; and history 119ff; concept of, in Bharata 111ff, 144ff,

159-160; vis-à-vis *mātṛkā* 116; vis-à-vis *pravrtti* 111fn
Vyākaraṇa 64
Vyāsa Bhāṣya (on the *Yogasūtras*) 257fn
vyavahāra; and *paramārtha* in music 272-273fn
vyutpatti (grasp of tradition) 8

Waley, Arthur 269fn
Walt Disney 184
weltanschauung 48
west 30, 100, 124; and Indian critical thinking 18; criticism in the 9; its cinema and Hindi films 124ff; its peculiar relation to modernity 2ff; the theatre of 152-153
western 15, 87, 94, 128, 152
westernisation (see also, 'west') and modernity 1ff
Winternitz, Maurice 218fn
words; and music 50-53, 102ff, 220, 286ff
writer 13, 126

yajña 43, 44, 48, 67, 284
Yājñavalkya 333
Yājñavalkya Śikṣā 236
Yājñavalkya Smṛti 49fn
Yāska 64, 69
yoga 258-259, 262 music as 282
Yogasūtra 257fn
Yoki 270ff
yoni (see also, 'transformation'); of *sāma* 296ff

Zinko, Christian 336

1239, 1240; its [illegible] — [illegible] 1250, [illegible] and
[illegible] 1170 — modernity 125
[illegible] — [illegible] Munro 1250
[illegible] — [illegible]
[illegible]
[illegible]
[illegible]
[illegible]
[illegible]
[illegible] 1240
[illegible] 1203
[illegible]
[illegible]
[illegible]
its cinema and other film[illegible] — [illegible]
1240; its peculiar relation to [illegible] — [illegible]
modernity 211; the meaning of — [illegible]
[illegible]
[illegible] — [illegible]